MOVIES of the SILENT YEARS

MOVIES of the SILENT YEARS

EDITED BY ANN LLOYD
CONSULTANT EDITOR
DAVID ROBINSON

ORBIS · LONDON

Acknowledgments

Many of the illustrations come from stills issued to publicize films made or distributed by the following companies: Artcraft, Art Film, Barker Films, Biograph Company, British International Pictures, Luis Buñuel/Salvador Dali, Butterfly, Charles Chaplin Productions, Chadwick Pictures, Cinégraphic/GPC, Cinès, Clarendon Pictures, Columbia, Comicque Film Corporation, Cosmograph, Decla/Bioscop, EMI, Edison Company, Elton Corporation, Epoch, Essanay, FRD, Douglas Fairbanks Productions, Famous Players/Lasky, Feature Productions, First National, Folly Films, Fox Film Corporation, Gainsborough, Gaumont, Goldwyn Company, Goskino, DW Griffith, Hepworth, Hillbilly, Homeland, Thomas Ince, Inspiration Pictures, Itala-Film, Buster Keaton Productions, Keystone, Lion's Gate, Harold Lloyd Corporation, London Films, Lumière Brothers, MGM, Märkische Film, George Méliès, Mercedes-Film, Metro Pictures, Mezhrabpomfilm, Mosfilm, Mutual, Nero-Film, New Era, Nordisk, Palladium, Pan-Film der Dafu-Film-Verleih, Paramount, Pathé, Pickford Corporation, Prana Film, Prometheus, RKO, Rank, Regent, Révillon Frères, Hal Roach, BP Schulberg, Selznick International, Larry Semon Productions, Mack Sennett, Sevzapkino, Shin kankaku-ha Eiga Renmei, Shochiku, George Albert Smith, Société du Film d'Art, Société Générale de Films, Sovkino, Stoll, Svenska Biograph, Svensk Filmindustri, Svensk Filminspelning, Tobis-Klangfilm, Transatlantic Pictures, Triangle, 20th Century-Fox, Ufa, Ukrainfilm, United Artists, Universal, VUFKU, Vitagraph, Vostok Kino, Walturdaw, Warner Brothers, Westi.

In addition we would like to thank: Peter Cowie, Culver Pictures Inc, Arnold Desser, Deutsches Kinemathek, Greg Edwards Archive, Joel Finler Collection, G Fuller, Thomas Gilcrease Institute, Japan Film Library Council, Kobal Collection, Raymond Mander and Joe Mitchenson Theatre Collection, Dan Millar, Museum of Modern Art Film Stills Archive, National Film Archive, National Film Archive/Nederlands, Rex Features, David Robinson Collection, Barry Salt, Tate Gallery, Thames Television, UPI, M Wanamaker.

Although every effort is being made to trace the present copyright holders, we apologize in advance for any unintentional omission or neglect and will be pleased to insert the appropriate acknowledgment to companies or individuals in any subsequent edition of this publication.

Abbreviations used in text

add: additional; **adv:** advertising; **anim:** animation; **art dir:** art direction; **ass:** assistant; **assoc:** associate; **chor:** choreography; **col:** colour process; **comm:** commentary; **cont:** continuity; **co-ord:** co-ordination; **cost:** costume; **dec:** decoration; **des:** design; **dial:** dialogue; **dial dir:** dialogue direction; **dir:** direction; **doc:** documentary; **ed:** film editing; **eng:** engineer; **ep:** episode; **exec:** executive; **loc:** location; **lyr:** lyrics; **man:** management; **mus:** music; **narr:** narration; **photo:** photography; **prod:** production; **prod co:** production company; **prod sup:** production supervision; **rec:** recording; **rel:** released; **r/t:** running time; **sc:** scenario/screenplay/script; **sd:** sound; **sp eff:** special effects; **sup:** supervision; **sync:** synchronization; **sys:** system. Standard abbreviations for countries are used. Most are self-evident but note: A = Austria; AUS = Australia; GER = Germany and West Germany after 1945; E.GER = East Germany.

Editor
Ann Lloyd
Consultant Editor
David Robinson
Editorial Director
Brian Innes

Senior Editor
Graham Fuller
Senior Sub Editor
Dan Millar
Chief Sub Editor
Maggie Lenox
Sub Editors
Lindsey Lowe, Susan Leonard

Research Consultant
Arnold Desser
Picture Researchers
Dave Kent, Liz Heasman
Research
Sally Hibbin, Barry Bliss

Designers
Ray Kirkpatrick, Wayne Léal

Facing title page: Ahmed (Rudolph Valentino) is about to ravish the dancing girl Yasmin (Vilma Banky) in *The Son of the Sheik* (1926), the great lover's last film/(*Kobal Collection*)

First published in hardcovers by Orbis Publishing Limited, London 1984
Reprinted 1985
First published in paperback 1985

Printed in Italy by Eurograph S.p.A., Milano
ISBN: 0-85613-641-7 (hardback)
ISBN: 0-85613-975-0 (paperback)

CONTENTS

INTRODUCTION

The silent cinema occupies a unique, isolated, distinguished place in the history of world art. It was a phenomenon unparalleled anywhere in that history. In the space of little more than thirty years, a medium had been invented and an art had progressed from first stumbling efforts and the discovery of elemental principles to an extraordinary culmination and then sudden extinction. In 1895 there were Lumière's *Arrival of a Train* and *Feeding the Baby*. In 1927 there were *October*, *Napoleon*, *Sunrise*, *The Wedding March*. Between times there had been Méliès, Griffith, King, Feuillade, Clair, Lang, Lubitsch, Flaherty, Chaplin, Pudovkin – a pantheon. With the art had grown up a vast industry that was itself unique in history, for its business was the marketing of dreams.

These years were eventful and epic, and very much the story of how the art and industry drew its resources from the nineteenth century to provide the most characteristic form of communication and entertainment of the twentieth. The first chapters in this collection illustrate how the desire for the motion picture existed long before the cinema itself came into being. We can see how the optical shows beloved of eighteenth- and nineteenth-century audiences exactly prefigured the experiences the cinema would more prodigally supply. The technology of the cinema, too, was more a matter of evolution than of invention. The elements that were combined in the 1890s to perfect the motion-picture camera and projector had been gradually assembled over decades and even centuries by scientists and experimenters.

Many men contributed to the cinema; but in the end those who perfected and exploited the new technology were the successful capitalist entrepreneurs like Edison and the Lumière brothers. From its very beginning money and industrial organization played a role in the progress of the cinema parallel to the imaginative flights of artists and the needs and demands of a vast audience.

As this book relates, America's domination of the cinema came only with time. The first decade or so belonged to Europe but particularly to France, which produced the cinema's first model of industrial empires – the Pathé and Gaumont organizations. France also produced the first film-maker with a conviction that the film might be an art capable of manipulation, rather than purely a technological tool to record what was set before it. This man, the movie's first artist, whose films retain all their charm after more than eighty years, was the magician Georges Méliès.

A variety of factors enabled America eventually to assume her leading role. One was the aggressive nature of American capitalism in the early part of the century. That aggressiveness was to give rise to a fierce internecine war within the infant industry, yet even that left a profitable legacy in revolutionary new strategies of entertainment and economics. America's forceful trading methods were to prove as effective in developing her foreign markets. Again, the United States had the luck to discover, at the crucial moment, the most influential and innovative film-maker in the whole history of the art. In ten astonishing years, between 1908 and 1918, D. W. Griffith discovered practically the whole expressive means of the cinema, and exploited them magisterially in two revolutionary masterworks, *The Birth of a Nation* and *Intolerance*. The greatest benefits to the rise of the American film, however, were provided by World War I, which impoverished and effectively eliminated European competition. After the war, with the advantage of the biggest home audience in the world, American film-making entered upon a period of phenomenal prosperity which enabled her in the future simply to buy up and absorb the major talents of foreign rivals. The Twenties and the Thirties were to be a period of mass emigration from Europe to Hollywood.

From this time on, right into the third quarter of the century, America's dominant role in the world's film industry, and as the universal purveyor of dreams, was to be virtually unassailed. A not insignificant part of America's political influence in the world has, since silent days, been due to the unconscious propaganda effect of its films. Their seductive vision of the American character and way of life has affected audiences the world over.

Elsewhere in the world throughout the silent period cinema flourished even despite Hollywood's artistic pillages and seizure of the major economic power. The new society of the Soviet Union was currently experiencing a period of artistic liberation that was unprecedented, and certainly never to be repeated. The young artists discovered new uses for the film in their Brave New World – stimulated by Lenin's shattering declaration that 'for us the cinema is the most important art' – and explored new styles and techniques. Like America, the Soviet Union was fortunate in finding at a strategic moment an artist of towering stature, Sergei Mikhailovich Eisenstein, who realized unprecedented intellectual potential in the visual art. Defeated Germany, too, experienced a great sense of artistic outbreak, expressed in the successive waves of Expressionism and the New Realism. Like the German cinema, the French film was deeply influenced by parallel developments in other fields of art: Dada, the Surrealists, and all the isms embraced by the Twenties resulted in two phases of avant-gardism which maintained the influence of French film art even at a time when its commercial cinema had declined fatally as a result of foreign competition. Before World War I, both Italy and Sweden had created strong national traditions of film-making – the Italians with their costume spectacles, the Swedes with the dramas and the indigenous saga films of the gifted Mauritz Stiller and Victor Sjöström – but these were early victims of the American hegemony. In these thirty years, the silent film spread throughout the world. In India and Japan, large industries and influential cultural forces, quite undiscovered by the Western world, were created in these years.

The silent film was to become extinct overnight with the arrival of talking pictures in the final years of the Twenties. But it had left its testament. The cinema's first lesson was the art of telling stories through pictures alone. Without this apprentice era of silent films, the cinema of our own times might easily have developed a more literary and visually less rich tradition. Some of the genres that have remained characteristic of the sound cinema were evolved in silent days. The need to stir audiences through visual impressions drew film-makers to exotic locations and romantic pasts, and the Western and the swashbuckler became staples of the silent era, as the musical and the gangster film, with the thrill of gunshot and roaring motor cars, were to become characteristic of the first years of sound. The greatest treasure of the silent cinema, though, was comedy. Never, in any form of art, was there a flowering of comedy as in the years between 1910 and the end of the silents. Linder, Chaplin, Keaton, Langdon, Lloyd, the Sennett circus – individually each would have been a remarkable phenomenon. Cumulatively they were a comic miracle.

"We didn't need voices. We had faces then," says Gloria Swanson, playing the silent star Norma Desmond, in Billy Wilder's tribute in 1950 to the silents, *Sunset Boulevard*. The faces of the silent years are memorable, like few other faces (Nefertiti, perhaps, the Mona Lisa, Napoleon) before or since. Chaplin and the comedians, Theda Bara, Nazimova, Valentino, Garbo, Clara Bow, Mosjoukine, Gloria Swanson herself: the images they created out of their own features were larger than life, superhuman. In the brief golden heyday of silence, they were more than mere stars. They were gods and idols, and the fabulous picture palaces of the era were cathedrals where the adoring multitudes worshipped. No small part of their mythical stature came from the very fact of silence. These fabulous beings inhabited a different plane, where they lived in light and spoke a universal language of pantomime, unshackled by the mundane conversation and Babel of ordinary voices.

Talkies came: the last silent film was taken off the screen; and it was the end. In the lifetime that has passed since then, the extinction has become virtually complete. We can admire the technique, the adventure, the invention and the courage of those early film-makers; but we can never again experience the thrill that the first audiences knew, the marvel and the emotions and the adoration that the dramas and the stars evoked in them. We cannot recapture the time when the prints were new and the images pristine and gleaming; when the picture palaces were opulent, the crowds eager, and the orchestras provided the musical accompaniments which were an essential part of the movie experience. Occasionally we are vouchsafed a brief glimpse into that enchanted past. To see the restored *Napoleon* in a big theatre, with its new orchestral score, is evidence enough that we can never again afford to patronize or underestimate the brief, miraculous time of the silent film.

David Robinson

THE LIVING IMAGE

In the cinema's long pre-history, shadows danced, projected pictures jerked into activity and scientists strove to capture the fleeting gestures of movement

Motion pictures were not so much an invention as an evolution, the confluence and culmination of a number of separate lines of research that stretched back decades, and even centuries. Men seemed always to be groping towards the kind of optical entertainment of which the cinema was to be the apogee. Myths, folklore and fiction frequently explored the theme of magic glasses in which the world may be viewed in microcosm. Long before the cinema, audiences marvelled at the shadow show and the vague images of the first magic lanterns.

The second half of the eighteenth century, however, witnessed a quite new passion for optical entertainments which was to continue practically unabated till the advent of the cinematograph, and which may be associated with the growth of popular illustrated publications as printing became cheaper.

The shadow show enjoyed an enormous vogue throughout Europe. In the 1780s a painter and theatrical designer from Alsace, Philippe-Jacques de Loutherbourg, delighted London with a show which he called the Eidophusikon. This was a theatre of effects, in which miniature scenes were animated by the cunning deployment of light and shadow.

Later in the 1780s a Scottish portrait painter, Robert Barker, took out a patent for his 'Panorama'; and Barker's vast landscape paintings, viewed on the inside of a great cylindrical building, deceived the eye with a thrillingly real *trompe-l'oeil* effect. Such works and their successors, often topical in their choice of theme and subject, were to delight London audiences for nearly seventy years. Meanwhile the public flocked eagerly to the display of realistic paintings of exceptional size, such as the 19-year-old Robert Ker Porter's opportunistically topical depiction of a famous military engagement in India, *The Storming of Seringhapatam*, which was the rage of London in 1799.

To please the eye with novelty was the universal aim of showmen and artists – and even toy-makers

The high point of this era of the painting as show was the Diorama, launched in Paris in 1822 by Louis Jacques Mandé Daguerre – whose work on photography, 17 years later, was to make another significant contribution to the evolution of the movies. The Diorama, which was re-created in London in 1823, consisted of huge paintings in which subtle effects of lighting and transformations were produced by the ingenious management of shutters and blinds controlling the light thrown from before and behind on the part-transparent image.

The names of the Panorama and Diorama were in time borrowed to describe a different method of bringing pictures to life. In Moving Panoramas and Dioramas, a long, continuous painting was passed through a proscenium opening, to give the impression of a constantly changing landscape – an effect anticipating the 'panoramic' (or 'pan') shot in the modern cinema.

Of all optical entertainments, the magic lantern was the most venerable and the most durable. The magic lantern – whose basic form still survives in the modern slide projector – embodies the same essential principles as every moving-picture projector: a powerful light source, concentrated by a condenser and passed through a transparent image to project an enlarged impression of that image, in all its colour and detail, on a white screen.

The magic lantern was first described by the Jesuit scientist Athanasius Kircher in 1671; but it was certainly known before that. Throughout the late seventeenth and eighteenth centuries, everywhere in Europe and beyond, itinerant showmen travelled with their lanterns to delight, astound and terrify their simple audiences. It was the *magic* lantern, and audiences thrilled to the supernatural and horrific effects that anticipated the twentieth-century preoccupation with horror films.

In the 1790s a Belgian showman, Etienne Robertson, scored a great and lasting success in Paris with his Phantasmagoria: the interior of his theatre was decorated as a Gothic chapel, and ghosts, witches and demons were projected on to the screen. Mounting the lantern on a wheeled carriage behind the translucent screen and adjusting the lens to maintain focus, Robertson made his fearsome images seem to grow or diminish, to startling effect.

Robertson's discoveries were exploited in London

Above: the first illustration of the magic lantern, in Athanasius Kircher's Ars Magna Lucis et Umbrae, *second edition, published in 1671. Below: an English triple or 'triunial' magic lantern, c.1890, about three feet high. By projecting from the three lenses on to the same screen, elaborate effects of superimposition could be created if the projectionist were skilful enough*

Above: Reynaud's Praxinoscope used a turning battery of mirrors in a rotating drum to reflect the phases of movement, giving a clear, bright image. Top left and right: a magic-lantern slide designed to produce the illusion of movement when projected on the screen; the techniques of the shadow show are borrowed – the articulated figures are cut out of thin brass and operated by levers. Above right: Plateau's Phenakistiscope, 1833. The spectator spun the disc in front of a mirror, viewing the reflected images through the slots. Right and centre right: a magic-lantern show in the home, c.1830, shown in a 'dioramic' print which produces a realistic lighting effect when illuminated from behind

by another showman, Niemiec Philipstahl. Rival lanternists developed other refinements, such as Henry Langdon Childe's effects of dissolving or superimposing images projected from two separate lanterns.

The magic lantern reached the height of sophistication in England in the late nineteenth century. English opticians developed magic lanterns, gleaming with the splendour of brass and polished mahogany, of such technical complexity that they required teams of people to operate them and whole libraries of explanatory literature as guides to their proper management.

From an early stage, showmen tried to give their audiences the extra thrill of movement on the screen. A slide pushed through the projector could give a persuasive impression of a procession of figures moving across the picture. Ingenious arrangements of levers and ratchets to manipulate or rotate circular glasses could produce mechanical movements in the pictures on the slides. Eyes could be made to roll, limbs to change position, fish to swim around a tank.

In the 1860s and 1870s, a more sophisticated and perfect means of producing the illusion of movement suggested itself. In the first third of the nineteenth century, physicists, including Michael

Faraday and Peter Mark Roget, had been studying a phenomenon already observed since classical times, persistence of vision. The retina of the eye appears to retain an impression for a fraction of a second after the image producing that impression has been removed. One easy illustration of this is the effect produced if a point of light – a pocket torch, for instance – is rapidly revolved in the dark, whereupon the eye receives the illusion of a continuous circle of light.

In 1833, quite independently of each other, two physicists – Joseph Plateau in Brussels and Simon Stampfer in Vienna – developed a toy to demonstrate this principle. Around the circumference of a disc were drawn a dozen little pictures representing successive phases of a continuing action. Slots were cut out between the pictures. When the disc was revolved rapidly, facing into a mirror, and the reflection was viewed through the slots as they passed before the eyes, the effect presented to the eyes was not a series of pictures but a single image in movement.

The device was quickly popularized as an instructive toy, the Phenakistiscope, and in time refined and varied. The Zoetrope, which came into vogue in the 1860s, replaced the system of disc and mirror by a hollow, open-topped drum, pierced with slots along its edge, around the inside of which were placed strips of paper printed with the appropriate series of phase drawings. In 1877, the Frenchman Emile Reynaud replaced the slots – the equivalent of the shutter in a modern movie projector – by a prismatic arrangement of mirrors in the centre.

When, in the 1850s and 1860s, the rotating disc of the Phenakistiscope was adapted to the magic lantern, flickering motion pictures could be cast

Far left: a Zoetrope manufactured in London by H.G. Clarke, c.1860. Left: the single moving image in the Zoetrope that the viewer saw by looking through the slots as the drum revolved. Below: the camera obscura, *from a mid-19th-century engraving. The viewers in the darkened chamber saw an image of the outside scenery projected, through an arrangement of lens and mirror, onto a table-screen*

onto a screen. In 1892, Reynaud's Théâtre Optique adapted the principles of the Praxinoscope, Reynaud's own invention, to project on to the screen what were virtually the first cartoon films.

One element was still missing. All these early moving-picture devices required the painstaking *drawing* of the images to be animated. But in 1839, with the perfection of Daguerre's Daguerreotype process in France and Henry Fox Talbot's Calotype (later Talbotype) in England, photography became a practical technique.

In the very early days of photography, Plateau suggested that the Daguerreotype and the Phenakistiscope could be combined; and in the 1860s and 1870s, there were a number of patents for the use of photographs in Zoetropes or similar devices. Henry R. Heyl's Phasmatrope, for instance, demonstrated in Philadelphia in 1870, gave movement to series of photographs obtained by a painful process of positioning models for each successive phase of action. The problem that thwarted all these early attempts was how to take a series of photographs in a succession rapid enough to capture the individual phases of the action as they actually took place.

The problem was eventually to be solved by a number of scientists and photographers who initially had no particular interest in creating moving pictures, but simply sought means to analyse human and animal movement for the purposes of scientific study. Eadweard Muybridge, an English photographer who spent most of his active life in the United States, arrived in 1878 at a brilliant solution with a battery of cameras which were triggered – at first mechanically, eventually electrically – as a moving person or animal passed before them. Muybridge added to this considerable achievement when in 1879 he reconstructed the movements by projecting a disc of drawings, closely based on the photographic images, in series to create an animated picture on the screen. The picture could be slowed down to show the details of motion. This development of the projecting Phenakistiscope was known as the Zoopraxiscope.

Above: a woman sitting down, photographed synchronously from three points of view by Muybridge at the University of Pennsylvania, c.1887–88. Below: Marey's photographic gun, 1882, could record phases of movement on a rotating photographic plate – the flight of a heron, for example (bottom)

In Europe, Muybridge met Etienne Marey, a physiologist who had long experimented with graphic methods of recording animal and bird movement, and contemporaneously with Muybridge was applying photography to his work. Marey noted the example of the astronomer Jules Janssen, who in 1874 had succeeded in recording the passage of the planet Venus across the face of the sun by means of a 'photographic revolver'. Shaped like a gun, this ingenious camera used a single circular plate, which revolved each time the shutter was opened, to expose one small area of its sensitized surface.

Animal locomotion was a challenge to science and a tricky puzzle to test the photographer's art

On much the same lines, Marey by 1882 had contrived a photographic gun (*fusil photographique*) which was capable of taking 12 individual photographs in one second. In 1885 in the USA, George Eastman perfected his paper roll film, which became very popular for still photography when he brought out a Kodak camera to use it in 1888. This development gave a new direction to Marey's experiments, and brought the motion-picture camera a considerable step nearer. Marey's Chronophotographe of 1888 used a continuous strip of paper film to record a sequence of individual photographs. When Eastman's celluloid roll film appeared in 1889, he promptly began to use that. In 1893, he suggested the construction of a projector to show the individual images he had recorded as a continuous action.

Marey's own assistant, Georges Demenÿ, in 1892 patented his Phonoscope, which used a sophisticated form of the Phenakistiscope to project a living photographic portrait on the screen. By this time, a great many other inventors, rich and poor, scientists and dabblers, visionaries and realists, had recognized the possibilities of a camera that would analyse movement and a projector that would reconstitute it on a screen. DAVID ROBINSON

Seeing is believing
Special effects in the early years

By 1896 Méliès was making the first of his trick films. By 1899 G.A. Smith was using a primitive montage technique. By 1900 reverse-motion printing had been achieved. So even by the end of the nineteenth century the technical skills were being learned and applied, and some have remained almost unchanged to this day

Although the programme of Lumière films that made up the first public film show in 1895 included the first fictional work, *L'Arroseur Arrosé* (Watering the Gardener), Louis Lumière and his company did not develop that side of film-making further, but concentrated on the production of actuality films. The workers at the Edison company who were making films for the Edison Kinetoscope peep-show machine, also neglected attempts at narrative in favour of recording music-hall acts and other pre-existing documentary material filmed outdoors. Nevertheless, the first Edison products did include one significant staged item, *The Execution of Mary, Queen of Scots*, made in 1895.

In this film the illusion of the Queen's head being struck off is created by stopping the camera before the axe falls and substituting a dummy for the actress kneeling at the block, then restarting the camera and continuing the action of decapitation. The two separate parts were later spliced together to give what would appear to be one continuous shot – were it not for the slight changes in position of some of the by-standing actors while the camera was stopped and the substitution made. Since many of the Edison Kinetoscope films were used for ordinary projection by the first cinema exhibitors in Europe and elsewhere, it seems quite likely that *The Execution of Mary, Queen of Scots* gave Georges Méliès the clue as to how to carry out his cinematic conjuring tricks when he took up film-making a year later.

Méliès' magical movies

Méliès, who had abandoned his father's shoe factory in 1888 for the staging of miniature spectacles of conjuring and illusionism in the Théâtre Robert-Houdin which he had bought in Paris, acquired a projector from Robert W. Paul in London after seeing the first Lumière show. He had a camera built to the same mechanical design as the projector, and began producing films that were direct imitations of the first films made by Lumière and R.W. Paul. Up to this point everybody's films had been restricted in length to the 65 or 80 feet strips in which Eastman Kodak and other manufacturers produced the film, but Méliès' *Sauvetage en Rivière* (1896, Rescue on the River) – an imitation of R.W. Paul's earlier *Up the River* (1896) – was made up of two parts, sold separately, each 65 feet long.

Towards the end of 1896, Méliès made the first of the trick films that created his fame. This was *Escamotage d'une Dame chez Robert-Houdin* (The Vanishing Lady), and it used the same device as *The Execution of Mary, Queen of Scots* but in the service of a magical effect. In it a woman was changed into a skeleton and back again by stopping the camera and substituting one for the other. It is even questionable whether Méliès was the first to use double exposure and photography against a black background, since G.A. Smith was also using these techniques at the same time in England, though it is certain that the Frenchman did the most striking things with them. In late 1898 he made *Un Homme de Tête* (The Four Troublesome Heads) in which the combination of the two devices allowed disconnected parts of the body to move round the set. After that date these methods, in combination with the 'stop-camera' effect, were his basis for large numbers of increasingly elaborate illusions.

Since trick films turned out to be merely a

Right: poster for Méliès' magic show at the Théâtre Robert-Houdin

Above: La Lune à un Mètre *(left to right), in which the astronomer falls asleep at work, dreams of a man-eating moon and an elusive goddess, and wakes a different man!*

passing fashion in the long view of history, Georges Méliès' most important contribution is that he led the way to making longer films made up of many shots. The earliest example of this was *La Lune à un Mètre* (1898, The Astronomer's Dream), closely based on one of the miniature fantastic shows that he had previously staged in his theatre. As such it indicates how not only *his* films, but also those of other film-makers of the early years were frequently indebted to the stage for their subjects.

La Lune à un Mètre was made up of three scenes, representing, first, 'The Observatory' in which an aged astronomer looks at the moon through a telescope and then falls asleep; next, 'The Moon at One Metre' in which the moon descends from the sky and swallows him up; and, lastly, 'Phoebe' in which he meets the goddess of the moon. The second sequence and the beginning of the third were intended to be understood as the dream of the astronomer who wakes up in the middle of the final scene when the goddess he is chasing vanishes by a stop-camera trick effect.

This was the first of a long line of films made over the next couple of decades that used the device of a dream story turning back to reality at the crucial moment, but the most important thing about *La Lune à un Mètre* was that the whole idea was not immediately apparent from the film itself. This was because there were only small changes made in the decor between one shot and the next, so that there was no way for the viewer immediately to realize the difference between what took place when the astronomer was awake and asleep. Since films in those days were nearly always shown with an accompanying commentary by the showman who projected them (just like the earlier lantern slide shows), this was not such a great handicap, but Méliès must have felt that the way he had treated the matter was not ideal, for in his next long fantasy film he joined all the scenes by dissolves, just as was the practice in slide shows.

He continued to put dissolves between all the shots in all his films ever afterwards – even when the action moved straight from one shot to the next without a time-lapse. *La Lune à un Mètre* was still not a very long film, being only three times the standard 65 feet (195 feet or 3 minutes running time), but in 1899 Georges Méliès moved on to films that lasted about 10 minutes and were made up of many scenes. The most important of these was *L'Affaire Dreyfus* (1899, The Dreyfus Affair), which restaged the recent events surrounding the trial of Captain Dreyfus in front of sets made of painted canvas.

Méliès had begun making 'reconstructed actuality' films as early as 1897, but those depicted unconnected events in the war between Greece and Turkey in single scenes that were sold separately. Although all the action in *L'Affaire Dreyfus* was still isolated incidents with no scene directly leading to another, it was sold as one film. Moreover, in one respect some of the staging looked forward to future developments. For the most part the actors were far from the camera and miming broadly – as was always the case at that time – but in showing an attack on Dreyfus' lawyer in the street, the framing and the way the passers-by move into the picture recall the look of actuality shots of street scenes. And when a brawl develops between pro- and anti-Dreyfus journalists in a courtroom, the action moves up close to the camera and past it in the way that was shortly to become standard for handling violent behaviour. It may be that these features were accidental rather than intentional, for Méliès himself did not develop them, but continued with his pantomime-like stagings of fantasy and his trick films.

Thrills of speed

One special style of actuality filming had a minor part to play in the evolution of the standard form of cinema that is now all too familiar. Of the large numbers of actuality films that already filled the producers' catalogues by 1898, most merely duplicated the kind of exotic and picturesque subjects – Spanish scenes, the pyramids of Egypt – that appeared on the cards of the stereoscopic viewers lying in a thousand front parlours. Yet there *was* one purely filmic variety of the travelogue shot. This was the 'phantom ride', which was produced by fixing a film camera on the front of a railway engine running along a suitable stretch of track. All

Left: the courtroom fight from L'Affaire Dreyfus. *Opposite page, far right: an early use of the inset shot – the children are asleep as* Santa Claus *makes his call*

the film-makers were producing these from 1898 onwards, but G.A. Smith – one of the many Englishmen with photographic businesses who turned to motion pictures – found a novel use for them.

In 1899 he made a film called *The Kiss in the Tunnel*, which was in essence a one-line joke of the kind that appeared in that other major source of early film content, the cartoons or comic strips of the pre-cinema period. The scene G.A. Smith shot showed the interior of a railway compartment with a single man and woman sitting on opposite seats. Nothing but blackness is visible through the windows of the compartment. Then the man stands up, takes off his hat and kisses the lady, who, after a token show of resistance, returns the embrace.

Although this was all there was to the film as it was sold, the maker's instruction to buyers was to splice a 'phantom ride' taken from a train entering and leaving a tunnel onto the beginning and end of the scene, and this is indeed the form in which the film exists today. Thus the complete *The Kiss in the Tunnel* contained a continuous action – both seen and implied – stretching across the cuts between the three shots, and when the film was re-staged and sold under the same title by Bamforth and Company of Holmfirth, Yorkshire in 1900, this point became even more obvious. In this version the kissing scene was preceded and concluded by shots taken from the sides of the tracks, which actually showed the train itself entering and leaving the tunnel. This kind of copying with interesting variations was extremely common in the first decade of the movies, and formed the main pattern for the evolution and development of film form.

Left: The Kiss in the Tunnel *(top to bottom) using the 'phantom ride' technique to amuse the audience of the day: train enters tunnel; man kisses girl; train leaves tunnel*

Shooting with sophistication

It was G.A. Smith who also invented the technique of breaking down a sequence into more than one shot or, to look at it another way, of making cuts within a scene, keeping continuity of action across them. He first did this in *Grandma's Reading Glass* (1900), showing a little boy playing with the large magnifying glass which his grandmother (who is also present in the scene) uses to read with. As the child looks at a newspaper, a bird in a cage, his grandmother's eye and so on, there is a cut to a

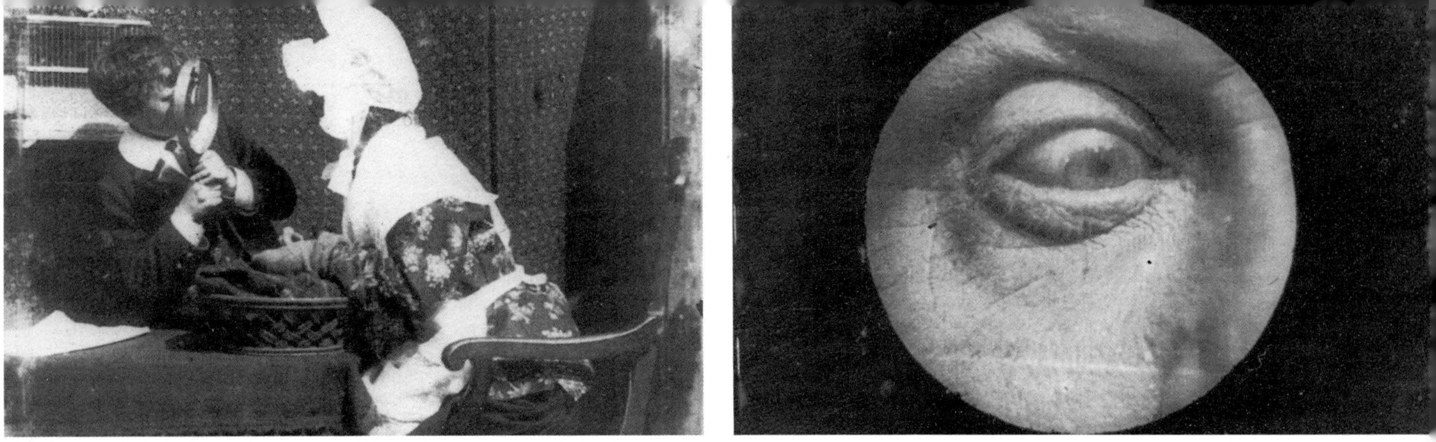

Above: on looking through Grandma's Reading Glass . . . *he sees grandma (right). Below right: the castle collapses at a touch but then re-forms in* The House That Jack Built

big close-up of each of the objects framed in a circular black vignette mask before the camera moves back to the more distant shot of the boy as he turns to look at something else.

Other innovations by G.A. Smith in these first years included the use of a second scene (inset within the main scene) to show what one of the characters was dreaming or thinking about, as in his *Santa Claus* of 1898. Here, two little children who have just been put to sleep on Christmas Eve have a dream of Santa on the rooftop climbing down into the chimney, and this dream is shown within a circular vignette in the top corner of the picture of their bedroom. This device was yet another taken over from the narratives of lantern slide shows, where it was used in the same way for the same purpose, and from that point onwards it became standard practice in films.

An even better example of Smith's technical mastery is given by *The House That Jack Built* (1901). The use of reverse motion in the cinema had existed from the outset, when it was achieved by the simple expedient of cranking the film backwards through the projector after it had been cranked through forwards. The Lumière film *Démolition d'un Mur* (1895, Demolition of a Wall) had always been a favourite for this treatment, and audiences had been fascinated to see the fallen wall rebuild itself. Smith decided to make a miniature version of the effect in permanent form, and he did it the hard way. In *The House That Jack Built* a little girl builds a castle of toy building blocks, and then a boy who is watching knocks them over. After a title announcing 'Reversed', the action appears in reversed motion, with the blocks flying up to reconstruct the original building. The scene was produced by making a print backwards one frame at a time from the original negative of the forwards action in a special projection-printer that Smith had constructed. In the very beginning (as is still mostly the case) positive prints were made from the negative by running them together in contact through a printer with light shining straight through. However, in a projection- or optical-printer the negative and the positive stock are separated, and the image from th negative is focused by a lens onto the positive so permitting the two films to be run i opposite directions if desired. A small numbe of comedy films were conceived aroun reverse-motion printing by other English film makers over the next few years, and it ha since remained part of the arsenal of purel filmic effects used for comedy purposes.

So, with all these developments, the cinem was already by 1900 taking on a life and shap of its own, independently of the older art forms and a number of its major features wer already in place and working. BARRY SAL

Below: in Smith's Let Me Dream Again *(1900, left to right) the changes of scene appear to follow without a break as the husband dreams of happier times*

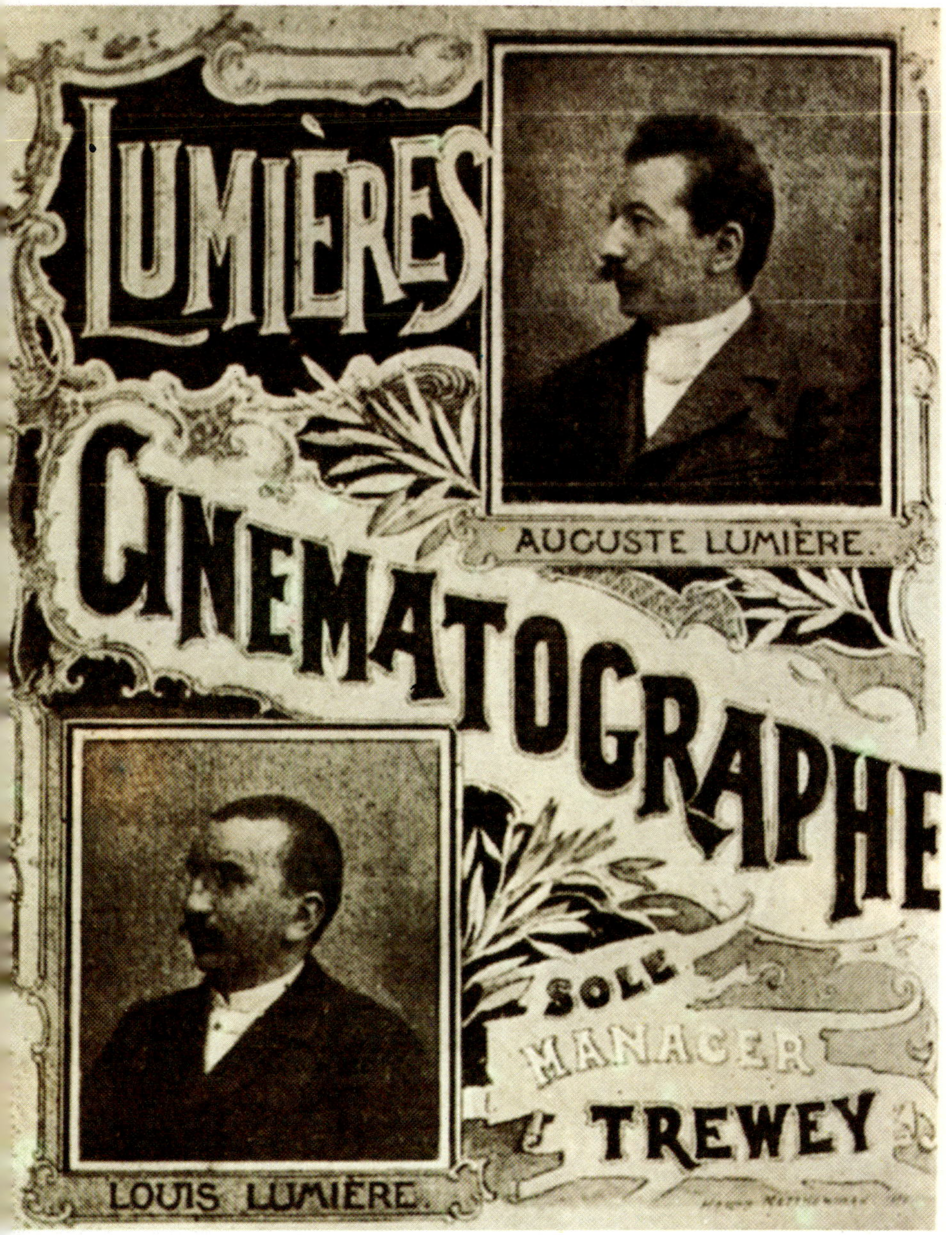

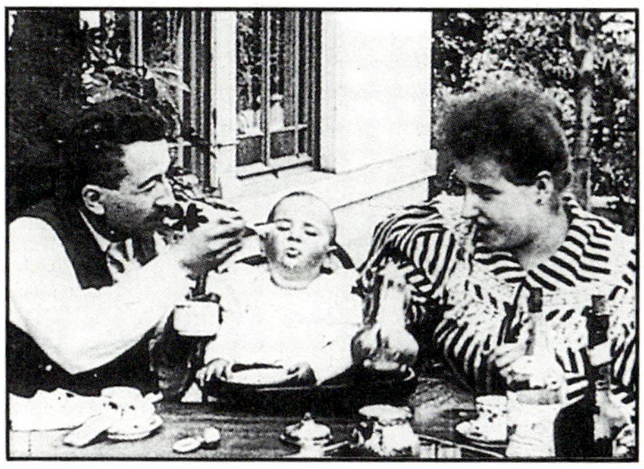

Left: the English poster for the Cinématographe. Scenes from the show (above): the workers leaving the factory (top) in the programme's opening film La Sortie des Usines; *Auguste and his wife feeding their already well-fed daughter (centre); an unsuspecting onlooker (bottom) about to be covered in dust after the demolition of a wall*

uguste and Louis Lumière were orn into the world of pictures; tatic pictures taken by their father, vho was a photographer and nanufacturer of photographic quipment. Edison's Kinetoscope nspired them to go one better and reate the Cinématographe. Thus t was more by accident than lesign that Louis Lumière became nown as the 'father of cinema'

)h, I never go to the cinema', admitted Louis umière in 1930; 'If I had known what it would ome to, I would never have invented it'. erhaps the latter was rather a sweeping atement, for the controversy over who was ctually the first to perfect practicable moving-icture apparatus still continues. However, in ne respect the Lumière brothers – Louis and uguste, who always worked as a team – have n incontrovertible claim: on December 28, 895 they presented the world's first show of rojected moving pictures to a paying public.

Louis Lumière (1864–1948) conquered the practical problems of constructing a camera and projector in the course of a sleepless night during the winter of 1894; and on February 23, 1895 Louis and Auguste (1862–1954) took out a patent for their Cinématographe. As constructed by the skilled French optician Jules Carpentier, the Cinématographe was an exemplary apparatus – compact, light, highly efficient, and combining the functions of camera, projector and optical printer.

A patently obvious success

Ten months passed between the patent and the first public showing, and during this time (according to the French historian Georges Sadoul) Louis Lumière shot some hundred one-minute films. Meanwhile, the brothers were also trying out their invention on learned societies, starting on March 22, 1895 with the Society for the Encouragement of National Industry. The following month there was a demonstration for the Congress of Learned Societies of France and the Provinces, and in June the Congress of French Photographic Societies took place on the Lumières' home territory of Lyon; the brothers delighted the Congress by filming its most distinguished members as they chatted and as they disembarked after a boat trip. These shows were followed by others in Paris and Brussels, and enthusiastic articles about the Lumières' work began to appear in the scientific press. It is hard to know whether or not these private showings were a deliberate advance campaign for the public launching of the Cinématographe, or whether the unanimously favourable reception eventually encouraged the Lumières to exploit the Cinématographe as a commercial, public entertainment.

Towards the end of the year Antoine Lumière, Louis and Auguste's father, began seeking a suitable place to house the show. The historian Jacques Deslandes says that among other sites considered was a photographer's studio over the Théâtre Robert-Houdin, which was run by the future film-maker Georges Méliès. Discussions with the Parisian waxwork show Musée Grévin came to nothing, perhaps because it was still running Emile Reynaud's Pantomimes Lumineuses. There were also negotiations with the Folies Bergère.

Finally, however, the Lumières settled on the Salon Indien of the Grand Café, Boulevard des Capucines. The Grand Café was situated on

the street level of the great Second Empire Grand Hotel; the Salon Indien was a room in the basement beneath. As the name implies, it had been extravagantly decorated in oriental style, but the proprietors of the Café seemed to have found no satisfactory use for it and were happy to let it to the Lumières for 30 francs a day. (Cautiously, but somewhat unwisely, they declined a counter-offer of 20 per cent of the receipts, which by the middle of January 1896 sometimes reached 2,500 francs a day).

The Lumières borrowed 100 gilt cane chairs from the Café, installed a house manager, Clément Maurice, and a projectionist, and on December 28 opened the doors to the public. The first advertising poster – a jolly affair looking as if the artist A. Brispot might have dashed it off at rather short notice – shows a moustachio'd policeman marshalling the enthusiastic hordes who press to the doors; though the first day of exhibition hardly justified this optimistic picture. The busy crowds were clearly too preoccupied with their New Year preparations to puzzle out the meaning of this bizarre new word, 'Cinématographe', and first-day admissions only numbered 35. However, by the second day word of the new marvel had evidently spread and queues stretched down the boulevard.

It seems likely that the programme was varied from day to day, since the Lumières already had an extensive stock of films to service the standard programme, but the opening picture seems to have remained constant: *La Sortie des Usines* (1895, Leaving the Factory) was probably the first film they had shot and was, as a tribute to their industrial success, a highly appropriate subject. The gates of the Lumière factory open; workers pour out – many of the men on bicycles, the women in long summer dresses and large hats. The last to leave is a little dog; and the gates close.

Like the rest of the following programme, this first film was technically faultless and composed with the visual sense of an

Below left: members of the Congress of French Photographic Societies leaving a pleasure boat. Below: Arrivée d'un Train en Gare *should have been a horror film judging by the audience reaction. Below right: Antoine Lumière making merry with friends. Below, far right: Madame Lumière and two children watching a rowing boat about to dock*

.eft: a colourful poster depicting the delight of n audience on seeing L'Arroseur Arrosé, *the 'rst of many Lumière gag films, in which above, far left to far right) the gardener hoses he garden; a boy sneaks up and steps on the ose, thereby stopping the water flow; a puzzled ardener looks down the nozzle; the boy takes is foot away, resulting in a soaking for the ardener; the punishment is seen to fit the rime*

ccomplished Victorian photographer. Above ll, the films were the Lumières' own home novies. They provided a faithful picture, sure o charm and flatter the public of the boulevards, of French middle-class life at the end of ne nineteenth century – a time when few eople could have foreseen the events that vere soon to destroy the illusion of unending ecurity, prosperity and peace.

Iappy families

n one film Auguste Lumière and his wife eed breakfast to their baby daughter who sits, umpling-like, between them; in another film ne same child is fascinated by a bowl of oldfish; elsewhere old Father Lumière plays ards and drinks a glass of beer with two ronies; a gentleman bathes in the sea; Iadame Lumière and two children stand on a anding stage watching the arrival of a small oat. There are scenes of the public square in yon and of soldiers exercising. The smoke ffects in a film about two blacksmiths, and the louds of dust raised by the demolition of a vall, were particularly popular with audiences.

There were two films that dominated the show and which for years were indispensable to every Lumière projection. *Arrivée d'un Train en Gare* (1895, The Arrival of a Train at the Station) is filmed looking up the platform so that the rails stretch obliquely into the distance. The express steams forward and passes the camera on the left; alighting passengers approach the camera and, again, pass it, this time to the right. The audience of the day is said to have bounded from their seats in shock at the approach of the train. Today the astonishing thing is the beauty and variety of composition achieved in a mere 50 feet of film. Louis Lumière was a highly accomplished photographer, sensitive to lighting and framing, and in addition the Cinématographe permitted a slow exposure rate with a consequently impressive depth of focus.

L'Arroseur Arrosé (1895, Watering the Gardener) earned its deserved success, and lasting fame, as the world's first film comedy. The gag is simple enough, though in 1895 it brought the house down and inspired the Lumières to feature it on a new poster. A naughty boy steals up on the gardener and treads on his hose. When the man peers into the nozzle to discover the cause of the trouble, the boy releases his foot, so spraying the poor man with water. The gardener administers a just boxing of the ears. Georges Sadoul points out that this was probably the first example of a film adaptation: the gag was inspired by a popular comic strip of the 1880s, which seems also to have been the source for later jokes.

Energetic exploitation

Perhaps because they had little confidence in the future of the cinema, the Lumières were energetic in its short-term exploitation. Their strategy was to equip projectionist-cameramen with machines and film, and despatch them to conquer new territories. Once at their destinations they would present the Lumière spectacle in theatres and music halls and at the same time film the local scenery to add to the range and exoticism of the repertoire. As their English representative the Lumières selected 'Professor' Lucien Trewey, who as a juggler and hand-shadow performer had often appeared in London's music halls. Trewey negotiated with the Empire Theatre of Varieties, Leicester Square for a fee of £300 a week. He opened there on March 9, 1896. The programme consisted of ten films, billed by English titles as:

'Dinner Hour at the Factory Gate of M. Lumière at Lyons; Tea Time; The Blacksmith at Work; A Game at Ecarté; The Arrival of the Paris Express; Children at Play; A Practical Joke on the Gardener; Trewey's Serpentine Ribbon; Place des Cordeliers (Lyon); Bathing in the Mediterranean.' Soon Trewey had added a scene of the Empire with its advertisements for the Cinématographe.

It is difficult to re-create the first impact of these films. Audiences marvelled at the limitless detail and were astounded that every figure moved, that even the leaves on the trees were given motion. The Lumières' mirror image of their world enchanted the people of the late nineteenth century, and instilled a taste that would make the movies – for all Louis Lumière's later reservations – the art of the twentieth century.

DAVID ROBINSON

If early film history is understood merely as a succession of 'firsts' (first close-up, first parallel montage and so on) and its key figures (Edwin S. Porter, D.W. Griffith, Thomas H. Ince) regarded chiefly as 'innovators', then *The Great Train Robbery* and other films of its vintage are in permanent danger of being viewed or 'read' from one perspective – how far back we can trace the key elements of today's cinematic story-telling style? This approach not only glosses over the considerable excitement of *The Great Train Robbery* itself, but also assumes that 'film language' emerged through the talent or discoveries of individual film-makers rather than as the result of the cultural and historical conditioning of how people *look at* and read movies.

The film historian Noel Burch has emphasized the early cinema's position alongside other popular entertainments of the period – melodrama, vaudeville, circuses, magic-lantern shows, and *tableaux vivants* among them. Indeed, the cinema at the turn of the century draws heavily on these popular art forms to establish a language that will be meaningful to its popular audience. But what makes *The Great Train Robbery* so compelling to watch is the way that each 'tableau' – the robbery, the passengers on the track, the barn-dance, the posse and the shoot-out – forms a fully articulated part of the narrative. The story flows from one incident to the next and builds in tension to a climax that, quite properly, is the conclusion of the film.

The resulting sense of narrative satisfaction is derived not just from the structure – plot elements decided at the script stage and dramatized in the editing – but also from the shooting. Here the director Edwin S. Porter achieves an unusual mixture of head-on, middle-distance studio shots – the barn dance for example – and exterior shots, including a remarkable panning movement as the camera follows the robbers away from the train and down the hillside. Recent research now confirms that 1903 is the correct date for *The Life of an American Cowboy*, which also concludes with an exciting chase. Porter's camera panned slightly to the right in order to hold the action – the capture of the robbers – in the centre of the frame. The lesson to be learned from this is clearly that, whatever else may be going on in the picture (in the frame), the action that is most significant for the story should be 'centred'. The best example of this in *The Great Train Robbery* occurs when the clerk interrupts the barn dance with the news of the robbery – a scene of diverse, almost documentary activity is suddenly focused by the narrative action.

Of all the specifically cinematic elements in the film, the most remarkable is the close-up of the bandits' leader (played by George Barnes, fiercely villainous in cowboy hat and kerchief) aiming his gun at the camera and, as the Edison trade catalogue states, 'firing point-blank at each individual in the audience'. The implications of this close-up and its shock value to audiences not accustomed to seeing film action from

2

1

6

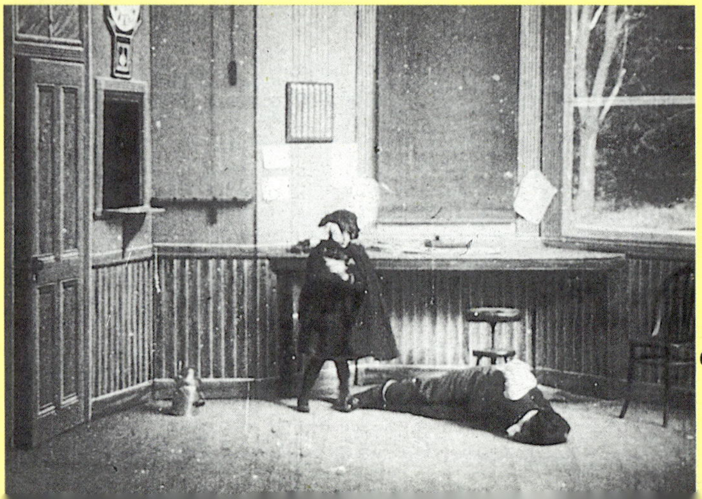
5

such proximity – let alone being made its 'victims' – are considerable. Even more significant is the fact that this shot was packaged separately from the rest of the film with exhibitors given the option of placing it at the beginning or at the end of the film – nowhere else. Thus in a film composed entirely of mid or long shots, it was impossible to *insert* the George Barnes close-up into the flow of the film simply because it could not be 'read' as part of the train-robbery narrative by an audience that had never encountered a close-up before.

Furthermore the shot complicated the narrative by introducing a recognizable human face – a character in the story – into an action that otherwise involves mere figures. Yet the film is not complete without its close-up: shown at the beginning, it is a kind of foretaste of the action; shown at the end, it serves as a 'parting shot', a warning and a triumph for the bad guy who appears to be resurrected after his death in the shoot-out.

Finally, it must be acknowledged that in a mere twenty shots, this film contains more variety of location, more fluid movement from scene to scene and more gripping action than anything that preceded it in the American cinema. For the early cinemagoer, the legend of the Wild West had been brought to life, vividly. And all for a nickel.

MARTYN AUTY

Directed by Edwin S. Porter, 1903
Prod co: The Thomas Edison Co.
Cast: Broncho Billy Anderson, George Barnes, A.C. Abadie, Marie Murray.

At a station two robbers attack a telegraph clerk (1), knock him out and tie him us as a train pulls in. While the engine is being refuelled, four more bandits join the robbery. The guard in the mail carriage hears shooting further up the train. As he tries to lock the strong-box, the robbers burst in and shoot him. They then blow up the strong-box (2).

The train has been stopped, meanwhile, and the passengers are lined up outside on the track. One by one they empty their wallets for the robbers. One man tries to escape but is shot in the back (3). Having disengaged the engine from the train, the robbers climb aboard (4) and travel a short distance before leaping off, running down a gorge and mounting their horses.

Back at the station the clerk is discovered by his daughter (5), who releases him from his ropes and sounds the alarm. At a nearby barn dance (6), townsfolk are enjoying themselves when the clerk rushes in and announces the robbery. The men form a posse and give chase to the robbers, one of whom is shot. The others come to a clearing and begin to share out the loot (7), but they are surrounded by the posse and killed in the subsequent shoot-out (8).

4

8

The Immigrant

1

4

7

Directed by Charles Chaplin, 1917
Prod co: Mutual. **sc:** Charles Chaplin. **photo:** William C. Foster, Rollie Totheroh. **r/t:** 30 minutes.
Cast: Charles Chaplin (*Tramp*), Edna Purviance (*the Girl*), Albert Austin (*Russian immigrant; a diner*), Henry Bergman (*the artist; fat woman on ship*), Stanley Sanford (*gambler-thief*), Eric Campbell (*head-waiter*), James T. Kelly (*the old tramp*), John Rand (*a customer*), Frank J. Coleman (*owner of the restaurant*), Kitty Bradbury (*the mother*).

In the summer of 1916 Charles Chaplin signed the most lucrative contract that the film industry had ever seen. It was with the Mutual company, and it brought him $10,000 weekly, a bonus of $150,000 and full creative control. For the company it was money well spent. The contract called for 12 two-reel films, and the 12 Mutual comedies that Chaplin made are thought by many to be his finest work. They included such masterpieces as *The Pawn Shop* (1916), *Easy Street* and *The Immigrant* (both 1917).

The Immigrant is perhaps the richest of all, and it conclusively gives the lie to the notion that Chaplin's ability as a director was less than his skill as a mime. From the opening rear shot of the Tramp kicking and wriggling over the side of the ship to the final happy flourish outside the marriage licence bureau, Chaplin's handling seldom errs.

Passages of staccato editing mingle comfortably with more sustained sequences. The close-ups are always effective. Gags are subtly worked into the pattern of the film, often quietly introduced for the sake of a pay-off sometime later – an example is the Tramp's appropriation of the artist's tip to pay his own bill, so setting up the marvellous look of disgust on the face of the head-waiter (Eric Campbell) at the end of the restaurant scene. Sentiment is easily controlled, and social comment is the more effective for being so unobtrusive.

The film is wonderfully economical. There are only four sets: the ship's deck, the ship's dining-room, a street exterior and the restaurant. There are very few actors. Chaplin creates the impression of a crowded immigrant ship; but the huddled masses are only about sixteen in number, carefully deployed, and they include Henry Bergman – who plays the artist at the end – disguised in scarf and apron as a plump lady immigrant rolling on the swaying floor with the Tramp.

Chaplin's own mime is at its most inventive. The rocking deck gives a new dimension to the familiar walk, and the crap game provides a delicious parody of a baseball pitcher, while the shuffle and deal at poker combine supreme elegance with two pieces of cheating that require very close observation to spot. The poker game leads to a lovely moment when the Tramp filches the gambler's pistol, turns to pick up his hat and suddenly aims the pistol backwards between his legs. As a final instance, the shadow-boxing in the restaurant when he fears that he will have to fight the monstrous head-waiter is a perfect blending of courage, defiance and despair.

The hard lot of the immigrants is never forgotten for long. They lie helplessly on the deck behind the Tramp's opening acrobatics. They are held back, roughly, by constraining ropes immediately after a shot of the Statue of Liberty has been ironically cut in. They are hustled off the ship into the utter

3

6

9

strangeness of the big city, a point beautifully made by the Tramp's unawareness that he has to take off his hat in the restaurant and by his inability to read the menu.

They need money, and money is continually and mockingly passing them by. The money that the Tramp gives to the Girl is in fact the mother's money, which the gambler has stolen and then lost at poker. The Tramp uses a coin the head-waiter has dropped, the same one he had found and lost, to pay his bill – but the coin is a dud, so he filches a tip meant for the head-waiter. The $2 he later borrows from the artist will go on the marriage licence. Where the gambling winnings have gone to is never made plain – nor does that matter. The important point being that money never stays.

There are still rough edges in *The Immigrant*. There is certainly too much crude fun with seasickness; and there is an odd continuity slip-up when a large axe, suspended on the wall behind the crap-shooters, clearly for a purpose, has vanished in the next scene. But the coarser slapstick of Chaplin's Keystone comedies, which persisted to some extent in the Essanay films too, has gone for good. There was one more Mutual film to come – *The Adventurer* (1917) – and then Chaplin would be off to the First National company with his feature films in sight.

But for his finest foil, Eric Campbell, *The Immigrant* and *The Adventurer* were to be the last films he would make. This gigantic Scot, remembered best for his sorely-tried head-waiter in *The Immigrant* and for his bully of the district in *Easy Street*, had, like Chaplin, come to America with Fred Karno's troupe, and was killed in a motor accident later in 1917. No-one could ever quite replace him.

JACK LODGE

On board a vessel bound for New York, the Tramp, seemingly sick, catches a fish (1). He strolls the deck (2), meeting the Girl and her mother, who are fellow immigrants. The Tramp wins money from the gambler at craps, and later at poker (3), and retains it by threatening him with his own gun (4). The gambler has stolen the money from the mother, the Girl tells the Tramp, who secretly replaces the cash (5).

Later, in the city, the Tramp is hungry and broke. He finds a coin and goes into a restaurant (6), not realizing that he has lost it again. There he meets the Girl, now an orphan, and then discovers his loss (7). The Tramp evades all the head-waiter's attempts to make him pay the bill, and is alarmed by a beating-up administered to a customer who is ten cents short.

The situation is saved by the artist (8), who wants the Tramp and the Girl to pose for him. The Tramp politely refuses the artist's offer to pay his bill, and manages to do so himself by appropriating the artist's tip. He borrows $2 on account from the artist, and leads the Girl into a marriage-licence bureau (9).

The spiritual purity of Lillian Gish; the earthiness of her sister Dorothy; the confident determination of Blanche Sweet and the youthful frailty of Mae Marsh are lasting images of the silent screen. D.W. Griffith's work with Mary Pickford is well known, but the other Griffith girls also embodied the characteristics that created his ideal of womanhood

The Griffith Girls

A personal choice of the five greatest actresses in early cinema might include – for no-one would produce the same list – Lillian Gish, Mae Marsh, Louise Brooks, (Renée) Falconetti and Greta Garbo. Of that imposing list two were formed by Mr Griffith. This was what D.W. Griffith was always called by his actresses; not 'David', 'Dave' nor even 'D.W.'. For them he was the master, and 'Mr Griffith' every time.

Lillian Gish and her younger sister Dorothy first went to the Biograph studio – so it is said – to see their friend Gladys Smith (Mary Pickford), whom they had recognized in *Lena and the Geese* (1912). There are half a dozen conflicting accounts of what happened that June day in 1912, but the sisters were immediately engaged, and made their first notable appearance soon afterwards in *An Unseen Enemy* (1912). Up until December 1913, Lillian and Dorothy worked for Griffith at Biograph. When he moved on to the Reliance–Majestic Company they went with him.

History in the making

Lillian Gish (born Lillian Guiche in Springfield, Ohio, on October 14, 1896) was on the stage at the age of 5. She was a mere 15 when she played the harassed young wife in *The Musketeers of Pig Alley* (1912), a performance that foreshadowed much that was to come; the gentleness, the fragility, the bruised innocence, the inner strength, all are there. But while at Biograph Lillian was very much third string to Pickford and Blanche Sweet. It was after Griffith's move to Reliance (and to features) that her talent flowered. Lillian played the lead in *The Battle of the Sexes* and *Home, Sweet Home* (both 1914), and then in 1915 came the role of Elsie Stoneman in *The Birth of a Nation*. The historian Edward Wagenknecht, a devoted Lillian admirer, found that this was the least effective of her major roles; but it is difficult to agree. Other parts in *The Birth of a Nation* offer showier opportunities but Elsie – daughter of a Northern politician who is in love with a Southern officer – is the still centre around which the film revolves. This was to be the keystone of any Lillian Gish performance. Threatened by wind or water, war or revolution, the small, self-sufficient figure was filled with its own private defiance. And audiences only had eyes for her – so sometimes had the extras. When she filmed the hospital scene in *The Birth of a Nation* an extra named Freeman gazed on her with adoration; Griffith noticed the expression, had Freeman repeat it for the camera, and an unforgettably comic moment resulted.

Because Lillian could express maternal concern with such conviction, the mother-child relationship was at the heart of many of her finest characterizations. In *Intolerance* (1916) she only appears in the linking tableau as the mother eternally rocking the cradle of history. People wondered why Griffith had not cast her in one of the other roles, saying that any extra could have rocked the cradle. But, as ever, Griffith was right. Only Lillian could have managed the same intensity of action and expression.

A series of marvellous Gish characters followed, and all for Griffith: the distraught bride in *Hearts of the World* (1918), wandering through the battlefield in her wedding-dress; her touching, resolute country girl in the charming (and very funny) *True Heart Sus[ie]* (1919); the little girl, scarcely more than [a] child, in *Broken Blossoms* (1919), arguably he[r] finest role. It was here that, when told to smi[le] in the midst of her wretchedness, she intro[-]duced that miraculous gesture of using he[r] fingers to force her lips into a smile. It was als[o] here that, shut into a cupboard, she betraye[d] hysteria not by any obvious means but b[y] turning rapidly round and round like som[e] tiny creature trapped on a treadmill. An[d] again, it was here that the photographe[r] Henrik Sartov, who had orchestrated he[r] close-ups since *Hearts of the World*, used h[is]

gauzes and special lenses to catch her ethereal beauty as no-one had done before.

Way Down East (1920) is remembered for the climax on the ice-floes, but still more moving was the amazing scene in which Lillian baptizes her dying baby. 'I do not know', wrote Wagenknecht in *The Movies in the Age of Innocence*, 'who [else] could have lifted the whole scene, as she did, away from squalor, beyond the physical, who could so beautifully have suggested the age-old miracle of the girl become mother.'

Far left: Lillian and Dorothy Gish as Orphans of the Storm, *sisters who are separated by cruel circumstances and are only re-united in the final reel. Left: Lillian as Lucy Burrows, soon to be battered to death by her father in* Broken Blossoms

Double acting

Lillian Gish's last film for Griffith was *Orphans of the Storm* (1921). (She and her younger sister Dorothy had appeared together three years previously in *Hearts of the World*, and under Griffith's auspices, Lillian had directed Dorothy in *Remodelling Her Husband* in 1920.) As the blind Louise, Dorothy has the bravura moments, and uses her chances well; Lillian, as her devoted prop, Henriette, once again conjures a world of emotion by the smallest and simplest of means. The sisters play together with charming naturalness and intimacy, culminating in a deeply moving moment when the blind Louise walks, singing, down a narrow street and Henriette, hearing, tries in vain to attract her attention from a balcony above. Silent movies were never really silent and watching this the audience 'heard' Louise sing, 'heard' Henriette cry out to her.

Then, as he often did with his more successful actresses, Griffith let Lillian go. She could earn more elsewhere and he would not hold her back. At MGM she had three great triumphs. King Vidor's *La Bohème* (1926), saw her opposite John Gilbert, ice against fire. In his autobiography *A Tree Is a Tree*, Vidor describes how she had control of director and script, and insisted – as her contract allowed – on rehearsals in Griffith style, with bare stage and imaginary props. He also tells of her preparation for Mimi's death scene:

'When she arrived on the set that fateful day, we saw her sunken eyes, her hollow cheeks, and we noticed that her lips had curled outwards and were parched with dryness.

Opposite page, bottom: Lillian Gish beginning to blossom in a very early one-reeler The Musketeers of Pig Alley *and (left) still blooming 66 years later in* A Wedding, *the black comedy about marriage*

Dorothy Gish: filmography

All shorts unless otherwise specified. **1912** An Unseen Enemy; The Musketeers of Pig Alley; The Informer; Gold and Glitter; The New York Hat; My Hero; A Cry for Help. **'13** Oil and Water; The Perfidy of Mary; The Lady and the Mouse; Just Gold; Almost a Wild Man; Her Mother's Oath; Pa Says; The Vengeance of Galora; Those Little Flowers; The Widow's Kids; The Suffragette Minstrels; The Adopted Brother; The Lady in Black; For the Son of the House; A Fallen Hero; A Cure for Suffragettes; The Blue or the Gray; The House of Discord; Judith of Bethulia. **'14** Her Old Father; Her Father's Silent Partner; The Mysterious Shot; The Old Man; The Floor Above (feature); The Mountain Rat (feature); Home, Sweet Home (feature); Classmates (feature); The Newer Woman; Silent Sandy; Their First Acquaintance; The Rebellion of Kitty Belle; The Tavern of Tragedy; Arms and the Gringo; The Suffragette Battle of Nuttyville; The City Beautiful; The Painted Lady; Man's Enemy; A Lesson in Mechanics; Her Mother's Necklace; Granny; Down the Hill to Creditville; The Warning; A Fair Rebel; Liberty Belles; Sands of Fate; Back to the Kitchen; The Availing Prayer; The Wife; The Saving Grace; The Sisters; A Question of Courage; The Better Way. **'15** His Lesson; An Old-Fashioned Girl; The Lost Lord Lovell; How Hazel Got Even; Minerva's Mission; Her Grandparents; Out of Bondage; The Mountain Girl; The Little Catamount; Victorine; Bred in the Bone (feature); Old Heidelberg (feature); Jordan is a Hard Road (feature); Her Mother's Daughter/The Nun. *All features unless otherwise specified.* **'16** Betty of Greystone; Little Meena's Romance; Susan Rocks the Boat (GB: Sweet Seventeen); The Little Schoolma'am; Gretchen the Greenhorn; Atta Boy's Last Race/The Best Bet; Children of the Feud. **'17** Stage Struck; Her Official Fathers. **'18** Hearts of the World; The Hun Within (GB: The Peril Within); Battling Jane; The Hope Chest. **'19** Boots; Peppy Polly; I'll Get Him Yet; Nugget Nell; Nobody Home (GB: Out of Luck); Turning the Tables. **'20** Mary Ellen Comes to Town; Remodelling Her Husband (+co-sc.); Little Miss Rebellion; Flying Pat; The Ghost in the Garret. **'21** Orphans of the Storm. **'22** The Country Flapper. **'23** Fury; The Bright Shawl. **'24** Romola. **'25** Night Life of New York; The Beautiful City; Clothes Make the Pirate. **'26** Nell Gwyn (GB). **'27** London (GB). **'28** Madame Pompadour (GB); Tiptoes (GB). **'30** Wolves (Released in the USA in 1936 as 'Wanted Men'). **'44** Our Hearts Were Young and Gay. **'46** Centennial Summer. **'51** The Whistle at Eaton Falls (GB: Richer Than the Earth). **'63** The Cardinal.

Lillian Gish: filmography

All shorts unless otherwise specified. **1912** An Unseen Enemy; Two Daughters of Eve; In the Aisles of the Wild; The One She Loved; The Musketeers of Pig Alley; My Baby; Gold and Glitter; The New York Hat; The Burglar's Dilemma; A Cry for Help. **'13** Oil and Water; The Unwelcome Guest; The Stolen Bride; A Misunderstood Boy; The Left-Handed Man; The Lady and the Mouse; The House of Darkness; Just Gold; Just Kids; A Timely Interception; The Mothering Heart; During the Round-Up; An Indian's Loyalty; A Woman in the Ultimate; A Modest Hero; So Runs the Way; The Madonna of the Storm; The Blue or the Gray; The Conscience of Hassan Bey; Judith of Bethulia. **'14** The Green-Eyed Devil; The Battle at Elderbush Gulch; The Battle of the Sexes (feature); The Hunchback; The Quicksands; Home, Sweet Home (feature); Silent Sandy; The Escape (feature); The Rebellion of Kitty Belle; Lord Chumley (feature); Man's Enemy; The Angel of Contention; The Wife; The Tear That Burned; The Folly of Anne; The Sisters. *All features unless otherwise specified.* **'15** The Birth of a Nation; His Lesson (extra) (short); The Lost House; Enoch Arden (GB: As Fate Ordained); Captain Macklin; Souls Triumphant; The Lily and the Rose. **'16** Daphne and the Pirate; Sold for Marriage; An Innocent Magdalene; Flirting with Fate; Intolerance; Diane of the Follies; Pathways of Life; The Children Pay. **'17** The House Built Upon Sand. **'18** Hearts of the World; The Great Love; The Greatest Thing in Life; Liberty Bond (short). **'19** A Romance of Happy Valley; Broken Blossoms; True Heart Susie. **'20** Remodeling Her Husband (dir. +co-sc. only); Way Down East. **'21** Orphans of the Storm. **'23** The White Sister. **'24** Romola. **'26** La Bohème; The Scarlet Letter. **'27** Annie Laurie; The Enemy. **'28** The Wind. **'30** One Romantic Night. **'33** His Double Life. **'42** The Commandos Strike at Dawn. **'43** Top Man. **'46** Miss Susie Slagle's; Duel in the Sun. **'48** Portrait of Jennie (GB: Jennie). **'55** The Cobweb; Night of the Hunter; Salute to the Theatres (appearance as herself) (short). **'58** Orders to Kill (GB). **'60** The Unforgiven. **'66** Follow me, Boys! **'67** Warning Shot; The Comedians; The Comedians in Africa (appearance as herself) (short). **'70** Henri Langlois (guest appearance as herself) (short). **'78** A Wedding.

Above: Carol Dempster as a homeless girl queuing for food to feed her father in post-World War I Europe in Isn't Life Wonderful? *Above right: Mary Pickford, Griffith's most popular lady, in* An Arcadian Maid *(1910). Right: Blanche Sweet in* Judith of Bethulia

What on earth had she done to herself? I ventured to ask about her lips, and she said in syllables hardly audible that she had succeeded in removing all saliva from her mouth by not drinking any liquids for three days, and by keeping cotton pads between her teeth and gums even in her sleep.'

As Hester Prynne in *The Scarlet Letter* (1926) she was perfect. Playing the girl's warmth, tenderness and instinctive passion against the Puritan rigour of her upbringing, Lillian made her character far more three-dimensional than the novelist Nathanael Hawthorne's had been. *The Wind* (1928), showing her driven to the edge of insanity by the unrelenting prairie wind and then trapped into murder, was her last *tour de force*. Here again no sound is needed. The images, and Lillian, still make that wind batter the ears.

She left MGM, displaced by Garbo and changing tastes, and returned to the stage. However, she still found time for character appearances in movies, and, as the indomitable protector of the children in *Night of the Hunter* (1955), is unforgettable. When she appeared, still very much alive and kicking in *A Wedding* (1978), she had been in movies for 66 years.

Her sister Dorothy (1898–1968) is unlucky in that the films in which she appears without Lillian are very seldom seen. There are glimpses of her in Biograph pictures; there is her French girl in *Hearts of the World*, for which Griffith wanted a comic walk and made her watch and imitate the gait of a London street-walker; and there is *Old Heidelberg* (1915). Here, in the role later played by Norma Shearer in *The Student Prince* (1927), she shows such charm and sense of fun that all her unseen films are regretted the more. She too continued into sound, but her appearances were rare and the films undistinguished.

Devilish rumours

No actress in the movies has been more unfairly criticized than Carol Dempster (b. 1902), who played leads for Griffith from 1919 to 1926. That she could not act, and was favoured by a doting Griffith who wished to marry her, has been said a hundred times.

Carol Dempster: filmography

1916 Intolerance (extra). **'18** The Hope Chest. **'19** A Romance of Happy Valley; The Girl Who Stayed at Home; True Heart Susie; The Fall of Babylon (extra) (The Babylonian story from 'Intolerance', 1916, with additional material); Scarlet Days. **'20** Way Down East; The Love Flower. **'21** Dream Street. **'22** Sherlock Holmes (GB: Moriarty); One Exciting Night. **'23** The White Rose. **'24** America (GB: Love and Sacrifice); Isn't Life Wonderful? **'25** Sally of the Sawdust; That Royle Girl. **'26** The Sorrows of Satan.

Blanche Sweet: filmography

All shorts unless otherwise specified. **1909** A Man with Three Wives; A Corner in Wheat; Choosing a Husband; The Day After. **'10** The Rocky Road; All on Account of the Milk; A Romance of the Western Hills. **'11** Was He a Coward?; The Lonedale Operator; How She Triumphed; Country Lovers; The White Rose of the Wilds; A Smile of a Child; The Primal Call; A Country Cupid; The Last Drop of Water; Out from the Shadow; The Blind Princess and the Poet; The Stuff Heroes Are Made of; The Making of a Man; The Long Road; Love in the Hills; The Battle; Through Darkened Vales; A Woman Scorned; The Voice of the Child. **'12** The Eternal Mother; For His Son; The Transformation of Mike; Under Burning Skies; The Goddess of Sagebrush Gulch; The Punishment; One is Business, the Other Crime; The Lesser Evil; An Outcast Among Outcasts; A Temporary Truce; The Spirit Awakened; Man's Lust for Gold; The Inner Circle; With the Enemy's Help; A Change of Spirit; Blind Love; The Chief's Blanket; The Painted Lady; A Sailor's Heart; The God Within. **'13** Three Friends; Pirate Gold; Oil and Water; A Chance Deception; Love in an Apartment Hotel; Broken Ways; The Hero of Little Italy; The Stolen Bride; If We Only Knew; Death's Marathon; The Mistake; The Coming of Angelo; The Vengeance of Galora; Two Men of the Desert; The House of Discord; Her Wedding Bell; The Massacre; Judith of Bethulia (feature). **'14** The Sentimental Sister; Ashes of the Past; Classmates (feature); The Soul of Honor; Strongheart; The Painted Lady; The Second Mrs. Roebuck; Men and Women; For Those Unborn; Her Awakening; For Her Father's Sins; The Tear That Burned; The Little Country Mouse; The Odalisque; The Old Maid; Home, Sweet Home (feature); The Escape (feature); The Avenging

Griffith may well have wanted to marry her, but the rest is an absurdity, for in *Isn't Life Wonderful?* (1924) she is direct, unmannered, utterly convincing and worthy to be Lillian's heir in this story of a starving family of Polish refugees (made by Griffith on location in Germany, and belying all rumours of his decline by showing a master at the height of his powers). Miss Dempster is undaunted by W.C. Fields in *Sally of the Sawdust* (1925), no mean feat, and charming in a sketchy role for *America* (1924). She had been with Griffith since *Intolerance*, in which she was one of the Denishawn dancers, but did not get her real chance until *The Girl Who Stayed at Home* (1919). The cinema historian Kevin Brownlow, virtually the only writer to do her justice, said of her performance in *The Sorrows of Satan* (1926):

'Griffith returned to his former methods to induce some shattering scenes from Carol Dempster. Again and again throughout the film a long-held close-up of Miss Dempster plays havoc with the audience's emotions. Seeing the film absolutely silent, with no music to help it, and just this lovely face in close-up on the screen, you can still feel something of the electricity that passed between director and actress and generated this extraordinary performance.'

Unhappily, it was her last. That same year she married a broker and retired.

The sour sweet

The first Griffith actress to become well known was Blanche Sweet (b. 1895). Like the Gishes and Pickford, Miss Sweet went on stage as a child, and when she was only 14 went to Biograph. At 15 she played her first famous role, that of the plucky telephonist in *The Lonedale Operator* (1911), a film noted for its superb cutting and camera placements. Belying her apparently genuine name, the typical Sweet character was far from sweet and pathetic, in fact she was very much the toughest and most self-reliant of the Griffith heroines. Her pioneer girl in *The Massacre* (1913) is an excellent example. But with the loss of almost all her later starring features for the Lasky company, the claim for her greatness rests on *Judith of Bethulia* (1913), Griffith's final Biograph film. Sent to kill Holofernes, the besieger of her city, she falls in love with him although she kills him all the same. Looking beautiful and acting with splendid authority, she generates a formidable erotic charge. Like Lillian Gish, Blanche Sweet returned to the theatre in the early days of sound and only made one film appearance thereafter.

Mary Wayne (Mae) Marsh (1895–1968) followed her elder sister Margaret to Biograph in 1911. She played the lead in *Man's Genesis* in 1912 because Pickford and Sweet, among others, refused to perform bare-legged. Her reward was the star part in *The Sands of Dee* (1912), a role that all Griffith's young ladies had set their hearts on. The two films firmly established her as leading player. As one of the young lovers in *Judith of Bethulia* she is radiant, and the Marsh persona is all there. The Mae Marsh heroïne is fragile in appearance, or was in her early days, but she has also been called 'helpless', and she was never that. 'Indomitable' would be a better word. The carriage, the set of the face, the ability to convey a sudden and overwhelming happiness, all these speak of an inner resource that nothing can touch. It is wrong to see the Little Sister in *The Birth of a Nation* as essential Marsh; the fluttering, bird-like movements, belong to the part and not to the off-screen actress. Indeed the character is a kind of allegory of the forlornly resisting South. Compare her with the Dear One in *Intolerance* (1916). Here are strength and determination personified, and the result is a great acting

Left: Sweet as she appeared in a series of star portraits. Below: Mae Marsh (here in The Escape, *1914) was never really a career woman, preferring to concentrate on her home*

onscience (feature) (GB: Thou Shalt Not Kill). *All atures unless otherwise specified.* **'15** The Wartens of Virginia; The Captive; Stolen Goods; The lue; The Secret Orchard; The Case of Becky; The ecret Sin. **'16** The Ragamuffin; The Blacklist; he Sowers; The Thousand Dollar Husband; The upe; Public Opinion; The Storm; Unprotected; he Evil Eye. **'17** Those Without Sin; The Tides of arnegat; The Silent Partner. **'19** The Unpardonble Sin; The Hushed Hour; A Woman of leasure. **'20** Fighting Cressy; The Deadlier Sex; mple Souls; The Girl in the Web; Help Wanted – ale; Her Unwilling Husband. **'21** That Girl ontana; Quincy Adams Sawyer. **'23** Souls for ale (guest appearance as herself); The Meanest lan in the World; In the Palace of the King; nna Christie. **'24** Those Who Dance; Tess of the Urbervilles. **'25** The Sporting Venus; His Supeme Moment; Why Women Love; The New ommandment. **'26** Bluebeard's Seven Wives; he Far Cry; The Lady from Hell (GB: The terrupted Wedding); Diplomacy. **'27** Singed. **9** The Woman in White; Blanche Sweet in lways Faithful (short). **'30** The Woman Racket B: Lights and Shadows); Showgirl in Hollyood; The Silver Horde. **'59** The Five Pennies.

Above: before returning to Griffith to make The White Rose, *Marsh starred in the British-made* Paddy the Next Best Thing *(1923). Right: Marsh beginning a new chapter in her career – with Peggy Ann Garner in* A Tree Grows in Brooklyn *(1945)*

performance. Griffith and his cameraman Billy Bitzer made it possible – never have close-ups been used more effectively or revealed such emotion – but it was Marsh who made her character live with such raw reality, such extremes of joy and grief.

After *Intolerance* Mae Marsh left Griffith for Goldwyn, and the quality of her films declined. She returned to Griffith, for *The White Rose* in 1923, then retired for a while before starting a new career as a character actress in the Thirties. In Borzage's *Little Man, What Now?* (1934), she plays a victim of the German depression – a tiny part, just two scenes, but she can still knock the rest of the film sideways.

Fording the years

But for John Ford, that would have been virtually the end. Ford had first met Miss Marsh while riding with the Klan in *The Birth of a Nation*, and he used her again and again. Often not even credited, she filled corners of the Ford canvas with her brave, undaunted ladies: standing firm as a rock as her home is razed in *The Grapes of Wrath* (1940); a quiet counterpoint to chattering Jane Darwell in *The Sun Shines Bright* (1953); the curate's proud mother in *The Quiet Man* (1952); rescued from Indian captivity in *The Searchers* (1956). In all these films she still carried an aura of the heroic days, and in her career linked two great masters of the American screen.

JACK LODGE

Mae Marsh: filmography

All shorts unless otherwise specified. **1912** One is Business, the Other Crime; The Lesser Evil; The Old Actor; When Kings Were Law; Home Folks; Lena and the Geese; The Spirit Awakened; Just Like a Woman; Man's Genesis; The Sands of Dee; Kentucky Girl; The Parasite; Brutality; The New York Hat. **'13** The Telephone Girl and the Lady; An Adventure in the Autumn Woods; The Tender-Hearted Boy; Oil and Water; Love in an Apartment Hotel; Broken Ways; Fate; The Perfidy of Mary; The Little Tease; The Wanderer; Her Mother's Son; The Reformers, or The Lost Art of Minding One's Business; Two Men of the Desert; Influence of the Unknown; The Primitive Man; Judith of Bethulia. *All features unless otherwise specified.* **'14** Brute Force (short); The Great Leap; Home, Sweet Home; The Swindlers; The Escape; Moonshine Molly; The Avenging Conscience (GB: Thou Shalt Not Kill); Paid with Interest; The Genius. **'15** The Birth of a Nation; The Outcast; The Victim; Her Shattered Idol; Big Jim's Heart. **'16** Hoodoo Ann; The Marriage of Molly O; The Wild Girl of the Sierras; Intolerance; A Child of the Paris Streets; The Little Liar; The Wharf Rat. **'17** Polly of the Circus; Sunshine Alley; The Cinderella Man. **'18** Fields of Honor; The Beloved Traitor; The Face in the Dark; All Woman; The Glorious Adventure; Money Mad; Hidden Fires; The Racing Strain. **'19** The Bondage of Barbara; Spotlight Sadie. **'20** The Little 'Fraid Lady. **'21** Nobody's Kid. **'22** Till We Meet Again; Flames of Passion (GB). **'23** Paddy the Next Best Thing (GB); The White Rose. **'24** Daddies; Arabella (GER); A Woman's Secret (GB). **'25** Tides of Passion; The Rat (GB). **'31** Over the Hill. **'32** Rebecca of Sunnybrook Farm; That's My Boy. **'33** Alice in Wonderland. **'34** Little Man, What Now? **'35** Black Fury; Bachelor of Arts. **'36** Hollywood Boulevard. **'39** Drums Along the Mohawk. **'40** The Man Who Wouldn't Talk; The Grapes of Wrath; Young People. **'41** Great Guns; How Green Was My Valley. **'42** Blue, White and Perfect; Tales of Manhattan. **'43** Dixie Dugan; Jane Eyre. **'44** In the Meantime, Darling. **'45** A Tree Grows in Brooklyn. **'48** Fort Apache; Deep Waters; Apartment for Peggy; The Snake Pit; Three Godfathers. **'49** Impact; The Fighting Kentuckian. **'50** When Willie Comes Marching Home; The Gunfighter. **'52** Night Without Sleep; The Quiet Man. **'53** Titanic; Blueprint for Murder; The Robe; The Sun Shines Bright. **'55** Prince of Players; The Tall Men; Hell on Frisco Bay; While the City Sleeps. **'56** Girls in Prison; Julie; The Searchers. **'57** The Wings of Eagles. **'58** Cry Terror. **'60** Sergeant Rutledge. **'61** Two Rode Together.

GIVING BIRTH...

D.W. Griffith welded together the techniques evolved by earlier pioneers and single-handedly created the art of screen narrative

On December 31, 1913, D.W. Griffith announced his departure from the American Biograph Company with whom he had worked since 1908. In an advertisement in *The New York Dramatic Mirror*, he summarized his achievements during the Biograph years, claiming that he had 'revolutionised motion picture drama' and 'founded the modern technique of the art'. To Griffith, on the strength of his own declarations, are normally credited the first uses of such devices as the close-up and the long-shot, the flashback (or, as he termed it, the 'switchback'), the fade-in and fade-out, the use of the iris lens to pick out details of action, the use of titles, the concept of editing for parallel action and 'dramatic continuity', the atmospheric use of lighting, and the encouragement of 'restraint in expression' in screen acting.

Some of these claims, particularly where restrained acting was concerned, were to find more substantial justification in the post-Biograph years. By 1920, Griffith could reasonably be said to have pioneered the expressionist use of colour tinting, the concept of widescreen cinema, and the commissioning of original musical scores. He had also sent a camera up in a balloon, and directed at least two of the greatest films the cinema would ever know. But there was no doubt, even at the time, that Griffith left both Biograph and film history the richer for a five-and-a-half-year output unequalled by any other film-maker in any other era.

That output, as has since been clarified, was not quite the one-man, technical revolution Griffith suggested. In the process of copyright registration, American motion-picture producers during 1894 to 1912 printed the individual frames of their work as photographs on paper for preservation by the Library of Congress. Thanks to these 'paper prints', and to the research into them by archivist Kemp Niver in the late Forties, it has become possible for Griffith's Biograph films to be studied in a more informative light.

What has emerged is at first sight contradictory to the Griffith claims; instead, Edwin S. Porter (for the Edison Company) and G.W. 'Billy' Bitzer (for Biograph) are amply illustrated as authentic pioneers. Porter's *The Great Train Robbery* (1903) has long been established as a primitive example of parallel storytelling, and ends up (or starts, according to taste) with the medium close-up, in colour, of a bandit shooting at the camera and thus at the audience. But Porter's other Edison productions, from the turn of the century, are also alive with dissolves, close-ups and camera movements. The effects are far from sophisticated – but they are there. Similarly, in such dramas as *Moonshiners* (1904) Bitzer pans fluently, if not particularly smoothly, around the countryside, while in *The Black Hand* (1906) he can be seen making use of titles, a two-shot, and a close-up. In both technique and subject (as with, for instance, *A Kentucky Feud*, 1905) he clearly marks out the territory that was subsequently to be assigned to Griffith. This indebtedness to the first film-makers is further reinforced by the irony that Griffith was directed by, among others, Porter in *Rescued From an Eagle's Nest*, when as an aspiring actor he first worked at Biograph in 1907, and by Bitzer in *The Sculptor's Nightmare*, made in 1908, by which time he had officially joined the company. (Bitzer subsequently worked as Griffith's cinematographer for the next 16 years.)

What Griffith brought significantly to the screen, then, was not a collection of technical tricks, but the skill to use them effectively to enhance his stories. It was a skill derived partly from the theatre – his first love – and partly from his family background, with its 'scholarly atmosphere'. But most crucially, the skill grew inevitably from the experience of maintaining an output of around nine films a month throughout his stay with Biograph. In the startlingly prolific context of nearly five hundred productions in five-and-a-half years, Griffith was given the unique opportunity – and had the responsive personality – to make every conceivable experiment in film-making at a time when the rules were few, the audience vast and enthusiastic, and the future unlimited.

Born on January 22, 1875 on a farm in Crestwood, Kentucky, Llewelyn Wark Griffith came of excellent Southern stock. His father had been a colonel in the Confederate army, and his domestic life seems to have been ordered along firmly ethical and devout (but not ardently militaristic) lines. 'My parents always directed our studies and our thoughts towards the noble, the great in literature', he later said, and from the age of six he was determined to become 'a great literary man'.

Numerous early jobs included being a salesman for the *Encyclopaedia Britannica*, a hop-picker, a newspaper reporter and drama critic in Louisville, and an actor under the stage name of Lawrence

Above: though the Indians butcher the whites in The Battle of Elderbush Gulch *(originally* The Battle at Elderbush Gulch*), Griffith makes it clear that the settlers are to blame. Below: Griffith (right) and his cameraman Billy Bitzer. Bottom: in* Man's Genesis*, the fight between 'Brute-force' and 'Weak-hands' is won by the latter, inventor of the axe*

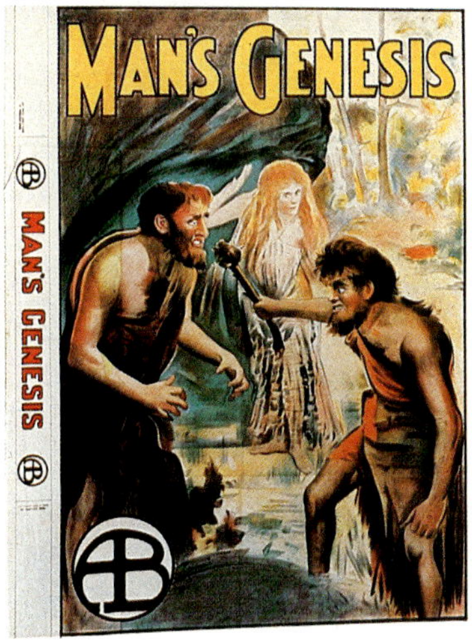

Griffith in stock and touring companies. He wrote a play, *The Fool and the Girl*, which was produced in Washington and Baltimore in 1907 without much success. Taken by a friend to his first picture show, he found it 'silly, tiresome, inexcusable; any man who enjoys such a thing should be shot at sunrise'. But it led him to offer film stories to the Edison and Biograph studios in New York, and it was only a short step to finding employment as a bit-player for the cameras, along with his wife Linda Arvidson.

Mrs Griffith has described in her autobiography (*When the Movies Were Young*, published in 1925) how the Biograph Company, originally created to make the peepshow devices called Mutoscopes in rivalry to Edison's Kinetoscopes, were by 1908 desperately searching for good material. At the suggestion of Billy Bitzer's camera assistant, Arthur Marvin (who happened to be the general manager's brother), the studio offered a story by staff-writer Stanner Taylor (later to write many of Griffith's one-reelers) to the reluctant Lawrence Griffith – only when established did he become known as 'David' or 'D.W.' – on the assurance that he could have his acting job back if the project did not work out. Photographed by Marvin, *The Adventures of Dollie* (1908) starred Linda Arvidson and Arthur Johnson, a young stage actor with no film experience whom Griffith picked for his suitable appearance. It was shot in a week, premiered in New York on July 14, 1908 and judged successful enough for Griffith to be granted a one-year contract which, with royalties, raised his salary from practically nothing to $500 a month. Apart from brief appearances when, in a crisis, there was nobody else to fill the walk-on roles, he never did go back to acting.

The torrent of films that poured from Biograph for the next few years has survived remarkably intact and has been carefully charted by, among other film critics, Robert Henderson (in his book *D.W. Griffith: The Years at Biograph*) and Edward Wagenknecht and Anthony Slide (in *The Films of D.W. Griffith*), although not too many film historians have had the stamina to voyage across the full flood of Griffith's early output. His one-reelers ventured into all conceivable territories long before they were defined (and later *confined*) as separate genres – in fact, the argument could be made that Griffith was the inventor of everything but fantasy cinema, which was pioneered by Georges Méliès and Thomas Edison, and the epic spectaculars, which he left to Italian film-makers until he could afford to outclass them.

His were among the first – if not *the* first – slapstick comedies (with *The Curtain Pole* in 1909 setting the scene for the Keystone antics of his Biograph colleague Mack Sennett), suspense thrillers, Westerns, gangster stories, social-realism dramas and romantic melodramas. He made costume films, adventure stories and war films, together with some adaptations, not always acknowledged, from such writers as Alfred Lord Tennyson, Leo Tolstoy, Guy de Maupassant, James Fenimore Cooper, and O. Henry. The variety of titles is astonishing in any month picked at random from the Biograph list: October 1908, for example, saw the release of *The Devil, The Zulu's Heart, Father Gets in the Game, The Barbarian Ingomar, The Vaquero's Vow, The Planter's Wife, Romance of a Jewess, The Call of the Wild* and *Concealing a Burglar*.

Today, just a handful of the Biograph works have a lasting reputation, though many more deserve attention. Among those most frequently reconsidered are *Pippa Passes*, which achieved the distinction of being the first film to be reviewed by the *New York Times* (on October 10, 1909); the Mary Pickford classic *The Lonely Villa* (1909), a suspense story of a family imprisoned in their own home by a marauder with a gun; *The Lonedale Operator* (1911), in which the camera was mounted on a locomotive to observe the struggle between the heroine (Blanche Sweet) and a railroad gang; and *Man's Genesis* (1912), a Stone Age parable in which an early screen dinosaur wobbled across the landscape.

If the one-reelers had anything in common (other

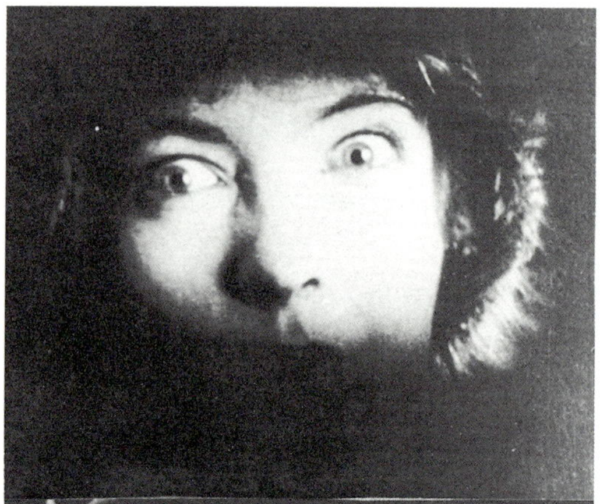

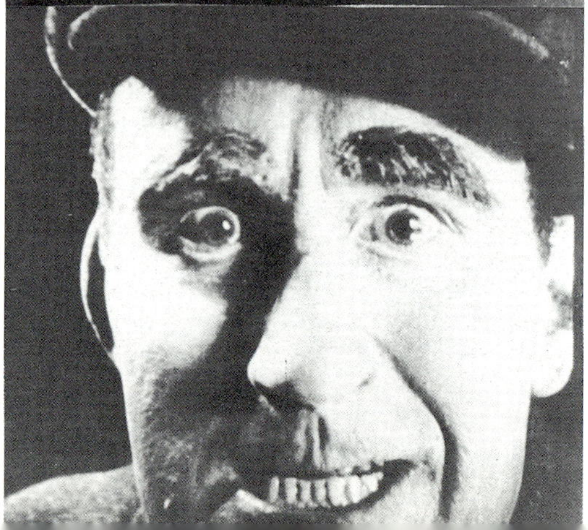

Far left: Griffith's screen debut as an actor in Rescued From an Eagle's Nest. *Left: scene from* Intolerance, *Griffith's epic portrayal of hypocrisy through the ages. Below: fragments of* Hearts of the World *(1918), a love story set during World War I, were actually shot at the Front. Bottom left: exemplary close-ups of a girl (Lillian Gish) and her brutal father (Donald Crisp) in* Broken Blossoms. *Bottom centre: Lillian and Dorothy Gish (blind girl in street) as the sundered sisters in* Orphans of the Storm. *Bottom right: Lillian Gish and Richard Barthelmess in* Way Down East

than the 'AB' logo that featured in all the backgrounds to protect copyright), not surprisingly it was a sense of speed. They could be made on any inspiration, even the slender basis of a change in the weather; the unit would make up a story on the spot to unfold against the background of a recent snowfall, or to take advantage of a vista of autumn trees. And since there was not time to show insignificant detail, Griffith used titles more creatively than had previously been tried, in the place of cumbersome or irrelevant action, pushing his stories headlong from climax to climax. Marriages were made, broken and mended in ten minutes, wars fought and lost in the space of a single shot. His stories, springing from this frantic schedule, frequently based themselves on a race against time, and the need to show widely separate events interacting with each other led him to the logical solution of cross-cutting.

Griffith had a vision of movies as 'the greatest spiritual force the world has ever known'

Despite the misgivings of the studio bosses, the obstinate vitality of Griffith's editing style never seemed to upset the one-reeler audiences:

'I borrowed the idea from Charles Dickens. Novelists think nothing of leaving one set of characters in the midst of affairs and going back to deal with earlier events in which another set of characters is involved. I found that the picture could carry, not merely two, but three or four simultaneous threads of action – all without confusing the spectator.'

As Griffith's experience grew, so did his ambition. His stories were increasingly complex, his cast ever larger, his budgets less comfortable to Biograph. His later one-reelers, straying occasionally into two reels despite his producers' certainty that no audiences would tolerate such lengths, looked more and more like sketches and episodes from far grander projects. *The Battle* (1911) can now be seen as a rehearsal for *The Birth of a Nation* (1915), *The Musketeers of Pig Alley* (1912) for the modern story in *Intolerance* (1916), while *A Feud in the Kentucky Hills* (1912) anticipates both *The Massacre* (1913) and *The Battle at Elderbush Gulch* (1914), brilliant and spectacular films which in turn were preparing for the sophisticated performances and magnificent photography of the later epics.

The parting of the ways came with *Judith of Bethulia* (1913), which Griffith made as a four-reeler at such casual expense, and in the teeth of such Biograph opposition, that there was no alternative but to fire him. As he left, he took his team with him – the teenagers who had matured to stardom in the same era that movie fandom had come into being as a direct response to the 'Biograph Girls', together with cameraman Bitzer, editor James Smith, and a score of designers and assistants. They moved to the Reliance-Majestic Company (distributing through Mutual) and between April and July 1914 they made the five-reel *The Battle of the Sexes* in five days for under $5000; the ill-fated (and ill-received) seven-reel melodrama *The Escape*; the six-reel, three-story *Home, Sweet Home*, which combined all the Griffith players in one film for the first time; and the six-reel oddity *The Avenging Conscience*, based on works by Edgar Allan Poe. None of these productions appears to have been successful, either dramatically or commercially. But it hardly mattered. Within six months, the Griffith team had created *The Birth of a Nation*, and the face of cinema was permanently changed.

Including the Reliance-Majestic productions, Griffith made 32 features after leaving Biograph. They were as disparate as his one-reelers had been, straying from the unargued (if controversial) classic status of *The Birth of a Nation*, *Intolerance*, *Broken Blossoms* (1919), and *Way Down East* (1920), to the ambitious but unsatisfying *Orphans of the Storm* (1921), *America* (1924) and *Abraham Lincoln* (1930), and to such largely peculiar and often plainly unattractive ventures as *Sally of the Sawdust*, *That Royle Girl* (both 1925) and the lavish *The Sorrows of Satan* (1926).

His final film, *The Struggle* (1931), a grim and obviously heartfelt warning of the perils of alcoholism, although vindicated by later critical re-evaluation, was a crushing commercial disaster, especially as it came within a year of his having won a 'best director' award for his first sound film, *Abraham Lincoln*. In the remaining 17 years of his life he made nothing further. Instead, he was avoided by the studios for whom he had almost single-handedly created the film industry, and he was forgotten by the public. When the D.W. Griffith Corporation went into bankruptcy and his films were auctioned, he picked up the rights to 21 of them for a mere $500.

'To us,' said Lillian Gish, his greatest star, 'Mr Griffith *was* the movie industry. It had been born in his head.' But the infant proved to be less respectful of past traditions than its creator, and as it grew his parental influence quickly lost its grip. Griffith's stories obsessively examined the theme of virtue under siege – he was repeatedly shutting his young lovers, his innocent heroines, his helpless children into traps from which they were usually (but certainly not always) rescued only at the last moment. With his affection for Dickensian romanticism, he held firmly and sentimentally to the view that entertainment and education were one, and that beauty and youth were their own justification – beauty not only of appearance but also of character and behaviour. If it was an approach that steadily lost headway against the accelerating cynicism of the times, it remained with Griffith himself as an undimmed faith. 'We are playing to the world', he would say jubilantly to his unit. 'We've gone beyond Babel, beyond words. We've found a universal language – a power that can make men brothers and end war forever. . . .'

PHILIP STRICK

1

4

Directed by D. W. Griffith, 1915

Prod co: Epoch. **prod:** Harry E. Aitken, D. W. Griffith. **sc:** D. W. Griffith, Frank E. Woods, Thomas Dixon Jr, from the novel *The Clansman* by Thomas Dixon Jr. **photo:** G. W. Bitzer. **ass photo:** Karl Brown. **ed:** D. W. Griffith, James Smith. **cost:** Robert Godstein. **mus:** Joseph Carl Breil, D. W. Griffith. **ass dir:** George Siegmann, Raoul Walsh, W. S. Van Dyke, Erich von Stroheim, Jack Conway. **length:** originally 13,058 feet (approx. 180 minutes) censored to 12,500 feet (approx. 165 minutes). Original title: *The Clansman*.

Cast: Henry B. Walthall (*Benjamin Cameron*), Violet Wilkey (*Flora Cameron as a child*), Mae Marsh (*Flora Cameron*), Miriam Cooper (*Margaret Cameron*), Josephine Bonapart Crowell (*Mrs Cameron*), Spottiswood Aitken (*Dr Cameron*), André Beranger (*Wade Cameron*), Maxfield Stanley (*Duke Cameron*), Lillian Gish (*Elsie Stoneman*), Ralph Lewis (*the Hon. Austin Stoneman*), Elmer Clifton (*Phil Stoneman*), Robert Harron (*Ted Stoneman; black-face spy*), Mary Alden (*Lydia Brown*), Sam de Grasse (*Senator Charles Sumner*), George Siegmann (*Silas Lynch*), Walter Long (*Gus*), Elmo Lincoln (*'White-arm' Joe; slave auctioneer; Confederate officer*), Wallace Reid (*Jeff*), Joseph Henabery (*Abraham Lincoln*), Alberta Lee (*Mrs Lincoln*), Donald Crisp (*General U.S. Grant*), Howard Gaye (*General Robert E. Lee*), William Freeman (*the mooning sentry*), Olga Grey (*Laura Keene*), Raoul Walsh (*John Wilkes Booth*), Tom Wilson (*Stoneman's negro servant*), Eugene Pallette (*Union soldier*), Madame Sul-te-Wan (*negro woman*), William de Vaull (*Jake*), Jennie Lee (*Dixie*), Erich von Stroheim (*man who falls from roof*).

The Birth of a Nation, D. W. Griffith's cinematic masterpiece, provokes controversy even to this day: it enjoys the uneasy honour of being both a technically innovative film as well as one of the most explicitly racist pictures ever made. It has been rightly venerated for its artistic achievements, and just as rightly condemned for its reactionary content.

The Birth of a Nation was one of the first films to establish the convention of story-telling in the cinema with now familiar techniques, such as use of parallel action in a chase sequence, and to exploit the full potential of close-ups and fades. Other, less-lasting devices like the iris-shot (whereby the film image is vignetted at the corners) were also used to good effect. It was the first of the 'big' pictures, complete with vast panoramic shots as carefully composed as epic paintings and splendidly staged battle scenes, all of which are intermingled with scenes of plantation life and coy romance.

The film deals with a prickly period in American history – the Civil War and the period of Reconstruction in the South, from which many Americans were still recovering when Griffith made the film. He himself was a Southerner, raised on the values and traditions of the Old South, though his depiction of that experience is laid out in epic proportions and succeeds in blurring sectional interests and antipathies. He does this by interweaving the lives of two families, the Stonemans and Camerons, respectively representing North and South, whose contrasting lives are eventually reconciled in the common interest of white supremacy or, as one of the film's intertitles puts it, 'in defence of their Aryan birthright'.

Such anti-black sentiments were not uncommon during the silent era, although most films tended to place emphasis on the traditional and relatively gentler image of devoted black servility, or use the black man for comic relief. Griffith's film follows the same pattern, but with greater force and with the emotive stress placed on the image of blacks as villains. These stereotypes play against the equally stereotyped whites in the film – men are aristocratic and paternalistic, women frail and vulnerable – but they do not express the interests of the blacks (played by whites in black-face) in the way that the white stereotypes express the interests of the whites.

The Birth of a Nation is one of few silent films to exploit the sexual stereotype of the black male in order to reinforce the doctrine of white supremacy. It achieves this through the use of the much-dreaded 'brute' figure – personified here by the renegade Gus, who not only betrays his former masters by joining the black revolt, but also commits the unspeakable crime of lusting after and causing the suicide of one of the Cameron daughters. This motif is duplicated in the character and actions of Silas Lynch, the mulatto leader of his people. The sexual racism that these characters exemplify plays a crucial part in the film's thematic development; and it comes to a head in the film's last-minute rescue finale which justifies the actions of the Ku Klux Klan, captioned by Griffith as 'the saviour of white civilization'.

Race feeling ran high wherever the film was shown, resulting in rioting in Boston and other cities. While the publicity this generated undoubtedly increased box-office receipts, Griffith himself was strongly attacked in the liberal and black press for his blatant racism and romanticizing of the murderous Ku Klux Klan (whose membership trebled within months of the film's release). Cinemas were picketed, and the newly-formed National Association for the Advancement of Coloured People (NAACP) managed to get the film banned in a number of states.

Today, at least in America, *The Birth of a Nation* is restricted largely to cinema 'club' showings, and to video-cassette. But the spectre of the film's original impact lingers, and it incurs the same wrath.

JIM PINES

3

6

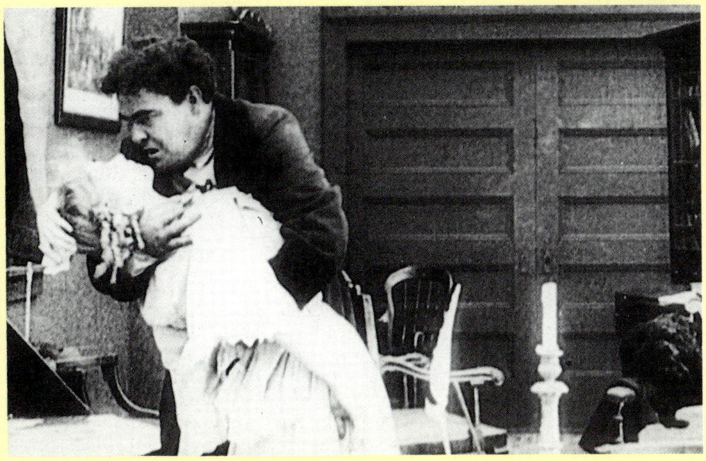

Pennsylvanians Phil and Ted Stoneman visit their boarding-school mates, the Camerons, at Piedmont, South Carolina. They are entertained by the black slaves on the plantation (1). Phil falls for Margaret Cameron, while Ben Cameron becomes enamoured of Phil's sister Elsie when he sees a daguerrotype of her.

Dr Cameron reads to his family and the Stonemans news of the South's threat to secede from the Union (2). With Civil War declared, the Stonemans leave to fight for the Union and the three Cameron boys join the Confederate army (3). Two of them are killed in action. Piedmont is devastated. Ben, wounded, is helped by Captain Phil Stoneman (4), who takes him prisoner. He recovers after being nursed by Elsie Stoneman.

After the war, Congressman Austin Stoneman, father of Phil and Elsie, agitates for the punishment of the South, but President Lincoln refuses to take revenge. Later he is assassinated (5). Stoneman sends Silas Lynch to take control at Piedmont. Ben is estranged from Elsie and Phil from Margaret because of wartime hostilities. Ben starts up the Ku Klux Klan to counteract 'the Black Menace'. They slay the renegade Gus (6) whose attempted rape of Flora Cameron has caused her to jump to her death.

Lynch seizes Dr Cameron for harbouring Klansmen, but he is rescued by two loyal servants and Phil and Margaret who flee to an isolated cabin. Meanwhile Lynch pursues the frightened Elsie (7). Ben leads the Klan to drive Lynch's black militia from Piedmont (8), then to save the besieged cabin and rescue Elsie. White supremacy is restored as the Klan rides back into town (9).

8

9

Music-hall mirth-makers

Before World War I, the British film industry tended to neglect the rich traditions of the music hall; and it was left to the variety comedians themselves to make their own way onto the cinema screen

The history of British screen comedy in the period preceding World War I is marred by the lamentable failure of film-makers to utilize the readily available talents of stage and music hall. Stars of the magnitude of Marie Lloyd and Vesta Victoria were seldom called upon to appear on screen and of the few films that they made virtually no examples survive. Following their first exhibition at the Empire and Alhambra music halls in March 1896, moving pictures rapidly became a staple ingredient of the music-hall programme. Yet, despite such an assured market and the willingness of variety performers to appear in films for next to no payment (the publicity alone was considered sufficient incentive), most film-makers were content to present anonymous, semi-professional actors in hackneyed situations and to trust to the novelty value of the medium. The few innovative ventures into screen comedy were more often than not undertaken by stage performers themselves.

By 1900 a number of well-known performers had appeared in filmed extracts from their variety acts. As early as April 1896 the director R. W. Paul had been producing short films, often using variety artists, in a makeshift studio on the roof of the Alhambra, Leicester Square, and in 1897 the British Mutoscope and Biograph Company built a studio at the rear of the Tivoli Music Hall in the Strand. Among the comedians to appear in these early productions were G. H. Chirgwin, a black-faced performer billed as 'The White-Eyed Kaffir', filmed by Paul (1896); Harry Tate in *Harry Tate Grimaces* pulling funny faces and in *Harry Tate Impersonations* imitating fellow artists; and Will Evans in *The Musical Eccentric* turning somersaults and dodging various objects thrown at him while he played the cornet, all filmed by the Warwick Trading Company in 1899. In 1900 Vesta Tilley, Alec Hurley (a barrow-boy comedian and the second husband of Marie Lloyd), Lil Hawthorne and the ever-popular Chirgwin made a number of synchronized sound films for Walter Gibbons' Phono-Bio-Tableaux. Primitive sound films remained popular throughout the period and from 1905 the Gaumont Chronophone

Above left: an 1895 music-sheet cover for songs sung by Dan Leno (inset, top right) and others at the Tivoli, where films were made from 1897. Right: among them were Dan Leno and Herbert Campbell Edit 'The Sun'

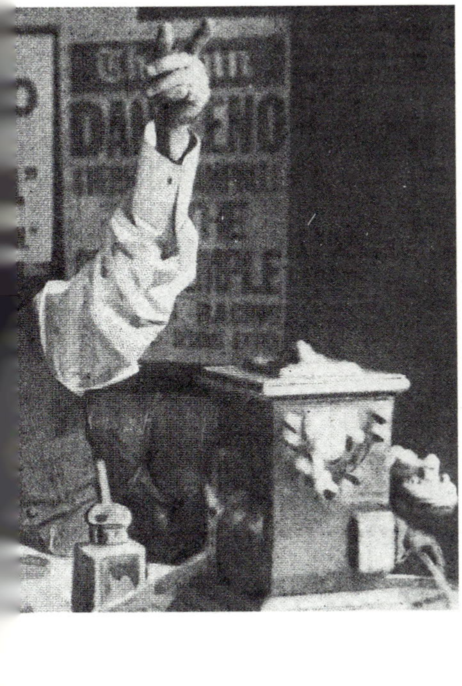

Above left and above: music-sheet covers depicting music-hall stars Alec Hurley and Chirgwin, who both made it into the movies. Above right: Billy Merson and Winifred Delavente in Billy's Stormy Courtship *(1916)*

presented many music-hall artists singing their latest song successes.

The funniest man

The leading music-hall star to appear on film and, potentially, the performer who had most to offer the development of British screen humour was the comedian Dan Leno. Leno, who was small in height but full of nervous energy, was famous for his sympathetic portrayal of humble, down-at-heel characters, but on film his chief asset was his unparalleled ability as a dancer and mime. Several of his short films were humorous newsreels, such as *Dan Leno, Musical Director* (1901), in which he was seen conducting the Metropolitan Police Band at Stamford Bridge Sports Ground, but others, like *Burlesque Attack on a Settler's Cabin* (made with fellow comedians Herbert Campbell and Joe Elvin for Warwick in 1900), *Bluebeard* (a scene from the Drury Lane pantomime made for Warwick in 1902) and *Dan Leno and Herbert Campbell Edit 'The Sun'*, Biograph (1902), were vehicles specially constructed to exploit his talents as a comic actor. Leno died at the early age of 43 in 1904 and, with no surviving films, his importance as a screen comedian has been largely neglected. He was, however, an established film performer long before Max Linder and other European and American stars created their own distinctive styles and it seems likely that given only a few more years he would have translated his unique stage artistry into the more lasting and influential form of film comedy. As it is there no longer remains a fragment of film by which to judge the publicity claim that he was 'The Funniest Man on Earth'.

Despite the efforts of Leno and a handful of other music-hall and stage performers, the years 1900 to 1912 were a period of stagnation. British companies lost ground steadily to foreign competition, yet continued to issue repetitive and often wretchedly-produced films in which enthusiastic slapstick was preferred to comic ability. Among the most effective comedies of this period were the long-running series of Tilly Girl films, beginning in 1908 and directed for the Hepworth Company by Lewin Fitzhamon. The films, such as *Tilly the Tomboy Visits the Poor* and *Tilly the Tomboy Plays Truant* (both 1910), were broad in humour but were lifted above the commonplace by the inspired mischief-making of their young stars Alma Taylor and Chrissie White. In *Tilly and the Fire Engines* (1911) the dreadful duo hijack a horse-drawn fire engine and scatter the pursuing firemen by soaking them with their own hose.

In the meantime the rapidly developing Continental and American industries were creating comedy stars, such as André Deed ('Foolshead'), Max Linder, Ferdinand Guillaume ('Tontolini') and John Bunny, whose popularity in Britain cruelly exposed the home film-makers' tardiness in harnessing the talents of the variety stage. It is a supreme irony that it was left to America to make an international star out of the skilful but minor music-hall comedian Charlie Chaplin.

Above: a batch of the Winky films – starring Reginald Switz, directed by Cecil Birch – from 1914. Below: Fred Evans in Pimple's Wonderful Gramophone *(1913). Bottom: Winifred Delavente, Blanche Kellino, Lupino Lane, unknown actor, J. Kellino, Polly Emery and Fred Toose in* A Wife in a Hurry *(1916)*

Signs of life

Although it was never to rival the world-wide successes of French and American comedy, the British market began to show signs of improvement from about 1912. In that year Will P. Kellino, a member of a famous troupe of comedy acrobats, helped form the EcKo film company, which immediately proceeded to produce a film a week, often featuring music-hall comedians like Billy Merson (a fine gymnast and the singer of 'The Spaniard That Blighted My Life') and the young Lupino Lane. The company had offices in Teddington in south-west London and several performers from the nearby Richmond Hippodrome and Kingston Empire theatres were persuaded to take part in a day's filming near the Thames.

Among the performers appearing for EcKo who attempted to do more than duplicate their stage routines were the brothers Seth and Albert Egbert, billed on the halls as 'The Happy Dustmen'. Their style of amazingly acrobatic knockabout humour was particularly well-suited to screen presentation and between 1912 and 1916 they made a long series of films including: *The Coster's Honeymoon* (1912), *Dodging the Landlord* (1913), *The Happy Dustmen's Christmas* (1914) and *The Dustmen's Nightmare* (1915).

A performer who, like the Egberts, drifted into cinematic obscurity was the variety comedian Sam T. Poluski. Sam, not to be confused with his more famous father of the Poluski Brothers music-hall act, appeared in a number of films with the Egberts, and also as Nobby in a series of shorts made for EcKo in 1913 and 1914. In *Nobby and the Pearl Mystery* (1913) he had to jump onto a car in Fleet Street and steal a lady's pearls. An accidental collision occurred and Sam was left with some amusing footage and a good deal of explaining to do to the irate police. Only one Nobby film apparently survives. In *Nobby the New Waiter* (1913) Sam is seen smoking on duty, flirting with a cook and finally getting the sack following an impromptu roller-skating display.

A series of laughs

As with Nobby and the Happy Dustmen, it made good box-office sense to establish a popular screen character and several attempts were made to launch bizarrely-named comedians into profitable series. The Yorkshire firm of Bamforth, famous for its lantern-slides and postcards, invented Winky who, as played by Reginald Switz, became involved in a wide range of farcical situations. An idea of the degree of subtlety exercized in these comedies is provided by *Winky's Weekend* (1914) in which, when left by his wife to clean the chimney, Winky steals his neighbour's chickens and uses them as brushes.

The most successful pre-World War I screen comedian was undoubtedly Fred Evans, a performer whose many films as the character Pimple extended over the period 1913–20. Evans was steeped in music-hall and pantomime tradition. His grandfather, also known as Fred Evans, was one of the country's leading clowns while both his father and his uncle Will were notable musical and knockabout comedians. Will Evans himself made a series of highly successful filmed adaptations of his music-hall sketches, including *Whitewashing the Ceiling* and *Building a Chicken House* (both 1914). Most of the Pimple films were devised and the humorous intertitles written by Fred's brother Joe Evans and were usually send-ups of contemporary events or were parodies of current film or stage successes, as indicated by such titles as *Miss Pimple, Suffragette* (1913), *Pimple, Anarchist* and *Pimple Enlists* (both 1914). In *Adventures of Pimple – Battle of Waterloo* (1913) – a spoof on a British epic of the same year – Napoleon and Wellington toss up for the first shot, a French soldier is dispatched to buy ammunition from a nearby shop and the Emperor is finally captured by a group of Boy Scouts.

The short-lived renaissance of British film comedy was curtailed by the outbreak of World War I. Comedies were still produced, however, notably by the Homeland Films Syndicate, another largely music-hall orientated company formed by Will Kellino and Billy Merson. Homeland's two- or three-reel comedies were made over the Boathouse Hotel, Kew, and featured Merson, the Egberts, Jack Edge, Winifred Delavente, Charles Austin and Lupino Lane. But with the concentration of resources on war dramas and propaganda the possibilities for screen humour were severely limited and it was to take many years before British comedy reasserted itself. Leading lights of the film world like Kellino and Lane left to recommence their careers in the more lucrative and professionally organized American industry and British comedy slid back into a state of torpor.

BARRY ANTHONY

ENGLAND EXPECTS...

The ups and downs of the British film industry between 1910 and 1929 make a tragi-comedy of hopes deferred, but optimism kept breaking through

Only one film, *The Blue Bird*, lasting longer than 15 minutes (or a whole reel), was made in Britain in 1910. There were many comic and dramatic 'subjects' turned out by the small British producers but most of them continued to be very short anecdotes rather than stories, and the lively and inventive spirit which had given Britain a lead in film technique had petered out. Pioneers like G. A. Smith, James Williamson and R. W. Paul had given up making films. Production was led by the staid Cecil Hepworth, with his stock company and studio beside the Thames at Walton. A former lantern-show lecturer, he took an interest in photographic quality and beauty of setting that made his films visually outstanding, and his players were encouraged to act with unusual restraint. The teenagers Chrissie White and Alma Taylor soon had a following of their own in the Tilly the Tomboy films, which started in 1910.

But the rest of the world was not standing still and it was clear that British producers were losing ground. A more adventurous approach was needed as films from abroad became longer and players began to be known by name. It was the arrival of a new producer, Will Barker, with his Bulldog brand, that signalled the revival. A rough diamond with big ideas and plenty of go, in 1910 he built the first Ealing studio, large for the time with two of its stages depending on sunlight and two on electricity. He made a sensation in 1911 with a shortened film version of Sir Herbert Beerbohm Tree's London production of Shakespeare's *Henry VIII*, which lasted over half an hour. After this, other eminent actors potted performances of their own favourite parts. Sir Frank Benson, for example, followed with spirited portrayals of Mark Antony in *Julius Caesar* and the title roles in *Macbeth* and *Richard III* (all 1911). Barker carried on with a couple of thumping melodramas, *East Lynne* and *The Road to Ruin* (both 1913), and broke new ground the same year with a film depicting scenes from the life of Queen Victoria called *Sixty Years a Queen*. Other companies made a conscious effort to get up to date – Cricks and Martin's futuristic airship story *The Pirates of 1920* (1911), although still just under a reel, had been hailed as the first British 'feature film'. British multi-reel films became longer and more frequent.

Hepworth, realizing that the faces of his stock company were becoming familiar to the public, began to publicize them by name. As Chrissie White grew up to be a fair-haired blue-eyed English rose, she and Alma Taylor, darker and softer, played in many love stories with two new members of the company, the stage actors Henry Edwards and Stewart Rome. *Oliver Twist* (1912), a long film directed by Thomas Bentley, who was well known in the halls for his impersonations of characters from the novels of Charles Dickens, was the first of

Top right: Edward IV's army triumphantly arrives in London in Jane Shore. *Right: filming Stoll's Sherlock Holmes series at Cricklewood studio*

Above: in 1925 Walter Summers reconstructed the World War I battles that occurred at Ypres – one of Harry Bruce Woolfe's series for British Instructional Films Above centre: Blood and Bosh *(1913) starred Chrissie White and Jack Hulcup as a couple whose baby is kidnapped; the villains are wiped out by an exploding gas meter. Top: on location at the seaside for the film-within-a-film in* Shooting Stars *are Ivy Ellison as a bathing belle and Donald Calthrop as the star Andy Wilkes*

many literary adaptations in costume. Hepworth's *Hamlet* (1913) showed the great actor Sir Johnston Forbes-Robertson, on the eve of retirement, as a very old Prince of Denmark in the Drury Lane production. These distinguished theatrical knights, ageing relics of the Victorian theatre, made little concession to the different medium and their larger-than-life style of classical acting contributed nothing to film technique, but they enhanced the prestige of the cinema. The beauty queen Ivy Close starred in films made by her husband, the Bond Street photographer Elwin Neame; self-consciously artistic, these also were part of a new tendency to take cinema seriously.

There were other newcomers before the war started in 1914. George Pearson, a kindly former schoolmaster who had been making educational films for Pathé, ventured into feature production and soon became a leading director. The incredible Maurice Elvey began 44 years of slick professional film-making in 1913. The Birmingham renter G. B. Samuelson established a studio at Worton Hall, Isleworth, and Percy Nash built one at Elstree, both near London. The London Film Company, a big public company with large capital resources, set new standards of business-like administration. Founded by Provincial Cinematograph Theatres, one of the biggest circuits, it turned an ice rink at Twickenham into a large studio and announced its intention of making films that reflected British life. Its top directors, writers and leading ladies, however, were all American. In fact, the American presence in British production was noticeable at this time.

By this time the chief British studios were scattered around the smoke-free edges of London. The longer film, with its greater demands on the script, had already caused producers to turn to the stage for material, and the nearness of the London theatres reinforced this dependence by providing a convenient pool of acting talent. Immediately war broke out, there was an outburst of activity in the belief that American imports would fall. The numerous dramas from the London Film Company, many of them from plays, tended to be longer and more colourful than those from Hepworth. But Hepworth's major productions included two important adaptations from the plays of Arthur Wing Pinero, *Sweet Lavender* (1915) and *Trelawney of the Wells* (1916), and more versions of Dickens' novels from Bentley. Barker's films were few but sensational, and his historical drama about Edward IV's mistress *Jane Shore* (1915) included spectacular crowd scenes of armies scattered over the hillsides.

The new Samuelson studio was enlarged in 1915, and Gaumont opened a studio at Shepherds Bush in west London, where Pearson filmed four adventures (1915–17) of his character Ultus the Avenger, created in answer to Léon Gaumont's request for a British equivalent of Louis Feuillade's Fantômas. Broadwest Film Company was founded during the war by Walter West. It specialized in racing dramas from the popular stories of Nat Gould, and daring society dramas and problem plays starring the beautifully-gowned Violet Hopson, formerly with Hepworth.

Serious films relating to the war were few, although a major series of authentic war films was made for the War Office by official cameramen such as J. B. McDowell and Geoffrey Malins. Beginning with *The Battle of the Somme* in 1916, these films seem unenterprising by the standard of later documentaries but were an advance on most films of the period, and for the first time gave people at home a real idea of the conditions under which servicemen lived.

Far from falling off during the war, American films had poured into Britain and vastly increased their share of the market. The multi-reel super-picture was common now, with costly stars and settings, big crowd scenes and elaborate costumes. The big American companies could in the first place spend more on their pictures because of their huge home market, and they were able with these attractive and well-advertised films to take over the British market as well.

The old 'open market' in films in which many copies of each film were sold was dead now, and the new expensive features were exploited by renters

who bid for exclusive rights for particular areas. This 'exclusive' system gave renters great power over exhibitors, who found that they had to book large blocks of films in order to get the few they wanted. British producers with their few films, already suffering by comparison with their more lavish competitors, now found that there were fewer and fewer booking slots left for them, often many months ahead. After the war, one by one the big American producing companies opened small renting subsidiaries in London so that this powerful weapon was in their own hands.

British producers had sought import protection as early as 1915, and in 1917 had suggested a quota system to guarantee them a proportion of screen time, but nothing had been done. In this unfavourable climate production tailed off. The London Film Company and Barker had given up and most of the small pre-war companies disappeared. Some tried to keep going with the mixture as before, but by about 1923 most had failed.

So, indeed, had two out of three much larger companies founded at the end of the war. The American firm Famous Players-Lasky had turned a barn-like former power station at Islington into a studio in 1919, bringing over technicians, stars and equipment from America. Using British actors, they claimed, like the London Film Company before them, that they wanted to make films with British themes, but they gave up after four years. The big renting company of Ideal, conscious of the importance of the story in these new longer films, took over the studio at Elstree and went into mass production of literary adaptations, mostly of English Victorian novels. Made on mean budgets, the films were poor and did not appeal to the more sophisticated post-war public. The theatre-owner Sir Oswald Stoll, also thinking of English writers as possible saviours of the British film, secured film rights to the works of many contemporary writers and went into even more massive production of the Eminent British Authors series in a former aircraft factory at Cricklewood in north London, with the directors Sinclair Hill and Elvey and many others. But as in the case of Ideal the films were churned out on the cheap and, despite three popular series of Sherlock Holmes films (1921–23), the unkind tag, 'Stoll films are dull films', was only too true. Stoll lasted a little longer than Famous Players-Lasky and Ideal, but faded out in the mid-Twenties.

So bad was the slump in production by 1923 that producers got together to hold country-wide British National Film Weeks, in which their films were specially promoted with exhortations to the public to support them for patriotic reasons. Unfortunately no standard of selection seems to have been imposed and many of the films were far from good.

One of them, *Comin' Thro' the Rye* (1923), was Hepworth's favourite of all his films, yet it was one of his last, in production while his company, which he had unwisely tried to expand, was heading for the financial crash that ended his career. It was a sentimental tale of a broken engagement, with Alma Taylor as a gentle Victorian heroine, but it was sadly out of touch with the jazzy post-war era. Pearson on the other hand just managed to survive the Twenties, although he too was a Victorian at heart. He opened his own studio after the war and made a number of thoughtful and interesting films. But the real success of his company was fortuitous,

Top left: Alma Taylor and Shayle Gardner as the engaged couple who are parted by a trick in Comin' Thro' the Rye. *Top: in* Moulin Rouge, *André (Jean Bradin) is engaged to Camille (Eve Gray, right) but loves her mother, the dancer Parysia (Olga Tschechowa). Above centre: this 1921 racing picture starred Violet Hopson as a woman whose husband tricks her lover into backing a horse fixed to lose. Above: Rose (P.G. Norgate) foils the Chinese rebels in a 1911 film in Clarendon's popular series*

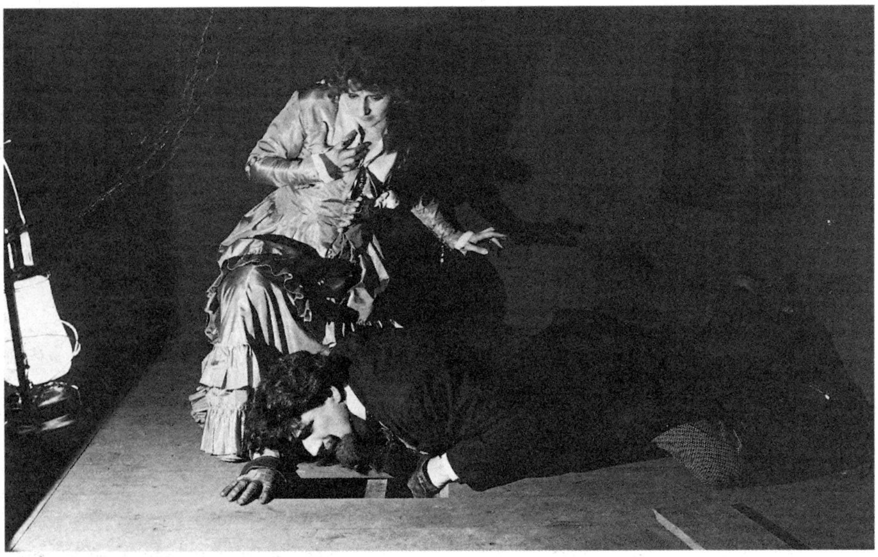

Top: in Ultus and the Grey Lady *(1916), Ultus the Avenger (Aurele Sydney) is helped by Mary Ferris (Mary Dibley) to find the man who betrayed him and killed her father. Above: despite its beefeater logo, the London Film Company depended heavily on its American producer-directors Harold Shaw and George Loane Tucker, and temporarily went out of production after 1917, by which time they had both departed*

and due to a series of comedies (1921–23) about a cockney flower girl, Squibs. Betty Balfour, bubbly and gay as Squibs, was the one true British film star, ranking with the Hollywood stars as far as the British public was concerned. But the unlikely partnership of the avuncular ex-teacher and the bouncy flapper finally ran out of steam, and after she had left the company it floundered.

Output hit bottom in 1926, with only 37 new features, compared with 103 in 1919. Among them, however, were some excellent films of far higher quality than before. For there were some post-war arrivals in the industry who had a more modern approach and by the mid-Twenties were making films which, although meagrely financed, could bear comparison with Hollywood films and were greatly enjoyed in Britain. Working in an old army hut at Elstree, Harry Bruce Woolfe, who had formed British Instructional Films in 1919, made an original contribution to cinema when he laboriously put together a compilation film with animated maps and diagrams, *The Battle of Jutland* (1921). Moving to a studio in Surbiton, he followed with a series of filmed reconstructions of famous wartime engagements, including *The Battles of the Coronel and Falkland Islands* (1927). This was made with Admiralty help, with naval vessels re-enacting their movements for the camera. Pioneering from the early Twenties onwards with *Secrets of Nature*, a brilliant series of films made by naturalists using stop-motion photography and microphotography, he led the way in the serious and factual film until the arrival of the documentarist John Grierson with *Drifters* in 1929. Harry Bruce Woolfe also turned to the production of features and gathered a band of young university graduates, one of whom, Anthony Asquith, the son of the former Prime Minister Herbert Asquith, dazzled the critics with a film about film-making, *Shooting Stars* (1927), which he wrote and co-directed. A display of technical virtuosity and wit, it showed the influence of German and Russian advances in film technique, and heralded the appearance of a more intellectual type of film-maker.

The British documentary was rooted in memories of the war and the investigations of naturalists

Two thrusting young businessmen, prepared to think big and promote each individual film as an important event, entered production from renting. Both believed a share of the American market was necessary if films were to cost enough to please British audiences used to Hollywood standards, and both tried hard to get their pictures released there. The Irishman Herbert Wilcox, producing and sometimes also directing, worked at first in hired studios and preferred stories with an obvious exploitation angle, often from stage successes and often in costume. He engaged American stars as part of his bid for American audiences, starring Dorothy Gish in five films. He hit the headlines when *Dawn* (1928) – in which Sybil Thorndike gave a memorable performance as Edith Cavell, the British nurse who had been shot as a spy by the Germans – was censored in case it offended Germany.

Michael Balcon, a young renter from the industrial Midlands, took over the Islington studio from Famous Players-Lasky with many of the staff, including a pudgy young assistant called Alfred Hitchcock. Hiring the American star Betty Compson at the unheard-of salary of £1000 a week, Balcon co-produced with Victor Saville the glamorous, tearful and rather daring *Woman to Woman* (1923), which was a smash hit. He went on to make many of the best British films of the Twenties. A number of them starred the romantic dark-eyed matinée idol Ivor Novello, whose popularity with the British public rivalled that of Betty Balfour. In *The Rat* (1925) the actor wrote himself a juicy part as a low-life Parisian apache, and the film was so successful that several sequels and remakes followed. Meanwhile Hitchcock rapidly showed himself to be an outstanding director: with the suspense and atmosphere of *The Lodger* (1926), in which Novello played the suspect for a series of Jack the Ripper murders, he hit the jackpot with both box-office and critics.

Even the old firm of Gaumont came up to date in the later Twenties with some successful films by Elvey, including *Mademoiselle From Armentières* (1926), starring the delightful Canadian Estelle Brody. Towards the end of the decade the Scottish solicitor John Maxwell, already the boss of a renting firm and a small circuit of cinemas, opened the huge new Elstree studio of British International Pictures. Hiring talent from all sides to fill it, including Hitchcock, he imitated Hollywood on a shoestring. Hitchcock's boxing story, *The Ring* (1927), was one of the better films to roll off the assembly line. Stars and technicians came from all over the world. Whereas Balcon entered into Anglo-German production agreements so that Alfred Hitchcock made his first two films in Germany, Maxwell brought German directors and cameramen over to Elstree. The sombre film about the troubles in Ireland, *The Informer* (1929), was directed by Arthur Robison; *Moulin Rouge* (1928) and *Piccadilly* (1929), two would-be sophisticated films, were made by E. A. Dupont. Elstree was frequently described as the British Hollywood, and it was appropriate that here in 1929 Hitchcock made the film which signalled Britain's leap into the talkie era, *Blackmail*.

When the Cinematograph Films Act of 1927, introducing a quota system at last, began operation on January 1, 1928, the initial reaction of the big American renters was to acquire for distribution the films of these few quality producers, in order to comply with their legal obligation. But the films were popular, and it soon became clear that the distribution on fair terms of pictures that would compete with their own was not good business. They looked around for cheap films that would pose no threat, and a whole industry was born. From now on, the production of 'quota quickies' was to account for at least half of British output.

RACHAEL LOW

Hollywood Dawn

Into the Californian land of sunshine and orange groves came an invading horde of itinerant showbiz folk who created their own movie worlds in vacant lots and empty stores. Soon they built up a great new industry and the name of Hollywood, a suburb of Los Angeles, was known around the world

Top: Hollywood in 1905, looking south across Hollywood Boulevard. Above: Sunset Boulevard, a main artery of Hollywood, as a crowded thoroughfare in recent times

A Kansas couple, Harvey and Daeida Wilcox, came to Los Angeles in 1883 and opened a real-estate office. Three years later, they owned a 120-acre tract that was subdivided and advertised for sale under the name 'Hollywood'. In 1903 the residents voted for incorporation into the city of Los Angeles. The geographic area of Hollywood was determined to be from Normandie west to Fairfax Avenue and from the Santa Monica Mountains south to Fountain Avenue. This area, annexed to Los Angeles in 1910, was to become the focus of film production in the United States, and its name 'Hollywood' covered film-making in all studios in the various outlying Los Angeles areas.

Los Angeles itself was far from an urban metropolis at the turn of the century. Most of its 100,000 residents were concentrated in the districts surrounding the downtown commercial hub. To the west lay great stretches of bean fields, orange groves and empty land all the way to the ocean. Entertainment was centred in the downtown area, paralleling the mostly dry Los Angeles River. The exhibitor Thomas Tally was among the first to show motion pictures in Los Angeles in 1896, and in 1902 he opened his Electric Theatre, installing 200 fixed seats and charging the high price of ten cents for admission. He showed *The Capture of the Biddle Brothers* and *New York in a Blizzard* (both 1902), made in the east by Thomas Edison's company.

First on the scene

Colonel William Selig of the Chicago-based Selig Polyscope Company sent his director Francis Boggs to the West Coast early in 1907 to photograph coastal locations for *The Count of Monte Cristo* (1907). In 1908 Boggs rented a lot on Olive Street in downtown Los Angeles, where he made the first dramatic film shot completely in California: *The Heart of a Race Tout* (1909), starring Thomas Santschi and Jean Ward. Location scenes were shot at the old Santa Anita Race Track, which was about to be closed down.

In August 1908 Colonel Selig began construction of a completely equipped studio in Edendale, where *In the Power of the Sultan* (1909) was made with Hobart Bosworth and Stella Adams. Selig expanded his holdings in 1910 by enlarging both this and a second studio, complete with zoo, in what is now the Lincoln Park area. The second studio was particularly used for jungle pictures, which were very popular. When Selig pulled out, the zoo was donated to the city of Los Angeles and renamed the Luna Park Zoo. He sold his Edendale studio in 1916 to William Fox. Fox also moved into the old Dixon studio at Sunset and Western Avenue, where he continued to produce while he was constructing the Fox Movietone Studio in 1927, and for years thereafter. The new ultra-modern complex bordered on Pico Boulevard on the south and on Santa Monica Boulevard on the north; 20th Century-Fox has continued to make important pictures there to the present day.

Edendale in 1909 was the choice also of another early film pioneer, the New York Motion Picture Company (NYMPC), which sent a unit of actors called the Bison Company to California. They located themselves near Colonel Selig in a converted grocery store and began shooting as soon as Indians and cowboys could be hired. If their unlicensed camera was threatened by an agent from the Motion Picture Patents Company, they would go into the mountains at Big Bear Lake and make Indian pictures. When the NYMPC brought Mack Sennett from New York to work at the Edendale studio, he improved the property by building one of the first enclosed concrete stages in the area for his two-reelers. The NYMPC also leased acreage in the Santa Ynez

Canyon, where Sunset Boulevard meets the ocean, and a young director brought from New York, Thomas Ince, took the Bison Company there. At 'Inceville' pictures were made with the resident village of Indians, who had previously been with a touring Wild West show.

One of the oldest studios in East Hollywood was the Lubin Manufacturing Company frame building at the corner of Sunset Boulevard and Hoover Street, established in 1912. It was later briefly occupied by Essanay, the Chicago-based company of George K. Spoor and Broncho Billy Anderson. They stayed long enough to make 21 Westerns before taking their unit back to their studio at Niles in northern California. Then, from 1913 to 1917, the studio housed Kalem, which had another West Coast studio in Glendale. Others who followed on the premises through the years included Monogram, Allied Artists and KCET, the Public Broadcasting television station, which bought the property in 1970.

Wild and free

Vitagraph, operating in Flatbush, Brooklyn, as early as 1907, came to Santa Monica in 1911, and in 1913 built a large plant in East Hollywood. Among its West Coast stars were Norma Talmadge, Anita Stewart, Lillian Walker and the comedian Larry Semon. The Santa Monica studio acquired an annex, described in *The Moving Picture World* of July 10, 1915 as:

'. . . a ranch up in the mountains near the studio . . . wild and free from civilization . . . which is used for big outdoors sets and Western frontier scenes.'

In 1919 Vitagraph absorbed the defunct Kalem's scenario properties, the first phase of the liquidation of the Kalem assets. By 1920 Vitagraph was very active in production on both coasts, and the East Hollywood studio had '. . . grown to enormous dimensions, with an extensive back lot, with sets, and street scenes of all genres'. Hundreds of actors and production people were on the payroll, earning from $100 to as high as $5000 a week in the case of some stars. Larry Semon headed the Vitagraph basketball team, and one of the team members was comedy actor, stunt man and later producer Joe Rock. Mr Rock recalls: 'When I worked at the Vitagraph western studio in 1916, I was paid at the front-gate pay window in gold coin every week.'

The *Motion Picture News* of January 1, 1921

Above: the famous old sign on Mount Lee became derelict in the Thirties and was eventually replaced by a new one in 1979. Below left: Selig's first temporary studio in Los Angeles, next to a Chinese laundry, 1908. Below: David Horsley, president of Nestor, wi[th] the principals of the Desperate Desmond series of serials in 1911

reported that Vitagraph was making a prison-life picture *Three Sevens* (1921), starring Antonio Moreno and directed by Chester Bennett:

'The exteriors were taken at Florence, Arizona, where the Governor of the State permitted 300 convicts to be turned loose outside the walls in a daring escape for the picture . . . a train-robbery scene was filmed at Newhall, near the San Fernando Valley and an excellent prison set was constructed at the studio to match the interior of the Arizona penitentiary where it was impossible to light the corridors sufficiently for photographing.'

Vitagraph was sold on April 20, 1925 to Warner Brothers for $735,000, including the copyrights of its scenarios, which enabled Warners to remake the Vitagraph hits for years to come.

The American Mutoscope and Biograph Company sent its most prolific director, D.W. Griffith, to California for three seasons in 1910, 1911 and 1912. Griffith was not limited to his studio in downtown Los Angeles. He travelled with his cameramen Arthur Marvin and Billy Bitzer, as well as his acting and production unit, to actual locations of places mentioned in poems, stories and books that had been dramatized for the screen.

Griffith left Biograph in 1913 to join the Mutual Film Corporation, an independent company not licensed by the Motion Picture Patents Company. Mutual took over the Kinemacolor Studio located in East Hollywood at the intersection of Sunset and Hollywood Boulevards. This was later to become known as the Griffith Fine Arts Studio. It was here that the controversial picture *Birth of a Nation* (1915) was planned and edited, and its interior scenes shot. The film was premiered in Los Angeles under the title of the book on which it was based, Thomas Dixon's *The Clansman*. To counteract the widespread turmoil over the 'White Supremacy' aspect of this film, Griffith went on to make his monumental epic *Intolerance* (1916). His huge Babylonian sets, several storeys high, stood for years afterwards before they were dismantled.

Negative impressions

The first studio in Hollywood itself was a converted tavern and grocery store on the north-west corner of Sunset and Gower. David and William Horsley, owners and operators of the Centaur Film Company in Bayonne, New Jersey, came to the West Coast in 1911 and

elow left: the East Hollywood studio of the 'hiladelphia-based Lubin Company in 1912. elow right: Elmo Lincoln and Louise Lorraine, ars of the Tarzan series, at the studio of the National Film Company in 1919. Insert above: a picture-postcard view of Universal City, the studio that is incorporated as a township and is a major tourist attraction

continued to produce as the Nestor Film Company. The film historian Kevin Brownlow quotes the cameraman Charles Rosher's description of conditions there:

'Although we had a developing room, we had no printing machinery. The picture was cut directly from the negative, and we thought nothing of running original negative through the projector. Scratches and abrasions were mere details.'

Across the street from Nestor, on the southwest corner of Sunset and Gower, the first West Coast studio of the Universal Film Manufacturing Company was set up in 1912. Carl Laemmle, president of Universal, planned a much larger complex across the hills from Hollywood, in an isolated valley, and he began to build there in spite of the lack of roads and the great distance from downtown Los Angeles, where the film-processing laboratories were located. Universal was the first studio to provide space for the public to watch a movie being made – special tours still take many thousands through the studio every day.

The Jesse Lasky Feature Play Company was established at Selma and Vine Streets in December 1913 and that year released the first feature-length Western made in Hollywood itself, *The Squaw Man.* Lasky joined forces with Adolph Zukor's Famous Players Company in 1916 to form the Famous Players-Lasky Corporation, which expanded the Lasky studio. Lasky and Zukor took over the Paramount distribution company and formed the Paramount Pictures Corporation, a major producing company to this day. By 1926 they had outgrown their premises and acquired the United studio at Melrose and Van Ness Avenue, which they proceeded to enlarge and equip with the most up-to-date inventions in

Top left: Rex Ingram directs The Four Horsemen of the Apocalypse *in 1921. Above: parade in downtown Los Angeles to publicize John Ford's epic* The Iron Horse *(1924). Right: John Travolta keeps up a Hollywood tradition by immortalizing his footprints outside Grauman's Chinese Theatre. Below: gunfight at the Universal corral today to entertain the tourists. Bottom left: Desi Arnaz warming up the studio audience for television's* I Love Lucy *show in the Fifties*

movies. The old Lasky studio at Selma and Vine was abandoned in 1927 to make way for a miniature golf course. In later years, NBC built its radio studios there.

The small Oz Studio in Hollywood, at the corner of Gower and Santa Monica Boulevard, produced the Wizard of Oz series, based on L. Frank Baum's famous children's stories. The National Film Company, headed by Edgar Rice Burroughs, who wrote the Tarzan novels, was the next tenant, occupying this studio from 1915 and making the world-renowned Tarzan film series starring Elmo Lincoln.

William H. Clune, a successful Los Angeles film exhibitor, went into the film-production business in April 1915, and took over a studio from Fiction Pictures on Melrose Avenue. The Clune Studio started production on large feature films, the first of which was a 12-reel version of the story of *Ramona*, the Indian maiden, released in 1917. (D.W. Griffith had previously filmed the same subject in California as early as 1910.) Sets were built across the street, including a representation of the Santa Barbara Mission; a Mexican village; and the 'Moreno Homestead' with mansion and grounds. A small pueblo street was constructed in the eucalyptus grove adjoining the studio grounds. Archbishop Gillow came from Mexico in October 1915 to visit the *Ramona* sets, and was shown around by the director Donald Crisp. In February 1921 Douglas Fairbanks moved into the Clune Studio with his production company to make *The Three Musketeers*, transforming Clune's back-lot into a French village. A succession of film-producing companies used the Clune Studio through the years, and in 1980 it was renamed Raleigh Studios.

Metro Pictures was a New York-based company that rented its first Hollywood studio in 1916 and the following year was housed in the Mutual 'Lone Star' studio used by Charles Chaplin for one year to make a dozen of his most famous two-reel comedies. By 1918 the company had moved all its eastern production to the Hollywood studio and proceeded to make noteworthy movies such as *The Four Horsemen of the Apocalypse* (dir. Rex Ingram, 1921), the Buster Keaton comedies and films with Mae Murray. Metro employed film favourites such as Alla Nazimova, Bert Lytell, Harold Lockwood, Renée Adorée, Ramon Novarro, the Dolly Sisters and Rudolph Valentino. Jackie Coogan, the child actor who had become famous working with Chaplin, signed with Metro in July 1923. Directors at Metro included Rex Ingram, who made *Scaramouche* (1923), and also Reginald Barker, Victor Schertzinger, Edward Sloman and Fred Niblo.

Charles and Sydney Chaplin acquired in 1917 an estate on the south-east corner of Sunset Boulevard and La Brea Avenue in Hollywood. They and their mother lived in the ten-room colonial-type residence, which could double as a set for filming. The land behind the house was developed into the Chaplin Studio, which was finished by March 1918. It consisted of six English Tudor-style bungalows with dressing rooms, storage facilities and two large stages, one open and one closed. The head cinematographer was Roland (Rollie) Totheroh, and the stock company in the main comprised actors from Chaplin's Essanay and Mutual days. Chaplin hired four-year-old Jackie Coogan and later starred him in *The Kid* (1921), which was considered a masterpiece and added to Chaplin's world-wide fame. He continued to work at this studio until 1942, the year in which he reissued *The Gold Rush* (1925) with an added soundtrack. The plant was leased to Monogram Pictures in 1944 and thereafter to a number of others, until 1951 when Chaplin returned to begin work on *Limelight* (1952), his last American film. The plant reverted to a rental studio again until the end of 1966, when the music-recording company A & M Records moved into it. Chaplin's footprints are in concrete in front of Sound Stage 3, which is now the entrance to the recording studio.

Loving Lucy

On December 4, 1920, the *Motion Picture News* noted that:

'The new Robertson-Cole studios, which have been in course of construction since last summer at the corner of Gower and Melrose Streets, Hollywood, will be informally opened within the next few days . . . The studio proper covers a little over sixteen acres of ground . . . [having] eight huge stages . . .'

The company began on the East Coast as a releasing agency, which joined forces with Mutual and the Affiliated Distributing Corporation to distribute the Tarzan films and others. The producer and director Hunt Stromberg worked in the Hollywood studios, and in 1922 Robertson-Cole shared studio facilities with the adjoining United Studios. That year the company name was changed to the Film Booking Office (FBO). The East Coast giant Radio Corporation of America took over FBO in 1929 and, in an amalgamation with the Keith-Albee-Orpheum cinema circuit, built an even more modern studio on the premises, known as Radio-Keith-Orpheum (RKO). In the Fifties and Sixties the Desilu Company acquired this RKO plant as well as the RKO plant in Culver City, and made the *I Love Lucy* television series there. After about fifteen years of Desilu ownership, the entire complex was incorporated into Paramount, which was adjacent to it.

The Triangle Film Corporation, founded in 1915, offering financial backing and studio space to its three prolific producers, operated the Fine Arts Studio for D.W. Griffith, the studio at Edendale for Mack Sennett, and the studio at Santa Ynez for Thomas Ince. By October 1915 plans were in the works for Ince to begin construction on a projected studio in newly-founded Culver City, midway between the city of Los Angeles and the ocean, on land made available by developer Harry Culver. After a series of mergers, this studio became the home of Metro-Goldwyn-Mayer in the Twenties.

Meanwhile, in 1919, Ince built a colonial-style studio on Washington Boulevard in Culver City, and produced films there until his early death in 1924. This studio was then occupied by Cecil B. DeMille; Pathé; RKO; David O. Selznick, who made *Gone With the Wind* (1939) there and built the 'Tara Mansion' which stood for decades; Desilu; the Culver City Studio; and most recently, in 1980, Laird International Studios.

A great number of these old film factories have disappeared and their product with them. But their history survives and is becoming of greater interest to a new generation. Many film studios operate in Hollywood today, the present built on the past.

MARC WANAMAKER

Ben-Hur is remembered today as MGM's most famous silent film and the studio's biggest box-office hit of the Twenties. But the picture was, in fact, one of the projects inherited by Louis B. Mayer and Irving Thalberg with the formation of MGM in 1924. As undoubtedly the most expensive and problematical of their early productions, *Ben-Hur* clearly presented the greatest challenge to the success of the new company. In completing the picture, Mayer and Thalberg demonstrated for the first time that ruthless and effective approach to film-making which was to transform MGM into the leading studio in Hollywood. With *Ben-Hur* they succeeded in turning a potential disaster into a triumph.

Lew Wallace's original novel had first been published in 1880 and immediately became a best-seller. An elaborate stage version was mounted in 1889 and achieved a big popular success, leading in turn to an unauthorized two-reel film directed by Sidney Olcott for the Kalem Company in 1907. After protracted negotiations during the early Twenties, the Goldwyn Company secured the feature-film rights, then tested numerous Hollywood leading men before George Walsh was selected to head the cast. The driving force behind the production was the chief scenarist at the studio, June Mathis, who chose Charles Brabin as director (in preference to the better-known and talented Rex Ingram), and pressured the company to shoot the film in Italy, beginning in 1923.

It was a production beset by troubles from the very beginning, and the usual difficulties of working in a foreign country were magnified by the unsettled political and economic conditions coinciding with Mussolini's rise to power. And when the initial rushes were viewed by the new management at MGM, it was apparent that the picture was in serious trouble. Recognizing the need for drastic action, they selected Fred Niblo as the new director and MGM star Ramon Novarro to play Ben-Hur, while scenarists Bess Meredyth and Carey Wilson replaced June Mathis. Among the many assistants hired to help in filming the crowd scenes was the young William Wyler, who directed the remake 34 years later.

Like many epics before and since, *Ben-Hur* stresses action and spectacle at the expense of the more personal and intimate qualities of the story. The great sea battle set-piece – including graphic close-ups of the killings and decapitations – is awkwardly staged, but provides the climax to the opening half of the picture. In the second half, the famous chariot-race is one of the most dramatic and exciting sequences ever filmed, reflecting the expertise and imagination of the various technicians and creative personnel who worked on the production. These included a small army of stuntmen; a team of cameramen (42 in all); a team of editors, headed by Lloyd Nosler who reduced the 200,000 feet of exposed film to 750 feet of pure action; and art director Cedric Gibbons and special-effects expert J. Arnold Gillespie who utilized a hanging miniature blended with model shots of the galleries in the stadium peopled by thousands of tiny moving puppets to create the illusion of a vast crowd.

Inevitably, with the race over, the final reels look anti-climactic, and a further major weakness of the film is the fact that the central relationship between Ben-Hur and Messala never appears convincing. Francis X. Bushman's part is rather small, and he is never more than a stereotyped villain, while – in spite of his big build-up from MGM – Ramon Novarro fits uneasily into the heroic mould required for Ben-Hur. Of lasting special interest are the few sequences shot in the then new two-strip Technicolor process.

The picture was finally premiered on December 30, 1925 at the George M. Cohan Theater in New York; it received generally favourable reviews and went on to become the studio's biggest grossing film. However, due to the extraordinary costs – estimated at about $4 million – and the Goldwyn Company's original agreement to pay half the income from the film for the rights to the novel, the picture failed to make a profit. That same year the top money-maker for MGM was *The Big Parade* (1925) which cost only a fraction of the budget of *Ben-Hur*. JOEL FINLER

Directed by Fred Niblo, 1925

Prod co: MGM. **prod:** Louis B. Mayer, Samuel Goldwyn, Irving Thalberg. **sc:** Bess Meredyth, Carey Wilson, from an adaptation by June Mathis of the novel by Lew Wallace. **titles:** Katherine Hilliker, H.H. Caldwell. **photo:** Rene Guissart, Percy Hilburn, Karl Struss, Clyde de Vinna, E. Burton Steene, George Meehan. **sp eff photo:** Paul Eagler. **ed:** Lloyd Nosler. **ass ed:** Bill Holmes, Harry Reynolds, Ben Lewis. **art dir:** Cedric Gibbons, Horace Jackson. **set des:** Arnold Gillespie, Ferdinand Pinney Earle, Camillo Mastrocinque. **mus** (for the original presentation): David Mendoza, William Axt. **add dir:** Al Raboch. **col. dir:** Ferdinand Pinney Earle. **2nd unit dir:** B. Reaves Eason, Christy Cabanne. **prod man:** Harry Edington. **prod ass:** William Wyler. **r/t:** 194 minutes. New York premiere, December 30. **Cast:** Ramon Novarro (*Judah Ben-Hur*), Francis X. Bushman (*Messala*), May McAvoy (*Esther*), Betty Bronson (*Virgin Mary*), Claire McDowell (*Princess of Hur*), Kathleen Key (*Tirzah*), Carmel Myers (*Iras*), Nigel de Brulier (*Simonides*), Mitchell Lewis (*Sheik Ilderim*), Frank Currier (*Quintus Arrius*), Leo White (*Sanballat*), Charles Belcher (*Balthasar*), Dale Fuller (*Amrah*), Winter Hall (*Joseph*).

Prologue: **The arrival of Mary (1) and Joseph in Bethlehem and the birth of Christ in the manger (Technicolor sequence) is observed by the Three Wise Men. *AD 26:* Messala arrives in Jerusalem to take command of the Roman military garrison, and meets his old friend Ben-Hur (2), whom he has not seen for many years. As the new governor passes in the street below, a roof tile is dislodged. This leads to the arrest of Ben-Hur (3) with his mother and sister.**

Ben-Hur is sentenced to the galleys on a Roman warship (4) which is attacked by pirates. He escapes and rescues Arrius, the Roman commander, who adopts him as his son (5). They make a triumphant entry into Rome.

Sheik Ilderim persuades Ben-Hur to enter the chariot-race against his arch-rival Messala. An Egyptian temptress, Iras, tries to seduce him in order to learn the identity of the mystery challenger. Ben-Hur confronts Messala and accuses him of treachery (6). The chariot-race (7) becomes a personal battle between the two men (8), with Ben-Hur emerging victorious while Messala is killed.

In the Holy Land Mary Magdalene is among those who join the followers of Christ. Ben-Hur goes with them and is reunited with his true love Esther and with his mother (9) and sister who had contracted leprosy while in prison. As one of the last acts before his crucifixion, Christ cures them.

3

5

7

9

'During those early years of motion pictures I was billed in theatre lobbies as "Blondielocks" and "Goldielocks". In other places I was known as "The Girl With the Curls", though the name that stuck longest was the "Biograph Girl" . . . There is, of course, one nickname, if I may be so bold as to call it that, which fastened upon me early in my career, a nickname involving an honour which has always touched me deeply but which I scarcely deserved or accepted'

Mary Pickford (America's Sweetheart)

Myths have persisted about Mary Pickford since the end of the silent era. One of them is that she invariably played a child. True, she often did, but when in 1968 a film historian as respected as Herman G. Weinberg could write, in his book *The Lubitsch Touch*, that Lubitsch's *Rosita* (1923) gave her her first adult part, it is evident that myth has taken over. Mary had played adults in D.W. Griffith's films when she herself was barely adolescent, and she continued to do so throughout her career.

A more dangerous myth is that Pickford was not really a serious actress. This idea was voiced long ago. Perhaps it began with Paul Rotha, who wrote in *The Film Till Now* in 1930 that she was not an artist and had no real idea of acting values (strictures he applied equally to Douglas Fairbanks). It was still a current notion in 1980 when the National Film Theatre programme notes on Frank Borzage's *Secrets* (1933) considered that Miss Pickford's presence was a handicap to a proper reading of a 'Borzage text'.

Far left: a portrait of Mary Pickford. Left: she often played children's roles, as in this 1917 film. Below: Pickford with (from left to right) her photographer, Charles Rosher, her cameraman, Henry Cronjager, and her director Marshall Neilan

The final myth, in which there is a fraction of truth, is that Pickford was a grasping and mercenary businesswoman. Reality was somewhat different. She certainly asked for, and frequently obtained, vast sums of money – and, in the process, transformed the industry into one where artists were the main gainers.

It all began in April 1909 when Gladys Marie Smith (born in Toronto on April 8, 1893), a child actress of ten years' experience whose name had been changed by the Broadway producer David Belasco to Mary Pickford, went to the Biograph studio in New York to ask for work. The girl was the main support of her widowed mother, her sister Lottie and her brother Jack. Accounts of her first meeting with Griffith vary, but he engaged her, and the following day she appeared in her first movie, a 'split-reel' (about six minutes long) comedy called *Her First Biscuits*. Griffith was turning out two films a week at this time and by the end of 1910 Mary had appeared in some eighty one-reelers, earning $40 weekly. Many of these films survive and some of them, like *An Arcadian Maid* and *Wilful Peggy* (both 1910), show her to great advantage: at 17 she is playing ingénues with considerable spirit and unmistakable enjoyment, and her acting reveals an instinctive understanding of the medium – as early as this, it is cool, naturalistic and poised. She was not known by name – that was against Biograph policy – but inter-titles had sometimes called her 'Little Mary', and that appellation stuck. (British distributors insisted on names, which they often made up, and for them she was Dorothy Nicholson.)

'We of the silent screen enjoyed a unique privilege. Through our voiceless images we were citizens of every country in the world'

Below far left: her last movie for D. W. Griffith was The New York Hat. *Below centre: a typical poverty-stricken child from* Rags *(1915). Below: in* Stella Maris, *she played both the pretty girl of the title and the ugly, slightly deformed Unity Blake*

These were the days of the war between the independent film-makers and the Patents Trust, and in 1910 Carl Laemmle, fighting hard for his Independent Motion Picture Company, lured her away from Biograph, billed her as Mary Pickford, and gave her $175 a week. She began a stormy marriage with actor Owen Moore (who appears to have been given a rough time by Mary's formidable mother and who drank too much), and she sailed to Cuba when the studio sent the director-producer Thomas Ince and a company there to escape the Trust's strong-arm men. The films she made for IMP are lost, but they got good notices in their day.

After a short stay at Majestic, another independent company (where she earned $275 a week), she returned to Griffith in 1912 for her last bunch of shorts before features took over. It was in 1912 that she made the best known of her early films, *The New York Hat*, with Lillian and Dorothy Gish, Mae Marsh and Lionel Barrymore. A quiet and gentle piece, it retains all its charm, but that cast hints at competition ahead and there may be some truth in the story that Pickford left Griffith for good because Mae Marsh got the role she coveted in *The Sands of Dee* (1912).

Briefly she returned to work for David Belasco, admitting with some shame that she had been in the movies, but now the stage could not hold her. In 1913 Pickford began her long association with Adolph Zukor when he signed her to appear in features for his Famous Players company at $500 a week.

She had become by now an actress of real versatility, playing children when required but equally adept as Latin-American girls, Indian maidens or Red Indian squaws. The Pickford of legend had not yet fully emerged.

Between 1913 and 1919 Mary Pickford made 34 pictures for Famous Players. If she was not so already, she became, unchallengeably, the best-known woman in the world. Her salary rose steadily, culminating in the famous agreement of 1916 by which she obtained $10,000 a week as a guarantee against 50 per cent of the profits of her own new Mary Pickford Motion Picture Company, together with lavish fringe benefits. Doubtless the memory of her childhood hardships – the years on the road, the lack of home and schooling – spurred her to fight for every comfort she could get, but there was another, more immediate, incentive. She was being exploited, and she knew it. Since 1914, Famous Players had been part of the giant Paramount distribution combine whose block-booking system forced exhibitors to take the company's pictures sight unseen in order to obtain the sure-fire Pickford successes, and the exhibitors also paid much higher rentals for the Pickford pictures. There are colourful tales about how Mary learned all this, but know it she certainly did.

'I sometimes wonder whether I had the right to cut off my hair. Were the choice ever given to me again, I am positive I would not do it'

The consequences were inevitable. Faced with such a high financial outlay, companies

Above: the tomboy Pickford, showing her spirit in Little Annie Rooney. *Below: she had her curls cut off before playing a society charmer in* Coquette

Above right: angelic side to the fore in The Poor Little Rich Girl. *Opposite page: the only film in which Douglas Fairbanks and Pickford acted together,* The Taming of the Shrew

would do everything to make the produc better. Films became longer and were mor carefully made; art directors, cameramen, dir ectors were given more time and scope. Artist generally became aware of their status. Film improved, not overnight, but steadily over th next ten years. The silent picture move towards perfection.

During her Famous Players period, Pickfor worked with one great director – Mauric Tourneur – and with many good ones – Cec B. DeMille, Marshall Neilan, Allan Dwan. I 1917, she began her long association with th great cameraman, Charles Rosher, whos lighting concealed the darkening of the famou golden curls and emphasized the better, le side of her face. To some extent now, an completely so after the formation of Unite Artists in 1919, Pickford was her own produce and her ability to discern and employ the be in every branch of film-making was as impor ant as her own acting skill.

Perhaps the greatest of her years wit Adolph Zukor, who controlled Famou Players, was 1917. In it she made the two mos famous of her 'little girl' pictures, *The Poc Little Rich Girl*, directed by Tourneur, an *Rebecca of Sunnybrook Farm*, directed b Neilan, followed in 1918 by the daring

Filmography

1909 Two Memories; The Violin Maker of Cremona; The Lonely Villa; Her First Biscuits; The Son's Return; The Faded Lilies; The Mexican Sweethearts; The Peach-Basket Hat; The Way of Man; The Necklace; The Country Doctor; The Cardinal's Conspiracy; Sweet and Twenty; The Renunciation; The Slave; A Strange Meeting; They Would Elope; His Wife's Visitor; The Seventh Day; Oh, Uncle!; The Indian Runner's Romance; The Little Darling; The Sealed Room; 1776, or the Hessian Renegades; Getting Even; The Broken Locket; In Old Kentucky; The Awakening; The Little Teacher (+co-sc); His Lost Love; In the Watches of the Night; The Gibson Goddess; The Restoration; What's Your Hurry?; A Light That Came; A Midnight Adventure; Sweet Revenge; The Mountaineer's Honor; The Trick That Failed; The Test; To Save Her Soul. **'10** All on Account of the Milk; The Call; The Woman From Mellon's; The Englishman and the Girl; The Newlyweds; The Thread of Destiny; The Twisted Trail; The Smoker; His Last Dollar; A Rich Revenge; As it Is in Life; A Romance of the Western Hills; The Kid; The Unchanging Sea; Love Among the Roses; The Two Brothers; An Affair of Hearts; Ramona; In the Season of Buds; A Victim of Jealousy; Never Again!; May and December (+sc); A Child's Impulse; Muggsy's First Sweetheart; What the Daisy Said; The Call to Arms; An Arcadian Maid; When We Were in our Teens; The Usurer; Wilful Peggy; The Sorrows of the Unfaithful; Muggsy Becomes a Hero; Little Angels of Luck; A Summer Tragedy; Examination Day at School; A Gold Necklace; The Masher; A Lucky Toothache; The Iconoclast; That Chink at Golden Gulch; Waiter No. 5; Simple Charity; Sunshine Sue; The Song of the Wildwood Flute; A Plain Song; White Roses. **'11** When a Man Loves; Their First Misunderstanding; The Italian Barber; The Dream; Maid or Man; At the Duke's Command; When the Cat's Away; The Mirror; Her Darkest Hour; Three Sisters; Artful Kate; A Manly Man; The Message in the Bottle; The Fisher-Maid; A Decree of Destiny; In Old Madrid; Sweet Memories of Yesterday; The Stampede; Second Sight; For Her Brother's Sake; The Fair Dentist; The Master and the Man; The Lighthouse Keeper; Back to the Soil; Behind the Stockade; For the Queen's Honor; In the Sultan's Garden; A Gasoline Engagement; At a Quarter of Two; Science; The Skating Bug; The Call of the Song; The Toss of a Coin; 'Tween Two Loves; The Sentinel Asleep; The Better Way; The Aggressor; His Dress Shirt; From the Bottom of the Sea; The Courting of Mary; Love Heeds Not the Showers; Little Red Riding Hood. **'12** The Mender of Nets; Honor Thy Father; Iola's Promise; Fate's Interception; The Female of the Species; Just Like a Woman; Won by a Fish; A Lodging for the Night; The Old Actor; A Beast at Bay; Home Folks; Lena and the Geese (+sc); The School Teacher and the Waif; An Indian Summer; The Narrow Road; The Inner Circle; With the Enemy's Help; A Pueblo Legend; Friends; So Near, yet so Far; A Feud in the Kentucky Hills; The One She loved; My Baby; The Informer; The New York Hat. **'13** The Unwelcome Guest; In the Bishop's Carriage; Caprice. **'14** Hearts Adrift (+sc); A Good Little Devil; Tess of the Storm Country; The Eagle's Mate; Such a Little Queen; Behind the Scenes. **'15** Cinderella; Mistress Nell; Fanchon the Cricket; The Dawn of Tomorrow; Little Pal; Rags; The Foundling (destroyed before release, remade in

ffbeat *Stella Maris*. Of Pickford's little-girl oles, one thing demands saying. The little girl no sweet young thing. She is full of fun, and ften naughty. She can hold her own with ough boys, notably in *Little Annie Rooney* (1925) and she is as much at home in a slum as in a castle. She bears no relation to the sugared moppets of later days.

There have been sympathetic studies of the motives behind Pickford's playing of children's parts even in her thirties, and it is easy enough to believe that she is compensating, once again, for that lost childhood. But it was only a part of her and *Stella Maris* brought out the other side. In it she plays a dual role. She is the crippled rich girl, Stella, and she is the plain and downtrodden, slightly deformed, servant, Unity Blake, who commits murder and suicide for Stella's happiness. The film went through against Zukor's opposition and Pickford was superb in both parts, Rosher's camerawork involving some of the finest double exposures yet seen.

She made three films at First National in 1919, including one of her greatest hits, *Daddy Long Legs*, again directed by Neilan, and then from 1920 to the end of her career in 1933 she worked exclusively for United Artists. The story of the company's formation is well known. What is perhaps less appreciated is how much Pickford and Douglas Fairbanks (whom she married in 1920, after a messy divorce from Moore) did to keep the company afloat. The other partners, D.W. Griffith and Charles Chaplin, contributed little (Chaplin only two films in seven years), and until fresh sources were tapped through a deal with Joseph Schenck in 1924, United Artists was virtually Fairbanks and Pickford. Pickford made 15 films (plus a guest appearance in Fairbanks' 1927 film *The Gaucho*) in 14 years. These included *Suds* (1920), a charming if slight story in which Mary rescues a broken-down horse; *Rosita* (1923), which was Ernst Lubitsch's first American film, and on which he and Pickford quarrelled lengthily and occasionally hilariously; and the delightful *Little Annie Rooney*. This has Mary as a spirited slum kid involved in street battles with her peers, local gang warfare and a successful hunt for the killer of her policeman father. The happy moments have an irresistible sparkle and there is an intensely moving scene when the child comes home to find that her father is dead. This had happened to Pickford too, when she was five, and she had never forgotten.

With the same director she made the marvellous *Sparrows* (1926) and then came *My Best Girl* (1927), her last silent film. Pickford plays opposite Buddy Rogers, whom she later married after her divorce from Fairbanks, and as a shop assistant in love with the son of the owner of the store, she is fresh and natural as she had been in those early Biograph movies almost twenty years before.

'I sometimes feel that my only real childhood was lived through the many children's roles I played, even into adulthood'

She made four sound films. For the first of them, *Coquette* (1929), she played a spoiled Southern flirt. She took chance after chance on this: the film was tragedy; she had cut her famous curls at last; she replaced Rosher with another cameraman, Karl Struss; and she was speaking for the first time. Yet she won the Best Actress Academy Award in this, the second year of the awards.

The Taming of the Shrew (1929) was her only film co-starring Fairbanks. In this adaptation, Petruchio is by far the richer part and it is Fairbanks' film. But Pickford's Kate, quietly seeing through him, is an engaging little devil, if not quite a shrew. *Kiki* (1931) was not a success, but her final film, *Secrets*, most emphatically was. As a pioneer woman, seen from youth to old age, she crowns her career with charm and dignity and grace. *Secrets* has never been much liked, and perhaps it was out of key with the brashness of much of the product of the time, but of the splendour of that last performance there is no doubt. As the film historian Kevin Brownlow wrote: 'She proved once and for all that she was among the greatest actresses of motion pictures, both silent and sound.'

And then she abdicated. There is no need to seek abstruse explanations. For 35 years she had not stopped working. She had cared for her feckless and often appalling family. Her first two marriages had been wearing, to say the least. She had had enough. In 1937 she married Buddy Rogers, who cared for her, for a change, and continued to do so until she died in 1979. She had once wanted her films to be destroyed on her death. Thankfully she had, slowly, changed her mind. JACK LODGE

16); Esmeralda; A Girl of Yesterday (+sc); adame Butterfly. **'16** Poor Little Peppina; The ernal Grind; Hulda From Holland; Less Than e Dust. **'17** The Pride of the Clan; The Poor ttle Rich Girl; A Romance of the Redwoods; The ttle American; Rebecca of Sunnybrook Farm; A ttle Princess. **'18** Stella Maris; One Hundred rcent American; Amarilly of Clothes-line lley; M'Liss; How Could You, Jean?; Johanna alists. **'19** Captain Kidd Jr.; Daddy Long Legs; e Hoodlum; Heart o' the Hills. **'20** Pollyanna; ds. **'21** The Love Light; Through the Back oor; Little Lord Fauntleroy. **'22** Tess of the orm Country. **'23** Garrison's Finish (title writer ly); Rosita. **'24** Dorothy Vernon of Haddon all. **'25** Little Annie Rooney; Waking Up the wn (prod only). **'26** Sparrows; **'27** My Best Girl; e Gaucho (guest); Potselui Meri Pikford SSR) (doc) (USA/GB: The Kiss of Mary Pickrd); Odna Iz Mnogikh (USSR) (doc) (USA/GB: e of Many). **'29** Coquette; The Taming of the rew. **'31** Kiki. **'33** Secrets. **'36** One Rainy fternoon (co-prod only); The Gay Desper-o (co-prod only). **'48** Sleep, My Love (co-prod ly).

Sparrows

1

No-one would expect to find a Mary Pickford picture included in the category of horror films. Yet *Sparrows* is not only one of Pickford's finest movies, it also has an honoured place in William K. Everson's book on the horror genre.

Perhaps its inclusion there is not quite fair. The villain, Grimes, superbly played by that great character actor Gustav von Seyffertitz, is certainly a horrifying creation, and though there is one scene which for sheer, sustained tension has seldom been equalled, the overall atmosphere is rather different. *Sparrows* is a melodrama – a cruel, frightening Dickensian melodrama – played perfectly straight and with utter conviction. It is also a film virtually without a hero. With Pickford as its heroine, and a villain like von Seyffertitz, it simply has no need of one.

The Southern swamp in which the film is set was constructed on the back-lot of the Mary Pickford Company studio on Santa Monica Boulevard, and no location shooting could equal the impact of this magnificent design by art director Harry Oliver, one of the great forgotten artists of the Twenties. This swamp has quicksands, a mass of hostile greenery and a lavish supply of alligators, and provides the nastiest of settings for the supremely nasty Mr Grimes, a baby-farmer of repellent mien and utter savagery.

The scene in which Mary Pickford as Mama Mollie – the girl who plays mother, nurse and comforter to the smaller inmates of Grimes' farm – leads them to safety across the swamp, has set historians at loggerheads. The climax of the journey sees Mollie walking along a log across a corner of the swamp, carrying one baby on her back with the others following, and alligators snapping their jaws within a couple of feet of the convoy. The story has it that Douglas Fairbanks visited the set, saw his wife in danger, was enraged and said that double-exposures should have been used. Miss Pickford herself told this to interviewers, and it was generally accepted.

The film historian Booton Henderson, however, interviewed Hal Mohr – one of three notable cameramen who worked on *Sparrows* – who gave a very different account. According to Mohr, the alligators were filmed first, with the top half of the picture matted out; Miss Pickford and the children did their bit two days later. Mohr adds a lovely detail. Out of camera range a trainer threw meat to the alligators; Mohr carefully timed the opening jaws; and two days later Mary could stumble at exactly the points of greatest danger. The more alarming version must have been circulated as studio publicity, and time and nostalgia have provided the rest.

Mary Pickford's own performance is of the kind she did superbly well, falling as it does mid-way between her little-girl roles and her adults. She was 32 at the time, playing a character of about 17, and she looks precisely right. It was the last occasion she would play a child, and her sturdy, spirited Mollie was a marvellous end to that side of her career.

There are other notable performances. William Beaudine, a skilful director of children, coaxes Mary's bedraggled brood into the most woebegone naturalism. Young Spec O'Donnell – splendid as the little Jewish kid in *Little Annie Rooney* (1925) – offers a very different characterization as Grimes' callous son, Ambrose. And the half-witted Mrs Grimes is nicely managed by Charlotte Mineau.

Perhaps the film's greatest virtues are those which were taken for granted in the Twenties, and rarely noticed in the criticism of the time, remarkable though they may appear today. *Sparrows* has not dated. It survives, and survives proudly, by virtue of its enormous care for detail, the perfection of its camerawork, and a total belief in what was being done, sufficient to inspire everyone involved.

Sometimes it seems as though the Twenties did not deserve their movies. Mordaunt Hall, film critic for the *New York Times*, had little use for *Sparrows*, and dismissed its 'puerile ideas' and 'exaggerated suspense'. Fortunately, the public generally knew better.

JACK LODGE

4

Directed by William Beaudine, 1926

Prod co: United Artists. **sc:** Winifred Dunn, George Marion Jr, C. Gardner Sullivan. **photo:** Charles Rosher, Hal Mohr, Karl Struss. **ed:** Harold McLernon. **art dir:** Harry Oliver. **ass dir:** Tom McNamara, Carl Harbaugh, Earle Brown. **length:** 7763 feet (approx. 103 minutes); recent soundtrack version 81 minutes.

Cast: Mary Pickford (*Mollie*), Roy Stewart (*Dennis Wayne*), Mary Louise Miller (*Doris Wayne*), Gustav von Seyffertitz (*Mr Grimes*), Charlotte Mineau (*Mrs Grimes*), Spec O'Donnell (*Ambrose*), Lloyd Whitlock (*Bailey*).

3

6

In the swamplands of one of the Southern states, Mr and Mrs Grimes and their son Ambrose run a baby-farm for unwanted children. The oldest child, Mama Mollie, protects the younger ones as well as she can (1) from the brutality of the Grimeses (2). In spite of Mollie's efforts, the children are half-starved, maltreated and quite without hope of escape.

A little girl, Doris, is kidnapped in the nearby city and brought to the farm (3, centre). Grimes fears that the police will learn of his activities, and tells Ambrose to throw Doris into the swamp (4). Mollie comes to her rescue, defies Grimes, defends herself with a pitchfork, and, encouraged by a vision of Christ (5), decides that she must try to get the children to safety (6).

She leads them through the swamp and eventually meets police who are searching for Grimes. He and his wife are finally arrested. The kidnappers are drowned after a pursuit by motor-boat, Doris is restored to her father (7), and Mollie's 'sparrows' are happily adopted by a friendly millionaire.

7

LAUGHTER IN THE DARK

Chuckles, guffaws and belly-laughs spread around the world as the movies' first comedians went about their business in France, Italy and finally America

Laughter is the surest of all best sellers. When things are bad, people want comedy to cheer them up; and when they are already happy, they want to seal their happiness with laughter. From the start film-makers recognized that they had in comedy a perennial money-spinner. From *L'Arroseur Arrosé* (1895, Watering the Gardener) onwards, comedy featured largely in the early film repertory.

These first films, barely one minute long, were confined to the sort of single-gag visual jokes that might have been inspired by cartoons in the comic papers – as, indeed, was *L'Arroseur Arrosé*. Even when films became longer and the action of comedies was extended and elaborated, what was funny was the happening, rather than the relationship to that happening of the people concerned. Of course it seemed funnier if the person who pulled the chair from under someone else was a cheeky-faced boy, and if the victim was a stout and irascible old person who might wave his arms or stick and otherwise express anger in an extravagantly comical way. Yet, despite the hints offered by the appearance in films of music-hall comedians who occasionally recorded fragments of their acts for the camera, and the strong characterization in Méliès' comic films, it was not until the middle of the first decade of the century that the cinema screen saw the regular emergence of character clowns – comedians who produced laughter by their relationship to the world and events around them.

It was in France, which dominated the world cinema industry in the decade before World War I, that a genre of comedy was introduced where the humour depended on the personality of the comic actor. The first true movie clown was André Deed (1884–1938), born André Chapuis. Trained as a music-hall singer and acrobat, and thus being part of a tradition of clowning that went back to the Italian pierrot and the Auguste of the circus, Deed entered films as a supporting player for Georges Méliès. In 1905, Charles Pathé saw him on stage at the Châtelet Theatre in Paris and at once engaged him. After appearing in a chase film, *La Course à la Perruque* (1905, The Wig Race), Deed went on to make a whole series of one-reel comedies, which within a few months established him as a favourite with audiences all over Europe.

Deed was the first of a generation of clowns who, though their proper names were unknown to the public at large, were lovingly styled by nicknames that were generally different in every country where their films were shown. In France, for instance, Deed was 'Boireau'. In Italy he was 'Beoncelli', in Spain, 'Sanchez', and so on. When in 1908 – perhaps nervous at the rise of a new rival, Max Linder, at Pathé – Deed accepted an offer to work for the Itala Film Company in Turin, his new Italian name was 'Cretinetti'. When the Cretinetti films were shown in France, he was renamed 'Gribouille'. The Spanish now named him 'Toribio', the Russians, 'Glupishkin', and the English, 'Foolshead'.

Perhaps this multiple nomenclature and change of nationality produced a kind of artistic schizophrenia, for Deed never established so clear-cut a personality as Linder and the later American clowns were to do. He was characterized by a glorious, irrepressible and incorrigible idiocy which, whether he was burning down his own house with a candle-lit Christmas tree or wrecking a cinema, generally resulted in apocalyptic destruction.

Deed was his own director and proved a good pupil of Méliès. He was the first director-comedian to exploit to the full the comic possibilities of accelerated action, stop motion and other comic

Above: André Deed made this 1910 film in Italy after he had l Pathé for Itala. He later returne to France but lost his popularity and ended his days in poverty. I was an agile clown, with hair t stood up and a nose and lower l that stuck out. He was also a talented director

ɔove: Rigadin Peintre Cubiste *ʀigadin, the Cubist Painter) was ɪe film in a long series, made tween 1910 and 1920, starring ɪarles Prince. He and the ncierge are dressed in vaguely bic clothes, but beyond that ere is little sign of comic spiration. Above right:* Kri-Kri ma la Tintura *(1913, Kri-Kri ves Dye) starred the Italian mic Giuseppe Gambardella. ght: Max Linder signed himself r the friends of the cinema' and r 20 years he graced film medy with his elegant presence*

trickery. His talent as a director was such that he continued to make films even when his own popularity as a star had waned, though his career did not survive the coming of sound. In his later days Deed worked as a night watchman at the Pathé studios, where once he had reigned.

Pathé had other comedians to succeed Deed after his defection to Italy. Charles Prince (alias 'Rigadin' in France, 'Whiffles' in England, 'Prenz' in Russia, 'Moritz' in Germany, 'Salustiano' in Spain, 'Timofeo Tartufini' in Italy, and so on) was blessed with a big clownish face and turned-up nose. An enormous favourite with audiences of the time, his comedy looks strained and repetitive beside that of Deed or Linder – not every comedian was equal to the pressures of making a film a week.

Other Pathé stars were recruited from the variety theatres, including Dranem, whose fame as a comedian was already sufficiently large for his name not to be adapted, and Louis-Jacques Boucot (known as Boucot or 'Peinard Gavroche'), who was blessed with a funereal face, epileptic movements and a disconcerting manner of suddenly sticking out his tongue. Roméo Bosetti, who had made his vaudeville debut at the age of ten with a plate-smashing act, joined Pathé as a comedian in

Send in the clowns – to keep the people happy in the days of innocence before World War I

1908, but showed such talent as a director and organizer that he was put in charge of Pathé's new Comica studio in Nice, established exclusively for the production of comedy on the Côte d'Azur, the beaches, boats and harbours of which provided rich material for the clowns to work on. The principal Comica stars were Sablon (alias 'Babylas') and a small, grimacing German clown called 'Little Moritz', who was generally in pursuit of Sarah Duhamel ('Rosalie'), a stout lady who stoically endured the humiliations devised by Bosetti's comic scenarios. Other Pathé stars were Cazalis ('Jobard' or 'Caze') and Léon Durac, who had particular success with the character of Nick Winter, a comic detective parodying the popular adventures of Nick Carter, the English sleuth.

Pathé's greatest star – indeed, the greatest comic star of the years before World War I – was Max Linder. Born Gabriel-Maximilien Leuvielle in 1883, he began his career as a legitimate actor, but in 1905 began to eke out his small salary from the Theâtre de l'Ambigu by working days at the Pathé studios. He played bit parts and occasional leads until 1909, when the departure of Deed decided Pathé to star Max in a series of his own. Max was different from the rest – suave, elegant and handsome in the garb of a young boulevardier, where they strove for grotesque eccentricity – and the special flavour of his comedy lay in the contrast between his personal elegance and the ludicrous situations in which he found himself.

Max was a brilliant and prodigal inventor of comedy, with a gift for endless variations on a single, simple theme, such as taking a bath or putting on a pair of tight shoes. Gags that he devised still enrich every comedian's repertory. He also had a greater and more sophisticated appreciation than any among his contemporaries of the demands and the potential, for the comedian, of the cinema screen. Max's career ended in tragedy. Dogged by ill health, disheartened by his failure to establish himself in America, fearful of his declining popularity, he took his own life in October 1925.

At the Gaumont studios the guiding creative force was Louis Feuillade (1873–1925), who had not yet discovered his forte as a director of serial thrillers. Gaumont comedies were altogether more extravagant than those of Pathé, with prodigal use of trick camerawork and an unrestrained fantasy that anticipated both Mack Sennett and the surrealist film-makers of the Twenties. Runaway perambulators are liable in Gaumont comedies to circle the earth; fashionable drawing-rooms are invaded by horses or camels. Images in the films about Onésime (originally Ernest Bourbon, though after 1916 the role passed to Marcel Levesque) and Calino (Mige) often have a delirious madness. René Clair's *Paris Qui Dort* (1923, *The Crazy Ray*) was probably inspired by *Onésime Horloger* (1912, Onésime the Clockmaker) in which time is telescoped, and all the activities of daily life are accelerated fourfold as a consequence of the hero's tampering with an electric clock in order to hasten the 20 years he has to wait for a legacy. Gaumont's most successful comedian between 1910 and 1912 was Léonce Perret, known as Léonce, who was himself to become a very distinguished and innovatory director of French silent cinema.

Feuillade hit upon a particularly effective formula with films starring two successive child comedians, first 'Bébé' Abélard and then 'Bout-de-Zan' – a particularly unappealing child who was maliciously, and no doubt unjustly, reputed to be a dwarf of advanced years. The pranks which these mischievous juveniles played at the expense of guileless elders contributed notably to the more innocent merriment of the last days of the pre-war world.

The styles of French comedy were imitated everywhere, and French clowns were much in demand in Italy. Deed's nearest rival there was Ferdinand (Ferdinando) Guillaume, whose screen name changed from 'Tontolini' to 'Cocciatelli' and 'Polidor' as he moved from one rival company to another in pursuit of higher rewards. He was small and quaintly shaped, with a beaming, foolish face. With the sudden burgeoning of American comedy in the early Keystone days from 1912 onwards, at least two French stars of Italian comedy, Emile (Emilio) Vardannes ('Totò') and Marcel Fabré ('Robinet') tried their luck across the Atlantic.

Below left: Onésime et le Chameau Reconnaissant *(1914, Meeting of Onésime and the Camel) featured Ernest Bourbon and an animal friend or two. Bottom left:* Little Moritz, Elève de Nick Winter *(1911, Little Moritz, Pupil of Nick Winter) was one of a series made in France by the German comedian Mauritz Schwartz. Bottom right:* Der Blusenkönig *(1917, The Blouse King) was directed by and featured Ernst Lubitsch. Later he was better known as the director of American comedies such as* Ninotchka *(1939) and* To Be or Not to Be *(1942)*

Other countries attempted to follow the Latin style. In Germany the popular Jewish star of a crude slapstick series, 'Meyer', was later to achieve international fame as a director under his real name, Ernst Lubitsch. The Russians were inclined to import their comedy. A favourite comedian, generally characterized as a foppish suitor, 'Antosha' was a Pole, Antoni Fertner. The clown 'Giacomo' was Milanese, and 'Reynolds' was probably English. The only two authentically Russian screen comedians of the period were V. Avdeyev, who played a stout, elderly bourgeois called Djadja Pud, and N. P. Nirov, who created a pleasant, truly native character in Mitjukha, a peasant boy constantly baffled by the ways and wiles of the big city. Slightly later another Russian artist, Arkady Boitler, was to base his character of Arkasha on the sophisticated, urbane manner of Max Linder, who had made a profound impression on Russian audiences during a theatrical tour shortly before World War I.

Britain and America lagged behind continental Europe in the production and development of film comedy in these early years of the century – surprisingly, because both countries had rich theatrical traditions of vaudeville comedy. Some of the great comedians of the time permitted their variety

Above: Sidney Drew at a touchy moment in Henry's Ancestors *(1917). Top:* C'Est la Faute à Rosalie *(1911, It's Rosalie's Fault) has Sarah Duhamel as the much-put-upon lady. Top right: Jimmy Aubrey (centre) wishes that he had not gone to the dentist in a typical low-comedy one-reeler*

acts to be filmed; but the only sustained English comedy series of the pre-war years were the films starring Fred Evans as Pimple; he had a grotesque clown face and a very broad style in knockabout comedy, and tended to topicality in his choice of themes. Infrequent revivals of these films suggest that the titles were often the best part of them: *Pimple Up the Pole*, for instance, or *Pimple, the Bad Girl of the Family* (both 1915) – Evans had a particular taste for playing roles in drag. Rival series, such as Bamforth's films about Winky and Clarendon's comedies featuring the character Jack Spratt, were short-lived.

Few American comedies of note have survived from the first decade of the century; and it was not until around 1910 that the American companies began to experiment with character clowns in the European style. In that year the American Mutoscope and Biograph Company launched a series with a character called Jonesy and another with Mumptious, a plump and pompous little man. At the same time Vitagraph discovered America's first true comedy star, John Bunny. Bunny had been a successful stage actor and manager before, with rare foresight, he perceived the potential of moving pictures. At first he had some difficulty in persuading Vitagraph to accept his services; but in a matter of months he had established himself as a major box-office attraction. Bunny was stout and cheery, with a huge and irresistibly comic face; he looked much older than his years – he was 46 when he made his first films for Vitagraph, and only 51 when he died in 1915. His usual partner was Flora Finch, generally playing the vinegary wife who frustrated his aspirations to amorous or other adventures.

Bunny's popularity launched American film comedy for the first time in the European market. In Russia, where he was known as 'Poxon', he was so well-loved that after his death a Russian 'Poxon', V. Zimovoi, attempted, without success, to take his place. American successors – Bunny's own brother, George, who had a strong family likeness to him, and the rotund Hughie Mack – proved equally unable to replace the much-loved fat clown.

The success of the John Bunny films produced new confidence among American makers of comic films. After 1910 comedy stars began to proliferate. Vitagraph enjoyed further success with the light domestic comedies of Mr and Mrs Sidney Drew as well as low-comedy one-reelers with Billy Quirk and an English comic from the Fred Karno music-hall troupe, Jimmy Aubrey. Essanay's long-running Snakeville Comedy series created characters who belonged to a comic-strip wild West, including Alkali Ike (played by Augustus Carney) and Mustang Pete (William Todd). Essanay, which was to score its greatest comic triumph a few years later, in 1915, when it captured Charlie Chaplin from Mack Sennett's Keystone Company, also promoted a popular series starring Wallace Beery as Sweedie.

The Selig company's answer to Snakeville was a Bloom Centre series. Tramp comedians had long been popular in vaudeville, and Kalem teamed Lloyd V. Hamilton and Bud Duncan as a knockabout hobo team, often directed by Marshall Neilan. Two shorter-lived hobo teams were Poke and Jabbas and Plump and Runt. In 1911 the Nestor Film Company translated Bud Fisher's strip-cartoon characters Mutt and Jeff to the screen; in later years the same characters were to be revived in the form of animated cartoons.

Comedies and their stars proved highly effective ammunition in the cut-throat industrial battles of the pre-war period. Character comedy had become a staple of the American silent cinema. It was to be carried to new heights of folk art and lunacy by Mack Sennett's Keystone studio.

DAVID ROBINSON

After the triumph of *Shoulder Arms* (1918) Chaplin made *Sunnyside* (1919), which was a comparative failure. In 1919, with his marriage to Mildred Harris already showing signs of strain, he was at a crisis of self-doubt. He relates in his autobiography that he would go to his studio, day after day, along with his stock company of actors in the hope of inspiration that never came.

Just when he had despaired of finding a new idea, he went to the Orpheum music hall where Jack Coogan was appearing in his eccentric dancing act. Coogan's four-year-old son Jackie made a brief appearance along with him, and Chaplin was so engaged by the little boy's personality and way with an audience that he promptly began thinking up a scenario that would team the child and the Tramp. Jack Coogan had just signed a short-term contract with Fatty Arbuckle but the child was still free and Chaplin quickly hired him; as he recalls in his autobiography, the father's words were: 'Why, of course you can have the little punk.'

Jackie Coogan played Charlie's younger son in *A Day's Pleasure* (1919) as a preliminary to his major role in *The Kid*. Chaplin found the child a natural performer and quick learner:

'There were a few basic rules to learn in pantomime and Jackie very soon mastered them. He could apply emotion to the action and action to the emotion, and could repeat it time and again without losing the effect of spontaneity.'

The very real affection that grew up between Chaplin and Jackie is quite evident in *The Kid*. According to Chaplin, the poignant scene where Jackie cries real tears as the orphanage men are taking him away was achieved by the simple ruse of Jackie's father threatening that if he did not cry, he would be taken away from the studio to the real workhouse.

The film opened with a title: 'A picture with a smile – perhaps a tear.' Although previous Chaplin films had introduced sentiment and pathos, this was the first time in the history of film comedy that anyone had risked mingling a highly dramatic, near-tragic story with comedy and farce.

The film was also much longer – six reels, or 88 minutes at silent running speed – than any he had previously made. With his customary care (the one-minute scene of Charlie and Jackie's pancake breakfast is said to have taken two weeks and 50,000 feet of negative to achieve), his shooting schedule was long and costly. The sum of nearly $500,000 which he claimed to have invested was enormous for a comedy at that date.

It was completed under extreme difficulties. Mildred Harris was in the process of divorcing him by the time he was editing. Fearing that her lawyers might attempt to seize the film, Chaplin smuggled 500 reels of film to Salt Lake City, where the picture was cut in a hotel room, with only a small, elementary cutting machine on which to view the material. Even when a preview was arranged at the local movie theatre, Chaplin had still not seen the finished picture on a screen. His inevitable apprehensions proved unfounded; from this very first screening, audiences responded wholeheartedly to the film, accepting totally the mixture of moods from high sentiment to low comedy.

Critics were not all so convinced. The playwright J. M. Barrie was among those who found the dream sequence out of place, which perhaps it is, though it is delightful with its slum angels (one of whom was, by chance, Chaplin's future wife, Lita Grey). Others were rather stuffy about 'vulgarities' such as Charlie's investigation of the foundling's sex, a joke about the child's dampness and the consequent devising of toilet facilities. Today such endearingly truthful touches have ceased to shock. The sentimental elements are more alien to modern audiences; and when, almost half a century later, Chaplin reissued the film with new music of his own composition, he trimmed some shots that he felt would be unacceptable to a new public. He need hardly have worried. The film, his comic invention and Jackie Coogan's remarkable performance have lost none of their power – it is one of the most durable of all silent movies.

The Kid made Jackie Coogan a star and world-wide celebrity. His trip to Europe, when he was received by the Pope, monarchs and presidents, was a royal progress. He went on to a highly profitable film career, playing such classic juvenile roles as the leads in *Peck's Bad Boy* (1921) and *Oliver Twist* (1922).

His beloved father, however, was killed in a road accident; and when, with adolescence and manhood, he found his star waning, his mother and stepfather withheld from him what was left of his earnings. Most of what remained was lost in lawsuits. This case had permanent results in the Californian legislation known as 'The Coogan Act' to secure half of the earnings of minors for their own future use. In later years Coogan, with no trace left of his cute baby looks, made occasional film appearances; and on television played the grotesque Uncle Fester in *The Addams Family*. DAVID ROBINSON

1

4

Directed by Charles Chaplin, 1921
Prod co: Charles Chaplin Productions, for First National. **prod:** Charles Chaplin. **assoc dir:** Charles (Chuck) Reisner. **sc:** Charles Chaplin. **photo:** Roland H. (Rollie) Totheroh. **length:** 5300 feet (approx. 88 minutes).
Cast: Charles Chaplin (*Tramp*), Edna Purviance (*mother*), Jackie Coogan (*boy*), Carl Miller (*artist-author*), Tom Wilson (*policeman*), Henry Bergman (*superintendent of the night shelter*), Chuck Reisner (*tough*), Lita Grey (*a flirtatious angel*), Phyllis Allen (*woman with the pram*), Nelly Bly Baker (*slum nurse*), Albert Austin (*man staying overnight in the shelter*), Jack Coogan (*pickpocket*).

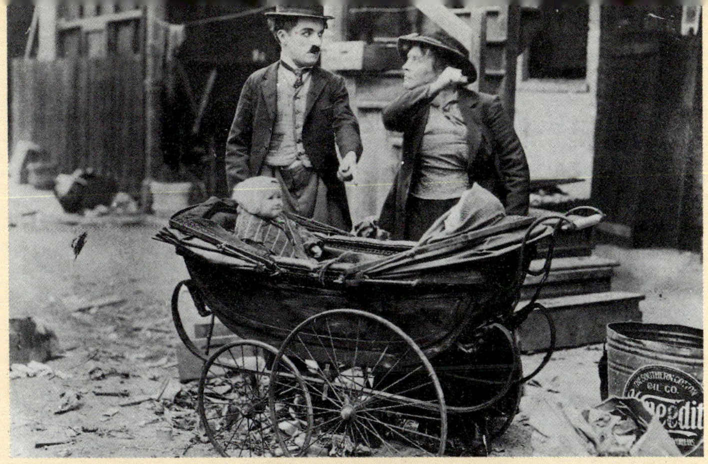

3

2

6

5

7

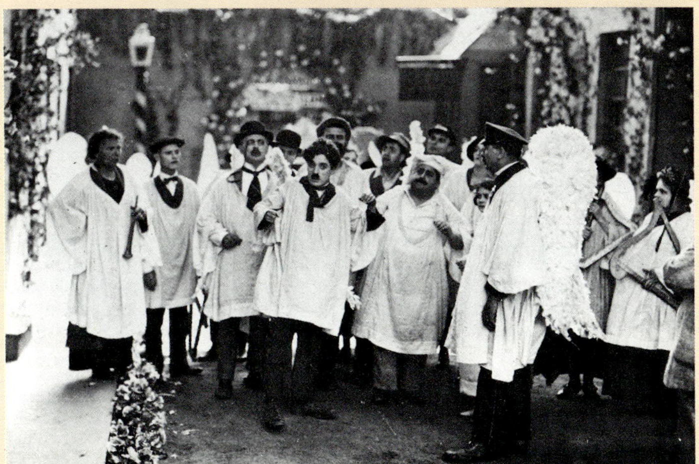

8

An unmarried mother (1) leaves her baby in an empty wedding limousine with a note asking the finder to care for the child. The car is stolen, and the thieves dump the baby in the slums where he is discovered by Charlie, a Tramp (2). Charlie's efforts to get rid of the child are all frustrated (3), and he is obliged to take him into his own garret room where he ingeniously devises a cradle, feeding bottles and other necessities.

Five years later (4) Charlie is a glazier; the boy precedes him around the street breaking windows. After a doctor has examined him (5), the child-care authorities try to take the little boy off to an orphanage (6); but Charlie manages to rescue him from the truck that is carrying him away. Now fugitives (7), they pass the night in a doss-house among outcasts and thieves.

Meanwhile the mother, who has become a rich and famous singer, has by chance discovered the whereabouts of her long-lost and sought-after child. Learning of the reward she is offering, the superintendent of the doss-house snatches the child while Charlie is sleeping and carries him off to the police station.

Later Charlie, exhausted from seeking the child, dreams that the slums have been transformed into a paradise inhabited by angels and kindliness (8). He is awakened by a policeman – the mother has sent for Charlie to reunite him with the boy.

Among the American paintings in New York's Metropolitan Museum of Art is a landscape by George Inness entitled 'Sunrise' and dated 1887. It is unlikely, for all the conscientiousness of Hollywood art directors in the Twenties, that this painting in any way influenced the set designers of F. W. Murnau's film, *Sunrise*, which appeared some forty years later. Yet both the picture and the film testify to the absolute importance of light in conveying the essence of space and landscape. So although Murnau's roots are in the Expressionist movement that flourished in German art, theatre and cinema from about 1914 to 1924, the stylistic origins of *Sunrise* can be traced back to the Impressionism of the 1880s, of which the Inness painting is a fortuitous example.

Should that reference seem pretentious, it must be admitted that *Sunrise* is a consciously artistic movie in which the problem of depicting space and light are paramount. It could hardly be argued that the plot – however much the viewer identifies with the protagonists – is anything but the flimsiest of frameworks, existing merely to contain Murnau's artistic experimentation in a format (namely melodrama) easily accessible to audiences.

In the event, the film was a flop, and since it was Murnau's first in America (after a spectacularly successful early career in Germany), it left his future with Fox uncertain. Few reviewers at the time registered the genius of the film's conception – a combination of sunlit

1

2

5

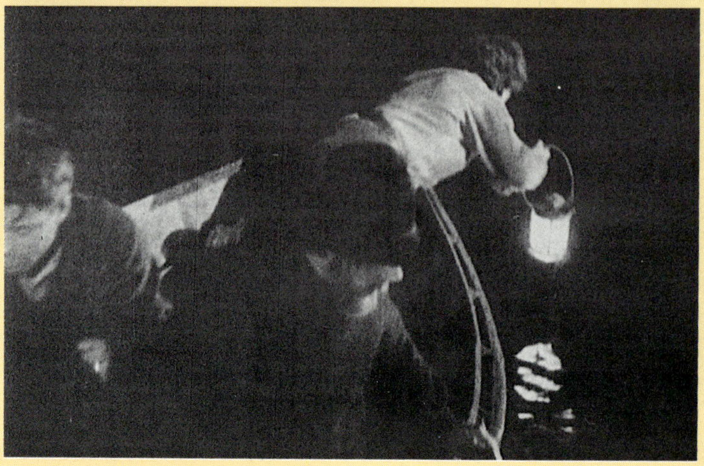
6

location shots and studio-lit exteriors and interiors that captured the essence of 'country' and 'city' and imbued each with metaphysical values. It is no accident that almost all the production team were German or Austrian (scenarist Carl Mayer, art director Rochus Gliese, assistant art director Edgar G. Ulmer, and Murnau himself) or of German parentage (assistant director Herman Bing and co-cinematographer Karl Struss). The look of the film, as Kevin Brownlow has noted in his book on silent Hollywood, *The Parade's Gone By*, is distinctively European, in spite of being made in California. The image of the city, as it appears to the country people, bears a closer resemblance to the modernist designs of the German Bauhaus style of architecture (founded 1919) than to any contemporary American reality, and is more reminiscent of films made at the Ufa studios in Berlin than in Hollywood. This is particularly noticeable in the amusement-park sequence where the miniature planes circling above a huge roller-coaster flashing with lights recall the city sets in Fritz Lang's *Metropolis* (1927).

But if *Sunrise*'s relationship to German Expressionist cinema is self-evident, it should also be recognized that the film is more realistic and 'American'. Murnau's sophisticated camera movements take the film beyond the painterly concept of the frame and create a fluid space that suggests a world outside it. The best illustrations of this are in the scenes where the trolley-car enters the city and where the couple go into the amusement park. In each case the studio sets – highly elaborate and built in diminishing perspective – appear to go on forever, and the illusion of depth is reinforced by the camera's tracking movement that leads the viewer into the fullest dimension of the image.

None of this precludes the use in the film of rear-projection scenes – a technique often considered a weakness in Hollywood cinema because it makes the image appear two-dimensional. But Murnau's use of it succeeds because it is either consciously stylized, as in the brief shot of the husband and wife appearing to walk into a wood as they step across a city street, or so full of action as to be virtually indistinguishable from the foreground action, as in the scene where the husband kisses his wife in the midst of the city traffic.

In the final analysis, however, it is Murnau's use of light – *the* metaphor of the movie, as one critic has suggested – that creates the atmosphere of *Sunrise*. Subtle oppositions between light and darkness determine the emotional tone of the different sequences: light breaking through the church when the husband and wife are reconciled in the wedding scene; the artificial light of the amusement-park scene that represents a state of ecstasy before the near-tragedy of the boat-accident; the darkness that adds extra tension to the night-time meetings of the husband and his mistress on the edge of the marshes.

That it is possible for the viewer to feel so anguished during the boat-accident sequence and at the husband's subsequent search by lamplight for his wife is attributable not simply to the bitter irony of the plot (he had originally intended to drown her) but also to the consummate skill of a director who creates out of light and space a world for the film that is at once abstract and concrete. *Sunrise* was underrated for years; now it is one of few films to be acknowledged – by a whole range of critics who disagree with each other on most aspects of cinema – as an undisputed masterpiece. MARTYN AUTY

A city woman, holidaying in the country, has an affair with a young married farmer (1) and eventually persuades him to murder his wife and move to the city with her. The husband plans an 'accident' in the boat he and his wife use to go to the city (2), stowing a bundle of rushes aboard to save himself from drowning.

Unable to go through with the plan, the husband breaks down and rows his wife ashore. In a state of extreme anguish, they take a tramcar to the city. Their tearful reconciliation is completed by a visit to a church where a wedding is taking place. In love once again (3), they visit a photographer and then a barbershop, where the husband ignores the advances of a manicurist and defends his wife from the attentions of a roguish admirer.

After visiting a huge amusement park (4), they return home in the boat. A storm blows up (5) and the sail snaps. Before the boat capsizes, the husband ties the rushes to his wife to save her. He is washed ashore but she is lost. A search party looks for her (6) – but to no avail. When the city woman arrives thinking the plan has been carried out, the husband attacks her in his despair (7). Word comes that the wife has been found, unconscious but alive. As the spurned mistress makes a hasty exit, the husband rushes to his wife's bedside and they are reunited (8).

Directed by F. W. Murnau, 1927
Prod co: Fox Film Corporation. **sc:** Carl Mayer, from the story *The Journey to Tilsit* by Hermann Sudermann. **titles:** Katherine Hilliker, H. H. Caldwell. **photo:** Charles Rosher, Karl Struss. **art dir:** Rochus Gliese. **ass art dir:** Edgar G. Ulmer, Alfred Metscher. **synch score:** Hugo Reisenfeld. **ass dir:** Herman Bing. **r/t:** 95 minutes. Premiere, 29 November 1927.
Cast: George O'Brien (*the man*), Janet Gaynor (*the wife*), Margaret Livingston (*the woman from the city*), Bodil Rosing (*the maid*), J. Farrell MacDonald (*the photographer*), Ralph Sipperly (*the barber*), Jane Winton (*the manicurist*), Arthur Housman (*the obtrusive gentleman*), Eddie Boland (*the obliging gentleman*).

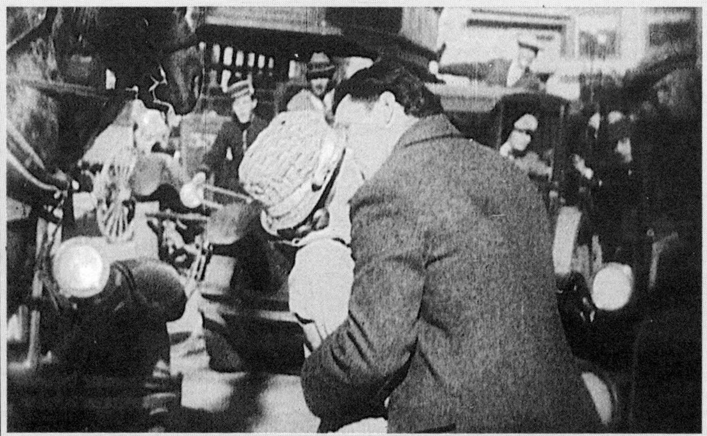

4

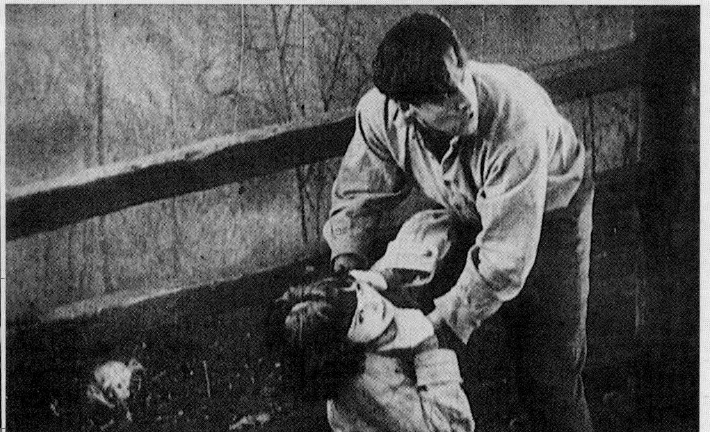

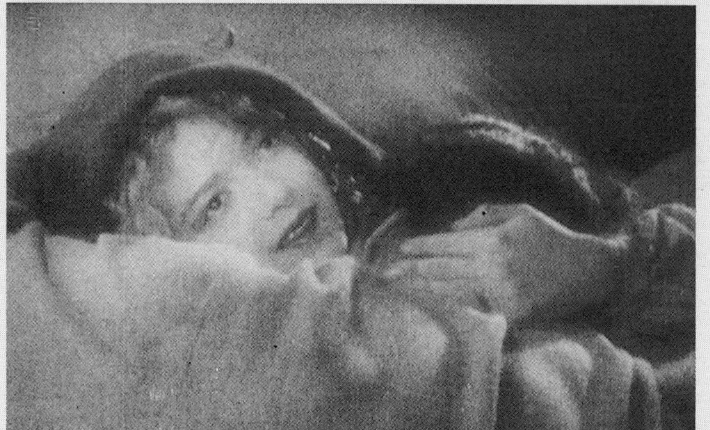

8

Above: Gösta Ekman as Faust *and Emil Jannings as the demon Mephisto. Above right: poster for* Tartuffe *showing Jannings in the title role of the hypocrite and Lil Dagover as the girl he lusts after. Below: George O'Brien as the peasant waiting on the edge of the swamp for his mistress in* Sunrise *– the shot shows Murnau's eloquent use of space*

doorman's fall from glory is realized in images just as haunting and atmospheric as those in which he clothed his vampire tales. And Emil Jannings' performance in the principal role – the one in which he first amazed international audiences with how much he could convey with his back to the camera – was also a potent factor in making the film the most universally noticed German feature of the year. It was, in fact, the immense American success of *The Last Laugh* which eventually brought both Jannings and Murnau to Hollywood.

Before he succumbed to the blandishments of the Hollywood producer William Fox, however, Murnau made two more films in Germany: both adaptations of theatrical classics, both with Jannings. *Tartüff* (1925, *Tartuffe*) was based on Molière's play, and *Faust* (1926) was based on Goethe's, and both opened in 1926. *Tartuffe* is an ingenious attempt to adapt a stage work in terms of a stage performance, distanced by a framing device but retaining all the theatricality of Molière's original concept. *Faust*, on the other hand, seizes the opportunity to make the whole into a thoroughly 'cinematic' film. Such is Murnau's skill in using the basic syntax of the cinema to his own purposes that it is hard to say which film is the more successful or the more genuinely cinematic.

California sunrise . . .

Then came the red-carpet treatment in Hollywood. All the resources of the Fox studios were placed at Murnau's disposal. He was able to use a script by his favourite writer, Carl Mayer, an adaptation of *The Journey to Tilsit*. Hermann Sudermann's Lithuanian story about a peasant wooing. He worked completely without interference, building giant sets, shooting and reshooting until he had got just the effect he desired. The result – *Sunrise* – is really a completely German film made in America with American stars (Janet Gaynor and George O'Brien). Visually stunning and atmospherically sublime, it is constructed in a European style; the story itself remains slight, though Murnau's treatment develops it like a symphony, reaching a crescendo with the storm on the lake in which the reunited husband and wife are nearly separated for ever. *Sunrise* was greeted with critical acclaim, and went on to win all kinds of awards. But the great American public did not buy it, and this relative failure overshadowed the progress of Murnau's two subsequent films for Fox.

The coming of sound did not help either, spreading uncertainty among the studios as to what they should do with the more expensive projects then in the works. Murnau's next film, a circus drama called *Four Devils* (1928), suffered from front-office interference designed to make it more general in its appeal. *Our Daily Bread* (1930) was begun with enormous ambition as a saga of the mid-Western grain lands, but got progressively cut down into a personal story of a city girl's problems with a hostile-seeming environment. Retitled *City Girl*, it was roughly re-edited with some talkie sequences (not by Murnau) to cash in on the new craze. Finally, though the silent version of the film contains some of the director's finest work, this was hardly noticed in the confusion of the talkies and his Hollywood career ended.

Paradise lost

He did, however, manage to make one more film: the privately financed and evidently noncommercial *Tabu* (1930), begun in collaboration with the documentary film-maker Robert Flaherty and intended as a semi-documentary, was filmed entirely in South Sea locations with a non-professional cast of Polynesians. Lacking the documentarist's ideals, Murnau insisted on making it into a rhapsody on the theme of fated young love, as elaborately structured as any of his studio pictures. The result was a perfect swansong for the director – a hymn to natural beauty, of people and of landscape, and a triumph of aesthetic cinema. But it did not open until a few days after his death, and what else he would have done – in America or Europe – remains one of the cinema's most intriguing fields of speculation.

JOHN RUSSELL TAYLOR

Filmography

1919 Der Knabe in blau/Der Todessmaragd. **'20** Satanas; Sehnsucht/Bajazzo; Der Bucklige und die Tänzerin; Der Januskopf/Schrecken; Abend – Nacht – Morgen; Der Gang in die Nacht (USA: Love's Mockery). **'21** Schloss Vogelöd. **'22** Nosferatu, eine Symphonie des Grauens (USA: Nosferatu, the Vampire) (German sound version: Die zwoelfte Stunde – Eine Nacht des Grauens, 1930); Marizza, genannt die Schmuggler-Madonna/Ein schönes Tier, das schöne Tier; Der Brennende Acker; Phantom. **'23** Die Austreibung. **'24** Die Finanzen des Grossherzogs. **'25** Der letzte Mann (USA/GB: The Last Laugh); Tartüff (USA: Tartuffe, the Hypocrite; GB: Tartuffe). **'26** Faust. *All remaining films USA:* **'27** Sunrise – A Song of Two Humans. **'28** Four Devils. **'30** City Girl/Our Daily Bread; Tabu (+co-prod; +co-sc).

Knock 'em flat

Mack Sennett's comic touch

Iack Sennett gave up playing heavy-handed country bumpkins to oncentrate on running his successful new company, Keystone. The ıame became a hallmark for pace-setting comedies that were turned ›ut by the hundreds: best loved and best known are those featuring hat immortal crew of crazy Kops, who perennially rush to the escue – arms flailing, feet slithering as they concertina into each ›ther, leaving mayhem in their wake

Iack Sennett was born Michael Sinnott n January 17, 1880 in Richmond, Quebec. Vhen he was 17, his family, who were of Irish escent, moved to Connecticut, where the lad ›und a job in a local iron foundry. He grew ıto manhood endowed with not much else esides a good bass voice, a yearning for the ıeatre and an obstreperous determination vhich was later to serve him well.

When the great comedienne Marie Dressler isited Northampton – where the Sinnotts had ettled in 1898 – Michael secured an introduc-on from a rising local lawyer, Calvin Coolidge vho was also to achieve future fame as President of the United States). In her turn Miss Dressler gave the young man an introduction to the great theatrical impresario David Belasco. Impatiently Michael rushed off to New York, where Belasco unfeelingly told him that he would do better to look for an opening in burlesque rather than in legitimate theatre or grand opera. Michael was not too proud to take the advice, and, changing his name to Mack Sennett, he took a job as utility comic in Frank Sheridan's Burlesque Company. The next few years were spent between burlesque and work as a chorus boy and comic support in a number of Broadway musicals.

Two faces of Sennett: (top) as actor with Mabel Normand and Charlie Chaplin in The Fatal Mallet *(1914), and (above) as director on the set of* Stolen Magic *(1915)*

Perhaps because of the scarcity of theatre work, in 1908 or 1909 Sennett enrolled in the regular stock company at the Biograph studios. Linda Arvidson, the wife of D. W. Griffith, Biograph's leading director, recalls that he was ready and eager to play any part, as well as to muck in with the rest of the company in building sets, or in doing any other odd jobs about the place.

First steps

Sennett's first big chance as a film comedian came with *The Curtain Pole* (1909), directed by Griffith who had to turn his hand to anything from farce to classical tragedy. Sennett, who thought French characters essentially funnier than English – 'the French go all the way' – played Monsieur Dupont who, slightly elated by absinthe, carries a long curtain pole through a crowded market place, wreaking comic havoc.

Mrs Griffith, who was playing a customer in the market place, had special cause to remember Sennett's first starring role, which she describes in *When the Movies Were Young*:

'He succeeded very well, for before I had paid for my cabbage, something hit me and I was knocked not only flat but considerably out, and left genuinely unconscious in the center of the stage. While I was satisfied he should have them, I wasn't so keen just then about Mack Sennett's starring ventures. But he gave a classic and noble performance, albeit a hard-working one.'

Sennett writes in his autobiography that he assiduously studied Griffith's methods both on and off the set. Mrs Griffith recalled that:

'When work was over, Sennett would hang around the studio watching for the opportune moment when his director would leave. Mr Griffith often walked home wanting to get a bit of fresh air. This Sennett had discovered. So in front of the studio or at the corner of Broadway and 14th Street he'd pull off the "accidental" meeting. Then for twenty-three blocks he would have the boss all to himself and wholly at his mercy. Twenty-three blocks of uninterrupted conversation. "Well now, what do you really think about these moving pictures? What do you think there is in them? Do you think they are going to last? What's in them for the actor? What do you think of my chances?"

'To all of which Mr Griffith would reply: "Well, not much for the actor, if you're thinking of staying. The only thing is to become a director. I can't see that there's anything much for the actor as far as the future is concerned".'

Changing direction

Sennett also recalls these evening conversations; and his disappointment that Griffith did not share his feeling for the comic possibilities of policemen in movies. However, he took seriously the advice about directing. In 1910 Biograph introduced a new director, Frank Powell, to take charge of a second unit, which henceforth undertook all comedy production. When Powell fell ill, Sennett eagerly took over as director. There is some dispute about which is the first picture that he directed, since he may have worked for a while as assistant to Griffith or Powell rather than as a fully-fledged director. His directorial debut appears, however, to have been in October 1910 with *A Lucky Toothache* or *The Masher*, or in March 1911 with *Comrades*. What is certain is that from March 1911 until the summer of 1912 all Biograph comedies – numbering around one hundred titles, ranging from four-minute split-reels to one-reelers – were directed by Sennett.

It was wonderful training in the invention and direction of comedy; and Sennett admitted cheerfully to extensive theft of ideas from his admired French clowns. His favourite actor at Biograph was the plump Fred Mace, with whom Sennett played in a series of films about a couple of comic detectives. His favourite actress was, and was to remain, Mabel Normand. This beautiful, graceful and witty comedienne was barely fifteen when Sennett first encountered her at Biograph. It was the beginning of a stormy romance that outlasted Mabel's short life (she died in 1930 aged only 35): Sennett's love for her continued till his own death. It was an affair constantly interrupted and impeded by quarrels and reconciliations between two incorrigibly volatile personalities.

Key to success

Though they did not collect the reverential press coverage accorded to the Griffith dramas, the Biograph comedies captivated the public and made money. So Sennett was able to convince a couple of bookmakers, Kessel and Baumann, to whom he owed money, that their interests would be best served by setting him up in his own studio. Thus Keystone was born and Sennett's backers were launched as moguls. The next years saw Sennett in whirlwind activity. He quickly convinced Kessel and Baumann to let him move his operation to California, and took over the old Bison studio at Edendale. He established regular production of two split-reels each week then moved on to issue first two and then three one-reelers every week, with a monthly two-reel production. He

ook Mabel Normand, Fred Mace and the ıctor-director Henry 'Pathé' Lehrman from Biograph, and created new artists. He introluced the Keystone Kops, animal comedies ınd child comedies.

Sennett's Keystone developed a unique, sureal style of visual comedy. It enriched the folkore of America and the world with a universe

Below: a comedy directed by Sennett for Biograph in 1912, the year he left to form Keystone. Below left: a gag typical of Keystone omedies, from Between Showers *(1914) with Emma Clifton, Charlie Chaplin, Ford Sterling ınd Chester Conklin*

of curious and colourful characters; and – quite incidentally to Sennett's aims, which were simply to make money out of comedy – advanced movie art, giving a new freedom to the camera which had to develop the same agility as the funny-men themselves.

Sennett recruited his artists from burlesque, circus, vaudeville, from building sites and mental hospitals. At first he directed all the films himself, but as the Keystone output grew, to keep several units occupied at any one time, he recruited or created other directors, among them the comedians Mabel Normand, Fatty Arbuckle, Dell Henderson and Charles Parrott (alias Charlie Chase). The films were largely improvised; and a single prop (car, telephone, boat) or setting (a grocery store or a garage) was enough to inspire endless comic variations.

Law and disorder

Keystone comedy drew its inspiration from comic strips, French slapstick cinema, vaudeville, pantomime; its techniques approached those of the old Italian *commedia dell'arte*; and yet it was different from all of these. The Keystone comedies remain a monument of twentieth-century popular art, transmuting the reality of the life and times of the teens and twenties of the century into a comedy that is basic and universal. The Sennett shorts were uncompromisingly anarchic, celebrating an orgiastic destruction of goods and possessions, cars, houses and crockery. Authority and dignity were regularly brought low – most notably by the Keystone Kops, that supremely incompetent law-enforcement troupe who were forever falling out of windows, tumbling down stairs or flying off their skidding patrol wagons, heading – brakeless – for imminent, cliff-edge catastrophes.

Left: Chester Conklin, nicknamed 'Fishface' because of his oversized moustache, was often the wide-eyed victim. Below: with the face and manner of a child, 'Fatty' Arbuckle nonetheless proved irresistible to the ladies in his many successful comedies

Star-studded casts

The inhabitants of this world were larger and wilder and far more colourful than life. They might be fat or thin, giants or dwarfs, with oversize pants and undersized hats, entangled spectacles and uncontrollable moustaches. They were monstrous, wonderful caricatures of reality. After Normand and Mace, Sennett's long procession of stars was to include Ford Sterling, with his angry face and ludicrous goatee (generally the superintendent of the Kops); baby-faced Fatty Arbuckle; cross-eyed Ben Turpin, with his phenomenal Adam's apple; gangling Charlie Chase; walrus-moustached Billy Bevan; confused Chester Conklin and the gigantic Mack Swain. Later Keystone stars included Charles Murray, Slim Summerville, Sydney Chaplin (brother of Charles), Hank Mann, Edgar Kennedy, Harry McCoy, Cary Brooks, Don Barclay, Harry Booker, Francis Wilson and Billy Walsh. Two

Keystone Kops, Eddie Sutherland and Edward Cline, became distinguished comedy directors, as did two Keystone gag men, Malcolm St Clair and Frank Capra. As well as the divine Mabel, the Sennett troupe of funny women included Polly Moran, Minta Durfee, Alice Davenport, Phyllis Allen, Louise Fazenda and Alice Howell. Of the greatest comedy artists who passed through the Keystone studios, Harold Lloyd failed to make his mark under Sennett; while his major discovery, Charlie Chaplin, left him after only one year and 35 one- or two-reel pictures. (Sennett, fearful of wage escalation, would never pay well enough to retain his most successful stars for long.)

In July 1915 Sennett was one of the Big Three – the others were D. W. Griffith and Thomas Ince – who were formed into the Triangle company. Triangle-Keystone, without forfeiting any of its allegiance to slapstick and to the public, was able to enlarge its ambitions. At first – in line with the aspirations of his sister companies for the prestige of famous names – Sennett engaged major stage comedy stars of the time, Raymond Hitchcock, Eddie Foy, Weber and Fields, though the results were uneven; and Triangle-Keystone tended quite soon to revert to its own stars, more accustomed to the demands of the screen.

More important, Sennett was able to extend his comedy production and embark on two- and three-reelers. Production values were more elaborate; characterization was more developed. The old *commedia dell'arte* improvisation began to give way – with no appreciable loss of invention and freedom – to more careful scripting and pre-planning of production.

By 1917 however, the Triangle partnership was breaking up. In June of that year, Sennett succeeded in extricating himself from the contract, though the Keystone company remained part of the Triangle grouping. Without Sennett, its creator and guiding force, the unit finally foundered in 1919.

In the swim

Though he had lost the company and the name, Sennett still retained his studio at Edendale, and continued in full production, releasing his films as 'Sennett Comedies' through Paramount. It was apparently at this period that the Sennett Bathing Beauties were first consciously introduced. Ornamental as their presence was in the films themselves, the object of the Bathing Beauties was rather to secure publicity for Sennett productions in magazines and newspapers. Sennett discovered early on that while picture editors were unenthusiastic about printing photographs of bewhiskered or cross-eyed comics, a photograph of a line of pretty girls in chic bathing dresses (and Sennett commissioned couturiers to design swim-suits that revealed more of the feminine shape than the usual patterns then in mode) was irresistible.

A longer laugh

In this period, too, Sennett's productions took new directions. Ben Turpin's grotesque style inspired him to a whole series of parodies of current Hollywood hits, with names like *The Shriek of Araby* (1923) and *Three Foolish Weeks* (1924). Love perhaps inspired Sennett to feature production. To placate Mabel, who had demanded more challenging parts, Sennett created the Mabel Normand Feature Film Company, and starred her in a full-length film, *Mickey* (1918). Hollywood was sceptical about the idea of a feature-length comedy; and Sennett invested his own money in the project. He was wholly vindicated when the public took this modern Cinderella comedy to its hearts: the film is said to have grossed $16 million. Sennett was to star Mabel Normand, whose later life was shadowed by drugs and scandals but whose charm was unimpaired, in the subsequent features, *Molly O* (1921) and *Suzanna* (1922).

In 1921 Sennett established Mack Sennett Inc., and released his films through First National. In 1923 he made further organizational changes, and from then until 1929 distributed his films through Pathé Exchange. The Pathé period was notable mainly for the series of films made with Harry Langdon, perhaps the oddest of the great comedy stars with his character of a middle-aged baby or a demented Pierrot Lunaire. Frank Capra, who directed or wrote Langdon's best features, notably *Long Pants* (1927), was later to claim that it was he, as a gag-man with Sennett, who first perceived Langdon's potential and modelled his screen character. Though it is true that Langdon's later efforts as his own director were less than successful, Capra's version, which has been accepted by history, disserves Langdon. For more than twenty years he had been a vaudeville star, with a very clearly defined comic character; and even before Capra, his whole essence was evident in the Sennett two-reelers directed by Harry Edwards.

Times were changing. Sennett responded uncertainly to the new audiences who felt that they were too sophisticated for the old styles of slapstick two-reelers. He knew that sound was not his element, though in 1928 he made his first sound feature, *The Lion's Roar*, and in 1930 experimented with colour.

Industrial reorganizations meant that Sennett films in 1929 were distributed by the ominously named Educational Film Company. In 1932 Sennett was obliged to close his studios. In 1935 the economic problems of Paramount had repercussions which resulted in Sennett's considerable personal fortune being wiped out.

He moved back to Canada, where he worked for a while as an associate producer for Fox. Even by this time Sennett and the Keystone Kops had passed into Hollywood legend. But legend was of small benefit to Sennett. He died still mourning his beloved Mabel, on November 5, 1960, in an old people's home in Hollywood.

DAVID ROBINSON

Above left: the Kop and ubiquitious fat man were staple fare of Keystone. Above: Mack Sennett Comedies, formed in 1917, used far more sophisticated sets and costumes as here in The Shriek of Araby, *a parody exploiting Ben Turpin's ocular disability*

Below and below left: called to the rescue, the patrol wagon roars off without its occupants. It swings round a corner and the Kops are spun round a pole – still hanging on

Pretty girls have always drawn publicity – a startled bevy with Mack Swain (above) and two of Sennett's Bathing Beauties (inset)

Filmography

All shorts unless otherwise specified. **1908** *Films as actor:* 6 films including The Song of the Shirt; Mr Jones at the Ball; The Sculptor's Nightmare. **'09** 39 films including the Jones series; The Curtain Pole; A Sound Sleeper; What Drink Did; The Violin Maker of Cremona; The Lonely Villa; Her First Biscuits; Pippa Passes, or the Song of Conscience; The Little Teacher. **'10** 27 films including All on Account of the Milk; The Englishman and the Girl; An Arcadian Maid; A Lucky Toothache; The Masher; Effecting a Cure. **'11** 58 films including Priscilla's Engagement Kiss (+sup); Comrades (+dir); The Lonedale Operator (sc. only); Cupid's Joke (+dir); Misplaced Jealousy (+dir); The Country Lovers (+dir); The Manicure Lady (+dir); The Beautiful Voice (+dir); Taking His Medicine (dir. only). **'12** 71 films including Brave and Bold (dir. only); The Fatal Chocolate (+dir); A Voice From the Deep (dir. only); Those Hicksville Boys (+dir); Their First Kidnapping (+dir); When the Fire Bells Rang (dir. only); Katchem Kate (dir. only). *Films as producer and director:* Pedro's Dilemma (+act); At Coney Island (+act); Mabel's Lovers; The Duel (+act); Mabel's Strategem (prod. only). **'13** 128 films including the Mabel series; The Sleuth's Last Stand (+act); The Sleuth's at the Floral Parade (+act); A Wife Wanted (prod. only); Murphy's IOU; Cupid in the Dental Parlour (prod. only); The Darktown Belle; Barney Oldfield's Race for Life (+act); The Speed Queen; Peeping Pete (co-dir; +act); For Love of Mabel (prod. only); Love and Rubbish (prod. only); Cohen's Outing; The Firebugs; Baby Day; Fatty's Day Off (prod. only); Mabel's Dramatic Career (co-dir; +act); Schnitz the Tailor; Fatty at San Diego (prod. only); Love Sickness at Sea (+act); Fatty Joins the Force (prod. only); The Champion (prod. only). *As producer only:* **'14** 145 films including the Mabel series and the Fatty series; Making a Living; Kid Auto Races at Venice; Mabel's Strange Predicament (+co-dir); Love and Gasoline; Between Showers; A Film Johnnie; Tango Tangles (+dir); His Favourite Pastime; Cruel, Cruel Love; The Star Boarder; Mabel at the Wheel (+act); Twenty Minutes of Love (+dir); Caught in a Cabaret; Caught in the Rain; The Fatal Mallet (+act); Mabel's Busy Day; Mabel's Married Life; Fatty and the Heiress; Laughing Gas; The Property Man; The Face on the Bar-room Floor; The Masquerader; His New Profession; The Rounders; Mabel's Last Prank (+dir; +act); Those Love Pangs; Dough and Dynamite; Gentlemen of Nerve; His Musical Career; His Trysting Place; Tillie's Punctured Romance (+dir) (feature); Getting Acquainted; His Prehistoric Past. **'15** 102 films including the Fatty and Mabel series, the Ambrose series and the Gussle series; Mabel's and Fatty's Wash Day; Ambrose's Sour Grapes; Miss Fatty's Seaside Lover; Gussle Tied to Trouble; Saved by Wireless; The Best of Enemies; Fatty and the Broadway Stars (+sc; +act); A Submarine Pirate (+sc). **'16** 67 films including A Modern Enoch Arden; A Movie Star; Bucking Society; The Surf Girl; The Fire Chief. **'17** 50 films including A Cream Puff Romance; Teddy at the Throttle; Roping Her Romeo; The Pullman Bride. **'18** 25 films including Sheriff Nell's Tussle; Mickey (feature). **'19** 25 films including Rip & Stitch, Tailors; East Lynne with Variations; Hearts and Flowers; No Mother to Guide Him; Yankee Doodle in Berlin/The Kaiser's Last Squeal (feature); Uncle Tom Without the Cabin; Salome vs Shenandoah. **'20** 22 films including The Star Boarder; Down on the Farm (feature); Married Life (feature); Love, Honour and Behave (feature). **'21** 16 films including A Small Town Idol (+sc) (feature); Molly O (+co-sc) (feature); Oh, Mabel Behave (+co-dir; +act) (feature). **'22** 15 films including The Crossroads of New York (+sc) (feature); Love and Doughnuts; Suzanna (+sc) (feature). **'23** 12 films including The Shriek of Araby (+sc) (feature); Where Is My Wandering Boy This Evening?; Nip and Tuck; The Extra Girl (+sc) (feature). **'24** 33 films including Picking Peaches; The Hollwood Kid (+sc; +act); The Lion and the Souse; Romeo and Juliet; The First 100 Years; East of the Water Plug (+sc); Lizzies of the Field; Three Foolish Weeks; Little Robinson Corkscrew; Riders of the Purple Cows; The Real Virginian; Galloping Bungalows; Love's Sweet Piffle; Feet of Mud; Bull and Sand. **'25** 42 films including The Sea Squaw; Boobs in the Woods (+sc); Water Wagons; He Who Gets Smacked; A Rainy Knight; Dangerous Curves Behind. **'26** 48 films including Whispering Whiskers; Gooseland; Spanking Breezes; Hooked at the Altar; Hoboken to Hollywood; A Harem Knight. **'27** 37 films including A Small Town Princess; His First Flame (feature). **'28** 32 films including A Finished Actor (+dir); The Good-Bye Kiss (+dir; +sc) (feature); The Lion's Roar (+dir; +sc) (feature). **'29** 36 films including Foolish Husbands; Caught in a Taxi. *Films as producer and director:* Midnight Daddies (feature). **'30** 23 films including Radio Kisses (+song); Hello Television (prod. only); Grandma's Girl. **'31** 33 films including A Poor Fish; One More Chance. *Films as producer only:* **'32** 32 films including Hypnotized (+dir; +sc) (feature). **'33** 21 films including Blue of the Night; A Fatal Glass of Beer; The Pharmacist; The Barber Shop. **'35** 5 films including Ye Olde Saw Mill (+dir; +co-sc). **'39** Hollywood Cavalcade (actor only). **'49** Down Memory Lane (appearance as self only).

The selected filmography above includes all of Sennett's major films.

It was both the shape and size of Erich von Stroheim's ambitions as a film-maker that defined him as a giant. What made him unruly was nothing more than the lengths to which he was willing to go in order to realize those ambitions

Erich von Stroheim was at once the creator and victim of a legendary status in the Hollywood of his time. It was a position which absorbed his various (fictional) acting parts as Prussian heavies in countless films, as well as his very real struggles with the studios in his directing of expensive productions, and Stroheim is remembered today for the figure he cut in both capacities, as anti-hero and as an exemplary victim of the industry. A glimpse of Hollywood's awed, fearful and guilty relationship with Stroheim can be seen in the central plot of George Archainbaud's *The Lost Squadron* (1932), which was made around the time Stroheim was being phased out of his *métier* as a director (about a quarter of a century before his death). In this film, Stroheim plays the German film director Erich Von Furst – a proud lunatic who sabotages the planes to be used by his three American stunt pilots, so that he can simultaneously avenge their real-life bombing of German towns during World War I and provide his own film with a spectacular climax. It seems significant (and disquieting) that the scriptwriter Dick Grace, a former ace flyer, initially wanted Stroheim to play this demented character under his own name, as Erich von Stroheim. It must have seemed mad to Hollywood for anyone to be as fanatically devoted to art as the real Stroheim was – especially since wealth and power are probably the two all-determining factors in his nine features as writer and director.

The Hun within . . .

That Stroheim was a passionate advocate of something that he called realism – and one who demanded and exacted complete precision in the naturalistic details in his sets and locations – obviously had a lot to do with Grace's idea to parody him as Von Furst. And clearly no less important were those assorted German and Prussian villains that Stroheim had been playing in American films since the late 1910s, when he was acquiring his reputation as 'The Man You Love to Hate'. Having started work in Hollywood as an extra for D. W. Griffith on *The Birth of a Nation* (1915) – a few years after unsuccessfully submitting a scenario written with his first wife to G. M. 'Broncho Billy' Anderson of Essanay – he quickly worked his way up to scene-stealing roles in other Griffith productions, and to such additional chores as assistant director and technical (usually military) consultant.

It was during the shooting of *The Heart of Humanity* (1918), a Universal extravaganza in which Stroheim played a super-villainous Hun who tosses a baby out of a window, that he asked studio boss Carl Laemmle to let him direct his own original scenario, called *The Pinnacle*, and somehow managed to win him over. Initially claiming that he could make the film for $5000 – a figure he quickly amended t[o] $10,000 as soon as he had Laemmle's atten[-]tion – Stroheim wound up making a film tha[t] cost nearly twenty times as much as that firs[t] projected amount. But the resulting work, which Laemmle called *Blind Husbands* (1919) over Stroheim's strenuous protests, proved t[o] be an enormous commercial success.

Already, with his first film, Stroheim wa[s] laying out the rudiments of a basic programm[e]

Erich von Stroheim The Unruly Giant

bove left: Count Karamzin (Stroheim in one of is beloved uniforms) seduces an American oman (Miss Du Pont) in Foolish Wives. *bove: 'Monte Carlo, California' at night – the afé de Paris was built for* Foolish Wives *by niversal art directors Richard Day and Elmer heeley at enormous cost. Above right: roheim and miles of wasted celluloid. Below: troheim, Gibson Gowland and Sam de Grasse* Blind Husbands

that, with the important exception of *Greed* (1925), was to characterize all his remaining silent features – a fantasy of European high and low life that sardonically passed judgment on every class in the social scale, from top to bottom. In *Blind Husbands*, this moral inventory leads all the way from the simply brawny innocence of Silent Sepp (Gibson Gowland) – a Tyrolean mountain guide and holy mystic fool, and the neighbouring mountain pinnacle he becomes associated with – to the stealthy charm of Erich von Steuben (played by Stroheim), a crafty young Austrian lieutenant on leave who attempts to seduce Mrs Armstrong (Francelia Billington), an American woman on holiday with her surgeon husband (Sam de Grasse) at the same Alpine resort.

After *Blind Husbands*, Stroheim was promptly assigned by Laemmle to direct *The Devil's Passkey* (1920), a lighter tale about the threat of marital infidelity, with Sam de Grasse once again playing the potentially wronged husband, this time an American playwright in Paris, and Clyde Fillmore playing the 'Stroheim part' of the would-be suitor (in this case an American captain innocent of any mischief) to the playwright's wife (Una Trevelyan). Like its predecessor, the film provided a *risqué* peek at the potential corruption of American innocents abroad, and was another hit. Unfortunately no prints of *The Devil's Passkey* seem to have survived.

Raising the stakes

It was with his next production for Laemmle that Stroheim's unruliness really began to take hold. Laemmle proposed a large-scale film about money and sex set in Reno, Nevada, where gambling casinos thrived and divorces were easily come by; Stroheim counter-proposed a film set in Monte Carlo shortly after the war. What emerged was probably Stroheim's first mature film – *Foolish Wives* (1922), a movie that, during production, Laemmle widely advertised as the first million-dollar picture ever made. On an electric sign in New York, the film's mounting budget was spelled out in lights, while the first letter in Stroheim's name was written as a dollar sign. As effective as this ploy was with audiences, it later backfired when Stroheim subsequently found that his reputation for lavishness scared off potential producers.

Foolish Wives features the definitive Stroheim performance as the unprincipled European scoundrel – here a counterfeiter and child-molester posing as the Russian count Karamzin – once again contriving to seduce an American married woman vacationing abroad. The fact that Stroheim this time played an impostor may lead one to speculate today how much of the portrayal might have contained autobiographical elements. For it was only in 1962, five years after Stroheim's death, that film historian Denis Marion published his discovery – made after getting in touch with a cousin and schoolmate of Stroheim – that the unruly giant's account of his Viennese past before he emigrated to America around 1909 was largely untrue. Contrary to Stroheim's claims about his aristocratic background and his supposedly life-long practice as a devout Catholic, he was the son – born in 1885 – of a Jewish hat manufacturer.

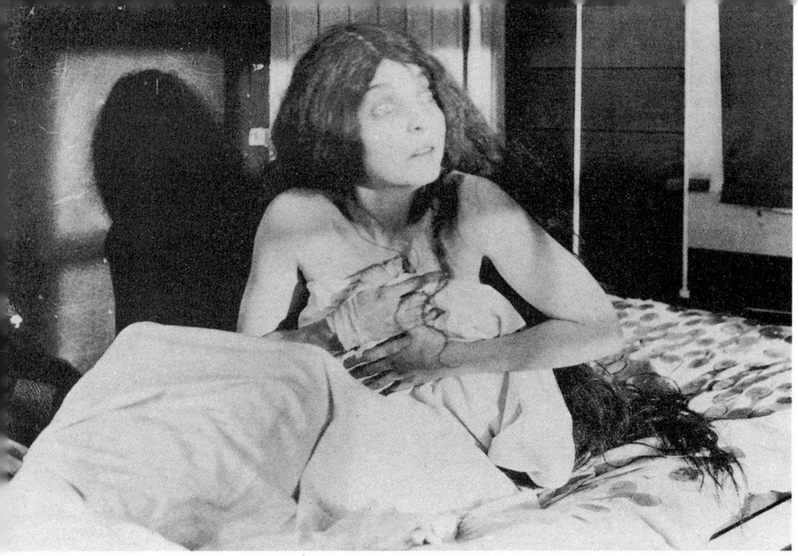

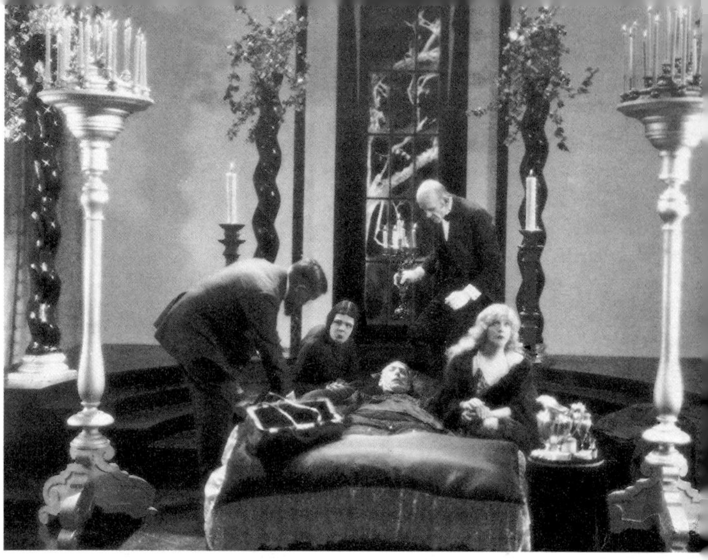

To cut a long story short

Apart from the director's remarkable performance in *Foolish Wives*, his full-scale reconstructions of Monte Carlo's casino, hotel and Café de Paris, which consumed much of his budget, allowed his art of nuance and detail to develop on a greater and more novelistic scale, in an imagined world of much greater density. But his first cut of the movie ran for almost six hours, and Laemmle and Irving Thalberg, then head of production at Universal, rejected Stroheim's request to show his film to the public over two consecutive nights. Instead, Stroheim had to re-edit a four-hour version for the premiere engagement, and then the studio recut this to a version slightly over half as long for general release; this version too was later drastically cut. It was the first of Stroheim's works to get savaged by a studio – setting an unhappy pattern that would dominate every subsequent film he directed.

Equally persistent were Stroheim's efforts to project what was essentially the same vision and story on the screen. As William K. Everson writes in *American Silent Film*:

'With the exception of *Greed*, not his own plot material, Stroheim seemed to have only one basic plot in him, and that a kind of wish-fulfilment fantasy of the aristocratic court-life of old Vienna. From *Merry-Go-Round* (1923) on, his major films other than *Greed* . . . were all variations on the same theme, and each one was approached as though it would be Stroheim's last chance. All of the previous themes and characters were refurbished and new excesses added.'

The widening canvas

Stroheim's last film for Universal was the abortive *Merry-Go-Round* (directed mainly by Rupert Julian after Stroheim had been fired by Thalberg). He next signed for the Goldwyn Company to work on a long-cherished project that was to become his supreme effort and masterpiece – a gritty adaptation of Frank Norris' naturalistic novel *McTeague*, set mainly in San Francisco and Death Valley, California. Unlike Stroheim's other films, *Greed* concentrated on low life in America – undoubtedly based in part on Stroheim's own early impoverished years as a European immigrant. It is somewhat curious, given the reputation of the film's realism and its fidelity to the novel, just how many creative liberties Stroheim was willing to take with both. Updating a story that was supposed to take place during the last years of the nineteenth century up to 1908 an just after, Stroheim wound up overlappin three separate time periods in many scene Major characters were dressed in clothes of th 1890s while extras in the crowd scenes wor the contemporary clothes of 1923 – and th stated time of the film's action fell almos in the middle of these two periods. And s great was Stroheim's absorption in Norris' plo and characters that he embellished them wa beyond the lineaments of the novel, yet per suasively so.

Though cut from over forty reels to ten fo release by MGM, *Greed* still burns with pr mordial power. Its memorable trio of doome characters – Mac (Gibson Gowland), his one

Above left: Trina (ZaSu Pitts) is visited at night in Greed. *Above right: death of an over-excited foot-fetishist in* The Merry Widow, *with Mae Murray (right). Below: pre-nuptial revels in* The Wedding March

time friend Marcus (Jean Hersholt) and Trina (ZaSu Pitts) – invoked the influential French critic André Bazin to remark that in Stroheim's films:

'. . . reality lays itself bare like a suspect confessing under the relentless examination of a police commissioner. He had one simple rule for direction. Take a close look at the world, keep on doing so, and in the end it will lay bare for you all its cruelty and its ugliness.'

A giant laid low

Yet in the silent films of Stroheim that followed *Greed*, 'cruelty', 'ugliness' and whatever else might be regarded as subversive comprised at most the spice or sauce rather than the daintily plucked royal fowl that Hollywood's glamour machine was otherwise providing. In *The Merry Widow* (1925), *The Wedding March* and *Queen Kelly* (both 1928) a few bitter almonds and cherished perversities of the old Stroheim are allowed to congregate, but chiefly just around the edges of the general portrait of static glamour, more mythic than novelistic. In both *The Merry Widow* and *Queen Kelly* this is effected through the grotesque character of a wealthy cripple (played by Tully Marshall) who dies after marrying the heroine; in *The Wedding March* the heroine is chased by a vulgar butcher, Schani (Matthew Betz). The narrative and psychological complexities of *Foolish Wives* and *Greed* were largely absent from these later films.

This compromise proved to be a tasty enough blend for future Hollywood directors – Billy Wilder among them – who could develop their own styles out of the bitter-sweet mixtures of cynicism and sentiment derived, indeed, from the films of Stroheim and Ernst Lubitsch. But for someone with Stroheim's wider and loftier aspirations it was a form of defeat. Although he reached the height of his popularity with *The Merry Widow*, his last film for MGM, he was prevented by the producers at Paramount from editing the final release version of *The Wedding March* (only the first half of which appears to have survived), while the producers of *Queen Kelly*, Joseph Kennedy and Gloria Swanson, halted that film in the middle of shooting.

If Stroheim was able to express himself only as an actor for the remainder of his film career – after the further débâcle of his only sound film *Walking Down Broadway*, which was mutilated, largely reshot and released as *Hello Sister* in 1933 – it is at least fortunate that many of his characters were more subtly portrayed than the mad Erich Von Furst of *The Lost Squadron*. From his memorable performance as Rauffenstein in Jean Renoir's *La Grande Illusion* (1937, *The Great Illusion*) and as a persecuted schoolteacher in Christian-Jaque's *Les Disparus de Saint-Agil* (1938, They Vanished From Saint-Agil) to a more complex partial self-portrait in Billy Wilder's *Sunset Boulevard* (1950), he left behind a unique gallery of characters in countless European and American films, continuing to act until his death in 1957. But it was for his prodigious – and blighted – work as a director in the Twenties that Erich von Stroheim will be chiefly remembered.

JONATHAN ROSENBAUM

Filmography

1914 Captain McLean (actor only). '15 Old Heidelberg (ass. dir; +tech. sup; +act); Ghosts (actor only); The Birth of a Nation (ass. dir; +act). '16 Intolerance (ass. dir; +act); The Social Secretary (ass. dir; +act); Macbeth (ass. art dir; +act. only); Less Than Dust (ass. dir; +act); His Picture in the Papers (ass. dir; +act). '17 For France (actor only); Panthea (ass. dir; +act); In Again, Out Again (sets; +act. only); Sylvia of the Secret Service (ass. dir; +sets; +act). '18 Hearts of the World (tech. sup; +act. only); The Heart of Humanity (military consultant; +act. only); The Hun Within (actor only); The Unbeliever (actor only). '19 Blind Husbands (+sc; +des; +act). '20 The Devil's Passkey (+sc; +des). '22 Foolish Wives (+sc; +co-cost; +act). '23 Merry-Go-Round (add. dir. only, uncredited). '25 Greed (+co-sc; +co-des; +orig. titles); The Merry Widow (+co-sc; +co-titles; +co-cost). '28 The Wedding March (+co-sc; +co-des; +act); Queen Kelly (unfinished) (+sc; +co-des; +co-cost). *All remaining films as actor only unless otherwise specified*: '29 The Great Gabbo. '30 Three Faces East; Friends and Lovers. '32 The Lost Squadron; As You Desire Me. '33 Hello Sister (some scenes only, uncredited). '34 Fugitive Road. '35 Crimson Romance; The Crime of Dr Crespi. '37 La Grande Illusion (FR) (USA: Grand Illusion; GB: The Great Illusion); Marthe Richard (FR); Mademoiselle Docteur (GB); L'Affaire Lafarge (FR). '38 L'Alibi (FR); Les Pirates du Rail (FR); Les Disparus de Saint-Agil (FR); Ultimatum (FR); Gibraltar (FR). '39 Derrière la Façade (FR); Rappel Immédiat (FR); Le Monde Tremblera/La Révolte des Vivants (FR); Pièges (FR); Tempête sur Paris (FR); Macao, l'Enfer du Jeu (FR); Menaces (FR). '40 I Was an Adventuress. '41 So Ends Our Night. '43 Five Graves to Cairo; The North Star. '44 The Lady and the Monster; Storm Over Lisbon; Rue de Montmartre. '45 The Great Flammarion; Scotland Yard Investigator; The Mask of Dijon. '46 La Foire aux Chimères (FR); On Ne Meurt Pas Comme Ca! (FR). '47 La Danse de Mort (FR–IT). '48 Le Signal Rouge (FR-A). '49 Le Portrait d'un Assassin (FR). '50 Sunset Boulevard. '52 La Maison du Crime (FR); Alraune (GER); Minuit, Quai de Bercy (FR). '53 L'Envers du Paradis (FR); Alerte au Sud (FR-IT). '54 Napoléon (FR). '55 Série Noire (FR); La Madone des Sleepings (FR). '56 L'Homme aux Cents Visages (FR).

Stroheim was uncredited for script contributions and as military consultant on several films.

Left: fact becomes fiction – Stroheim as Erich Von Furst, the mad film director, on location in The Lost Squadron. *Below: Seena Owen and Walter Byron in* Queen Kelly *– a film abandoned by its producers because of its unprintable scenes of debauchery*

GREED

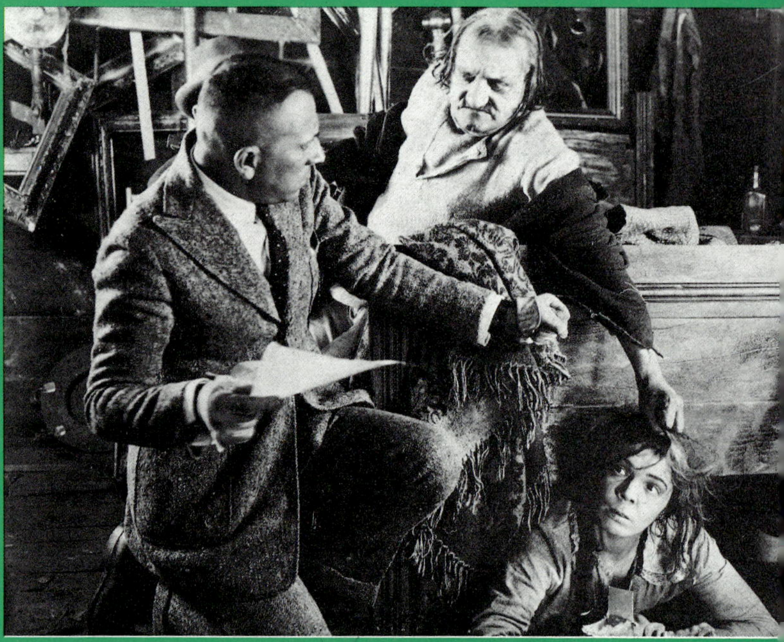

Erich von Stroheim's quarrel with Universal over the production of his film *Merry-Go-Round* (1923) left him Hollywood's most notorious free agent. But he was not unemployed for long, for he soon signed with the Goldwyn Company, an exhausted studio that had fallen on bad times since co-founder Samuel Goldwyn was ousted by stockholders in 1922. In an effort to reverse the downward trend of its fortunes the company hired such major talents as the screenwriter June Mathis and directors Marshall Neilan, King Vidor and the noted Swede Victor Sjöström. The accountants in the front office planned to allow this new group considerable production freedom, just the opposite of Irving Thalberg's policy at Universal, where the studio hierarchy was growing increasingly assertive. Stroheim saw that there was no-one on the Goldwyn lot who could effectively meddle in his projects, and that his new contract gave him a 25 per cent share of the profits of his pictures, something denied him at Universal. Both sides jumped at the opportunity to join forces, but neither really knew what it was getting into.

Stroheim had long been fascinated with Frank Norris' novel *McTeague*, and had announced it as a film project as early as 1920. But although the screen rights were acquired he could never get the project off the ground at Universal, and it became his first priority at Goldwyn.

History notes that Stroheim took his cast and crew out on location for the entire production of *Greed* (as the project soon came to be called), reversing a growing Hollywood tendency towards studio shooting. On one level this move away from the studio gained Stroheim an added sense of surface realism, but far more was involved than mere authenticity of setting. Stroheim wanted to express the *theme* of Norris' novel on screen, not just its story, and to do this he needed to find a stylistic equivalent of Norris' literary Naturalism. In other words, how this film was to be made was as important to Stroheim as the narrative content – an extraordinary notion for the period.

Frank Norris was the chief American exponent of Naturalism, an informal literary school developed out of the writings of the nineteenth-century French novelist Emile Zola. The Naturalists stressed the influence of heredity and environment and eliminated any notion of free will; fatalism also played a major role. To express these ideas, tremendous space was given in the Naturalists' work to 'milieu detail' – involved descriptions of places and events which served to underline the oppressive effect of the material world on the lives of the characters. Stroheim knew that his film would succeed or fail on his ability to make this world a living presence on the screen, so he decided to leave the studio stages and take up residence at the 'real' locations that inspired the Norris novel. Prior to this he had had no problems with a back-lot Paris, Vienna or Monte Carlo, but *Greed* would be different.

All elements of the film's style, not simply the production design, helped emphasize this concern with the forces that oppress human life. Stroheim gave instructions to his cameramen – Ben Reynolds and William Daniels – to maintain a crisp depth of focus throughout the film, even in hard-to-light interiors. There would be no scenes where the background blurred fashionably out of focus – it was always to make its presence known. Where Norris used many short descriptive sentences to introduce his readers to a room filled with cracked plates and dirty dishes, Stroheim employed a series of brief close-ups for the same purpose. It is not true, as the French critic André Bazin claimed, that the editing style of *Greed* was based on the long take. Much more characteristic of the film's cutting is this accumulation of detail in short shots.

Unfortunately, Stroheim's efforts at uniting content and style made little impression on the studio (which, despite its policy of 'creative freedom', infamously cut it from an estimated seven and a half hours running time to barely two), on the critics or on audiences. Few were able to see past the surface concern of the story with moral decay, which Stroheim had rendered in so graphic a fashion. His direct assault on the capitalist financial structure also failed to win Stroheim many friends. 'The filthiest, vilest, most putrid picture in the history of the motion picture business,' one critic wrote of it. 'In Austria, where Erich von Stroheim comes from, they may enjoy this picture, but I doubt if a single normal American can be found to feel that way about it.'

This assessment, in the trade paper *Harrison's Reports*, was wrong on all counts, even, surprisingly, the last. Audiences in Europe rejected *Greed* even more strenuously than those in America. The film had cost $585,000, a considerable amount for the time. Studio records show a disappointing $227,000 domestic gross. But foreign receipts, which might have been expected to reach at least 50 per cent of this total, were a minuscule $47,000. Needless to say, Stroheim never saw a penny of his 25 per cent. RICHARD KOSZARSKI

Directed by Erich von Stroheim, 1925

Prod co: Goldwyn Company. **sc and original titles:** Erich von Stroheim, June Mathis, from the novel *McTeague* by Frank Norris. **release titles:** Joe W. Farnham. **photo:** Ben Reynolds, William Daniels. **ass photo:** Walter Bader, H. C. Van Dyke. **ed original version:** Erich von Stroheim (sup), Frank Hull. **ass ed:** Marguerite Faust. **prod des:** Richard Day, Erich von Stroheim. **mus:** *Greed* theme by Leo A. Kempinsky. **mus dir:** James Bradford. **ass dir:** Eddy Sowders, Louis Germonprez. **length:** 10,212 ft (approx. 113 minutes).

Cast: Tempe Piggot (*Mother McTeague*), Gibson Gowland (*McTeague*), Günther von Ritzau (*Dr 'Painless' Potter*), Jimmy Wang (*Chinese cook*), Jean Hersholt (*Marcus Schouler*), Chester Conklin (*'Popper' Sieppe*), Sylvia Ashton (*'Mommer' Sieppe*), ZaSu Pitts (*Trina*), Austin Jewel (*'Owgooste' Sieppe*), Oscar and Otto Gotell (*Max and Moritz*), Joan Standing (*Selina*), Frank Hayes (*Old Grannis*), Fanny Midgley (*Miss Baker*), Max Tyron (*Rudolf Oelbermann*), Hughie Mack (*Heise*), E. 'Tiny' Jones (*Mrs Heise*), J. Aldrich Libby (*Mr Ryer*), Rita Revla (*Mrs Ryer*), Dale Fuller (*Maria Miranda Macapa*), Lon Poff (*lottery agent*), S. S. Simon (*Joe Frenna*), William Mollenheimer (*palmist*), Hugh J. McCauley (*photographer*), William Barlow (*minister*), Jack McDonald (*Cribbens*), James Fulton (*sheriff*), James Gibson (*deputy sheriff*). Roles cut from final release version: Jack Curtis (*McTeague Sr*), Florence Gibson (*hag at saloon*), Cesare Gravina (*Zerkow*).

McTeague, a young miner in the California gold country, is sent off to better himself as apprentice to a travelling dentist. He settles on San Francisco's Polk Street where he meets Marcus Schouler (1), assistant in the local dog hospital. Other residents of Polk Street include McTeague's cleaning woman Maria, and Zerkow, a crazed old junk collector who later marries her. McTeague falls in love with Trina (2), Marcus' cousin and prospective fiancée. Marcus gives her up to his pal, and McTeague courts Trina during visits to her family in Oakland. But when Trina wins $5000 in a lottery, Marcus feels he has been cheated (3).

McTeague and Trina marry (4) – but money soon begins to dominate Trina's life. Marcus leaves town to work on a cattle ranch, but not before informing the dental board that McTeague has been practising without a licence. His livelihood gone, McTeague takes to drink (5) and begins to brutalize Trina (6). Zerkow, meanwhile, kills Maria, and the McTeagues move into his shack. McTeague abandons Trina, but returns after she finds work as a scrubbing woman at a nursery school (7) and murders her for her money. McTeague flees to Death Valley where Marcus catches up with him. A final meeting (8) leaves both to die under the blistering desert sun.

This synopsis is based on the original version of Greed *before it was edited for release. Top: Stroheim directs Cesare Gravina and Dale Fuller in one of the scenes that were cut from the film*

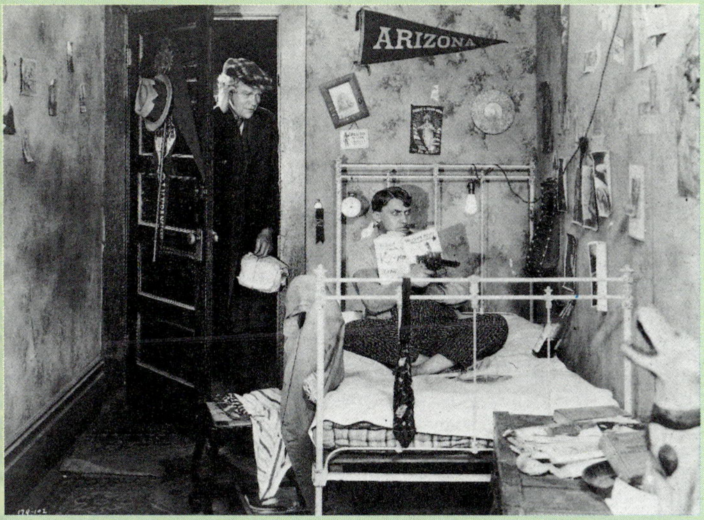

2

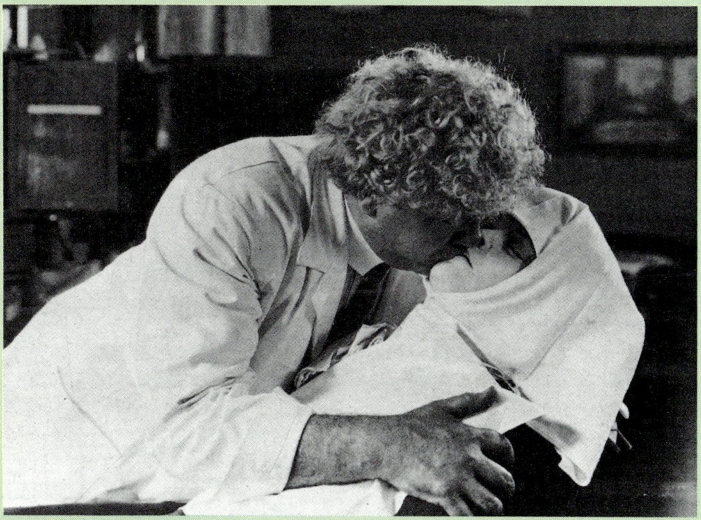

4

6

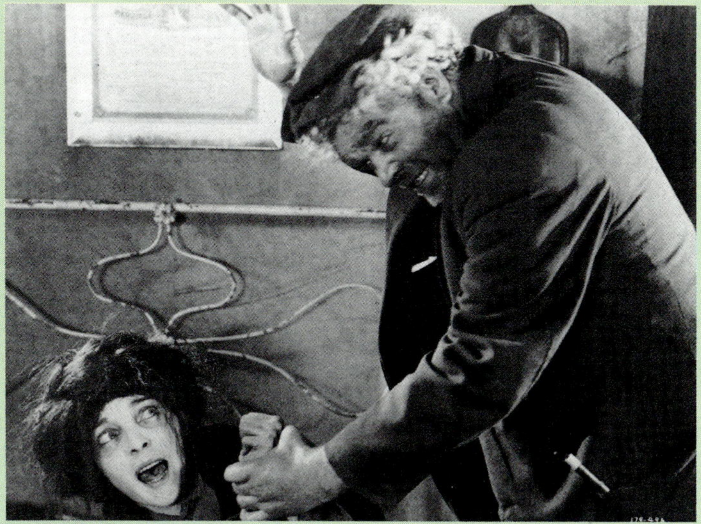

8

Glorious Swanson

Gloria Swanson is a movie legend. She has survived the rigours of a superstar's life, she has made and lost fortunes, married and re-married, and has worked with the greatest names in Hollywood. She is witty, charming, elegant, intelligent and is one of the most sought-after characters from cinema's past

People always think that Gloria Swanson was Norma Desmond, the flamboyant, crazed heroine she plays in Billy Wilder's acid *Sunset Boulevard* (1950) – for, like Desmond, Swanson was a big movie star in the silent days. She was directed by Cecil B. DeMille and Erich von Stroheim, both of whom appear in *Sunset Boulevard* as figures from Norma Desmond's past. Moreover, the extract from *Queen Kelly* (1928) which illustrates how Stroheim used to direct Norma is in fact from the film in which Stroheim directed Swanson for her own production company. Thus the identification seems complete; except that Norma Desmond is living in the past and is quite out of touch with the modern world, while Swanson was truly-up-to-date until her death in 1983, a successful businesswoman in many areas, a busy actress on stage and screen, a world-famous proselyte for macrobiotic foods and a member of the international jet-set.

Second sunrise

However, it was undoubtedly *Sunset Boulevard* that made Swanson into a modern cult figure, and it contains her best performance, no doubt partly because it is overall the best film she has made in her long career. It is also the most spectacular and newsworthy comeback in the whole history of cinema, for in 1950 she had made only three films in the previous 17 years, and had not had a hit since *The Trespasser* in 1929. Suddenly handed a role which most actresses should have given their eye-teeth for, she seized on it with such unsparing relish as to make it totally her own – and seemingly to disappear into it.

The real Gloria Swanson was no tragedy queen like Norma Desmond but a 'lightweight' and often a comedienne. She was also a famous clothes-horse, and when scenarists could think of nothing else for her to do, she could always be relied upon to take an audience's breath away by sweeping on to screen in yet another stunning confection.

Swanson was born in Chicago, according to her own account, on March 27, 1899 – although other sources suggest a year or two earlier. She was brought up mainly in Florida, where her father worked with the army, and returned to Chicago just long enough to be 'discovered' at the Essanay studio at the age of 15. She was tested by Chaplin for one of his pictures but was turned down as lacking in comedy sense – and also, perhaps, because she was physically too similar in type, as can be seen from her stunning impersonation of him in *Sunset Boulevard*.

On her way to the Philippines to join her father in 1915, she and her mother stopped off in Los Angeles. She decided to try the studios there, and at once managed to get noticeable roles, several of them in films with Wallace Beery, whom she married in 1916. Most of her first Hollywood films were slapstick comedies for Mack Sennett; she often said later on that she was so determined to be a dramatic actress at that time that she always played dead straight, not realizing that the more genuine her emoting, the funnier the final effect. In 1917 she decided to move away from Sennett and found herself employed at another studio, Triangle, starring in a series of dramas about marital misunderstandings and the mishaps of courting couples. They had titles like *Society for Sale*, *Everywoman's Husband*, *Shifting Sand* and *Wife or Country* (all 1918), and in most of them she starred opposite her boyish partner from Sennett days, Bobby Vernon. Although

she was playing drama she became restive of the restrictions at Triangle and was eager to take up an offer to star in a Cecil B. DeMille film, but Triangle prevented her on a contract technicality. In 1919 she was finally free to go over to Paramount and the first film she made for DeMille was *Don't Change Your Husband* (1919), one of his biggest successes.

Youthful old-timer

Thus at the age of 20 Gloria Swanson became an 'important star', with five years of film experience already behind her. 'Working for Mr DeMille', she recalls in her autobiography, *Swanson on Swanson*, 'was like playing house in the world's most expensive department store'. If this is taken to mean that there was a lot of getting elaborately dressed in Swanson-DeMille films, that is quite possible, for at this time DeMille was going through his period of specialization in 'mature', sophisticated society dramas. In *Don't Change Your Husband*, for instance, Swanson plays the wife who does, only to discover at the end that the first husband was better than the alternative, who proves to have a roving eye. In *For Better, for Worse* (1919) she is a woman who wrongly believes her sweetheart to be a coward, but experience showed otherwise. And both films had comfortingly happy endings.

But the best and most famous of the six films she made in a row for DeMille was *Male and Female* (1919), a free version of J. M. Barrie's *The Admirable Crichton* which gave scope for grand society goings-on at the beginning, drama in the shipwreck, comedy on the island and then a bitter-sweet conclusion back in Mayfair – plus a typical DeMille dream-scene set in ancient Babylon, with Swanson being sacrificed to the lions. This was one of the peaks of her career. Otherwise her roles became rather repetitious as she suffered in gorgeous gowns through *Why Change Your Wife?*, *Something to Think About* (both 1920), and finally *The Affairs of Anatol* (1921), where she had mainly to wait at home while vamps like Bebe Daniels had all the fun with tame cheetahs and the like.

Left: Gloria Swanson and Warwick Ward in Madame Sans-Gêne. *Far left: the comedienne Swanson with Juanita Hansen in an early Mack Sennett movie. Above: in* Queen Kelly *as a madame in Africa – this final section of the film was cut out before release. Below right:* Indiscreet *(1931) included a scene that showed a silhouetted Swanson in the shower. Below left: in* Why Change Your Wife? *Swanson plays a wife who regrets her divorce*

Changing affairs

It was time for DeMille and Swanson to part company, and in *The Great Moment* (1921) she was handed on to Sam Wood, a director who was to guide her through a string of ten films.

For this one, which was actually made before *The Affairs of Anatol*, she first received billing above the title, and had the story specially devised for her by Elinor Glyn, the great resident expert in high passion and higher society. In her later Sam Wood films she ranged from heavy suffering in *Under the Lash* (1921) through further problems in *Don't Tell Everything* (1921), and an extra-marital relationship opposite Rudolph Valentino in *Beyond the Rocks* (1922), to the light comedy of the French farce *Bluebeard's Eighth Wife* (1923). By this time she was the top star at Paramount, and her 1923 contract was almost without parallel in the powers it gave her to choose her own films. This she used to good effect in order to vary her roles constantly: *Zaza* (1923), a strong story of the French music-hall was followed by others such as *Manhandled* (1924), directed by Allan Dwan, in which she gives a brilliantly funny performance as a gum-chewing shop girl who finds out that society life is not all it is supposed to be, and *Wages of Virtue* (1924), in which she surpassed even her own previous extravaganzas by wearing a wedding dress alleged to have cost $100,000.

Below: Swanson's greatest triumph – Sunset Boulevard. *Below left: during a visit to London in 1981. Left: Swanson as* Sadie Thompson *the tough lady who gains the attentions of a reformer (Lionel Barrymore); he commits suicide when she leaves him*

In 1925 she insisted on going to France to make *Madame Sans-Gêne* on the right locations under the direction of a real Frenchman, Léonce Perret, and returned with a real Marquis (de la Falaise de la Coudraye) as a husband. In her autobiography she gives a frightening account of her apparently triumphant return to America – after a near-fatal abortion in a Paris hospital – but the film was another career highpoint. After four more films she left Paramount to set up her own company (with the help of her then lover Joseph Kennedy), and began with *The Love of Sunya* (1927), which was something of a misfire, and *Queen Kelly* (1928), which was never properly finished due to Stroheim's extravagances and the inopportune arrival of sound. Two other pictures, however, were complete triumphs: she played a briefly reformed prostitute in the tropics in *Sadie Thompson* (1928), her last silent film, and in *The Trespasser* (1929) she wowed audiences by not only talking but singing too.

Comedy comebacks

After that her career went rapidly downhill through four wishy-washy comedies, the last of which, *A Perfect Understanding* (1933), was shot in Britain and co-starred a very young and inexperienced Laurence Olivier. There followed contracts with MGM and Columbia; ambitious projects were announced, but none was fulfilled, and the only film she did make, *Music in the Air* (1934) when on loan to Fox, was a flop. Her first official comeback, a comedy with Adolphe Menjou, *Father Takes a Wife* (1941) did not do much better. Finally in 1950 Billy Wilder, after thinking of Pola Negri, Mary Pickford, Mae Murray and various other silent movie stars, settled for her in *Sunset Boulevard*. She portrays an ex-movie queen, from the silent era, who is adamant that with the help of an out-of-work screenwriter (William Holden) she will make a dramatic comeback. But she becomes jealous of his girlfriend and eventually murders him. Even as she is being taken away by police she believes she is making a triumphant return to superstardom.

The rest is history. She then made only a few more films: a negligible farce, *Three for Bedroom C* (1952); a rather funnier parody costume epic, *Mio Figlio Nerone* (1956, *Nero's Weekend*), in which she was a redoubtable Agrippina to Alberto Sordi's Nero; a stint as one of the long-suffering airline passengers in *Airport 1975*; and *Killer Bees* (1974) for television and several stage appearances as well as numerous chat shows, discussing life and diet, her career and her book. She really did not have to do anything more: she was more than a star; she was a legend. Norma Desmond says defiantly in *Sunset Boulevard*, 'We had faces then!' Gloria Swanson always did.

JOHN RUSSELL TAYLOR

Filmography

1915 The Fable of Elvira and Farina and the Meal Ticket; Sweedie Goes to College; The Romance of an American Duchess; The Broken Pledge (credited as Gloria Mae). **'16** A Dash of Courage; Hearts and Sparks; A Social Club; The Danger Girl; Love on Skates; Haystacks and Steeples; The Nick of Time Baby; Teddy at the Throttle. **'17** Baseball Madness; Dangers of a Bride; The Sultan's Wife; The Pullman Bride. **'18** Society For Sale; Her Decision; You Can't Believe Everything; Everywoman's Husband; Shifting Sands (reissued as: Her Wanton Destiny); Station Content; Secret Code; Wife or Country. **'19** Don't Change Your Husband; For Better, For Worse; Male and Female (GB: The Admirable Crichton). **'20** Why Change Your Wife?; Something to Think About. **'21** The Great Moment; The Affairs of Anatol (GB: A Prodigal Knight); Under the Lash; Don't Tell Everything. **'22** Her Husband's Trademark; Beyond the Rocks; Her Gilded Cage; The Impossible Mrs Bellew; My American Wife. **'23** Prodigal Daughters; Bluebeard's Eighth Wife; Zaza; Hollywood (as herself). **'24** The Humming Bird; A Society Scandal; Manhandled; Her Love Story; Wages of Virtue. **'25** Madame Sans-Gêne; The Coast of Folly; Stage Struck. **'26** Untamed Lady; Fine Manners. **'27** The Love of Sunya. **'28** Sadie Thompson; Queen Kelly (unfinished). **'29** The Trespasser. **'30** What a Widow! **'31** Indiscreet; Tonight or Never. **'33** A Perfect Understanding (GB). **'34** Music in the Air. **'41** Father Takes a Wife. **'50** Sunset Boulevard. **'52** Three for Bedroom C. **'56** Mio Figlio Nerone (IT-FR) (USA: Nero's Mistress; GB: Nero's Weekend). **'74** Airport 1975.

IN PURSUIT OF REALITY

Many film-makers of the late Twenties were searching for the 'truth' and 'reality' of the actual world, but 'realism' remained as always a controversial idea

By the late Twenties, an earnest, self-righteous search for 'realism' was under way in most major film-producing countries. It entailed a host of different approaches, confused, contradictory and so diverse that the flexibility of the concept 'realism' must immediately be recognized. Sound itself was a decisive step towards greater naturalism in the movies. It added the actuality of speech *and* silence to that of visibility, for it is only in sound pictures that people can choose to stay silent. But sound also permitted the precisely synchronized atmospheric accompaniment of music that seldom plays so appositely in real life.

As a medium, film is as romantic as it is real. The thing most crucial to its understanding is that it confuses these two modes – offering life itself, but allowing the audience a safe vantage never possible in fact. Film separates the lifelike from life. It does not vouchsafe to give its spectators reality. But, time and again, its slippery dealings with life force them to ask themselves what is real. It is as if the photograph had uncovered depths of ambiguity and doubt in a commodity previously taken for granted. 'Realism', therefore, is not a sure and easy contact with actuality; it is an expression of some pressing urge to tell the truth, and it is invariably a response of social and political convictions that the truth has been neglected or suppressed.

Thus it is hardly possible to comprehend the mood of realism among silent film-makers without recognizing the disillusion wrought by World War I, the devastation that lingered long afterwards (especially in Germany), the onset of the Depression (coming like retribution after the frenzied excitement and boom years of the Twenties), the new sense of industrialization and the developing phenomenon of modern urban alienation, the success of one communist revolution and the various fears that the new world was a battleground of radical socialism and reactionary fascism in which democracy might be squeezed dead. Besides all these larger issues, several film-makers believed that the picture business had wilfully ignored its 'objective' nature in order to make money from escapist entertainment.

All over the world, in the Twenties, artists were convinced that society had lost sight of unpleasant truths. In post-war Germany, Expressionist techniques were often employed to get at those truths: *Metropolis* (1927) does not nowadays seem a realistic film, but its makers were attempting to uncover the real relationship between power and the masses in an industrial society. At the same time, writers, as well as painters and film-makers, strove to find access to the authentic stream of private consciousness, which is as real as the stock market. The nineteenth-century French novelist Emile Zola had been called a realist, but he wrote in formal sentences. The Irish writer James Joyce believed that when people thought they did so in a more fluid form of consciousness. His *Ulysses* (1922), Virginia Woolf's *Mrs Dalloway* (1925) and William Faulkner's *The Sound and the Fury* (1929) are novels of intense subjectivity – but their authors believed that was far more 'real' than telling the story through an all-knowing narrator.

Of special interest is the work of John Dos Passos, who deliberately experimented with literary equivalents of newsreel and what he called 'Camera Eye' in his epic trilogy of novels *USA*, published in 1930, 1932 and 1936. It is a collage of conventional story, illustrations by Reginald Marsh, flickering and remote newsreel sections (drawn from newspapers and popular songs) and passages of observation that seem to be free from a personal consciousness – the mood of 'I am a camera, I see without thinking'. It was an age in which many were inclined to trust the hope that the camera could not lie, and in which they jumped to the conclusion that it therefore told the truth.

That approach was central to the new documentary method, though its claims for neutrality or honesty never smothered the personality of the film-maker. 'Realism' is only another style, despite

Above: the Empire Marketing Board gave John Grierson the opportunity to put his documentary ideas into practice with Drifters, *a study of the herring fleet, filmed in Scotland (mainly Lerwick) and England, partly off Lowestoft. The ship's cabin was reconstructed in Lerwick fish market, and tank shots of fish were made at Plymouth. Below: Dziga Vertov's* Man With a Movie Camera *combined footage shot in several Soviet cities, notably Kiev, Odessa and Moscow*

Kein Haushalt
Bullrich Magensalz

Far left: in the realist Mutter Krausens Fahrt ins Glück *(Mother Krausen's Journey to Happiness), Max (Friedrich Gnass), a left-wing worker, rejects Mother Krausen's daughter when he learns that she is not a virgin, but is later reconciled with her. Top left: Jean Vigo captures the underside of life in the Riviera city in* A Propos de Nice. *Above: the Berlin street is enlivened by carnival-like figures advertising a cure for indigestion in* The Symphony of a Great City. *Left: George Grosz's 1916 painting* Suicide *demonstrates his flair for caricature as well as his desire to get to grips with the harsh realities of modern city life. Below left: a small crowd of the impoverished middle class gathers in* The Joyless Street, *in the hope of getting some meat from a gross and dictatorial butcher (Werner Krauss). Below right: Conayou, one of the wives of* Nanook of the North, *with their son Allee*

the fierce idealism of men like the documentary producer John Grierson that it might reassert common sense and social community. Grierson lamented in 1937 the false direction of some forty years of commercial movie-making:

'Here is an art based on photographs, in which one factor is always, or nearly always, a thing observed. Yet a realist tradition in cinema has emerged only slowly. When Lumière turned his first historic strip of film, he did so with the fine careless rapture which attends the amateur effort today. The new moving camera was still, for him, a camera and an instrument to focus on the life about him. He shot his own workmen filing out of the factory and this first film was a "documentary". He went on as naturally to shoot the Lumière family, child complete. The cinema, it seemed for a moment, was about to fulfil its natural destiny of discovering mankind. It had everything for the task. It could get about, it could view reality with a new intimacy; and what more natural than that the recording of the real world should become its principal inspiration? . . . Hardly were the workmen out of the factory and the apple digested than it was taking a trip to the moon and, only a year or two later, a trip in full colour to the devil. The scarlet women were in, and the high falsehood of trick-work and artifice was in, and reality and the first fine careless rapture were out.'

That was the spirit which inspired the one film directed by Grierson, *Drifters* (1929), and which spearheaded the British documentary movement. It was a non-partisan, educationally-driven crusade to let a people know how their institutions, their machines and their system functioned. In that it guessed how close society had come to abandoning reading for some more complete confrontation with actuality, British documentary was not unlike the Bolshevik adoption of movie as a way of inspiring the multitudes of the new Russian state.

Lenin's early choice of moving pictures as a dominant form of propaganda led to a decade of Soviet films motivated by actuality and the revealed 'truth' of class conflict. That could mean the highly stylized films of Sergei M. Eisenstein, which fused painting and theatre in reinventing history. Or it could mean the work of Dziga Vertov, the most significant pioneering figure in the history of documentary. When still in his early twenties, he set up the weekly newsreel series *Kinonedelya* (1918–19, Cine-Week) and the more occasional series *Kino Pravda* (1922–25, Cine-Truth). Vertov had a great eye: his films have a formal beauty that repays close scrutiny. But they also vibrate with immediacy. He believed in the camera's eye serving as a social conscience, and as a model of inquisitive, good-natured alertness. No other film-maker so loved the camera as a machine that mimicked human sensory function. In his best-known work, *Cheloviek s Kinoaparatom* (1929, *Man With a Movie Camera*), he gloried in mundane life, the various processes of film-making, the cameraman as a folk hero and in film as a magic that danced with the real. Using hidden cameras, long tracking shots and natural light on the one hand, Vertov also enjoyed trick effects, opticals and startling cuts. In one sense, his films are naive: they give scant indication of the compromises in the Russian Revolution, or the suffering. But it is arguable that no other film-maker had so revelled in the loveliness of common sights. For that reason, Vertov is now regarded as a seminal influence on *cinéma-vérité* (cinema truth), the candid-camera documentary movement of the Sixties that has continued to dominate the style and methods of much of the best television documentary.

Vertov's younger brother, Boris Kaufman, went to live in Paris, carrying some of the Russian enthusiasm for actuality. It was he who served as cameraman to Jean Vigo on the satirical documentary *A Propos de Nice* (1930), as well as on his later films, *Taris* (1931), *Zéro de Conduite* (1933, *Nought for Behaviour*) and *L'Atalante* (1934). Kaufman was personally attuned to Vigo's mordant poetic vision, but in *A Propos de Nice* he demonstrated several Russian tricks and attitudes. Moreover, Vigo, the son of an anarchist, had no doubt about the decadence of Nice, no matter how idyllic it might look on film. He shows the Riviera playground as a place where gambling and death conspire against the rich – the realism of the film's approach cannot resist the social forebodings that preoccupied Vigo.

Also in France, the Brazilian director Alberto Cavalcanti had made *Rien que les Heures* (1926, Nothing But the Hours). It is another study of a city, observing the passage of a day. There are many moments of commentary: a shot of a steak cuts into a slaughterhouse; at the very beginning of the film, a view of beautiful women descending a staircase – as if out of a Hollywood extravaganza – becomes a freeze-frame, and hands tear up the picture, tossing the pieces on to a real street. But Cavalcanti's film expresses a belief that the city has a life of its own and a history, in which individual thoughts and social movements are like passing phases. More cheerful still was Marcel Carné's first film *Nogent, Eldorado du Dimanche* (1929, Nogent, Sunday's Eldorado), a movie essay on Parisians going to a weekend pleasure spot on the river. That film accepts the notion of simple enjoyment – it has a freer camera than ever operated in the composed fatalism of Carné's subsequent feature films.

The emphasis on the city in these documentaries has much to do with the real evolution of cities into huge concrete grids, lit by night, and so arranged that the crowd and loneliness coexist – it should be remembered that T.S. Eliot's poem *The Waste Land*, with its bleak view of London, was published in 1922. But it was in Germany, the land of *Metropolis*, that the city dominated as a subject, and aspirations towards realism were often accompanied by heavy stylistic overlays. Historians stress the importance of the *Neue Sachlichkeit* ('New Objectivity') art exhibition at Mannheim in 1925. It was a collection of paintings – by such as George Grosz and Otto Dix – that sought ordinary subjects and journalistic approaches. But many of the paintings were visually exaggerated and pessimistic in tone. Similarly, the photo-montages of John Heartfield juxtaposed and treated photographic images to reveal inner political realities. To see reality in Germany in the late Twenties was to recognize depravity and danger – the eye could not help but be soured and alarmed.

Above: Ernest B. Schoedsack and his Debrie camera during the making of Chang, with some of the Siamese (Thai) cast, including Bimbo the white gibbon. Below: Stark Love was filmed on location in the Great Smoky Mountains of North Carolina, part of the southern Appalachians. All but one of the roles were played by genuine mountain people, an isolated group of Scots-Irish origin. The death of Mrs Warwick (Mrs Queen) early in the film precipitates a violent rivalry between her husband and her son over a young girl

Still, the *Neue Sachlichkeit* movement did bring about a number of films with realist themes, styles or sentiments. Piel Jutzi made a working-class documentary *Ums tägliche Brot* (1929, *Hunger in Waldenburg*) that was banned; and then a feature film *Mutter Krausens Fahrt ins Glück* (1929, Mother Krausen's Journey to Happiness), co-scripted by the painter Otto Nagel and made as a tribute to the naturalistic illustrator Heinrich Zille. A similar impulse inspired several young men, including Robert Siodmak, Edgar G. Ulmer, Billy Wilder and Fred Zinnemann, to collaborate on a low-budget, real-location, slice-of-life feature *Menschen am Sonntag* (1929, *People on Sunday*). Most influential of all was the work of Walter Ruttmann, originally a painter who had helped Fritz Lang on the 'Dream of Hawks' sequence of *Siegfried* (1924). In 1927 Ruttmann completed *Berlin, die Sinfonie einer Grossstadt* (*The Symphony of a Great City*), which was started before Cavalcanti's *Rien que les Heures* but released after it. As his co-scenarist, Ruttmann had Carl Mayer, the writer of *Das Kabinett des Dr Caligari* (1919, *The Cabinet of Dr Caligari*) and of several of F.W. Murnau's pictures. *The Symphony of a Great City* attests to the hope that a film could be as sweeping, and as aesthetic, as a symphony; it is also as formal as a painterly background might ensure. This is reality distilled by design, but the documentary of the Twenties and Thirties generally looks over-studied when seen today.

Influenced by recent painting, German directors looked at the modern city with a realist eye

G.W. Pabst deserves some credit as a realist director. His subjects included street-life scenarios, and he was familiar with the new discoveries of psychoanalysis. Some of his films dwell on the sordid life of Austria and Germany after World War I – *Die freudlose Gasse* (1925, *The Joyless Street*) and much of *Die Büchse der Pandora* (1929, *Pandora's Box*), which follows its characters from an expensive city apartment to the slums of London. But there are no real places in *Pandora's Box*, and its sharpest truths are to be found in the spontaneity of the actress Louise Brooks. *Geheimnisse einer Seele* (1926, *Secrets of a Soul*) is a conscientious exposition of Freudian theory, but still a claustrophobic melodrama. The essence of German cinema was always atmosphere, and that could be furnished as easily on a stage with lights as on the streets.

In America, newsreels became common during World War I, and they were given a great boost of narrative authority by sound. But the reputation of documentary depended largely on a remarkable maverick, Robert Flaherty. He was a traveller who loved far places and noble savages. His early film on Eskimo life had accidentally been destroyed; but Révillon Frères, a fur company, hired him to make *Nanook of the North* (1922). Flaherty believed in long takes, long shots and 'unarranged' action. He was also a romantic so drawn to his subject that he did not notice how far Révillon Frères was a leading exploiter of the Eskimo.

Nanook of the North was a sensation, the first documentary to get a wide public showing in America. Famous Players-Lasky put Flaherty under contract and sent him off to the South Seas to make *Moana* (1924). It was as great a flop as *Nanook of the North* had been successful – perhaps because the distributor, Paramount, promoted it badly, perhaps because Flaherty had been carried away by primitive beauty. It was effectively the end of his Hollywood career, and a sign that the large audience equated 'documentary' with the boring. That antagonism is still central to the urgency of good documentary, films made in a mood of rebuke for the escapist entertainment picture.

More authentically American as documentarists are Merian C. Cooper, a pilot-journalist, and Ernest B. Schoedsack, a news cameraman. Their first collaboration was *Grass* (1926), about tribal migration in Turkey and Persia. Very spectacular, but indifferent to political background or human hardship, *Grass* ended on a note of breezy self-congratulation. After *Grass*, they made *Chang* (1927), which was filmed in Siam, now Thailand. Cooper is generally thought to be the model for the 'gung-ho', sensationalist film producer Carl Denham (Robert Armstrong) in *King Kong* (1933). This fictional treatment of documentary ideas that he and Schoedsack made for David O. Selznick used a studio jungle and a special-effects ape.

There were other documentaries made in America, but they reached far smaller audiences. Paul Strand and Charles Sheeler had made *Manhatta*, a study of New York, in 1921, and it was a forerunner of later 'New Deal' films of the Thirties by Pare Lorentz, Willard Van Dyke and Ralph Steiner. Karl Brown, once an assistant cameraman on several of D.W. Griffith's most famous films, made a dramatized documentary, *Stark Love* (1927), shot in the mountains of North Carolina.

Apart from attempts at documentary as such, reality can be seen and felt in the background of some American feature films – for example, Erich von Stroheim's *Greed*, Josef von Sternberg's *The Salvation Hunters* (both 1925) and King Vidor's *The Crowd* (1928). In all of these movies, the city is a model for man's fall and the setting of alienation. One of the great romantic visions of feature movies – the dark, hostile city in *film noir* – owes a great deal to documentary. DAVID THOMSON

The Avenging Spirit of

By the late 1900s, French film-makers began to exploit a new form of cinema entertainment – serial films, or ciné-novels, as they were called at the time. Especially popular during the years of World War I were the detective crime serials, which romanticized the fantastic exploits of pulp heroes and villains. The most successful director in the genre was Louis Feuillade, whose uncanny blending of realism and dream-like imagery added a new and exciting dimension to the screen's range of film fantasy

Louis Feuillade

Louis Feuillade is undoubtedly one of the most fascinating figures of early French cinema. He worked for Léon Gaumont for 20 years – 18 of them as artistic director and head of studio – and directed between 500 and 700 films, all but a handful from his own stories or scripts.

Feuillade had his eye firmly fixed on making money and pleasing the public, and felt nothing but contempt for experimentation and 'art'. Yet in the middle of a pedestrian career, churning out a relentless stream of trivial comedies and lachrymose melodramas, he made several great fantasy serials – *Fantômas* (1913–14), *Les Vampires* (1915–16), *Judex* (1916) and *La Nouvelle Mission de Judex* (1917, The New Mission of Judex). Rediscovered in the Sixties, these films have been hailed as landmarks in art cinema.

Feuillade, the son of a wine-merchant, was born at Lunel, near Montpellier, on February 19, 1873, and educated in the Catholic seminary at Carcassonne. All his life he remained a devout Catholic and a fervent monarchist; and from the time of his arrival in Paris in 1898 until 1902, he worked as a book-keeper to the Maison de la Bonne Presse, the celebrated Catholic publishing house.

He turned his hand to journalism, and founded his own magazine, *La Tomate*, a satirical weekly which lasted only for three months. For the more prestigious *Revue Mondiale*, Feuillade wrote a long historical essay, 'La Genèse d'un Crime Historique' (The Origin of a Historical Crime), which explored the fate of the boy who would have been Louis XVII, and who may, or may not, have been killed in the Revolution.

This theme had obsessed Feuillade ever since two alleged descendants of the Dauphin had visited Lunel in his childhood; and it inspired some of the historical films which he directed between 1910 and 1913. It may also have had much to do with the taste of mystery, impersonation, and hairbreadth escapes so vividly displayed in the great works to follow.

In 1905, Feuillade was engaged by the Gaumont company. At first he simply provided scripts, but within months he was directing little comedies and dramas. Then in late 1906, the studio head, the remarkable Alice Guy (the first woman director), married the English cameraman Herbert Blaché, and went with him to head Gaumont's operation in Berlin, then in New York. Gaumont wanted Albert Capellani to replace her in Paris, but Alice Guy persuaded him to give Feuillade a chance.

Top: a portrait of Louis Feuillade as the foppish gentleman. Above: a poster from L'Oubliette *(1912, The Secret Dungeon), in the* Le Détective Dervieux *series, aptly evokes Feuillade's knack for nightmarish fantasy*

Thus, on January 1, 1907, Feuillade became artistic director of Gaumont, with a salary of 125 fr. a week plus a cut of the sales. He worked with prodigious energy and, until 1913, turned out some eighty films a year – including comedies, religious and historical spectacles, detective thrillers, and series.

A realist manifesto

In 1911 financial problems led Léon Gaumont to demand economies of his staff. Feuillade responded with the series *La Vie Telle Qu'Elle Est* (1911–13, Life As It Is). These 18 films were designed as simple slices of domestic realism, and were very cheaply made. Feuillade changed necessity to advantage with a resounding manifesto proclaiming that the films 'attempt to bring reality to the screen for the first time,' and that the 'scenes represent people and things as they are, not as they ought to be.'

Unhappily, the public did not welcome these early examples of reality, and soon the series was including controversial items like *La Souris Blanche* (1911, The White Mouse), in which two old maids inherit an establishment of doubtful reputation, learn how profitable it is, and gleefully take it over. Trade reviews accused Feuillade of pornography, but the customers were coming back.

Feuillade made two very popular series featuring child stars: the Bébé series (1910–13), utilizing the talented child actor Clément Abélard; and the Bout-de-Zan series (1912–16), which was built round the engaging imp of the title, whom Feuillade used again in *Judex* as the character Le Môme Réglisse (The Liquorice Kid).

The master of crime

Meanwhile two popular writers, Pierre Souvestre and Marcel Allain, had published their fantastically successful series of crime thrillers concerning the exploits of the master criminal, Fantômas.

There were 32 Fantômas stories, and for 6,000 fr. Gaumont bought the film rights. Feuillade made the films in harmonious collaboration with the authors, often present during the shooting and lending a hand with the constant improvisation. However, Feuillade's *Fantômas* was not a genuine serial. It consisted of a series of self-contained films, released at intervals over a year (1913–14), and varying in length from three to five reels. But with it, the essential Feuillade was born.

Vigorous and enjoyable as it is, *Fantômas* loses slightly today by being shown in one piece, that is, in a form for which it was never intended. Its repetitions become obtrusive and its climaxes misplaced. Also, René Navarre as the villain-hero lacks the kind of solidarity and the panache evoked so strikingly by the central figures in *Les Vampires* and *Judex*. But there is still much to admire in the film.

Realism and fantasy blend in the manner unique to Feuillade; evil may lose in the end, but on the way there it flourishes with a cheerful anarchism. The locations take on a personality of their own, and the beautifully choreographed battle among the wine-casks on the dockland provides one of the memorable moments in cinema history. All that is needed is a great central performance and a touch more poetry. This would come in Feuillade's next serial, *Les Vampires.*

The devilish criminals

After the *Fantômas* series Feuillade marked time until the war. In fact, until he was mobilized in March 1915, he returned to the little farces and historical pieces he had cut his teeth on, with the odd patriotic drama thrown in. In July he was discharged for medical reasons, and returned to a different Paris. Most of the actors and technicians were in the forces, money was scarce, and electricity not to be wasted. Yet all of this contributed to his next masterpiece, as did the competition soon to come from the Pearl White serials, which were about to be released by the New York branch of Pathé.

Feuillade's immensely popular *Les Vampires* was a true serial, a continuous story released in ten episodes at irregular intervals during 1915–16. The Vampires are a band of criminals; they have a chief (the Great Vampire), but their inspiration is the ruthless, voluptuous Irma Vep (an anagram of Vampire), played with superb relish by the actress Musidora.

The locations are the great glory of *Les Vampires*. Forced onto the streets by studio conditions affected by the war, Feuillade turned the bleak suburbs of Paris into his star. Grey, cobbled side roads, melancholy wasteland, gaunt factories, scattered bystanders, the occasional car gleaming with brass, all bathed in the light of a grey dawn or in a threatening twilight – this was the backcloth to Feuillade's drama of precarious good versus elemental (and exultant) evil.

The plot was largely improvised from episode to episode. Actors would be written out as they were called up, others written in as they returned. When Jean Ayme, who was playing the Great Vampire, was late for work one day, Feuillade had him killed off, and the following episode sees Louis Leubas as the new, and quite unexplained, Great Vampire.

The sheer unpredictability of *Les Vampires* is one of its greatest strengths. Its raw spontaneity, added to its total contempt for law, order and normality, especially appealed to the Surrealists. Thus Louis Aragon and André Breton, two of the leading spokesmen of the Surrealist movement, commented in 1928: 'It is in *Les Vampires* that one must seek the great realities of this century. Beyond fashion. Beyond taste.'

The film is magnificently acted. Feuillade had built his stock company mainly from people with little or no stage experience, and had taught them restraint above all. Their naturalism amid all the wild developments of the plot lends the whole an uncanny conviction.

The first caped hero

Here and in the next serial, *Judex*, the hero' henchman was played by the great comi actor Marcel Lévesque. Tall, balding, sardonic slow-moving, Lévesque was a vital part of th pattern, periodically bringing a disillusione commonsense to bear on the story's wilde flights.

Judex is almost as good as *Les Vampire* Though less pleasurably shocking because, fo the first time in Feuillade, the central figure o the Avenger is on the side of good, it is as ric in poetry and as extravagant in invention. also has the child Bout-de-Zan as The Liquoric Kid forming a marvellous partnership of un equals with Lévesque.

Feuillade felt he had to play it a little safe this time. The censor had held up *Les Vampire* for nearly ten weeks, until vamped into sub mission by Musidora in person, and the pres had been shocked by the film's potenti for corruption. They still found *Judex* beneat serious attention, but Feuillade worked for h audiences – and, without knowing it, for th future.

JACK LODG

Above: the black-hooded bandit hero Fantômas strikes in Fantômas. *Above right: a publicity poster for the same film evokes the genre's vision of urban fear. Above far right: an illustration for the newspaper serialization of the* Judex *saga. Below: René Cresté as the black-cloaked crusader of justice in* La Nouvelle Mission de Judex *(The New Mission of Judex). Below left: the madhouse villa at Nice, a candid scene from* Tih Minh *(1918)*

Filmography

All shorts unless otherwise specified: **1905** Le Coup de Vent/Attrapez Mon Chapeau (sc. only). **'06** La Course au Potiron (sc. only); Le Billet de Banque; C'Est Papa Qui Prend la Purge; Les Deux Gosses; La Porteuse de Pain; Mireille (co-dir); N'Te Promène Donc Pas Toute Nue. **'07** La Course des Belles-Mères; Un Accident d'Auto (sc. only); Un Facteur Trop Ferré; La Légende de la Fileuse; Un Paquet Embarrassant; L'Homme Aimanté (sc. only); La Sirène; Le Thé Chez la Concierge; Vive le Sabotage. **'08** La Grève des Apaches; Nettoyage par le Vide; Une Nuit Agitée; Un Tic; Les Agents Tels qu'on Nous les Présente; Une Dame Vraiment Bien; Prométhée; Le Roman de Soeur Louise; Le Récit du Colonel. **'09** Les Heures (4 eps); Histoire de Puce; L'Aveugle de Jérusalem; Judith et Holopherne; La Mère du Moine; Le Printemps; La Mort de Mozart; La Possession de l'Enfant; Le Savetier et le Financier; Vainqueur de la Course Pédestre; Le Collier de la Reine; La Légende des Phares; La Chatte Métamorphosée en Femme; Fra Vincenti; Le Huguenot; Le Mort; Les Filles du Cantonnier; La Cigale et la Fourmi. **'10** Le Festin de Balthazar; Esther; Maudite Soit la Guerre; Le Pater (first film of Le Film Esthetique series); La Fille de Jephté; Benvenuto Cellini; L'Exode; Le Roi de Thulé; Les Sept Péchés Capitaux (3 eps); Mater Dolorosa; La Nativité; Bébé Fume (first of 75 films in Bébé series, 1910–13); Mil Huit Cent Quatorze; Le Christ en Croix; L'An 1000. **'11** Dans la Vie; Les Doigts Qui Voient; Le Fils de Locuste; La Fille du Juge d'Instruction; Sous le Joug; Les Vipères (first of 18 films in La Vie Telle Qu'Elle Est series, 1911–13); Le Fils de la Sunamite; Le Bracelet de la Marquise; Les Petites Apprentices; L'Aventurière, Dame de Compagnie; Fidélité Romaine; Le Trafiquant; La Vierge d'Argos; Aux Lions les Chrétiens; Quand les Feuilles Tombent; Charles VI. **'12** L'Aventurière; La Demoiselle du Notaire; La Fille du Margrave; La Mort Vivant; Les Cloches de Pâques; La Maison des Lions; La Prison sur le Gouffre; Androclès; Le Château de la Peur; Dans la Brousse; La Cassette de l'Emigrée; Le Proscrit (first of 4 films in Le Détective Dervieux series, 1912–13); Préméditation; Le Témoin; Le Tourment; Au Pays des Lions; Le Coeur et l'Argent; Amour d'Automne; L'Anneau Fatal; Tyrtée; L'Attrait du Bourge; La Hantise; Le Petit Poucet; Bout-de-Zan Revient du Cirque (first of 52 films in Bout-de-Zan series, 1912–16); La Course aux Millions; Haut les Mains!; L'Homme de Proie; La Vie ou la Mort; Le Maléfice; Le Noël de Francesca; Les Noces Siciliennes; Les Yeux Qui Meurent. **'13** Les Audaces du Coeur; La Conversion d'Irma; Erreur Tragique; L'Intruse; La Mort de Lucrèce; La Vengeance du Sergent de Ville; Le Bon Propriétaire; Le Mariage de Miss Nelly; Le Revenânt; Le Secret du Forçat; Les Yeux Ouverts; L'Angoisse; Le Browning; Fantômas (3 parts); Les Chasseurs de Lions; L'Effroi; Le Ménestrel de la Reine Anne; La Petite Danseuse; L'Agonie de Byzance; Juve Contre Fantômas (4-part feature); La Gardienne du Feu (3 parts); La Rose Blanche; Un Drame au Pays Basque; Les Millions de la Bonne (first of 25 films in La Vie Drôle series, 1913–18); Le Mort Qui Tue (6-part feature); Au Gré des Flots; La Marche des Rois; Bonne Année; Un Scandale au Village. **'14** La Rencontre; Fantômas Contre Fantômas (4-part feature); Les Lettres; Manon de Montmartre; L'Enfant de la Roulotte (5 parts); Pâques Rouges; Le Faux Magistrat (feature); Le Calvaire; Severo Torelli (5 parts); Les Fiancés de Séville; Le Coffret de Tolède; Les Fiancés de 1914; Le Diamant du Sénéchal; L'Epreuve; La Gitanella; La Neuvaine; La Petite Andalouse. **'15** L'Expiation; Celui Qui Reste; Le Coup de Fakir; Deux Françaises; Fifi Tambour; Union Sacrée; Les Noces d'Argent; L'Angoisse au Foyer; La Barrière; Les Vampires (10-ep. serial); Le Noël du Poilu; Le Blason; La Course à l'Abîme. **'16** C'Est le Printemps; Le Double Jeu; Le Malheur Qui Passe; L'Aventure des Millions (feature); Un Mariage de Raison (feature); Notre Pauvre Coeur (feature); Le Retour de Manivel; Judex (12-ep. serial). **'17** La Déserteuse (feature); Le Passé de Monique (3-part feature); Herr Doktor (3 parts); L' Autre (3 parts); Le Bandeau sur les Yeux (3 parts); La Nouvelle Mission de Judex (12-ep. serial); La Fugue de Lily (3 parts). **'18** Les Petites Marionnettes (4-part feature); Vendémiaire (feature); Tih Minh (12-ep. serial). **'19** L'Homme Sans Visage (4-part feature); L'Engrenage (4-part feature); Le Nocturne (4-part feature); L'Enigme/Le Mot de l'Enigme (4 parts); Barabbas (12-ep. serial). **'20** Les Deux Gamines (12-ep. serial). **'21** Zidore ou les Métamorphoses (first of 7 films in Belle Humeur series, 1921–22); L'Orpheline (12-ep. serial); Parisette (12-ep. serial). **'22** Le Fils du Flibustier (12-ep. serial). **'23** Vindicta (5-part feature); La Gosseline (feature); Le Gamin de Paris (feature); L'Orphelin de Paris (6-ep. serial). **'24** La Fille Bien Gardée (feature); Pierrot, Pierrette (feature); Lucette (feature) (co-dir); Le Stigmate (6-part feature) (co-dir).

The handsome young Comte de Trémeuse is one of the two sons of a Corsican banker who committed suicide after being ruined by his former friend Favraux. Sworn by his mother to avenge his father, the Comte, disguised in a black cape and broad-brimmed hat, becomes Judex. He gains the confidence of Favraux, who fails to recognize him, and strikes him down in the course of a grand reception. Believed dead, Favraux is in fact buried alive, and reappears. Meanwhile Judex has fallen in love with Favraux's beautiful daughter, the widow Jacqueline, and so far relents as merely to imprison the villain in the dungeons of the ruined castle where he has set up a laboratory. . . .

1. The banker Favraux (right), with Cocantin, receives a warning from the avenger Judex

4. Judex sends Jacqueline some homing pigeons, to be released when she is in peril

7. Diana Monti conspires with Moralès, watched by Judex's henchman Cocantin

This basic story of *Judex* is the starting point for endless variations and digressions, whose nature and variety is indicated by the titles of the twelve episodes listed in the credits. Both his *Fantômas* (1913–14) and *Les Vampires* (1915–16, The Vampires) had been attacked for glorifying crime and ridiculing the police, and Louis Feuillade exhibited a nice balance of moral duty and commercial discretion in deciding to make the hero of his next serial, written by himself in collaboration with Arthur Bernède, an avenger and defender of the law who renounces, like every classic Western hero, the use of weapons and the shedding of blood.

The audiences of 1917 took *Judex* to their hearts – though in retrospect it must be confessed that virtue offered slightly less excitement than vice. However, Feuillade's ingenuity in inventing suspense and surprise was unflagging. The discursive adventures of Judex and his enemy the banker Favraux provided excuses for Feuillade to introduce his stock company of favourite players – the fine comedian Marcel Lévesque as a detective, Musidora as the sinister Diana Monti and his child-star Bout-de-Zan as The Liquorice Kid.

Above all, *Judex* exemplified Feuillade's discovery of the special piquancy that lay in creating his extravagant and fantastic happenings in a landscape that was both modern and familiar, as well as revealing the visual beauty and magic that was to be found in that landscape. Feuillade's biographer Francis Lacassin observed that, long before Antonioni, Feuillade understood:

'. . . that there is nothing more beautiful than that urban poetry which springs from uneven streets, bleak, crumbling districts, silent and deserted, stretches of waste-land with strange buildings silhouetted in the distance.'

For the original programme of the film, Feuillade and Bernède wrote an introduction. Never reprinted since 1917, their statement remains a masterly résumé of the state of the French cinema during World War I, and of the role which (allowing for the hyperbole of a master publicist) Feuillade saw for his film:

'After the beginning of the war, the French cinema was to pass through a fatal crisis, whose deplorable results we are experiencing today. Everywhere in France production was severely curtailed, if not entirely stopped.

'The Americans profited by this to launch on our markets a stock of films whose merits it would be unjust and childish to deny. But if our clever competitors, marvellously served by circumstances, have succeeded, thanks to first-class equipment, and a strength of invention that has to be admired, in making real progress in our art . . . we must nevertheless keep ourselves from concluding that French production is definitively outclassed by the Americans and that we are condemned always to be following after others.

'We possess too many solid and durable elements of success to reconcile ourselves to taking a second place. . . .

'Nowhere are there authors more gifted with the sense of action, movement, the picturesque, which are the essential qualities of a good scenarist.

'Nowhere, equally, do actors play with a more exact notion of life, a more minute care for truth, a more discreet sense of tact and proportion. Nowhere do we find all together such an abundance of marvellous locations, varied in style, making natural pictures and evoking splendid atmospheres of poetic grace and ascendant beauty.

'All these elements associated and established in perfect harmony must give excellent results. . . . Such is the conception which has prevailed in the creation of *Judex*.

'What is *Judex*? . . . A film in twelve episodes, or rather twelve weeks, appearing in *Le Petit Parisien* in the form of a novel designed to capture in advance the attention of three or four million readers who form the loyal clientele of the greatest daily paper in the whole world, and who will become equally faithful habitués of the cinemas

---

Directed by Louis Feuillade, 1916

Prod co: Gaumont. **sc:** Arthur Bernède, Louis Feuillade. **photo:** Klausse, André Glattli. **length:** 26,849 feet (approx. 450 minutes). Serial in 12 episodes: 1. *L'Ombre Mystérieuse* (The Mysterious Shadow); 2. *L'Expiation* (Expiation); 3. *La Meute Fantastique* (The Fantastic Hounds); 4. *Le Secret de la Tombe* (The Secret of the Tomb); 5. *Le Moulin Tragique* (The Tragic Mill); 6. *Le Môme Réglisse* (The Liquorice Kid); 7. *La Femme en Noir* (The Woman in Black); 8. *Les Souterrains du Château-Rouge* (The Dungeons of the Château-Rouge); 9. *Lorsque l'Enfant Parut* (When the Child Appears); 10. *Le Coeur de Jacqueline* (The Heart of Jacqueline); 11. *L'Ondine* (The Water Sprite); 12. *Le Pardon d'Amour* (The Forgiveness of Love). Paris premiere: 16 December 1916.
Cast: René Cresté (*Henri de Trémeuse alias Judex*), Edouard Mathé (*Roger de Trémeuse*), Yvonne Dario (*Comtesse de Trémeuse*), Louis Leubas (*Favraux the banker*), Yvette Andreyor (*Jacqueline*), Musidora (*Diana Monti alias Marie Verdier*), Jean Devalde (*Robert Moralès*), Georges Flateau (*Vicomte de la Rochefontaine*), Gaston Michel (*Pierre Kerjean*), Olinda Mano (*Jean*), Juliette Clarens (*Gisèle*), Marcel Lévesque (*Cocantin*), Bout-de-Zan (*The Liquorice Kid*).

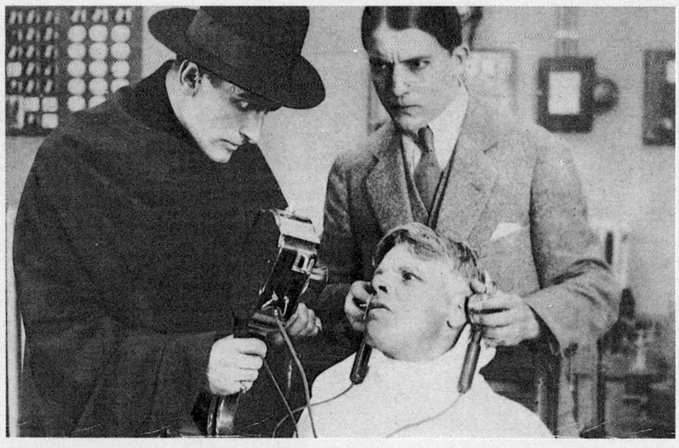

2. **Judex and his brother force Favraux, believed to be dead, to speak to his daughter. . . .**

3. **. . . and Jacqueline is astonished to hear her father's voice from beyond the tomb**

5. **Judex gives his judgment in letters of fire, blazoned on the wall of the prisoner's cell. . . .**

6. **. . . commuting Favraux's sentence to life imprisonment, because of his daughter**

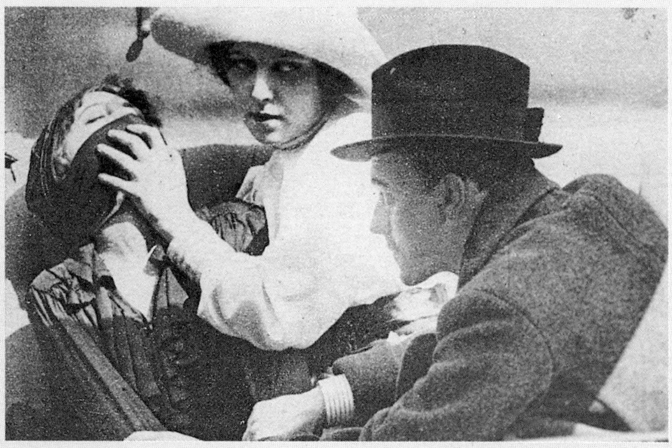

8. **Diana Monti, disguised as a nurse and aided by Moralès, kidnaps the helpless Jacqueline**

9. **The Liquorice Kid saves Jacqueline from Diana Monti's plot to drown her in the river**

which show on their screens the cinematographic realization, that is to say the bringing to life of the novel which they will have read with interest during the week.

'A film . . . which we have wished to be popular in the largest, best sense of the word, a family show, exalting the finest sentiments and in which we have endeavoured to please great and small, thanks to the most diverse and unusual incidentals to the action.

'Conforming to the traditions of those who, like the great Dumas, remain the masters of the French imagination, we have sought to bring to life a real story of adventure, love, laughter and tears.

'To ensure its realization, as we have dreamed of it ourselves, Messrs Gaumont have spared no sacrifice. Not only have they engaged the most celebrated stars of the cinema, Mmes Andreyor, Musidora, Juliette Clarens, MM Lévesque, René Cresté, Ed. Mathé, Leubas, G. Michel, not to speak of the popular Bout-de-Zan; but they have desired that the production should be at once magnificent and varied and at the same time in the most perfect artistic taste.

'A spectacle of emotion, joy and art, that is what we have sought to attain, with the aid of the precious and rare support that has been so generously given us, together with our ardent wish to make our contribution to an industry which must become and remain national.'

Even before Feuillade's death in 1925 serious critics and bourgeois filmgoers dismissed his mystery serials as cheap and out-dated, and it was only with the ardent admiration of the Surrealists that the beauty and fantasy of his world was fully appreciated.

Judex has been twice remade: in 1933 a version was directed by Feuillade's son-in-law Maurice Champreux; a new version made in 1963 by Georges Franju was co-scripted by his grandson, Jacques Champreux. DAVID ROBINSON

Asta Nielsen
A star in her own light

Like Louise Brooks after her, Asta Nielsen made a virtue – and erotic capital – of her androgynous looks. The helmet of black hair, the flat chest, the languorous limbs all became world famous. But in defying the stereotype of the screen goddess, she was, as a consequence, never wooed by Hollywood

Had Asta Nielsen been American, she would probably now be a household legend throughout the English-speaking world as the first true superstar. Being Danish, and working for most of her career in Germany, she found her success – though remarkable – sadly short-lived. To the end of her days, however (her death came in May 1972 at the age of 90), Asta Nielsen remained a *monstre sacré* for many film enthusiasts.

Brought up to know poverty in Vesterbro, a suburb of Copenhagen, she was an orphan at 14, and earned her keep by working in a city bakery, studying in the evenings in the tough school constituted by the chorus at the Royal Theatre. By the age of 8 she had read Ibsen's *Brand* and become fixated with the idea of the theatre, making her first appearance as an angel suspended from the stage loft in Boito's opera *Mephistopheles*.

Within a few months of leaving the Royal Theatre School, she had won acclaim for her stage work on tour in Norway, and soon became enshrined as the leading lady at the New Theatre in Copenhagen. At first she declined offers to appear in the new-fangled medium of the cinema, setting her sights too high for the producers of the period, who were after a quick profit. Copenhagen impresarios were condescending towards her talents, claiming that her nose was crooked, her lips too thin and her voice and figure too mannish. Her wide-set eyes (dark but never lugubrious), her regal mien and pencil-thin appeal made her ahead of her time – but also timeless.

A name for fame

But in 1909 she was approached with a screenplay by Urban Gad, who was to become her first husband. It was entitled *Afgrunden* (1910, The Abyss), and was shot in eight days in an old prison yard and on location in the streets of Copenhagen – the budget was minuscule. Asked why she had opted for the cinema at a time when it was not accepted as an art form, she said:

'Only to show Denmark that I *was* an actress, and all the world gave me the chance to prove that I was not wrong . . .'

She was referring to the extraordinary word-of-mouth success of her first film. Only 153 people had attended the premiere of *Afgrunden*, and the city's theatre directors were especially conspicuous by their absence. And yet, the word spread like wildfire. Her name was marketed on a scale that would have made even today's media publicists envious. There were 'Asta' cigarettes, 'Asta' skin cream and – as her films began to earn release abroad – cinemas named after Miss Nielsen in places as far apart as San Francisco and Nagasaki. In her autobiography *The Tenth Muse*, she

Top: Asta Nielsen in Hamlet, *the first film produced by her own company. Above: with Alfred Abel in* Rausch. *Above right: Nielsen aged 34 plays a 16-year-old impersonating a 12-year-old in* Engelein. *Above, far right: the poster for* Das Haus am Meer *(1924, The House by the Sea) shows the gaunt face that personified the actress. Right: Nielsen at 50 in her first talkie and last film,* Unmögliche Liebe *as a mother longing for her lost youth*

marked that:

'In spite of *Afgrunden* being distributed with-
ıt our names being mentioned on it, my
ame everywhere rose like a phoenix out of the
.hes. Letters from all corners of the world
gan to pour in to me, the adventure of the
m had become my reality.'

In 1911 Paul Davidsohn, the original foun-
r of the UFA (Universum Film Aktien Ges-
lschaft) studio in Berlin, persuaded her and
rban Gad to work in Germany. During the
st four years Nielsen and her husband made
fewer than thirty full-length features, and
hat seemed likely to be a brief sojourn in fact
sted some twenty-five years, with only short
ips home to Denmark from time to time.

Although she often asserted that she had no
ir for comedy, she graced a series of witty
ıd lively satires for Neutral Films – among
em Magnus Stifter's *Das Liebes-ABC* (1916,
he ABC of Love), in which she played a young
oman in drag, taking a male friend from one
ve to another to show him the facts of life. In
as Eskimo-baby (1917, The Eskimo Baby) she
as an Eskimo girl introduced by an Arctic
xplorer into the stuffy vastness of his aristo-
atic home. Two more of her many films
om this period are certainly worthy of men-
on. *Engelein* (1913, Little Angel) delighted
ns with her impersonation of a 16-year-old
ho has to convince her visiting uncle that she
a mere stripling innocent of 12. Asta Nielsen was 34 at the time! In *Zapatas Bande* (1914, The Zapata Gang) – which pokes fun at the movie-making process – Miss Nielsen and her actor colleagues are forced to become bandits in Italy after their costumes have been stolen.

Filmography
1910 Afgrunden (DEN). **'11** Nachtfalter; Den Sorte Drøm (DEN); In dem grossen Augenblick (USA/GB: The Great Moment); Heisses Blut; Zigeunerblut; Der fremde Vogel; Balletdanserinden (DEN); Die Verräterin. **'12** Die arme Jenny; Die Macht des Goldes; Zu Tode gehetzt; Der Totentanz (USA: The Dance of Death); Die Kinder des Generals (USA: Children of the General); Wenn die Maske fällt (USA: When the Mask Falls); Jugend und Tollheit (USA: Youth and Folly); Das Mädchen ohne Vaterland (USA: The Girl Without Home); Komödianten (USA: The Comedians). **'13** Die Sünden der Väter (USA: Parents' Sins); Der Tod in Sevilla (USA: Death in Sevilla); Die Suffragetten; Die Filmprimadonna; S. I.; Engelein. **'14** Das Kind ruft; Zapatas Bande; Das Feuer. **'15** Vordertreppe und Hintertreppe; Die Tochter der Landstrasse; Aschenbrödel; Die ëwige Nacht; Engeleins Hochzeit; Die falsche Asta Nielsen; Weisse Rosen. **'16** Dora Brandes; Die Börsenkönigin; Im Lebenswirbel; Das Liebes-ABC. **'17** Die Rose der Wildnis; Der erste Patient; Das Eskimo-baby. **'18** Das Weisenhauskind; Des Meeres und der Liebe Wellen. **'19** Mod Lyset (DEN); Rausch; Nach dem Gesetz; Das Ende vom Lied. **'20** Der Reigen; Kurfürstendamm; Graf Sylvains Rache; Hamlet (+co-prod); Steuermann Holk. **'21** Irrende Seelen/Sklaven der Sinne; Die geliebte Roswolskys; Fräulein Julie. **'22** Brigantenrache; Vanina; Der Absturz; Die Tänzerin Navarro. **'23** Erdgeist; I.N.R.I. (USA: Crown of Thorns). **'24** Das Haus am Meer; Lebende Buddhas; Die Schmetterlingsschlacht; Die Frau im Feuer; Hedda Gabler. **'25** Athleten; Die freudlose Gasse (USA: Streets of Sorrow; GB: The Joyless Street; reissued as: The Street of Sorrow); Die Gesunkenen. **'27** Laster der Menschheit; Dirnentragödie (USA: Women Without Men); Gehetzte Frauen; Kleinstadtsünden (USA: Small Town Sinners); Das gefährliche Alter. **'32** Unmögliche Liebe. **'68** Asta Nielsen (doc. short) (appearance as herself only) (DEN).

A woman beyond men

It was in the years immediately after World War I that Asta Nielsen's fame reached its peak. Georg Brandes, the major Scandinavian literary critic, pronounced:

'If I borrowed the wings of the morning dawn and travelled unto the farthest ocean, I would meet the name of Asta even there.'

Even the French poet Guillaume Apollinaire greeted her work ecstatically:

'Ah, she is all! She is the vision of a drinker, and the dream of a lonely man. She laughs like a girl completely happy, and her eye knows of things so tender and shy that one could not speak of them.'

In 1920 she formed her own company, Art Film A.G., to produce a screen version of *Hamlet*. Her notion – taken from an American book on the subject – was that Hamlet had been in reality a woman, whose sex had been disguised to enable her to inherit the throne of Denmark. The film was directed by Sven Gade and Heinz Schall, and photographed by the brilliant Curt Courant. While in Germany, Asta Nielsen assumed a remarkable degree of influence over the details of each film appearance – selecting the costumes, checking the props, and hiring artists to design imaginative posters.

Her one contact with Ernst Lubitsch came immediately after the Armistice, when she appeared in *Rausch* (1919, Intoxication), the German director's screen version of Strindberg's play *There Are Crimes and Crimes*. Then in 1925 came *Die freudlose Gasse* (*The Joyless Street*), Pabst's first major film and a vehicle for Greta Garbo as well as Miss Nielsen. The two great actresses did not appear in a single scene together, but featured in parallel stories set in the inflation-ridden Vienna of the post-war period. Two years later she played a prostitute who becomes the victim of her own romantic yearnings in *Dirnentragödie* (1927, *Women Without Men*). Her first talkie was the last film she made in Germany – *Unmögliche Liebe* (1932, Unlikely Love Affair). Erich Waschneck cast Nielsen as a middle-aged mother trying to keep up with her swinging daughters.

She departed Germany in 1936 in revulsion at the actions of the Nazi Party, although not before she had reputedly been offered the chance of establishing her own studio. In the last 35 years of her life, Asta Nielsen devoted much time to writing and painting. She was – both on screen and off – a prototype of the independent woman, and, indeed, as such one of the pioneers of feminism.

PETER COWIE

The Cabinet of Dr Caligari

1

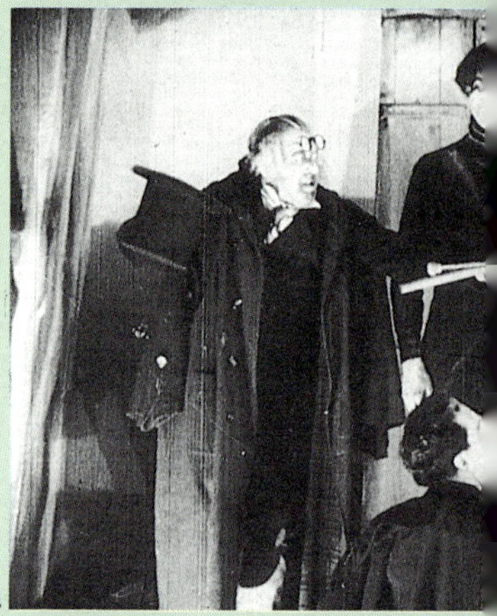
4

7

When it was released in Britain in 1922, *The Cabinet of Dr Caligari* was billed as 'Europe's greatest contribution to the motion picture art' and it remains one of the cinema's landmarks. But its making and its meaning continue to give rise to controversy, with the sometimes conflicting accounts left by the participants playing a significant part.

Evidently, Hans Janowitz and Carl Mayer, two young writers, devised a script in which they mingled their own memories of a notorious Hamburg sex murder and an unsympathetic army psychiatrist Carl encountered while on military service with several archetypal themes from German Romanticism. They apparently intended their story to be a modern pacifist parable, with Cesare as the symbol of the people and Caligari as the state, seemingly benign and respected but in fact ordering the people to kill (in wars). The meaning of the ending, in which Caligari is unmasked and overthrown, is therefore clearly anti-authoritarian.

Erich Pommer, head of the small Decla company, agreed to produce a film of the script and assigned Fritz Lang to direct. But when Lang's work on *Die Spinnen* (1919, *The Spiders*) went on longer than expected, the job fell to Robert Wiene, who, it was felt, was equipped to handle a story involving insanity because his own father, a once-famous actor, had gone mad towards the end of his life. Then either Pommer or Wiene or both insisted on adding a framing device to the script (a prologue and an epilogue), making the story a tale told by a madman. The result of this is to completely reverse the meaning of the original story and rob it of its subversive intent.

In his classic book, *From Caligari to Hitler*, Siegfried Kracauer elaborated the theory of the German cinema directly reflecting the mentality of the German people and foreshadowing the rise of the Nazis. In particular he saw Caligari as the first of a series of power-crazed tyrants in German films, to whom the other characters in the story situation submit without question. But this view is now regarded as too precise and mechanistic.

Equally untenable is the view advanced by scholars like Lotte Eisner that the Germans are somehow peculiarly obsessed with death, madness and twilight. Interestingly, although Hollywood in the Thirties produced horror films in the same style and on the same themes as Germany in the Twenties, no one suggests that the Americans are therefore peculiarly pessimistic or doom-laden. It seems more likely that the popularity of tales of horror in Weimar Germany and Depression America has the same cause – a turning to stylized horrors to escape the real horrors of depression and inflation.

What is incontrovertible is that *The Cabinet of Dr Caligari* is an Expressionist film. But to what extent? Expressionism was a movement in the arts beginning before World War I. It involved painters whose work was characterized by subjectivism, emotionalism and anti-naturalism. This is significant because Hermann Warm, Walter Reimann and Walter Röhrig, who designed *The Cabinet of Dr Caligari*, were themselves Expressionist artists. In literature, Expressionism embraced the themes of 'alienation, anti-authoritarianism, pacifism, salvation through love, and hostility to bourgeois society'. Some of these elements were certainly present in the original script but were negated by the framing device.

The visual style of the film was distinctly Expressionist – with painted backcloths, dominated by curves and cubes, deliberately distorted perspectives, and furniture unnaturally elongated. The effect was to disorientate the viewer, and it was enhanced further by the Expressionist style of acting – with Werner Krauss' top-hatted and bespectacled Caligari a shuffling, gesticulating, totally malign presence; and Conrad Veidt's somnambulist, a slender, hollow-eyed, ashen-faced, living corpse. There were only a few totally Expressionist films like *The Cabinet of Dr Caligari*, which drew themes, styles and visual motifs directly from the movement; but elements of Expressionism in art direction and the plastic, externalized acting style it fostered nevertheless became distinguishing features of the German cinema until the late Twenties.

Over the years considerable attention has been devoted to the political, psychological and artistic importance of *The Cabinet of Dr Caligari*, but only recently has its perhaps most obvious importance – as horror film – been more fully appreciated. For whatever else it was, the film also represented the latest manifestation of German Romanticism with a pedigree stretching back to the novelist E.T.A. Hoffman, the folklorists Jakob and Wilhelm Grimm, and the dramatist-poet Schiller. It is from these roots that the themes of death, tyranny, fate and disorder, and the subjects of haunted students, mad doctors, ghosts, mummies, vampires and somnambulists spring. *The Cabinet of Dr Caligari* was as much a product of this tradition as such contemporary horror classics as *Der Golem: wie er in die Welt Kam* (1920, *The Golem*), *Nosferatu, eine Symphonie des Grauens* (1922, *Nosferatu, the Vampire*), *Orlacs Hände* (1925, *The Hands of Orlac*) and *Der Student von Prag* (1926, *The Student of Prague*).

In the Romanticism of its content and the Expressionism of its form,

2

3

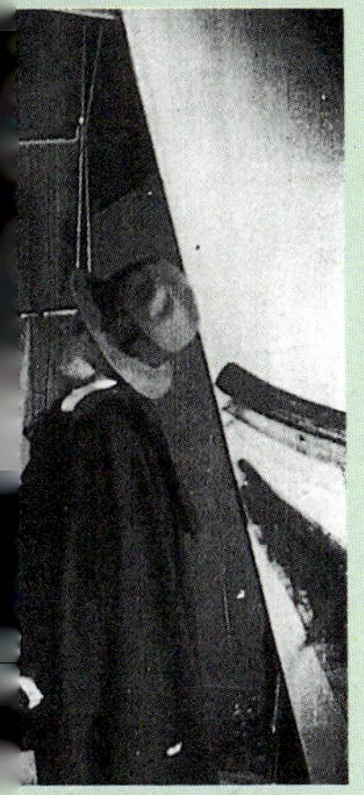

5

6

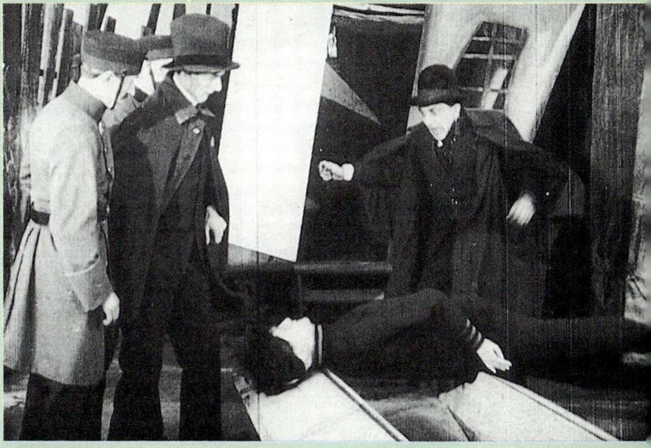

8

9

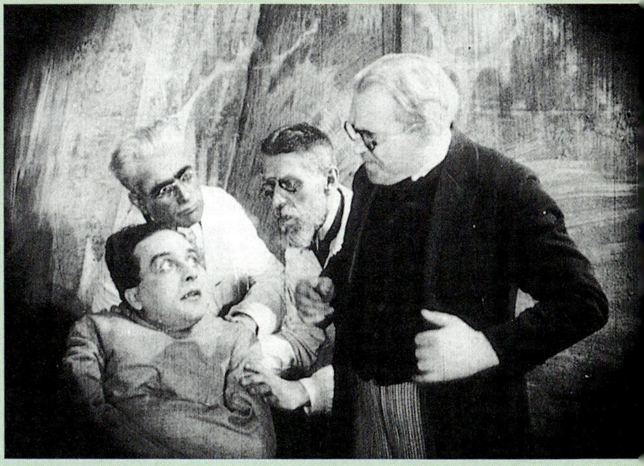

The Cabinet of Dr Caligari not only exercised a decisive influence on other German horror films, but also on the later Hollywood horror genre – where, for instance, in the films of Robert Florey, the students, fairground, mad doctor and killer ape of *Murders in the Rue Morgue* (1932) and the madman's fantasy of persecution in *The Beast With Five Fingers* (1946) are recognizably akin to the milieu of *The Cabinet of Dr Caligari*. JEFFREY RICHARDS

Seated on a bench in a lane, Francis tells his story to a companion (1) . . .

In the north German town of Holstenwall a travelling fair appears, and Francis persuades his friend Alan, a student, to visit it with him (2). Dr Caligari, one of the showmen, asks the town clerk to grant him the necessary licence. The clerk mocks him and next day is found murdered.

Francis and Alan, now at the fair, go to see Caligari and his somnambulist Cesare (3). Cesare foretells Alan's future (4) – he will live until dawn. Next day, Alan is found killed in the same manner as the town clerk. Francis, suspecting Caligari, takes the doctor father of Jane, the girl he loves, to examine Cesare but the doctor can find nothing amiss. Francis, however, continues to watch Caligari, not knowing that he has replaced Cesare with a dummy, which now rests in the coffin where the somnambulist sleeps.

Sent to kill Jane, Cesare carries her off instead (5), chased by her family. Eventually he falls dead of exhaustion. The police discover the dummy in the coffin (6), but Caligari escapes. Francis follows Caligari to the asylum and entering, discovers he is the Director (7).

Next night, Francis and three of the asylum staff search the Director's papers (8) and discover an account of an eighteenth-century Italian showman called Caligari who used his somnambulist Cesare to kill people. Francis confronts the Director with Cesare's corpse and, raving, he is put in a strait-jacket.

Having finished his story, Francis returns to the courtyard of the asylum, where he, Cesare and Jane are inmates. The Director appears and Francis attacks him. Attendants overpower Francis (9) and the Director declares that now he has realized that Francis thinks he is Caligari, he can cure him of his madness.

Directed by Robert Wiene, 1919

Prod co: Decla-Bioscop. **prod:** Erich Pommer. **assoc prod:** Rudolf Meinert. **sc:** Carl Mayer, Hans Janowitz, from a story by Hans Janowitz. **photo:** Willy Hameister. **art dir:** Hermann Warm, Walter Röhrig, Walter Reimann. **cost:** Walter Reimann. **length:** 4682 ft (approx. 78 minutes). German title: *Das Kabinett des Dr Caligari*. Released in GB as *The Cabinet of Dr Caligari*. **Cast:** Werner Krauss (*Dr Caligari*), Conrad Veidt (*Cesare*), Friedrich Feher (*Francis*), Lil Dagover (*Jane*), Hans H. von Twardowski (*Alan*), Rudolf Lettinger (*Dr Olsen*), Rudolf Klein-Rogge (*captured murderer*).

Clara Bow

The 'It' Girl

Clara Bow was the 'It' girl – the star whose nickname survived after she, and the era that she had lit so brightly, had been long forgotten. She was an uninhibited, exuberant flapper, the embodiment of the Jazz Age and its pursuit of love and laughter

Had Clara Bow died at the peak of her popularity in the late Twenties her face would probably have remained as familiar as that of Jean Harlow and Marilyn Monroe, who both died young. The mention of her name would then have instantly conjured up that vibrant, tousle-haired prettiness which rushed from the screen with so much life to give. But if Clara Bow is remembered at all it is as the 'It' girl, the personification of sex appeal. 'It' was the term coined by the romantic novelist Elinor Glyn and defined, in the hit song by Sigmund Romberg, as 'That improper fraction, of vague attraction, that gets the action, somehow'. Asked to say who she thought had 'It', Madame Glyn mentioned Rex the Wonder Horse, the doorman at her hotel . . . and Clara Bow. She even wrote a script around it for Clara, and in *It!* (1927) the star played a sexy, rumbustious shop-girl who ends up marrying the boss of the department store where she works.

The 'It' girl did not die young. She lived on and faded away, to die at 58 in a Los Angeles sanatorium in 1965. But Clara Bow had packed more living, loving, tragedy and fame into her first twenty-five years than most people do in a lifetime.

It is hard to see Clara Bow's films and not respond to the direct, simple, outgoing charm that had made her the idol of her generation. But while her on-screen image was one of great vitality and a compelling open-heartedness, underneath Clara was wracked by mistrust and nervous instabilities that were the result of a miserable childhood.

She was born on July 29, 1907, the third daughter – and the only one to survive birth – of Robert and Sarah Bow, a poor couple living in Brooklyn, New York. Her mother never recovered from losing her first two children and became increasingly ill. At five Clara watched her grandfather die from a stroke while swinging her in the makeshift swing he had built in the family's two-room apartment; at eight she held her young playmate in her arms as he died from burns.

Left: . . . butter wouldn't melt in her mouth. Below far left: all eyes on the star of Mantrap *– they belong to actors Ernest Torrence (left) and Percy Marmont, director Victor Fleming and cinematographer James Wong Howe. Below left: as* Rough House Rosie *(1927), with sparring partner Reed Howes*

But she wasn't without friends, most of them boys:

'When they played baseball in the evening in the streets, I was always chosen first and I pitched. I wasn't a pretty child at all. . . my eyes were too black and my hair was too red. When I was little, people always took me for a boy.'

The young Clara took solace in the movies and early on decided that she wanted to be a film actress. When she was 14 – and working as a telephone receptionist in a doctor's office – she entered a 'Fame and Fortune' contest run by some of the movie fan magazines. The winner got a silver trophy, an evening gown and a contract for a part in one film. Encouraged by her father, Clara had two pictures of herself taken at a cheap Brooklyn photographer's, sent them in and was one of 12 girls chosen for a screen test – in which she impressed the judges with her range of emotional expression. In November 1921 they announced that Clara was the winner. 'You are going straight to hell,' her mother said, 'I would rather see you dead.'

The small role she won as part of her prize was as a flirt in W. Christy Cabanne's *Beyond the Rainbow* (1922), starring Billie Dove. With no previous screen experience, Clara had to teach herself how to act as well as do her own makeup and provide her own wardrobe. When the film was released her five scenes had been cut out (when she became famous they were reinstated for the movie's reissue), and there was no work forthcoming. She was turned down by the studios for being too young, too little or too fat: 'Usually I was too fat.' But in 1922 she was sent for by the director Elmer Clifton who needed a small, tomboyish girl to play the second lead in *Down to the Sea in Ships*, and had spotted Clara's photograph in *Motion Picture* magazine. The night she got the part her mother came into her room with a butcher's knife, threatening to kill her. While Clara was doing a bit in *The Enemies of Women* (1923), in which she played a flapper who dances on a table, she was home at nights nursing her mother:

Left: in Clarence Badger's film Elinor Glyn expounds on 'It' to store-boss Cyrus (Moreno) – but Clara doesn't bother with words. Below left: as college flapper Cynthia in The Plastic Age, *with Gilbert Roland and Donald Keith. Below: in* Children of Divorce, *with Gary Cooper as the man she ensnares*

'I remember thinking then that fun didn't seem to last very long, that something terrible always happened, and maybe it was the best to get *all* you could get out of it *when* you could.'

While the film was shooting, Clara 'used to be half-hysterical, but the director thought it was wonderful.' Her mother died in a mental hospital at this time and Clara said it was then that her childhood ended. She was 16.

After her first few film appearances audiences had begun to notice her and critics to single her out. She signed with the New York agent Maxine Alton who got her a successful test with former Paramount producer B. P. Schulberg at Preferred Pictures. Clara signed a three-month contract with Preferred at $50 a week, and went to Hollywood. The studio certainly got its money's worth out of her. It was nothing for Clara to shoot two or three movies at once, playing all sorts of parts in all sorts of pictures – nine in 1924, including Frank Lloyd's *Black Oxen*, in which she had a prototype flapper role; fifteen in 1925, including Ernst Lubitsch's *Kiss Me Again*, in which she was a lawyer's stenographer. She also fell in love – with Gilbert Roland, a young Mexican actor then also starting out on his career, whom she met on the set of *The Plastic Age* (1925). They were engaged but parted after 18 months. The affair was no secret. As public interest in Clara Bow registered with the press, they started to feed it with gossip. A rumour became a date, a date a romance, a romance an engagement – which would be broken so there could be further instalments. Clara, simple, open and spontaneous, saw nothing wrong in that, and continued to speak straight, hide little and set herself up to be hurt. She eventually discovered that her directness was rewarded with ridicule.

'If I'm different, if I'm the "super-flapper" and "jazz-baby" of pictures, it's because I had to create a character for myself. They certainly didn't want me'

Meanwhile her career leapt ahead. Her zest for life, her immense capacity for understanding and love of excitement made people rush to see her films. When Schulberg rejoined Paramount he took Clara with him and her contract was bought up by Jesse L. Lasky for a reputed $25,000. No-one yet realized just how sensationally popular she was about to become. Her first film for Paramount, *Dancing Mothers* (1926), gave her third billing as the flapper-daughter of the heroine (Alice Joyce). Soon afterwards the colossal success of *Mantrap* (1926), directed by Victor Fleming, forced the studio to promote her to stardom, over Clara's own objections. Fleming, one of Hollywood's finest directors of women in action, brought out hitherto unknown depths and nuances in her performance as a wise-cracking city manicurist who catches a simple backwoodsman, goes up river with him as his wife, flirts with a lawyer on a hunting trip, only to go back to her lonely husband.

Above: in The Wild Party *Clara's nasal Brooklyn voice was heard for the first time; she played college girl Stella. Above right: in* Dancing Mothers *as the flapper whose man is stolen by her mother. Right: as the golden-hearted ambulance-driver Mary in* Wings

For a time Clara and the older Fleming were a romantic item. Then came her affair with Gary Cooper, whom she met on the set of *Children of Divorce* and who also appeared with her in *It!* and *Wings* (all 1927). Their romance made the headlines, but it fell victim to his jealousy and to her reluctance to settle down.

Increasingly salacious stories of her love life were exaggerated. She spoke of her three affairs up to that time:

'Is that so many romances for a girl of twenty-two? Yet just because I am Clara Bow and it is always printed, it sounds as though I were a regular flapper vamp.'

But the public preferred any news about her

'Being a sex symbol is a heavy load to carry, especially when one is tired, hurt and bewildered'

to none. She had become their idol – the wildest of flappers, the hottest of hot mamas, a woman dedicated to hedonism. *It!* made her their symbol and gave her a tag that she could not shake off. She was branded. Now her films became more lavish but her roles remained the same. Elinor Glyn was not alone in thinking that had Clara not retired from films:

'She would have become one of the greatest artists on the screen, particularly in tragic parts for which she had a far greater aptitude than for the comic scenes which I had to make her act in my films.'

Her directors – Victor Fleming, Clarence Badger, Frank Lloyd – thought the same, but Paramount knew that she would remain a gold-mine as long as they kept casting her as the predatory 'It' girl. Towards this end screen-writers contrived as many situations as possible where Clara would have to strip down as far as was permissible. And as she played an ever steamier succession of virginal hoydens so her fame rose – much faster than her salary, which in 1929 was $2800 a week compared to the $10,000 less popular stars were drawing.

Clara made her talkie debut in *The Wild Party* (1929), which was a personal hit though the idea of sound scared her so much that she delivered her opening line – 'Hello everybody!' – with such force that she broke the light valve in the recording room. But she was not to stay in talkies for long. By now, private mistakes, scandals and studio pressures were beginning to effect her health. An alienation-of-affection case brought against her by a Texan doctor' wife, the scandal of unpaid gambling debts an her on-again off-again romances with othe stars all helped to tarnish her image an damage her popularity. The last straw cam with a court case against her secretary, Dais DeVoe, who had been pilfering Clara's money Found guilty and sentenced to jail, DeVoe sol stories about her employer's supposed privat life to a weekly tabloid, *The Coast Reporter*, t explain how she had been lured into he criminal actions by Clara's loose way of living The ordeal shattered Clara and she had nervous breakdown. She withdrew from *Cit Streets* (1931), which would have reteame her with Gary Cooper, and was admitted to sanatorium for rest.

Left: Clara as Bubbles in Red Hair *(1928), a girl who indignantly returns gifts of clothing to her admirers at a party – only to lose her coat. Above: the fiery Nasa finds true love with Moonglow (Gilbert Roland) in* Call Her Savage, *Clara's penultimate film*

In June 1931, after work had been stopped a another of her films, Schulberg announced at her contract with Paramount had been ncelled at her request. Said Clara years later: 'The thing that burned me up was that the idio did nothing but scold me and threaten e all through the DeVoe trial . . . I had made em millions with what I and many critics ought were lousy pictures, but I received thing but a salary, untrained leading men, d any old story they fished out of astebaskets.'

In 1932 Clara married cowboy actor Rex Bell and announced:

'I can live perfectly well on what Rex earns. . . . Until the right role turns up, I shall continue to turn down all offers. I won't ever play again the sort of stereotyped part I used to have to play. If all producers want me to do is register 'It' and show my underwear, they can keep their parts.'

She made her comeback for Fox, who reputedly offered her $125,000 for two films. In *Call Her Savage* (1932), opposite Gilbert Roland, she played a half-breed Texan wildcat who horse-whips men for laughing at her. After *Hoopla* (1933), in which she played a hula dancer, Clara retired. She made the headlines again when she gave birth to two sons, in 1934 and 1938. But her health was wrecked (she was a chronic insomniac) and she spent more and more time in sanatoriums and mental homes. When her husband – who had been elected Lieutenant Governor of Nevada in 1954, and again in 1958 – died in 1962 they had been living apart for several years.

Shortly before she died, Clara Bow told a reporter about film stardom in the Twenties:

'We had individuality. We did as we pleased. We stayed up late. We dressed the way we wanted. Today, stars are sensible and end up with better health. But *we* had more fun.'

JOHN KOBAL

Filmography

1922 Beyond the Rainbow; Down to the Sea in Ships. **'23** The Enemies of Women; The Daring Years; Maytime. **'24** Grit; Poisoned Paradise; Daughters of Pleasure; Wine; Empty Hearts; This Woman; Helen's Babies; Black Oxen; Black Lightning. **'25** Capital Punishment; The Adventurous Sex; My Lady's Lips; Eve's Lover; The Scarlet West; Lawful Cheaters; Parisian Love; Kiss Me Again; The Primrose Path; The Keeper of the Bees; Free to Love; The Best Bad Man; The Plastic Age; My Lady of Whims; The Ancient Mariner. **'26** The Shadow of the Law; Two Can Play; Dancing Mothers; Fascinating Youth; The Runaway; Mantrap; Kid Boots. **'27** It!; Children of Divorce; Rough House Rosie; Hula; Get Your Man; Wings. **'28** Red Hair; Ladies of the Mob; The Fleet's In; Three Week-Ends. **'29** The Wild Party; Dangerous Curves; The Saturday Night Kid. **'30** Paramount on Parade; True to the Navy; Love Among the Millionaires; Her Wedding. **'31** No Limit; Kick In. **'32** Call Her Savage. **'33** Hoopla.

1

2

4

It comes as a surprise to the viewer to find himself falling for a movie actress in the middle of a war film. But maybe it is because *Wings* is such a male-buddies, danger-charged action picture that the appearance of Clara Bow as Mary – winking at the boy next door, driving an ambulance to the front and dancing in a Paris nightclub – is even more erotic than in those films that exploited her unique sex appeal more conventionally.

Not that the love interest short-changes the action. *Wings* is one of the very few films about aerial warfare that is at once authentic and highly watchable. The familiar problems in films about the war in the air – such as identifying who is piloting which plane and who was shot down in the last exchange of fire – are often produced by the routine intercutting of close-ups of the characters and long shots of the aircraft whose markings must be recognized first before the ensuing action makes any sense. But the director William Wellman had flown with the Lafayette Flying Corps, attached to the French Air Corps, during World War I and the direct experience that he brought to the scenes of aerial combat enabled him to create and sustain the tension of bombing raids and dogfights on the screen.

Another problem encountered in many aerial-warfare movies is that the fields beneath the action look neatly ploughed and hedged rather than scarred with trenches and shell holes. There are no such lapses in *Wings*. Wellman's unit took over a vast tract of land in Texas; the US Army moved in, dug miles of trenches, excavated bomb craters and blasted the few sparse trees to re-create, in all its stark authenticity, the landscape many of them had known at first hand only nine or ten years previously.

Wellman has described how he made the company wait over thirty days until there were clouds in the sky before shooting the epic dogfights. His authority on the set was absolute. When an important banker interrupted him during the shooting of a ground attack, Wellman's concentration lapsed momentarily and as a result an explosion went off in the wrong place, injuring two extras. According to the story, the banker was lucky to escape injury himself – at the hands of the director.

Although Wellman was an active director in the silent era, only *Wings* and *Beggars of Life* (1928) survive from that period of his work. World War I had been strong box-office ever since Chaplin's comedy *Shoulder Arms* (1918) and big star features such as Rex Ingram's *The Four Horsemen of the Apocalypse* (1921) and King Vidor's *The Big Parade* (1925) added to the genre's popularity. Thus *Wings* benefited from a substantial budget that allowed Wellman his cast of thousands and the freedom to use (and blow up) as much artillery as he needed.

Made in the same year as *The Jazz Singer*, the film was, as it turned out, one of the last silent movies about World War I and seems, with hindsight, to be the definitive film on the subject. The scenes of trench warfare and the action behind the lines (the friendship of David and Jack, the 'romance' of Jack and Mary) are as entertaining as any of the aerial sequences, though these remain outstanding as Kevin Brownlow notes in his book *The Parade's Gone By*:

'The camera is in an aircraft for the most memorable scenes; the audience is given the vicarious thrill of shooting down balloons, engaging the enemy in a dogfight, bombing a village, machine-gunning columns of troops, and

A production shot shows the set-up for the complex Paris-café scene, with its big camera boom

3

Directed by William A. Wellman, 1927
Prod co: Paramount. **exec prod:** Adolph Zukor, Jesse L. Lasky. **prod:** Lucien Hubbard. **assoc prod:** B. P. Schulberg. **sc:** John Monk Saunders, Hope Loring, Louis D. Lighton, Julian Johnson. **photo:** Harry Perry, E. Burton Steene, Cliff Blackston, Russell Harland, Bert Baldridge, Frank Cotner, Faxon M. Dean, Ray Olsen, Herman Schoop, L. Guy Wilky, Al Williams. **sup ed:** E. Lloyd Sheldon. **ed:** Lucien Hubbard. **sp engineering effects:** Roy Pomeroy. **mus:** J. S. Zamecnik. **song:** J. S. Zamecnik, Ballard MacDonald. **flying sequences sup:** S. C. Campbell, Ted Parson, Carl von Hartmann, James A. Healy. **length:** 12,267 feet (136 minutes).
Cast: Clara Bow (*Mary Preston*), Charles 'Buddy' Rogers (*Jack Powell*), Richard Arlen (*David Armstrong*), Jobyna Ralston (*Sylvia Lewis*), Gary Cooper (*Cadet White*), Arlette Marchal (*Celeste*), El Brendel (*Patrick O'Brien*), Gunboat Smith (*sergeant*), Richard Tucker (*Air Commander*), Julia Swayne Gordon (*Mrs Armstrong*), Henry B. Walthall (*Mr Armstrong*), George Irving (*Mr Powell*), Hedda Hopper (*Mrs Powell*), Nigel De Brulier (*French peasant*), Dick Grace and Rod Rogers (*aviators*), James Pierce (*military policeman*), Roscoe Karns (*Lt. Cameron*), Carl von Hartmann (*Kellerman*).

chasing and destroying a general's staff car.'

The 'thrill' is reminiscent, for today's filmgoers, of the aerial attack in Francis Coppola's *Apocalypse Now* (1979) and while its power cannot be resisted, there are other notable visual pleasures in the ground-based scenes. Chief among these is the scene in the Café de Paris for which the Paramount technicians constructed a mammoth camera boom that enabled Wellman to film his establishing shot of troops on leave in one extended tracking shot with the camera gliding over the table-tops.

Elsewhere Wellman's subtle visual style is notable in the use of certain motifs: for example, as the critic Richard Combs has pointed out, David's habit of making the motion of a turning propeller as a signal for take-off is echoed in the montage sequence (train wheels turning, a band leader's baton twirling) as Jack arrives home to his hero's welcome after unintentionally bringing about David's death.

Critics quibble about the standard of the acting; but Gary Cooper's cameo as Cadet White made its mark on producers and audiences, and Clara Bow's 'come-and-get-me' flapper at the front is among the most treasurable performances in silent cinema. Unquestionably a worthy winner of the first-ever Oscar for Best Picture, *Wings* was the film its director was most proud of. He had good reason to be.

MARTYN AUTY

Jack Powell, a small-town boy in America in 1917, is in love with the sophisticated Sylvia Lewis and irritated by the constant attentions of the girl next door, Mary Preston (1). But Sylvia's passion for the wealthy heir David Armstrong is interrupted when the two boys enlist in the US Army.

After training they enter the Air Corps (2), where Jack (left) and David (centre) meet Cadet White, who is subsequently killed in a flying accident. Their first aerial engagement (3) is against German air ace Kellerman, who chivalrously lets David go when the young American's machine-gun jams. Jack is shot down but escapes safely via the British lines.

Meanwhile Mary has joined the Women's Motor Corps (4) and follows Jack and David to Paris where, after helping to shoot down a giant German bomber, the boys have gone to celebrate their newly-won medals. She lures Jack away from another girl but is discovered in a state of undress by military policemen and packed off home to America.

Jack and David quarrel over Sylvia. On his next mission David is shot down behind enemy lines (5). He escapes in a German plane only to be attacked and killed by Jack who fires when he sees the plane's markings (6). Jack returns home to a hero's welcome and a new-found love for Mary (7).

7

A Gentleman's Fate: the career of *John Gilbert*

Although the name of Rudolph Valentino remains a household name more than half a century after his death, the same cannot be said of the man who was his nearest rival, and successor, as the foremost romantic idol of the Twenties. John Gilbert, like Valentino, died tragically young, but unlike Valentino he did not die at the height of his fame, and unfortunately the sadness surrounding Gilbert's last years has tended to blot out the success that preceded them. Furthermore, the very distinction of the more significant films in which Gilbert appeared has tended to work against recognition of his own contribution to them: he may have been overlooked amid the attention paid to directors like Erich von Stroheim or King Vidor, and to his leading lady of several pictures, Greta Garbo. Be that as it may, John Gilbert is one of the cinema's neglected luminaries.

John Gilbert was one of the best-known lovers on the silent screen. His great eyes could flash with passion and anger or soften to show pity and remorse. His screen presence was totally dominating, and audiences adored him. And then the fans deserted him, critics panned his films and the studios wouldn't give him work. With the advent of a wonderful new technical innovation – the coming of sound – his career was in ruins

Gilbert, christened John Pringle, was born in Utah – and into show business – in 1897. His father ran a theatrical troupe in which his mother was a performer; after his parents separated he took his stepfather's surname. But it was to his own father that he turned when – after an education in California that was cut short by lack of parental funds – he became set on a show-business career. And, following some experience in repertory, it was through his father's contacts that he gained an introduction to Thomas H. Ince's Triangle studio in 1916. This led to his employment as a bit player at the less than princely salary of $15 a week. Gilbert later described himself as having always been 'movie struck'; it was on Hollywood, rather than Broadway, that his professional sights were set.

Right: Gilbert and Lillian Gish making their own kind of music in the silent La Bohème. *Below: the charming Prince Danilo (right) and* The Merry Widow *(Mae Murray) with a connoisseur of embroidery. Below right: Garbo and Gilbert provided the fire with the smoke in* Flesh and the Devil

Left: a pin-up shot from The Cossacks *(1928), an adaptation of a Tolstoy story. Above: Gilbert's first leading role, opposite Enid Bennett, in* Princess of the Dark *(1917)*

at first . . .

e first film in which he appeared was one of me note, *Hell's Hinges* (1916), now recog-zed as an early landmark in the Western nre, and a key work in the career of cowboy r William S. Hart. A sufficiently sharp-eyed ectator should spot Gilbert in several of the owd scenes.

Advancement could be rapid in those oneering days of the cinema, and within a ar Gilbert – who for several years was billed Jack, the name by which he was known to ends – had progressed to leading roles. The st of these was in *Princess of the Dark* (1917), d two years later he played opposite no less an Mary Pickford in *Heart o' the Hills.* owever, despite this apparent success he idently felt little confidence as a performer, and his insecurity was increased by a brief and unhappy first marriage.

The figure responsible for brightening his professional horizon was the French-born director Maurice Tourneur. Tourneur became Gilbert's mentor, encouraging the screenwriting aspirations with which Gilbert sought to bolster his misgivings about acting. In rapid succession Gilbert contributed to several Tourneur films, starting with a prison drama *The White Circle* and continuing through *The Great Redeemer* and *Deep Waters* (all 1920) to *The Bait* (1921): Gilbert not only acted in the first three, but also served as Tourneur's unofficial assistant and occasional scriptwriter.

Gilbert was then hired by the millionaire Jules Brulatour – at a weekly salary of $1500, a considerable improvement on his earnings of five years before – to direct films starring Brulatour's 'discovery', Hope Hampton. But without Tourneur, Gilbert's confidence evaporated and the only film he directed, *Love's Penalty* (1921), was a complete flop. Gilbert severed the connection with Brulatour and reluctantly returned to acting.

Trying and trying

From 1921 to 1924 he worked for the Fox studio in a variety of indifferent pictures. Studio boss William Fox apparently did not rate Gilbert highly, making the rather ridiculous objection that his nose was unphotogenically large and bulbous. In fact it was in an attempt to offset this alleged disability that Gilbert cultivated the pencil moustache, later to become one of his salient characteristics as a screen idol.

But if most of the Fox films were undistinguished, there was one exception, John Ford's *Cameo Kirby* (1923), a romantic melodrama about the Mississippi river boats of the nineteenth century. (Some of the footage later appeared in Ford's *Steamboat Round the Bend*, 1935.) It is perhaps in *Cameo Kirby* that Gilbert's screen persona first definitively appears. To the role of the Southern aristocrat of the title, reduced by circumstances to being a riverboat gambler, Gilbert brings both a brooding authority and a magnetic sense of refined sexuality. After the film's release Gilbert found himself on the threshold of professional triumph, although his domestic situation was rather less happy – his second marriage, to the actress Leatrice Joy, ended after barely two years, partly, it would seem, because of his dalliance with the Broadway star Laurette Taylor.

Success at last

In 1924, Irving Thalberg signed him up for MGM, and in his first film there, King Vidor's *His Hour* (1924), his playing of a dashing Russian nobleman amplified the romantic appeal he had displayed in *Cameo Kirby*. Over the next few years Gilbert appeared in a wide variety of notable movies: in particular he brought an outward dash and elegance, combined with an affecting suggestion of weakness and vulnerability, to the figure of Prince Danilo in Erich von Stroheim's *The Merry Widow* (1925). That same year he worked again for Vidor on *The Big Parade*. The director has admitted that Gilbert's casting was 'suggested' by the studio – Vidor had initially felt that an anonymous player would be more in keeping with the project – but has also been unstinting in his admiration for the unerring sensibility that the (clean-shaven) actor contributed to the role of a young American recruit in war-torn France.

Certainly *The Big Parade* proved that Gilbert's forte was not merely in glamorous costume roles, although his next two films were of that ilk. *Bardelys the Magnificent* (1926) saw him as a Fairbanks-style swashbuckler, whilst in a version (inevitably non-operatic) of *La Bohème* (1926), his leading lady was the ethereal Lillian Gish, whose painstakingly academic approach to her craft evidently clashed somewhat with his penchant for the spontaneous effect.

Heading for a fall

It was in the following year, however, that Gilbert was first teamed with his most celebrated co-star – Greta Garbo. Their first film together was *Flesh and the Devil* (1927). Ironically, Gilbert was opposed to appearing with Garbo – presumably fearing that she would steal his thunder. However, the pairing proved inspired, and the intensity of romantic feeling in the film, which managed to defy the conventions of the time by including love scenes in a prone position, seems to have derived from a genuine attachment. According to the director Clarence Brown:

'They were in a blissful state of love . . . sometimes I felt I was intruding on the most private of emotions.'

Hollywood legend has it that Gilbert proposed to Garbo and even got her to the door of a Justice of the Peace; but whatever the real story, Garbo eluded him off screen. They made two further silent films together, *Love* (1927) and *A Woman of Affairs* (1928), but though their relationship may by this time have been purely professional, the on-camera chemistry was still highly effective.

Gilbert's last silent films showed his command of the screen undimmed, but with the advent of sound his career disintegrated. The traditional contention that Gilbert's high-pitched voice was his undoing scarcely withstands scrutiny: after all, MGM retained his costly services, and in 1933 again co-starred him with Garbo (apparently at the latter's bidding, after Laurence Olivier proved unsatisfactory to her) in *Queen Christina*. The soundtrack evidence from that film testifies that his voice in talkies was perfectly acceptable. Perhaps Gilbert's *style* of acting did not easily translate to the changed conventions of sound pictures, or perhaps the primitive sound recording of the earliest talkies undermined his self-confidence; in any event, the routine vehicles the studio subsequently found for him can scarcely have helped.

Queen Christina was his last film at MGM The next – his last film of all – was fo Columbia. By this time his private life was i poor shape. There were two more brief mar riages – to actresses Ina Claire (1930–32) an Virginia Bruce (1932–34), the latter his co-sta in *Downstairs* (1932), scripted by himself – an Gilbert's drinking problem was worsening Ironically, his last screen role was as a alcoholic trying to lay off the bottle in *Th Captain Hates the Sea* (1934).

He died of a heart attack shortly after th

Below: gathering the usual crowd as a sideshow barker in The Show *(1927). Below right: Gilbert in his last screen role, as a drunken writer in* The Captain Hates the Sea

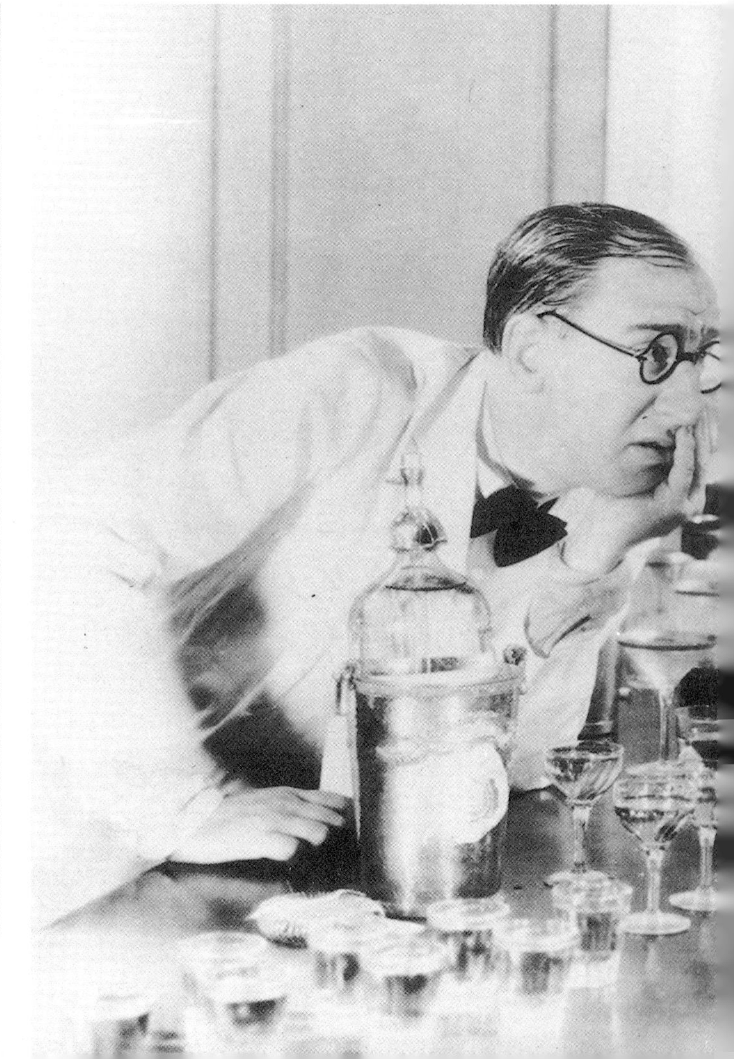

film was released. But despite all the glum attention that his decline and fall have compelled, in the long view of film history he should be remembered as the star of *The Merry Widow* and *Flesh and the Devil* – and as one of the silent screen's Great Lovers.

TIM PULLEINE

Below: although Gilbert minus 'tache was unpopular in The Big Parade, *it was again shown a blade for* Way for a Sailor *(1930). Right: Garbo and Gilbert in* Love *– a silent version of the Anna Karenina story*

Filmography

1916 Hell's Hinges; Bullets and Brown Eyes; The Apostle of Vengeance; The Phantom; The Eye of the Night; Shell 43. **'17** The Mother Instinct; The Devil Dodger; Golden Rule Kate; Doing Her Bit; Princess of the Dark; The Millionaire Vagrant; Happiness; Hater of Men. **'18** Nancy Comes Home; Sons of Men; Shackled; More Trouble; Wedlock; The Mask/The Mask of Riches; Three X Gordon; The Dawn of Understanding. **'19** The Red Viper; The White Heather; The Busher; Widow By Proxy; Heart o' the Hills; Should Women Tell? **'20** The White Circle (+co-sc); The Great Redeemer (+co-sc); Deep Waters (+co-sc); While Paris Sleeps (released 1923). **'21** The Bait/The Bait, or Human Bait (sc. only); The Servant In the House; Love's Penalty (dir; +sc. only); Shame; Ladies Must Live. **'22** Gleam o' Dawn; Arabian Love; Monte Cristo; The Yellow Stain; Honor First; Calvert's Valley; The Love Gambler; A California Romance. **'23** Truxton King; The Madness of Youth; Saint Elmo; The Exiles; Cameo Kirby. **'24** Just Off Broadway; The Wolf Man; A Man's Mate; The Lone Chance; Romance Ranch; His Hour; Married Flirts; He Who Gets Slapped; The Snob; The Wife of the Centaur. **'25** The Merry Widow; The Big Parade. **'26** La Bohème; Bardelys the Magnificent. **'27** Flesh and the Devil; The Show; Twelve Miles Out; Love; Man, Woman, and Sin. **'28** The Cossacks; Four Walls; Show People (as himself); The Masks of the Devil; A Woman of Affairs; Voices Across the Sea (short). **'29** Desert Nights; A Man's Man (as himself); The Hollywood Revue of 1929; His Glorious Night. **'30** Redemption; Way for a Sailor. **'31** Gentleman's Fate; The Phantom of Paris; West of Broadway. **'32** Downstairs (+co-sc). **'33** Fast Workers; Queen Christina. **'34** The Captain Hates the Sea.

1

4

It seems characteristic of the genre that the finest war films only begin to emerge some six or seven years after the historical events that 'inspire' them: *Apocalypse Now* (1979), for instance, is a notable recent example. The pattern was no different for films about World War I. Although Rex Ingram's *The Four Horsemen of the Apocalypse* (1921) was one of the earliest pictures to examine how the experience of war could be related to romance and escapism without compromising the seriousness of the events depicted, it was not until *The Big Parade*, made seven years after the Armistice, that Hollywood attempted to assess the effects of World War I on ordinary people.

In an interview with the critic Richard Schickel, King Vidor described the context of his film:

'Up until that time all the war pictures had been glamorous – fellows with shiny boots, epaulettes and medals and beautiful costumes. And there had never been one about a GI. Just the ordinary guy.'

This populist approach is characteristic of Vidor's most widely admired works – *The Big Parade*, *The Crowd* (1928) and *Our Daily Bread* (1934) – subjects ideally suited to the scale and sweep of Vidor's epic style. The critic Andrew Sarris has noted that: 'Vidor's is an architectural cinema . . .' and illustrates his remark by citing the director's skill in playing off individuals against masses, both social and physical. The role of Jim Apperson (John Gilbert) in *The Big Parade* provides a good demonstration of this point: from the moment of his joining up we see him become, in Vidor's words, 'one of the mob', yet at the same time he remains the point of contact with a larger story that concerns millions of people. Another example of the same counterpointing occurs in the celebrated sequence where the troops move out and Jim's French girlfriend (Renée Adorée) pushes her way through the massed ranks of soldiers to bid farewell to her man.

An even more impressive sequence is that of the American troops' advance through the wood. The audience's concern for Jim's safety (developed through the narrative) becomes an all-embracing empathy that also wills his comrades to survive the German machine-gunning. Here, by tracking in long shot and forcing his actors and extras to keep up a good pace, Vidor succeeds in extending the rhythm – already established in the earlier route-marching scenes – into a crescendo of suspense, culminating in a hand-to-hand battle at the German trench lines.

This moving scene may well have been drawn from the war experiences of the screenwriter Laurence Stallings, who had lost a leg (as does Jim) while serving in the Marines in northern France. Vidor recalled, in conversation with Kevin Brownlow (*The War, the West and the Wilderness*), that it was not so much through Stallings' script as through the conversations the writer and director shared that the scenario for *The Big Parade* was gradually pieced together.

6

7

Authenticity certainly mattered, but it was not Vidor's paramount concern. War Department advisers were attached to the film and many of the extras had seen service in France, as had the art director James Basevi, whose most memorable contribution was the painted-perspective set for the church that is used as a field hospital. But when the second unit was filming in Texas, they shot a spectacular sequence of troops and tank reinforcements being brought up to the front along an endless straight road under frequent aerial attack. Someone remarked that such roads were not to be found in France; for Vidor, however, the power of the image was more important and the sequence remains in the movie.

For all its 'epic' scale and 'universal' subject-matter, *The Big Parade* is a film of surprising intimacy and incidental humour. The scenes with Jim's family, and the food parcel he receives from home containing a rock-hard cake, testify – though somewhat sentimentally – to the strength of family feeling. The episode in which the French girl experiments with chewing gum provides just the right kind of light relief. Most intimate of all, however,

3

8

is the scene in the shell hole into which Jim pursues a wounded German soldier but is unable to finish him off. Jim gives him a cigarette and then, with a gesture of disgust, pushes the German's face away. Moments later the German dies and Jim, shattered by the proximity of death, retrieves the cigarette and smokes it himself. The scene may bring to mind a similar episode at the close of *All Quiet on the Western Front* (1930), but the latter uses action and dialogue to assert its message about pacifism and human brotherhood, whereas the Vidor film conveys as much tragic irony and achieves the same impact through the eloquence of silence. MARTYN AUTY

Jim Apperson watches a parade of volunteers leaving his American home-town for the battle-front of World War I. After an emotional parting from his parents (1) Jim joins up and is soon trained as an infantryman and packed off to France.

Once disembarked, Jim makes friends with fellow soldiers Tim and Slim (2) and meets a young French peasant girl with whom he falls in love (3). The column of troops leaves the town where they are billetted and the girl and Jim are parted (4).

Jim's unit is put through final preparations for battle within earshot of the shelling. The next day, having cleared the forest of snipers (5), Jim, Tim and Slim are cornered and take on a German machine-gun post (6). Several of his comrades are killed but Jim escapes with a minor leg wound (7) and is nursed back to health in a vast church serving as a field hospital. Driven to his girlfriend's village he finds it deserted and is caught in shellfire. This time his leg has to be amputated and, fitted with an artificial limb, he is sent back behind the lines to be reunited with his girl (8) whom he later marries and prepares to take home to America.

Directed by King Vidor, 1925
Prod co: MGM. **prod:** King Vidor. **sc:** Harry Behn, from a story by Laurence Stallings. **photo:** John Arnold. **ed:** Hugh Wynn. **art dir:** Cedric Gibbons, James Basevi. **cost:** Ethel P. Chaffin. **titles:** Joseph W. Farnham. **mus:** William Axt, David Mendoza.
Cast: John Gilbert (*Jim Apperson*), Renée Adorée (*Mélisande*), Hobart Bosworth (*Mr Apperson*), Claire McDowell (*Mrs Apperson*), Claire Adams (*Justyn Reed*), Robert Ober (*Harry*), Tom O'Brien (*Bull/Tim*), Karl Dane (*Slim*), Rosita Marstini (*French mother*).

Pandora's Box

G. W. Pabst's film *Pandora's Box* immortalized Louise Brooks. The American actress' portrayal of the doomed beauty, Lulu, with her startling helmet of black hair, is charged with alluring sensuality combined with a powerfully tragic sense of childlike innocence and vulnerability. Brooks personifies the joy and craving of sex; she is part predator, part supplicant – she both lures men to their death and attracts, like a magnet, her own lewd downfall.

Pandora's Box is based on the plays *Erdgeist* (Earth Spirit) and *Die Büchse der Pandora* (Pandora's Box) by Frank Wedekind, which were first performed in 1893 and 1905 respectively. The Lulu figure is an extension of the mythical Pandora, who, according to Greek mythology, was sent to earth with a box containing all the disorders of the world. In Pabst's film she is surrounded by admirers, though none more fervent than the proper if passionate Dr Peter Schön. Compelled by lust to marry Lulu, Schön himself becomes fatefully intwined in the zestful progress of the *femme fatale*. Lulu is sentenced to prison for Schön's murder, but she manages to escape to continue the good life with Schön's infatuated son, Alwa. Together they flee to England where Lulu, one fog-bound London evening, crosses the path of Jack the Ripper. Legend meets legend, each fulfilling the other's destiny.

Louise Brooks was under contract to Paramount in the autumn of

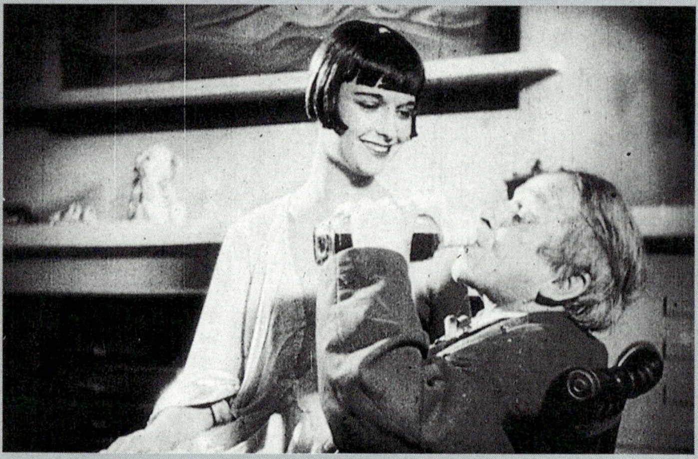
1

2

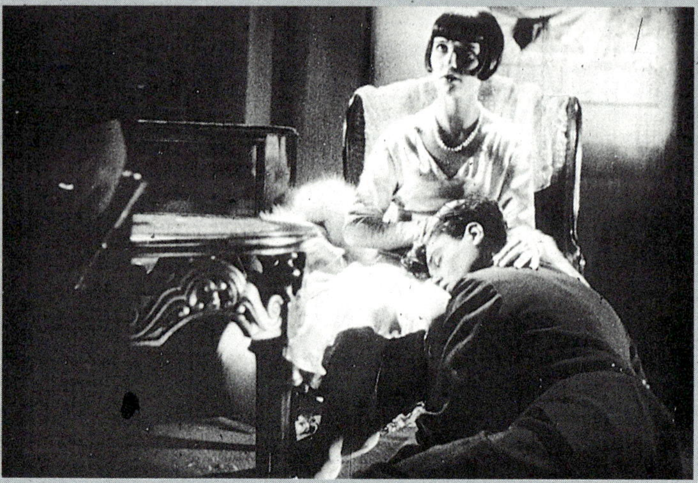
5

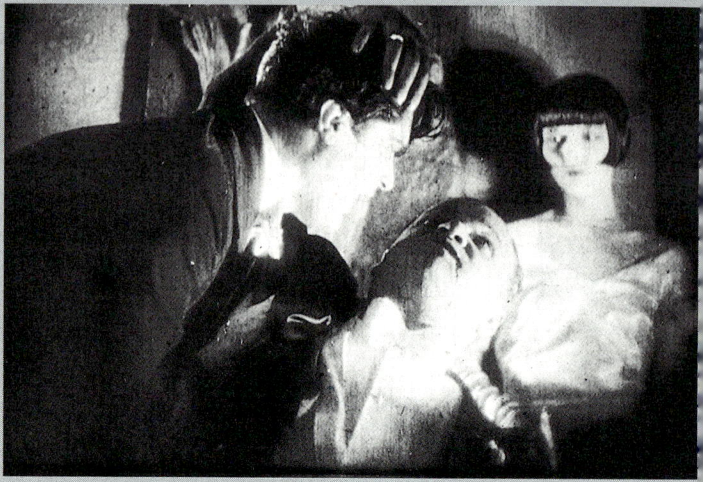
6

1928, when the request arrived from Berlin: could she appear in Mr Pabst's *Pandora's Box?* Marlene Dietrich, two years before *Der blaue Engel* (1930, *The Blue Angel*), had been considered and rejected as being 'too old and too obvious'. Although Brooks' career was by now beginning to languish, because of her inability to make the transition to sound, Pabst nevertheless hit at once on the dualism of the American's appeal. In contrast to her alluring beauty, Pabst placed Lulu in an environment of unutterable degeneracy, attended by the suave and prosperous Schön, his fawning son (played by Franz Lederer, subsequently to become a leading man in Hollywood), a brutish acrobat named Rodrigo Quast, and a sinister, perverse character called Schigolch, also known as Papa Brommer, who clings to Lulu's side like some faithful terrier through all the phases of her ruin.

The artificial gaiety of the opening scenes soon gives way to an almost stifling iconography of humiliation. At the wedding reception for Lulu and Schön, Lulu creates an embarrassing scene with her flirtatious dancing. Schön later discovers his wife in the bedroom embracing Schigolch. He loses his temper and threatens Schigolch with a gun. Schön's humiliation is further aggravated, when he discovers his son, Alwa, with his head on Lulu's lap. Schön reacts with appalling drama: 'Kill yourself!' he hisses at Lulu, thrusting the gun phallus-like towards her face; 'It is the only way to save both of us.' In a clumsy, yet also classical, struggle between the couple, the gun goes off, and Schön is mortally wounded. So the white satin of her wedding gown yields to the black veil of mourning and guilt, as Lulu stands in the court and hears sentence pronounced against her for manslaughter.

The symbols proliferate. A Cairo nightclub owner buys Lulu for 6,000 marks. The hefty trapeze artist, Quast, lurks within range, threatening to blackmail her and return her to Germany unless she joins his variety act. As he leers, a stuffed alligator on the wall behind him reflects his guile.

The epilogue, in London, carries the grace and inevitability of an operatic coda. Lulu's smile is so plangent, even in the bleakness of London's East End, that it beguiles the notorious murderer. She gazes at a candle as though rapt in some mysterious chapel of the mind, as though anticipating the significance of her death. Then the Ripper catches sight of the gleam of a breadknife, and Pabst's close-up of his hand clasped urgently around Lulu's plump white arm has all the force of a violation.

Pandora's Box belongs as much to Pabst as to Louise Brooks. Her brilliance does not efface his talent, as Garbo's does many a journeyman director's. Pabst, after all, had seized and enhanced the gifts of Asta Nielsen, Brigitte Helm, Garbo herself. By opposing the American actress' beauty to the grotesqueries of Berlin high life, he created a rare dialectic, in which the characters are at the mercy of their images. Decadence has seldom appeared so enticing as in *Pandora's Box*. PETER COWIE

Directed by G. W. Pabst, 1929

Prod co: Nero-Film. **prod:** George C. Horsetzky, Seymour Nebenzahl. **sc:** Ladislaus Vajda, from the plays *Erdgeist* and *Die Büchse der Pandora* by Frank Wedekind. **photo:** Günther Krampf. **ed:** Joseph R. Fliesler. **art dir:** Andrei Andreiev. **cost:** Gottlieb Hesch. **r/t:** 131 minutes cut to 120 minutes. German title: *Die Büchse der Pandora*. Released in USA/GB as *Pandora's Box*.

Cast: Louise Brooks (*Lulu*), Fritz Kortner (*Dr Peter Schön*), Franz Lederer (*Alwa Schön*), Carl Goetz (*Schigolch/Papa Brommer*), Alice Roberts (*Countess Anna Geschwitz*), Daisy D'Ora (*Marie de Zarniko*), Krafft-Raschig (*Rodrigo Quast*), Michael von Newlinsky (*Marquis Casti-Piani*), Siegfried Arno (*the stage director*), Gustav Diessl (*Jack the Ripper*).

Lulu is visited in her expensive flat by the shabby Papa Brommer, an old friend (1). He helps himself to her money and liquor and then asks her to dance for him. Lulu's lover, newspaper editor Dr Peter Schön, comes by to tell her he is going to get married. Schön discovers Brommer hiding, and leaves in disgust (2) when Lulu introduces Brommer as her first sugar-daddy.

Schön's son Alwa, who is infatuated with Lulu (3), is writing a musical revue in which she will star. Sometime later Schön, with his respectable fiancée, visits the theatre to see his son's show. Lulu gets upset and refuses to go onstage. While Schön comforts her, his fiancée walks in and catches them embracing. Schön decides to marry Lulu.

On their wedding night Lulu entertains her low-life friends to the dismay of her new husband. Schön enters their bedroom and sees Lulu embracing Brommer. Schön threatens him with a gun (4). The other guests hurriedly leave and Schön, already feeling betrayed, discovers Alwa with his head in Lulu's lap (5). Schön attempts to appease his honour by getting Lulu to kill herself but he is accidentally shot instead (6). She and Alwa flee the country. They are later forced to leave their refuge on a ship after Alwa has gambled away all his money and is caught cheating at cards (7). Lulu, Alwa and Brommer then escape to London where they are reduced to living off Lulu's earnings as a prostitute. But a killer is stalking the streets of the East End. On Christmas Eve Lulu brings a strange client back to her flat (8) . . .

4

8

Louise Brooks

A lust for life

She danced, she acted, she scandalized, she seduced – during her life Louise Brooks has embraced near superstardom and near poverty, but her individuality has always shone through

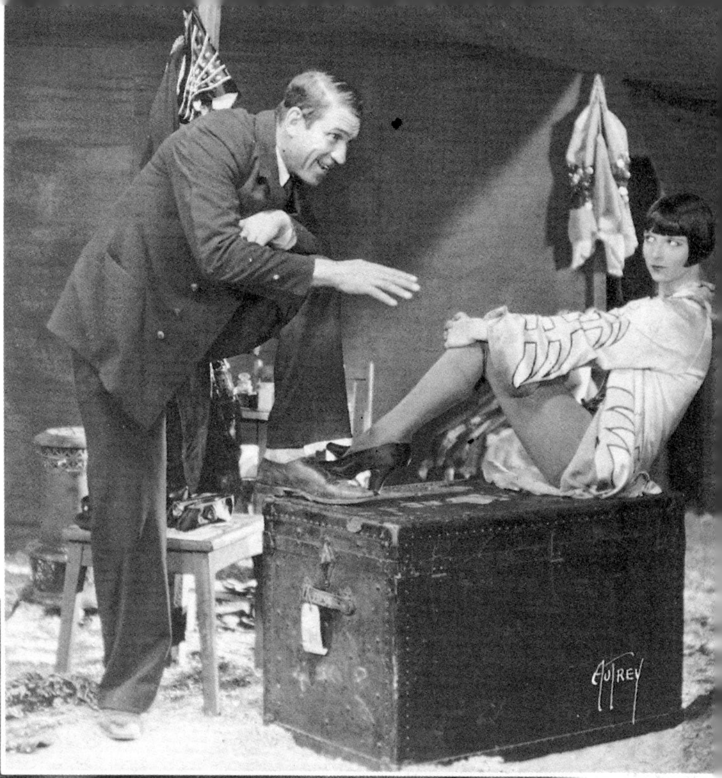

The legend of Louise Brooks is like her screen work: it depends on moments of intense, behavioural immediacy, an animalistic aura that transcends or plumbs far beneath conventional morality. Gazing at her fluctuating appearance – as consuming and as short-lived as breathing – is like looking at the face of a wild animal. The beauty seen is in direct relationship to the creature's freedom from guilt or responsibility. In watching her the basis of the viewer's seriousness is threatened. The very sight of Louise Brooks urges the thought that nothing is as important as the present, and that is why her scattered and frustrating career is so vital to the movies. It is also what makes *Die Büchse der Pandora* (1929, *Pandora's Box*) a lyrical plunge into self-destruction in which the audience is carried deeper by the wanton liveliness of Brooks. This one film is persuasive enough to make it believable that all movies are about the people they show; that actors and actresses always have a large claim on authorship; and that looking at dangerous beauty is the dynamic of all movies.

Stepping out

Louise Brooks was born in Cherryvale, Kansas, in 1906 – although some sources say it was 1900. Her mother encouraged her to dance, and subsequently Louise abandoned high school and went to New York with her dance teacher. Men could no more resist her than they could control her. She would be married twice, involved in countless affairs, and an occasional experimenter in lesbianism. It was a careless life, yet she has survived, arthritic and alone, but seemingly undiminished in her faith in instinct and the moment. That she lived for sex, for its manifestation of life in desire and gratification, is not a scandalous or libellous comment, and that is what is so shocking about her. That, and her sublime refusal to wear the gloomy look of degradation, suffering or ruin that is normally expected to accompany total hedonism. How pleasant to think of the actress now living in Rochester, New York, open to visitors and 'happily in bed with my books, gin, cigarettes, coffee, bread, cheese, and apricot jam'.

In New York City, in 1921, she joined the Denishawn Dancers and began touring the country. But she was fired, not because she was a poor dancer – her body was seethingly mobile, expressive and insolent – but because she was not obedient and not prepared to be a placid servant of boredom. It could be said that she took nothing as seriously as her own pleasures and moods. She joined the George White Scandals; she danced at the Café de Paris in London; and she worked for Ziegfeld – all before she was 20, if the 1906 birth date is to be believed.

Inroads to stardom

Then in 1925, at the Astoria Studio on Long Island, New York, she made a movie for Paramount, *The Street of Forgotten Men*. She was a drifter, fond of movie-making, but unimpressed with Hollywood. In New York, she was still in the Follies, escorted around town by screenwriter Herman Mankiewicz, and already treasured for a biting wit that seemed incongruous in an uneducated Kansas girl. She made *The American Venus* (1926), and then signed a contract with Paramount which led to a run of pictures in which she usually played Manhattan sophisticates – with her jazzy eyes darting out from beneath her glossy cap of black hair, like a child or a nymph hiding, the hair a metaphor for attraction and death. She pouted, she lounged, she danced, and she looked at men as if their wishes were naked; her agile body swayed with amusement and longing. Her silk-sheath dresses were like water on her lean body. And this uncompromising erotic force knew no sentimental saving grace, like love or happy endings. She was utterly demanding, clearly insatiable.

She made *A Social Celebrity* (1926) with Adolphe Menjou; *It's the Old Army Game* (1926) with W.C. Fields, directed by Edward Sutherland, one of her official husbands; *The Show-Off* (1926); *Love 'em and Leave 'em* (1927), seducing the boyfriend of her sister (Evelyn Brent) – testament to her being hotter than the film's nominal star.

Staying till dawn

She moved to Hollywood, made more films, and thrived as an habituée of all-night parties who still managed to look fresh on camera the next day for films such as *Evening Clothes, Rolled Stockings, The City Gone Wild* and *Now We're in the Air* (all 1927). Then in 1928 she was loaned to Fox to play a circus-girl who is loved by two men in Howard Hawks' *A Girl in Every Port*. This situation is not uncommon in Hawks' work, but seldom would he find a woman who so toyed with men, whose erotic energy was so much more ruthless than theirs. It was a key film for Brooks, for it was seen by the German director G.W Pabst, who was looking for an actress who could play the lead role of Lulu in his film *Pandora's Box*.

But first, there were two more American films. In *Beggars of Life* (1928), Brooks spends part of her time masquerading as a boy, in a suit and a flat cap – only to dress up later as a little girl. There is no other film that so clearly

Below, far left: sultry and mysterious – Louise Brooks. Left: she plays a circus performer in A Girl in Every Port, *with Victor McLaglen as one of two men out to gain her affections. Below left: in* Love 'em and Leave 'em *Brooks is a shop-girl who refuses to step down when vying for the attention of her sister's lover*

Top left: her first major role was as the winner of a beauty contest in The American Venus *with Ford Sterling. Left: in* Rolled Stockings *– a glamorous interpretation of college life*

shows her appetite for perverseness, and the innocent delight that removes all traces of guilt from it. Then came *The Canary Murder Case* (1929) with William Powell.

With the coming of sound, Paramount tried to bully Brooks – no salary rise or quit. She walked away and went to Germany at the suggestion of one of her lovers, George Marshall, to make *Pandora's Box*. Pabst, respectably married, adored her – thus, his normally staid directing style burst into nervy life. He deplored the way she lived off screen because it was exactly like Lulu. Brooks merely laughed at this and made even more outrageous what is one of the greatest performances in the movies.

The film is a succession of moments: Lulu swinging on the arm of the strong man; her brow startingly revealed in a lesbian romance; preening like a cockatoo in an early dance of happiness; and, particularly, Lulu's skin and her flimsy dress appearing alike in the fiery light of a theatre props room. With the stout, dignified figure of her lover Dr Schön lost and lovelorn in her burning lap, she looks up with carnal triumph as his fiancée and son appear at the door.

Transient triumphs

She was, briefly, in her element. Pabst hurried her into another film *Das Tagebuch einer Verlorenen* (1929, *Diary of a Lost Girl*) and she also made *Prix de Beauté* (1930, *Miss Europe*) for the director Augusto Genina. In the end, though, she was too demanding for the cautious film industry, too animated, too direct and too aware for its insidious form of sexual exploitation. She made more films in the Thirties, back in America, but they were all duds and humiliations. Her downfall is not easily explained, perhaps because she regarded it as nothing more than the way of a stupid world. She had offended Paramount; she had aligned herself with art pictures, and she had blazed more brightly in *Pandora's Box* than any Hollywood film could countenance; she was bored by old tricks; she was also difficult, volatile and indifferent to money. Hollywood tycoon Harry Cohn offered her renewed stardom if she would be his mistress, but she decided that such a choice would always have to rest with her. She played a supporting part in *It Pays to Advertise* and a smaller role in *God's Gift to Women* (both 1931). She took part in a play, but was fired from the company for being a disruptive force.

She married again, to Deering Davis – a coupling that lasted six months. She appeared in cabaret, and she was all set to play Helen of Troy in Pabst's proposed film of *Faust*. When that fell through she sank to a B Western, *Empty Saddles* (1936), with Buck Jones. Cohn took his revenge for her rejection of him by putting her in the chorus of *When You're in Love* (1937), and she made her last film in 1938, a John Wayne Western called *Overland Stage Raiders*.

Thereafter, by her own account, she lived off rich men, hovering between being a call-girl and taking her own life. She returned to Kansas and tried to teach dance. Restored to New York, she acted in radio soap operas, did odd jobs for publicity agencies, and by 1946 was an unknown sales clerk at Saks Fifth Avenue, a department store. She wrote an autobiography but burnt it, because she felt 'unwilling to write the sexual truth that would make my life worth reading'. She flirted briefly with the Roman Catholic Church and by the mid-Fifties she was broke and nearly as low as Lulu at the end of *Pandora's Box*.

In praise of Louise

Then gradually she was rescued by new admirers. In France, Henri Langlois made much of her at the Cinémathèque, and she might have noticed tributes to her in *Lola Montès* (1955), *Lola* (1961) and *Vivre Sa Vie* (1962, *It's My Life*). In America James Card, curator of film at Eastman House, encouraged her to move to Rochester, New York, where the archive held several of her films. Since then she has written occasional articles on movie personalities – so shrewd and eloquent that her destroyed autobiography must be mourned. She has been the subject of a documentary film by Richard Leacock, and of a *New Yorker* profile by Kenneth Tynan. She emerges from these without bitterness or regret, vibrant and demanding still, always a Lulu.

DAVID THOMSON

Above: Brooks gives a magnificent performance as Lulu in Pandora's Box *– a* femme fatale *who finally becomes a prostitute in London's East End and dies at the hands of Jack the Ripper. Below left: dressed as a boy in* Beggars of Life. *Below right: as Thymiane Henning she finds herself slipping into a sordid existence in* Diary of a Lost Girl

Filmography
1925 The Street of Forgotten Men. **'26** The American Venus; A Social Celebrity; It's the Old Army Game; The Show Off; Just Another Blonde. **'27** Love 'em and Leave 'em; Evening Clothes; Rolled Stockings; Now We're in the Air; The City Gone Wild. **'28** A Girl in Every Port; Beggars of Life. **'29** Die Büchse der Pandora (GER) (USA/GB: Pandora's Box); The Canary Murder Case; Das Tagebuch einer Verlorenen (GER) (GB: Diary of a Lost Girl/Diary of a Lost One). **'30** Prix de Beauté (FR) (GB: Miss Europe). **'31** It Pays to Advertise; God's Gift to Women (GB: Too Many Women); Windy Riley Goes to Hollywood (short). **'36** Empty Saddles. **'37** When You're in Love (GB: For You Alone); King of the Gamblers. **'38** Overland Stage Raiders.

SILENTS OF THE NORTH

Scandinavia filmed its brief summers and snowy winters in the great outdoors, while Germany explored the secrets of the soul in claustrophobic studio interiors

Etymologists often point out that the Scandinavian languages are inextricably bound up with German. Certainly in the pioneering days of silent cinema, the fate of Denmark and Sweden depended in large measure on what was happening south of the Baltic, and vice versa. In modern times, this connection has withered away; but the fact remains that during the second decade of the century the German film industry would actually have collapsed had it not been for an injection of successful movies and talent from Denmark.

Sweden, however, pointed the way forward as early as 1907, when Charles Magnusson was appointed production manager at AB Svenska Biografteatern – the company that still flourishes to this day as Svensk Filmindustri. Magnusson's gifts included a flair for cinematography – he had made his reputation with newsreels – and an administrative efficiency that enabled him to stay at the top as the firm grew under him. He was also anxious to secure respectability for the new medium; he believed that the cinema could fulfil a reforming role and actually influence the way society acted – and reacted. He felt more closely tied to the Swedish countryside than to the urban areas with their theatres and music halls, and he resolved to make more films on location, in natural surroundings.

So this stalwart pioneer, a legend in the Swedish film industry, laid the foundations for a tradition that has continued right through the work of Ingmar Bergman and Bo Widerberg. The virtues commonly associated with Nordic cinema – fine acting, luminous photography, ageless themes, social commitment – may all be ascribed to Magnusson's influence.

Early in 1912, Magnusson gave contracts to Mauritz Stiller and Victor Sjöström. The three men became close friends and, through the next ten years or so, Sjöström and Stiller directed literally scores of films, an achievement that would establish the Golden Age of Swedish cinema, and that led eventually to their both being recruited by Hollywood.

Mauritz Stiller was born in Helsinki in 1883, in a Russian Jewish family who named him Mowsche. At the age of 21, he emigrated to Sweden in order to escape military service (Finland was still at that time under Russian control) and, like Sjöström, was engaged in the theatre until the summons came from the astute Magnusson.

Victor Sjöström was born in 1879, in the heart of one of Sweden's most beautiful provinces, Värmland, near the Norwegian border, and by his early thirties had built up a modest reputation as a travelling actor in Finland and Sweden, eventually running his own repertory company in tandem with another actor. He was startled when Magnusson offered him 15,000 crowns (a tidy sum in those days) to join Svenska Bio, and had his first taste of the movies when he accompanied his new boss to Paris to watch some shooting at the studios of Pathé Frères:

'We saw a scene with Mistinguett, I remember, and the comedian Lehman came in and stumbled over the Diva's legs. It was all enormously amusing, but personally I was more interested by the construction of the studio.'

The two men had to learn the craft of film-making together. They worked in a hot and glaring studio, built of glass, out on the island of Lidingö, to the east of Stockholm. Julius Jaenzon, one of the greatest photographers of the silent period, was already in residence and showed the new directors the ropes. Georg af Klercker (1877–1951), now unjustly forgotten, was head of the studio, although he directed his own best films for another studio, the Hasselblad company in Gothenburg – for example, *Kärleken Segrar* (1916, The Victory of Love) and *Mysteriet Natten Till den 25:e* (1917, The Mystery of the Night of the 25th), which revealed him as a master of both comedy and melodrama.

But Sjöström and Stiller were not merely geniuses in isolation. Both men were undoubtedly impressed by the neighbouring Danish cinema, which had set a fair course long before 1912. Nordisk Films Kompagni had been founded in November 1906 by Ole Olsen, once a penniless farmhand, later a fairground showman and subsequently a cinema owner. Under his leadership, the company became known throughout the world under its trademark – a polar bear atop the globe. All filming was done in the open air, with a hand-cranked camera and a few actors (paid only a derisory sum) posing in front of fragile sets painted to look like interiors. Olsen's early successes were two documentaries, *Bjørnen Løs* (1906, Hunting a Polar Bear) and *Løvejagten* (1908, *Lion Hunting*),

Top: Benjamin Christensen's 1922 survey of Witchcraft Through the Ages *mixed horror and humour in its sceptical view of the occult. It was revived in 1968 with a commentary spoken by the novelist William Burroughs.*
Above: founded in 1906, Nordisk is the world's oldest surviving film company

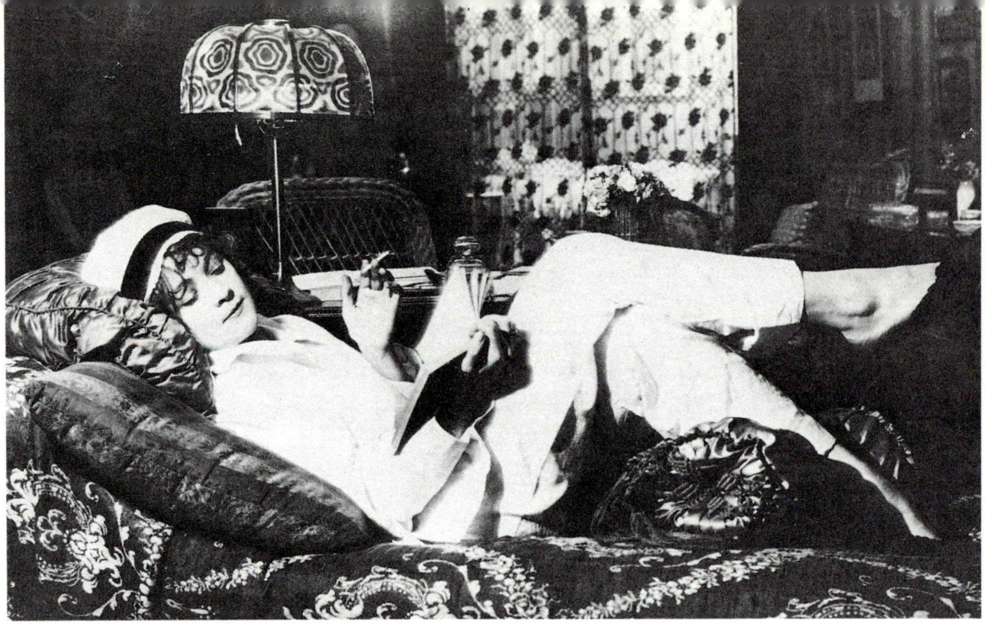

Above: Asta Nielsen played an early prototype of the vamp in her first film Afgrunden. *Top: in* Luffar-Petter *(1922,* Peter the Tramp*), Greta Garbo's first story film, she was one of the Mayor's daughters, taken bathing by a pompous fire-officer (Erik A. Petschler). Top right: Karin Molander in* Love and Journalism *as a reporter who tries to get a story about an explorer by taking a job as a maid in his house – but ends up falling in love with her quarry. Above right: a production shot shows Victor Sjöström as* Terje Vigen, *a fisherman apparently alone at sea in a small boat; in fact the fisherman is standing on a rock into which the mast is fixed*

the sales of which reached as high as 191 and 259 copies respectively, though Olsen's killing of two imported lions for the sake of realism incurred the wrath of the Minister of Justice, who promptly withdrew the showman's exhibitor's licence.

Lion Hunting marked a breakthrough on the international market for Nordisk, and between 1907 and 1910 more than 560 films were produced by Olsen's company. Celebrated stage actors were brought to the screen, among them Bodil Ipsen,

Denmark was an early power on the film scene and reached a peak in World War I, only to fade slowly away during the Twenties

Clara Pontoppidan, Olaf Fønns, Poul Reimert and the legendary Asta Nielsen. Valdemar Psilander was relatively unknown before joining Nordisk, but within a few years he was a household name throughout Europe. He committed suicide, buckling beneath the pressure of his unexpected fame.

Nordisk also housed some of the liveliest directors of the period, including August Blom, Carl Theodor Dreyer, Holger Madsen and George Schnéevoigt. Dreyer began his career in the so-called 'Poets' Caravan' where Nordisk scriptwriters met and worked. He made his debut with *Praesidenten* (1919, The President), the story of a judge with a past, but also completed *Blade af Satans Bog* (1920, Pages From Satan's Book), an imitation of Griffith's *Intolerance* (1916) based on a Marie Corelli novel, before leaving Nordisk. The link with Germany was emphasized when Dreyer made one of his most imposing films there, *Michael* (1924, *Heart's Desire*), from a novel by Herman Bang, about a painter's love for his adopted son, already transposed to the screen eight years earlier by Stiller, under the title of *Vingarne* (1916, The Wings).

Two other significant Danes of the pre-war period were Urban Gad (1879–1947), who helped to turn Asta Nielsen into a star with such films as *Afgrunden* (1910, The Abyss) and *Heisses Blut* (1911, Hot Blood); and the enigmatic Benjamin Christensen (1879–1959), who asserted himself as a master of the horror film before it became a genre, with *Det Hemmelighedsfulde X* (1913, The Mysterious X) and *Haevnens Nat* (1916, Night of Revenge). Christensen produced an extraordinary quasi-documentary in Sweden, *Häxan* (1922, *Witchcraft Through the Ages*), and after a spell in Germany he sailed for Hollywood, where a clutch of horror movies (the best being *Seven Footprints to Satan*, 1929) proclaimed him worthy of comparison with Louis Feuillade and Tod Browning.

Meanwhile, Sjöström and Stiller matched each other stride for stride, with Sjöström often acting in the films of his Finnish colleague. Of the 62 features they directed between 1912 and the end of 1916, virtually all have disappeared or been destroyed by fire. Sjöström's most important work, however, *Ingeborg Holm* (1913, *Give Us This Day*) has survived to attest to its director's attention to detail and fierce sense of social commitment. Ingeborg Holm is flung into the poor-house when her husband dies, and one by one her children are taken from her. She becomes distraught, and by the close of the film is a woman old before her time, nursing a piece of wood and her apron as though they were her long-lost babe-in-arms. The film provoked enormous controversy in Sweden – where it helped to secure an improvement in the Poor Law – and admiration abroad. In England it was reviewed as early as January 1914 under the title *Give Us This Day*.

Stiller's earliest masterpiece was *Kärlek och Journalistik* (1916, *Love and Journalism*), a sparkling comedy about a young female journalist who poses as a maid in the household of a top Antarctic explorer in order to obtain a scoop for her paper. Karin Molander was a delightfully insouciant heroine of this and two other Stiller comedies (which also starred Victor Sjöström): *Thomas Graals Bästa Film* (1917, *Thomas Graal's Best Film*) and its sequel *Thomas Graals Bästa Barn* (1918, *Thomas Graal's Best Child*).

Sjöström embarked on a series of literary adaptations, each more striking than the last. His *Terje Vigen* (1917, *A Man There Was*) was based on the epic poem by Henrik Ibsen about a fisherman who pierces the English blockade of Norway during the Napoleonic Wars, is captured, and after a miserable life finally has the chance of avenging himself on his enemy; instead he relents and his hatred of humanity subsides. Sjöström also adapted several works of the Swedish novelist Selma Lagerlöf.

A Swedish writer who contributed to the major screenplays of both Sjöström and Stiller from 1916 onwards was Gustaf Molander (1888–1973). He eventually became a director in his own right and enjoyed a distinguished career right up to the Sixties – his last film was an episode, shot in 1964 and featuring Ingrid Bergman, in the portmanteau film *Stimulantia* (1967). Molander had a flair for writing dialogue and for directing actresses – for example, Ingrid Bergman in *Intermezzo* (1936).

Below left: Siegfried (Paul Richter) is the heroic adventurer whose murder ends the first part of Fritz Lang's Die Nibelungen, *based on a 13th-century German epic. The British director and film historian Paul Rotha commented: 'For sheer pictorial beauty of structural architecture,* Siegfried *has never been equalled.' But twenty years later the French critic André Bazin complained that the concrete studio-built forest gave no sense of open space*

German exhibitors depended for a livelihood on a flow of films from Denmark prior to the outbreak of World War I and even beyond. Few local directors made any impact, although Richard Oswald, Max Mack and Max Reinhardt all came to the cinema around 1910. Significantly, when the Germans did make their first important film, revealing the themes that would obsess them in the years ahead, it was directed by a Dane, Stellan Rye. This was the first version of *Der Student von Prag* (1913, *The Student of Prague*), which was seen by Sjöström on its release and made a great impression on him. *The Student of Prague* reflected the bizarre, intense vision of the actor and co-writer Paul Wegener (1874–1948), who had acted under Reinhardt, and drew on the work of such writers as E.T.A. Hoffman and Edgar Allan Poe and on the Faust legend, as well as Robert Louis Stevenson's novel *Dr Jekyll and Mr Hyde*, to paint the story of a man whose soul is divided fatally between two conflicting personalities.

Wegener acted in and co-directed *Der Golem* (1913, *The Golem*), which also displayed the penchant for the fantastic that was to distinguish German cinema in the Twenties. Seven years later he remade the picture, with greater resources and power. The Golem is the sacred monster, fashioned from clay, who can rise to help the Jews at times of crisis. Astrology and superstition hold sway, and Wegener as the monster is a curious ancestor of Boris Karloff's monster in *Frankenstein* (1931), awesome yet tender.

At the height of the war, General Ludendorff created a new office under the High Command to co-ordinate photography and film for the war effort. This initiative led to the gathering together of most of the main film companies under one organization: Ufa (Universum Film AG). Nordisk, which itself owned several companies in Germany, had to succumb. The irony of the situation was that within a year Ufa was denationalized; in the wake of military defeat, the Reich abandoned its shares and control passed into the hands of the Deutsche Bank, which bought out even Nordisk. Ufa remained bent on promoting the image of Germany at home and abroad, and to ensure distribution even signed exclusive exhibition deals with cinemas in Switzerland, Scandinavia, Holland, Spain and elsewhere.

Siegfried Kracauer, in his seminal study of the German cinema *From Caligari to Hitler*, has emphasized the mood of intellectual excitement that swept through Germany after the Armistice, a mood described as *Aufbruch* (start, departure). The avant-garde, Expressionist painting and enthusiasm for the film as a medium were all as much to the fore in

Germany as they were in the Soviet Union.

The omens were favourable. Ufa, with its immense financial resources, could offer film-makers every facility they could dream of, and during the last years of the war several directors had emerged, often working with one another, stimulating each other and responding to the atmosphere of revolutionary optimism. Lupu Pick and Emil Jannings stood prominent among players. Joe May, a specialist in thrillers, worked from screenplays written by a young Viennese, Fritz Lang. Arthur Robison and Ewald André Dupont had proved themselves skilled directors. And there was Lubitsch.

Ernst Lubitsch (1892–1947), like practically every bright young member of the German film world at this time, had begun his career under Max Reinhardt in the theatre. He had become an adroit and popular comedian, and by the end of the war was established as his own director. But his real surge to fame coincided with the expansion of Ufa. *Madame Dubarry* (1919, *Passion*) inaugurated Ufa's spectacular new showcase cinema in Berlin, the Ufa Palast am Zoo. One of Lubitsch's protegées was the fiery Polish actress Pola Negri, who had already smouldered in his 1918 version of *Carmen*, but who reached her apotheosis as a vamp in *Sumurun* (1920, *One Arabian Night*), Lubitsch's devastating parody of the Italian epic genre, with Negri as the vixen who dances her way to dusty death at the hands of a lecherous sheik. Lubitsch's gifts encompassed also the traditional German operetta, and he brought a delicate touch to the comedies *Die Austernprinzessin* (1919, The Oyster Princess) and *Kohlhiesels Töchter* (1920, Kohlhiesel's Daughters). Within a couple of years, Lubitsch was resident in the United States, transplanting his singular satirical talent to American soil with remarkable ease.

History has granted the glory to German directors for the great films of the Twenties in Berlin; but Fritz Lang, Robert Wiene, F. W. Murnau and others would have been severely handicapped without the contributions of several distinguished screenwriters. Outstanding among these writers was Carl Mayer, an Austrian, who joined with the Czech poet Hans Janowitz in concocting the script for the most renowned of all German silent films, *Das Kabinett des Dr Caligari* (1919, *The Cabinet of Dr Caligari*). Directed by another Czech émigré, Robert Wiene, this nightmare of a movie, this living testament to the graphic powers of film expression, produced one of the cinema's immortal characters – Caligari (Werner Krauss), a maniac charlatan who exhibits his somnambulist giant Cesare (Conrad Veidt) at fairgrounds. Walter Reimann, Hermann Warm and Walter Röhrig created the brilliant sets for *The Cabinet of Dr Caligari*, with their twisting passages and triangular windows reflecting the vision of a madman. The characters shift in hideous harmony with the objects surrounding them, and in the dormant menace of Cesare lies the embryo of Nazism itself – the true 'serpent's egg' to which Ingmar Bergman referred later in his film *Das Schlangenei* (1977, *The Serpent's Egg*).

Mayer wrote *Hintertreppe* (1921, Backstairs) for Leopold Jessner and Paul Leni, and some key pictures for Murnau: *Schloss Vogelöd* (1921, Vogelöd Castle), a crime story; *Der letzte Mann* (1925, *The Last Laugh*); *Tartüff* (1925, *Tartuffe*); and Murnau's greatest film of his American period, *Sunrise* (1927). His genius comprised both subtle fantasy and social documentary – the documentary streak represented by his outline for Walter Ruttmann's *Berlin, die Symphonie einer Grossstadt* (1927, *The Symphony of a Great City*).

The winding path of fantasy and terror pursued by many of the German directors ended in a cul-de-sac. Films like Arthur Robison's *Schatten* (1923, *Warning Shadows*) and Paul Leni's *Das Wachsfigurenkabinett* (1924, *Waxworks*) have lost their hallucinatory quality with the years and linger, heavy-footed, as mere parodies of Expressionist art.

Above: this tale of love, jealousy and murder in the circus was shown in Ufa's top Berlin cinema. Right: Madame Dubarry *(Pola Negri), once mistress of the late Louis XV, dies in the French Revolution. Far right: Fritz Kortner as the jealous husband in* Warning Shadows. *Bottom far right: Max Schreck as* Nosferatu, the Vampire. *Below right: Paul Wegener as the monster in* Der Golem: Wie er in die Welt kam *(1920,* The Golem*)*

Fritz Lang (1890–1976) may be regarded as the most versatile of all German directors of the Twenties, able to turn his hand to everything from legend to fantasy, from thrillers to melodrama. In 1920, with the two-part commercial hit *Die Spinnen* (1919–20, *The Spiders*) behind him, he began writing screenplays with his future wife Thea von Harbou, and the following year earned his critical spurs with *Der Müde Tod* (1921, *Destiny*), an allegory about the struggle between Love and Death, notable for its awesome decors. Lang was attracted to figures of colossal dimensions, whether in the past or the present. His arch-criminal, Dr Mabuse, seemingly harbours a yearning to rule the world in *Dr Mabuse der Spieler* (1922, *Dr Mabuse, the Gambler*) and a similar villain predominates in *Spione* (1928, *The Spy*). These films were set in the present or immediate past. *Die Nibelungen* (1924) – made in two parts, *Siegfried* and *Kriemhilds Rache* (*Kriemhild's Revenge*) – plunged back into the Middle Ages, searching for a mythical, epic hero to inspire the Germans once more. The two films were shot in the months of 1923 that saw Germany reach its post-war nadir, with the currency plummeting in value, members of the ultra-left manning the barricades in Hamburg, and Hitler leading an abortive *Putsch* in Munich. They were dominated by massive sets, enormous staircases, vast artificial forests – a feat of production design, curiously combining ancient and modern.

Yet Lang's insatiable imagination drew him to visions of the future too. The most spectacular of all

his films remains *Metropolis* (1927), and if the early scenes appear lugubrious in pace, as groups of workers relieve each other with the metronomic shuffle of robots, this seems justified by the dynamic climax when the 'slaves' run riot, destroying the machines that oppress them and thereby flooding their own homes. The acting mars *Metropolis*, and its false sentimentality and genuflection to power are less repulsive than ludicrous. Less trumpeted, yet more accurate in its prognosis of the future, was Lang's *Frau im Mond* (1929, *The Girl in the Moon*), a science-fiction story that anticipated the use of spacecraft in the Sixties and Seventies.

Around the middle of the decade, German artists came to contemplate their society with a numbed, somewhat cynical gaze, a feeling known as the *Neue Sachlichkeit* ('New Objectivity' or 'New Realism'). Resigned, disillusioned, appalled, these film-makers recorded the reality around them with a jaundiced eye. Walter Ruttmann, in *The Symphony of a Great City*, follows the life of the German capital from dawn to night; he shows a girl drowning herself, and observes the cold disdain mingled with curiosity in the faces of those watching from a nearby bridge. This indifference is stressed again and again, with shots of tailors' dummies standing in shop windows. The inhabitants of Berlin respond to the promptings of the city as automatically as do machines when the levers are depressed.

The director G. W. Pabst also embraced the New Realism: 'What need is there for romantic treatment? Real life is too romantic, too ghastly.'

But the film that bridged the past and the contemporary, taking pleasure in nostalgia while at the same time opting for a naturalism of tone, was E. A. Dupont's *Varieté* (1925, *Vaudeville*), based on a novel by Felix Holländer about a circus director who abandons his wife for a luscious young trapeze artiste, only to be ousted by a handsome acrobat, whom he subsequently kills. Emil Jannings, as the showman forced to experience first elation and then spiritual degradation, is acknowledged by the director Ingmar Bergman as the model for his similar character Albert Johansson (Åke Grönberg) in *Gycklarnas Afton* (1953, *Sawdust and Tinsel*). Dupont, who in 1911 had flourished as one of the first film critics at work in Germany, here achieved the summit of his career; and Karl Freund, the cameraman, follows the curling flight of the trapeze with as much voluptuous delight as he follows the doomed man's sojourn in prison, the huge number 28 on his back conveying at once anonymity and disgrace.

F. W. Murnau (1888–1931) survived the vicissitudes of the German cinema in the Twenties, and succeeded in his brief Hollywood heyday in establishing a name there also, above all for *Sunrise*, which won for its leading actress, Janet Gaynor, one of the first Academy Awards in 1928. Murnau sought in his first major work, *Nosferatu, eine Symphonie des Grauens* (1922, *Nosferatu, the Vampire*), to tackle the extremes of fantasy with a realism that involved shooting in streets rather than in studios and testing the potential of deep-focus photography. The texture of *Nosferatu, the Vampire* (based on Bram Stoker's *Dracula*) is boldly naturalistic. In *The Last Laugh*, Murnau dispensed with titles, letting the story come across by visual means, and gave Karl Freund the chance to strap a camera to his chest and reel around, simulating the drunken stupor of the old porter (Emil Jannings) whose self-respect has been stripped from him by the hotel management. With its sense of outrage against a decadent society and its unerring sense of the visual panache of which cinema is capable, *The Last Laugh* abides as the greatest German film of the Twenties – a perfect union of form, content and style.

PETER COWIE

Sweden's silent masters
Victor Sjöström and Mauritz Stiller

In the clear early light of the Swedish cinematic dawn, two giants stood out – Victor Sjöström and Mauritz Stiller – great directors who were destined to make a mark in Hollywood but flourished best under a northern sky

Although Victor Sjöström and Mauritz Stiller each directed about five or six films a year between 1912 and 1916, their genius only began to blossom from about 1917 onwards. Their hectic pace slowed. They devoted more time to each production. The result was a steady stream of excellent, often brilliant, films that brought the Swedish cinema to the forefront – impressing even the Americans.

American producers have a long history of coveting foreign talent. The undoubted gifts – and success – of *two* Swedish directors were indeed proof that Sweden knew a thing or two about film-making. In the early Twenties both were invited to Hollywood. But what the American moguls had failed to perceive was that Stiller and Sjöström – like many artists – drew direct inspiration from their country's emotions, experience and daily rhythm. In 1917, for example, Victor Sjöström took his tiny crew and his actors up to the mountains of Lappland to shoot *Berg-Ejvind och Hans Hustru* (1918, *The Outlaw and His Wife*), a dour story of a man, played by himself, who steals a sheep to feed his starving family, is outlawed, and – in spite of the love of the loyal Halla (played by Sjöström's wife, Edith Erastoff) – comes to a miserable end in the mountains. But nature has at least granted the outlaw and his wife a brief summer to enjoy together, and in the throes of his hunger, huddling in the tiny mountain hut, Berg-Ejvind summons up moments of sunshine and happiness from his youth. Sjöström's skill at knitting together past and present in a series of short, wrenching spasms, and his own intrepid performance (dangling by rope from a high cliff at one point) as the hero mitigate the puritanism of the piece. Man may be at the mercy of nature, but is also ennobled by its all-pervasive presence, and in *The Outlaw and His Wife* Sjöström was articulating a kind of pantheism that would distinguish many Swedish films of the future.

The sweet smell of the States

Sjöström had grown up in the same province as the Nobel Prize-winning authoress Selma Lagerlöf, and brought to his adaptations of her work a lively sympathy and understanding. *Tösen Från Stormyrtorpet* (1917, *The Woman He Chose*) took pity on a peasant girl saddled with an illegitimate child. *Ingmarssönerna* (1919, The Sons of Ingmar), released in two parts, was a morality about a stolid Swede who clambers towards heaven on a gigantic ladder in order to consult his ancestors about his difficulties on earth; and *Körkarlen* (1921, *The Phantom Carriage*) was a severely cautionary tale about the dangers of alcoholism.

And yet *The Phantom Carriage* must be accounted a Sjöström masterpiece: not so much because of its content (as an actor Sjöström himself was, like Douglas Fairbanks, at his best in action roles, and rather ponder ous in introspective ones), but rather oı account of its dazzling technique. Sjöström ha already proved himself imaginative at usin flashbacks; and here the drunken past of th hero David Holm (Sjöström) is reconstructed ı a skein of recollections while he himself wait in a churchyard for Death's wagon to bear hir away. Julius Jaenzon's photography excels ı enabling the director to superimpose as man as four images on a single frame, creating ghost-like effect so that in a very palpabl fashion Holm's soul seems to take leave of hi body.

Soon after making *Vem Dömer?* (1922, *Love' Crucible*) – a lavish, rather portentous evo cation of Renaissance Italy – Sjöström wa contacted by MGM. Charles Magnusson, hea of Svensk Filmindustri, supported the idea c his most prominent director's departure, bot because he sensed that his vitality was ebbin and needed a fresh stimulus, and also becaus Svensk Filmindustri was anxious to secure th sole rights to MGM pictures in Sweden. So, o

Above left: Sjöström (left) and Stiller with Garbo in Hollywood. Below: in The Wind, *Letty (Lillian Gish) buries the man she has killed*

January 10, 1923, Victor Sjöström set sail for America, confident of the future and aware that, due to his having lived in the States for the first few years of his life (his father had settled there briefly), his fluency in English would enable him to cope with the rigours of filming in Hollywood.

Mauritz Stiller's saga

Stiller, too, was destined to make the journey to Los Angeles, but his achievements in the six years between 1918 and 1924 if anything surpassed those of his great friend and rival. In *Erotikon* (1920, *Bonds That Chafe*), he established the pattern of sophisticated, upper-class comedy that would be elaborated upon in the years ahead by Lubitsch and DeMille. *Erotikon* remains an elegant pirouette of a film, sensational at the time because of its lack of inhibitions and its *risqué* innuendoes.

Like Sjöström, Mauritz Stiller turned to the stories of Selma Lagerlöf for some of his greatest works. *Herr Arnes Pengar* (1919, *Sir Arne's Treasure*) unfolds in sixteenth-century Sweden, with the discovery of a conspiracy among the Scottish mercenaries of King Johann III. The mercenaries escape from prison, loot and pillage a splendid manor belonging to Sir Arne, and make off with his treasure. But the box is too heavy, and the robbers have to abandon it on the ice. Their rapacity leads to the death of the waif-like Elsalill (Mary Johnson), who has fallen in love with the mercenaries' leader; and the scene of her funeral cortège slowly wending over the ice at Marstrand constitutes one of the most enduring of all Swedish film images.

Yet another Lagerlöf novel, *Gunnar Hedes Saga* (1923, *Gunnar Hede's Saga*) breathes a strange power and fervency in its screen version by Stiller. An introspective young man, devoted to the violin, suddenly flings up his life and treks to the north of Sweden, where he buys a herd of reindeer and drives them southwards. Half-fantasy, half-documentary, *Gunnar Hede's Saga* demonstrates Stiller's ability to cope with both the epic genre and the fluctuations of memory – a fascination common to Lagerlöf, Sjöström and Stiller.

Stiller looked to a novel by one of his Finnish fellow-countrymen, Juhani Aho, for the equally impressive *Johan* (1921), which encapsulates the now familiar Nordic theme of the 'Dark Stranger' who comes out of the wilds to enlarge the vision of a staid and sheltered housewife. Stiller's treatment lends it an irony as well as a whirling passion.

Gösta Berlings Saga (1924, *The Atonement of Gösta Berling*), based on one of Selma Lagerlöf's greatest novels, was to be Stiller's last Swedish film, but the one destined to set a young Swedish actress, Greta Garbo, on the path to fame. The film survives as a swansong to the glory of the Swedish silent cinema, rich in tableaux, yet laborious in pace.

Stiller was restless. He took Garbo and his cameraman, Julius Jaenzon, to Istanbul in the hope of shooting a film in Turkey for a German company. But the finance never materialized, and Stiller returned to Berlin, where he managed to strike a contract for Garbo to appear in G. W. Pabst's *Die freudlose Gasse* (1925, *The Joyless Street*). While in the German capital, he met Louis B. Mayer, who screened *The Atonement of Gösta Berling* and saw in Greta Garbo a potential star for MGM. Reluctantly, he took Stiller along on her coat-tails, although at this stage Garbo relied totally on her mentor for any decision concerning her career. And on July 5, 1925, they both arrived in New York, a little bewildered and somewhat neglected by the officials of MGM.

He who gets trapped

Although Victor Sjöström, with his command of the language and his sunnier nature, fared better than Stiller in Hollywood, the cruel fact is that neither of them really fulfilled the high hopes vested in him. For Sjöström, as he said in an interview, the worst moment came when, fresh from Sweden:

'. . . my wife and all the associations of a lifetime left behind, I felt lost among the big sets and technical facilities of which I understood next to nothing, and wondered if the day would come when I'd be on my way back to Sweden, a failure.'

For Stiller, the first year in America was hell. He suffered from rheumatism, was left without an assignment by MGM, and when at last he was allowed to direct Garbo in *The Temptress* (1926), he told Sjöström that:

'. . . they engage me because they think I have good ideas about how films should be made, and then I'm not allowed to do anything without the busybodies interfering everywhere.'

Sjöström's name was changed to Seastrom

Right: Sjöström and his wife Edith Erastoff as The Outlaw and His Wife. *Below right: the soul of David Holm (Sjöström) leaves his body in* The Phantom Carriage. *Below: Marianne (Greta Garbo) and her true love Lucien (Lars Hanson) in* The Divine Woman

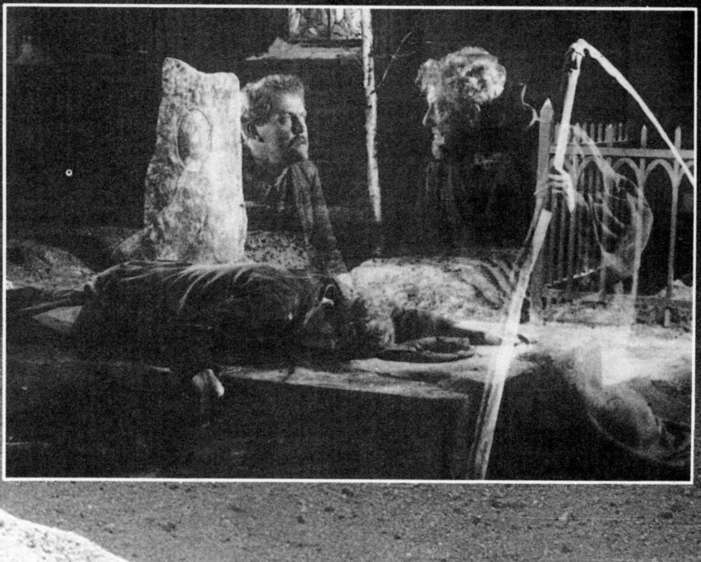

so that Americans might be spared the rotundities of Swedish pronunciation, and he completed nine features – including one with Garbo, *The Divine Woman* (1928) – during his six-year stay in Hollywood. From this point of view, he proved infinitely more successful than Stiller, who worked on a mere five films, three of which were swept out of his hands and completed by journeyman directors.

Few of the American films of either man have survived. But *He Who Gets Slapped* (1924) is an astonishing achievement, in which Sjöström not only masters the more sophisticated technical apparatus available to him in Hollywood, but brings to the story of humiliation and revenge a blistering irony quite absent from his Swedish pictures. Lon Chaney, as the embittered scientist turned clown, gives a superb performance, and the film opened to record business throughout the country. By August 1925, Sjöström was earning $30,000 a film and had even, in *The Tower of Lies* (1925), been allowed to make a screen version of a Selma Lagerlöf novel, set in their native Värmland.

The victors return

It was his two films starring Lillian Gish that assured the success of Victor Sjöström's career in Hollywood. *The Scarlet Letter* (1926) was based on Nathaniel Hawthorne's novel, a stern tale of intolerance, tinged with a ghastly humour reminiscent of *The Phantom Carriage*. Scripted by the versatile Frances Marion, *The Scarlet Letter* also featured Lars Hanson, who had joined his expatriate friends in the movie colony and was under contract to MGM.

The Wind (1928) marks perhaps the peak of both Sjöström's and Gish's careers. Although inspired by a book by Dorothy Scarborough, set in a desolate stretch of Texas, the film exemplifies a particular theme of Sjöström's – that man drifts ultimately at the mercy of his environment and the elements. Wind and sand are all-pervasive. The ranchers live with the threat of starvation constantly at hand; men and beasts alike are helpless in the harsh landscape. As Letty, the demure young woman forced to murder a mysterious assailant during a storm, Lillian Gish gives as convincing a portrayal of raw-nerved hysteria as she had done in *Broken Blossoms* (1919). Few scenes in silent cinema are so gripping as the climax of *The Wind*, with the gale whipping the sand inexorably away from the shallow grave where Letty has buried her victim.

In *The Masks of the Devil* (1928), Sjöström again made skilful use of superimposed imagery, as he had done in *The Phantom Carriage*. His final Hollywood picture was *A Lady to Love* (1930), a screen version of the stage comedy b Sidney Howard, in which the young Edward G Robinson had a role. In April 1930, Victo Sjöström returned permanently to Sweden where he made the occasional picture bu turned increasingly to acting, becoming father-figure to many a new Swedish director Among them was Ingmar Bergman, who pai homage to the master by starring him in bot *Till Glädje* (1950, *To Joy*) and *Smultronställe* (1957, *Wild Strawberries*). He died in 1960.

Of the various productions on whic Mauritz Stiller was unhappily involved, *Hote Imperial* was accorded the best reception. Re leased in 1927, it was based on an espionag romance by the Hungarian writer Lájos Birć and starred Pola Negri. Both reviews and box office figures were excellent, and Stiller wa whipped away from MGM by Paramount, t the tune of $2500 a week. But poor health combined with a refusal on Stiller's part t immerse himself in American life or society contributed to the decline of his career. Hi final assignment, *The Street of Sin* (1928), wa completed by Ludwig Berger, and Stiller, ailin and disillusioned, departed for Sweden. Les than a year later he collapsed and was rushe to hospital. Sjöström, home for a trip, manage to visit his bedside just before Stiller died, i 1928, at the age of only 45. PETER COWI

Victor Sjöström: filmography

1912 Trädgårdsmästaren (+act); De Svarta Maskerna (actor only); I Lifvets Vår (actor only); Lady Marions Sommarflirt; Äktenskapsbyrån; Ett Hemligt Giftermål/Bekännelsen på Dödsbädden. **'13** Löjen och Tårar; Halvblod; Barnet (actor only); Vampyren/En Kvinnas Slaf (actor only); När Kärleken Dödar (actor only); Blodets Röst (+sc; +act); Livets Konflikter (co-dir; +act); Ingeborg Holm (GB: Give Us This Day). **'14** Prästen: Kärlek, Starkare Än Hat; Miraklet; Bra Flicka Reder Sig Själv; Dömen Icke; För Sin Kärleks Skull (actor only); Gatans Barn; Högfjällets Dotter (+sc; +act); Hjärtan som Mötas; Det Var i Maj. **'15** En av de Manga (+sc); Sonad Skuld (+co-sc); Strejken (+co-sc; +act); Skomakare Bliv Vid Din Läst; Judaspengar. **'16** Landshövingens Döttrar (+sc); Havsgamar; I Prövningens Stund (+co-sc; +act); Skepp som Mötas; Hon Segrade (+co-sc; +act); Thérèse (+co-sc); Guldspindeln (actor only); Dodskyssen (+co-sc; +act). **'17** Terje Vigen (+co-sc; +act) (GB: A Man There Was); Thomas Graals Bästa Film (actor only) (GB: Wanted, a Film Actress; retitled: Thomas Graal's Best Film); Tösen Fran Stormyrtorpet (+co-sc) (GB: The Woman He Chose). **'18** Berg-Ejvind och Hans Hustru (+co-sc; +act) (USA: You and I; GB: Love, the Only Law; retitled: The Outlaw and His Wife); Thomas Graals Bästa Barn (actor only) (GB: Thomas Graal's Best Child). **'19** Ingmarssönerna (two parts) (+ sc; + act); Hans Nåds Testamente (GB: His Grace's Last Testament). **'20** Klostret i Sendomir (+sc) (GB: Secret of the Monastery); Karin Ingmarsdotter (+co-sc; +act) (GB: God's Way); Mästerman (+act). **'21** Körkarlen (+sc; +act) (USA: The Stroke of Midnight: GB: Thy Soul Shall Bear Witness/The Phantom Carriage). **'22** Vem Dömer? (+co-sc) (USA: Mortal Clay; GB: Love's Crucible); Det Omringade Huset (+co-sc; +act). **'23** Eld Ombord (+act); Name the Man (USA). **'24** He Who Gets Slapped (USA). **'25** Confessions of a Queen (USA); The Tower of Lies (USA). **'26** The Scarlet Letter (USA). **'28** The Wind (USA); The Divine Woman (USA); The Masks of the Devil (USA). **'30** A Lady to Love (USA). **'31** Markurells i Wadköping (+act) (German version: Väter und Söhne); Brokiga Blad (actor only). **'34** Synnöve Solbakken (actor only). **'35** Valborgsmässoafton (actor only). **'37** John Ericsson Segraren vid Hampton Roads (actor only); Under the Red Robe (GB). **'39** Gubben Kommer (actor only); Mot Nya Tider (actor only). **'41** Striden Går Vidare (actor only). **'43** Det Brinner en Eld (actor only); Ordet (actor only). **'44** Kejsarn av Portugallien (actor only). **'47** Rallare (actor only). **'48** Jag Är Med Eder . . . (actor only). **'49** Farlig Vår (actor only). **'50** Till Glädje (actor only) (GB: To Joy); Kvartetten som Sprängdes (actor only). **'52** Hård Klang (actor only); Kärlek (actor only). **'55** Männen i Mörker (actor only). **'57** Smultronstället (actor only) (GB: Wild Strawberries).

Mauritz Stiller: filmography
1912 Mor och Dotter (+sc; +act); De Svarta Maskerna (+co-sc); Trädgårdsmästaren (sc. only); I Lifvets Vår (actor only); Den Tyranniske Fästmannen (+sc; +act). **'13** Vampyren/En Kvinnas Slaf (+sc; +act); När Kärleken Dödar (+co-sc); När Larmklockan Ljuder (+sc); Barnet (+co-sc); Den Okända (+sc); Kammarjunkaren (+sc); På Lifvets Ödesvägar/Smugglarne; Gränsfolken; Den Moderna Suffragetten/I Mrs Pankhursts Fotspår (+sc); Livets Konflikter (co-dir. uncredited; +sc); Mannekängen (+sc) (unfinished). **'14** Bröderna (+co-sc); For Sin Kärleks Skull (+sc); Stormfågeln; Skottet; Det Röda Tornet (+co-sc); När Konstnärer Älska; När Svärmor Regerar/Så Tuktas-Äkta Män! (+sc; +act). **'15** Lekkamraterna (+co-sc); Hämnaren; Hans Hustrus Förflutna; Madame de Thèbes (GB: Son of Destiny); Hans Bröllopsnatt/Bröllop Med Förhinder; Mästertjuven; Minlotsen. **'16** Lyckonålen (+co-sc); Dolken; Kärlek och Journalistik (GB: Love and Journalism); Kampen om Hans Hjärta; Vingarne (+co-sc; +act); Balettprimadonnan (GB: Anjala, the Dancer). **'17** Thomas Graals Bästa Film (GB: Wanted, a Film Actress; retitled: Thomas Graal's Best Film); Alexander den Store (+sc) (GB: Alexander the Great). **'18** Thomas Graals Bästa Barn (+co-sc. under pseudonym) (GB: Thomas Graal's Best Child). **'19** Sången om den Eldröda Blomman (+co-sc. under pseudonym) (GB: The Flame of Life); Herr Arnes Pengar (+co-sc) (USA: Sir Arne's Treasure; GB: Snows of Destiny; retitled Sir Arne's Treasure). **'20** Fiskebyn (+co-sc) (GB: Chains); Erotikon/Riddaren av Igår (+co-sc) (GB: Bonds That Chafe). **'21** Johan (+co-sc); De Landsflyktige (+co-sc) (USA: In Self Defence). **'23** Gunnar Hedes Saga/En Herrgårdssägen (+sc) (USA: The Blizzard; GB: The Judgment; retitled: Gunnar Hede's Saga). **'24** Gösta Berlings Saga (two parts) (+co-sc) (USA: The Legend of Gösta Berling; GB: The Atonement of Gösta Berling). **'26** The Temptress (co-dir; +co-sc) (USA). **'27** Hotel Imperial (+co-sc) (USA); The Woman on Trial (+co-sc) (USA); Barbed Wire (co-dir) (USA). **'28** The Street of Sin (co-dir) (USA).

Top far left: Lon Chaney as the clown, with Norma Shearer and John Gilbert, in He Who Gets Slapped. *Top left: Sjöström's last role, with Bibi Andersson, in* Wild Strawberries. *Top right: Nils (Einar Hanson) plays for Ingrid (Mary Johnson) in* Gunnar Hede's Saga. *Right: Sir Archie (Richard Lund) woos Elsalill (Mary Johnson) in* Sir Arne's Treasure. *Below right: Pola Negri as a servant and George Siegmann as a drunken officer in* Hotel Imperial. *Below: Greta Garbo as* The Temptress

No-one now will ever see Mauritz Stiller's last Swedish film, *The Atonement of Gösta Berling*, in its original form. A vast fresco of life in early nineteenth-century Sweden, drawn from a long and complex novel by Selma Lagerlöf, the film was released, as Stiller had planned, in two parts totalling some three hours. After Stiller's death in 1928, his script assistant, Ragnar Hyltén-Cavallius, cut the film by about half and added a musical score. In the Seventies, the Swedish Film Institute completed what restoration was possible, but even that version is some way short of the original.

The cutting of the film had of course been motivated by the desire to emphasize the part played by Greta Garbo, making her second film appearance. But as the film deals with the interlocking lives of three families, the Elisabeth Dohna character (played by Garbo) is in fact no more important than eight or ten others in the film. Thus the shortened version loses all balance.

The Atonement of Gösta Berling was the last great work of the golden period of Swedish silent film. Two directors, Stiller and Victor Sjöström, had given the period its shape and richness; Sjöström later went to America, followed by Stiller in 1925. *The Atonement of Gösta Berling* was a summation, an epitaph, of the period. The great virtue of the Swedish school had been the use it had made of natural landscape. This is aptly reflected in *The Atonement of Gösta Berling*, which is set in Värmland, on the Norwegian border, an area dominated by its great lakes. Not only in the famous pursuit by wolves at the climax, but throughout the film, Stiller uses the forests, the frozen lakes, the huge stillness of the region, as a complementary backdrop to his turbulent plot.

Stiller treated Selma Lagerlöf's novel, *Kavaljererna pä Ekeby*, in a cavalier fashion, excising scenes and adding others, and drastically altering the chronology. He had already incurred Lagerlöf's hostility by inserting a reindeer stampede as the climax of *Gunnar Hedes Saga* (1923, *Gunnar Hede's Saga*), and, inevitably, this time she had asked for the utmost fidelity. But Swedish Biograph had bought the film rights years before and, perhaps mercifully, there was nothing Lagerlöf could do. Stiller could proceed as he desired.

Contrary to popular belief, Stiller did not discover Greta Garbo. Needing two young girls for the roles of Elisabeth and Ebba, he asked Gustaf Molander, himself a distinguished director and at that time head of the dramatic school attached to Stockholm's Royal Dramatic Theatre, to send him his two best pupils. Molander sent Mona Mårtensson and Greta-Lovisa Gustafsson. Stiller engaged them both, and changed the latter's name to Garbo.

The Garbo of *The Atonement of Gösta Berling* was, in *Variety's* inimitable words, 'totally unlike the sleeky dame MGM experts made of her.' With luxuriant hair piled high above her head, eyebrows of their natural size, and fuller lips, she looks very young (she was only 18), very fresh and very lovely. Her acting is inevitably a little hesitant, owing far more to direction than was ever the case later, but Stiller and the experienced Lars Hanson, playing opposite her, see Garbo through, and her star quality shines out.

1

The best Swedish cinema of the time was justly famous for its development of a genuine cinematic style of acting. In *The Atonement of Gösta Berling*, the acting is in general restrained and subtle; Stiller never allows his players to be swamped by the elaborate interiors, the majestic landscapes, or the melodramatic artifices of the story.

Stiller's reputation had been made in comedy, of a refined and incisive kind; and his masterpiece in the genre, *Erotikon* (1920, *Bonds That Chafe*) was greatly admired by such directors as Ernst Lubitsch. The timing and exactitude of his comic style, however, carry over easily into the more melodramatic milieu of *The Atonement of Gösta Berling*.

Stiller was equally adept at great set-pieces. Of the two in *The Atonement of Gösta Berling*, the burning of the château of Ekeby is a masterpiece of scurrying confusion, while the chase over the frozen lake, superbly edited, has a taut excitement which quite obliterates its essential absurdity. Stiller was a complete film-maker. Writing his own scripts and editing his own films (like so many of his European colleagues), he could not fit into Hollywood's more sharply defined categories, and returned to Sweden disillusioned, to die in 1928 at the age of 45. The loving restoration of *The Atonement of Gösta Berling* was an overdue memorial.

JACK LODGE

The Countess Märtha Dohna engages Gösta Berling, an unfrocked priest, as tutor to her stepdaughter, Ebba, at her home in Borg (1). If Ebba marries a commoner she will be disinherited in favour of Märtha's son, Henrik. Märtha hopes that Berling, who is notoriously attractive to women, will marry Ebba. Ebba later overhears Märtha explaining her plot to Elisabeth (2), Henrik's wife. Now in love with Berling, Ebba becomes distressed. Berling, ashamed, leaves to seek refuge with the Samzelius family, who keep open house for all kinds of spongers at their château of Ekeby (3). Ebba subsequently dies, heartbroken.

Elisabeth assures Berling of her friendship. During a gala at Ekeby, Berling is caught embracing Marianne Sinclair, whose father drives her from their house. Meanwhile, Major Samzelius learns that the previous owner of Ekeby, from whom he inherited the estate, had been a lover of his wife, Margareta. It transpires that the lover, a rich and generous man, had intended Ekeby for Margareta but bequeathed it to Major Samzelius in order not to betray the illicit love affair. Angered and shamed by this revelation, Major Samzelius promptly turns his wife out (4).

Later, Berling finds the destitute Marianne exhausted in the snow (5), and takes her back to Ekeby. Henrik is informed that, through a technical error, he and Elisabeth are not legally married. This offers a glimmer of hope for Elisabeth, who gazes from her window towards Ekeby (6), longing for Berling, whom she really loves.

Margareta returns to Ekeby and sets fire to the château, hoping to wipe out all trace of her sin. Berling rescues Marianne from the flames (7), but she dies. Seeing the fire, Elisabeth hurries to Ekeby, meets Berling, and is carried off by him across the frozen lakes. They confess their love for each other. Escaping from a wolf pack, they eventually return to Borg. Elisabeth then sends Berling away, to rebuild Ekeby and his own life. She also refuses to regularize her marriage with Henrik (8).

Later, Elisabeth, who is about to leave for Italy, is, with Margareta's help, reunited with Gösta Berling.

3

5

7

Directed by Mauritz Stiller, 1924
Prod co: Svensk Filmindustri. **sc:** Mauritz Stiller, Ragnar Hyltén-Cavallius, from the novel, *Kavaljererna pä Ekeby*, by Selma Lagerlöf. **photo:** Julius Jaenzon. **prod des:** Ragnar Bratten, Vilhelm Bryde. **cost:** Ingrid Günther. length: 8700 ft (approx. 145 minutes). Swedish title: *Gösta Berlings Saga*. Released in GB as *The Atonement of Gösta Berling*.
Cast: Lars Hanson (*Gösta Berling*), Gerda Lundeqvist (*Margareta Samzelius*), Hilda Forslund (*Margareta's mother*), Otto Ely-Lundberg (*Major Samzelius*), Sixten Malmerfeldt (*Melchior Sinclair*), Karin Swanström (*Gustava Sinclair*), Jenny Hasselqvist (*Marianne Sinclair*), Ellen Cederström (*Countess Märtha Dohna*), Mona Mårtensson (*Lady Ebba Dohna*), Torsten Hammaren (*Count Henrik Dohna*), Greta Garbo (*Elisabeth Dohna*), Sven Scholander (*Sintram*), Svend Kornbaeck (*Captain Kristian Bergh*), Hugo Rönnblad (*Beerencreutz*), Knut Lambert (*Rutger von Örneclov*), Oscar Bergström (*Julius*), Gaston Portefaix (*Major Anders Fuchs*), Albert Stahl (*Uncle Eberhard*), Anton de Verdier (*Cousin Kristoffer*), Axel Jacobsson (*Lilliencrona*), Jan de Meyere (*Löwenborg*), Edmund Hohendorf (*Kevenheuler*), A.T.H. Buch (*Ruster, a drummer*).

8

Carl Theodor Dreyer

In search of the spiritual self

Had he lived to film his treasured project on the life of Christ, Carl Theodor Dreyer might have definitively enshrined the spiritual truths after which his career as a film director seems to have been a constant striving. Though unfulfilled, he still managed to leave behind a body of work of uncompromising idealism and terrible beauty

The greatest figure in the Danish cinema, Carl Theodor Dreyer made nine films in the last decade of the silents. Forty working years remained to him after that, but in all that time the pressures of the industry restricted him to five features and a few shorts. It is a classic instance of the waste of an enormous talent.

Dreyer was born on February 3, 1889 in Copenhagen, orphaned in early childhood, and brought up by foster-parents in a strict Lutheran environment. For some years he worked as a journalist before joining the Nordisk film company in 1912. Hired as a title-writer, he gained further experience as an editor, and also wrote a number of scripts, at least twenty of which had been filmed by 1918. With that apprenticeship, he wrote and directed his first film, *Praesidenten* (1919, The President). Though long and often sentimental, the film showed (according to those who have seen it) a precocious mastery of technique, fluid editing and a gift for expressive close-ups of perfectly chosen faces (a characteristic of the mature Dreyer's films). His second picture, *Blade af Satans Bog* (1920, Pages From Satan's Book) – derived from a novel by the Victorian writer Marie Corelli and clearly influenced by

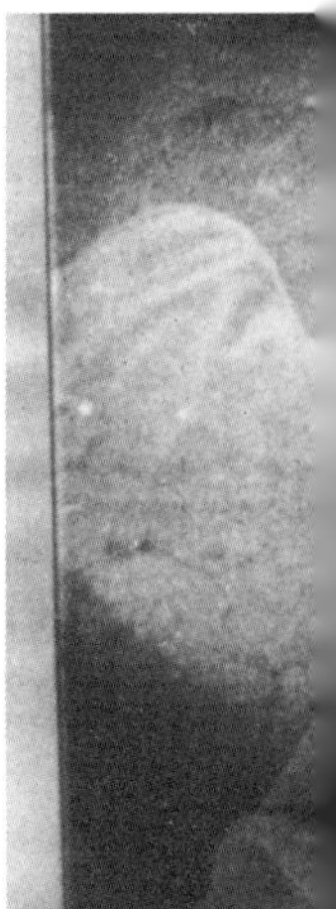

Right: Marte (Anna Svierkier) brought to the stake in Day of Wrath. *Above right:* Michael *(Walter Slezak) and the artist (Benjamin Christensen). Above, far right: the premature burial of David Gray (Nicolas de Gunzburg) in* Vampyr. *Far right: Nina Pens Rode as* Gertrud *with Bendt Rothe as her husband*

W. Griffith's *Intolerance* (1916), which
eyer had seen – dealt with the havoc caused
Satan at four different historical periods.
it before this film received a belated release in
921, Dreyer's third film – and his first master-
ece – had been completed and shown.

he parson's tale

ästänkan (1920, *The Parson's Widow*) was a
vedish film, but shot at Lillehammer in
orway in the locations of a preserved medi-
al village. Warm, serene and often very
nny, the film is set in a country parsonage
here a young man has just taken his place as
e new incumbent. He has brought his
ncée with him, but local custom decrees that
e new parson must marry the late parson's
dow. The lady is very old and the young
an will be her fourth husband. He agrees,
d the fiancée is engaged as a maid. All this
uld have made a coarse rustic comedy, but
th a flow of radiant images, Dreyer makes it
to a tranquil celebration of old age and
ath. The lady knows very well what is going
, accepts its naturalness and, in her own
ne, gently dies. She was played by a very old
tress, Hildur Carlberg, who herself knew
at she would not long survive the making of
e film; this is the first of the great per-
rmances Dreyer drew from his actresses.

Dreyer filmed *Die Gezeichneten* (1922, Love
ne Another), the story of a Russian village
ring the 1905 Revolution, at Lankwitz near
rlin. This little-known piece, once thought
st but rediscovered, is one of the director's most fascinating works. It is the account of a pogrom in which the crowd, unusually for Dreyer, is more important than any individual – and in which the scenes of swirling disturbance have a vivid reality. The cast was drawn from Russian émigrés, many from the Moscow Arts Theatre, from Poland, Germany and Scandinavia, and the villain was played by a Polish cavalry officer who had done some film work in Russia – the future Hollywood director Richard Boleslavsky.

After *Der Var Engang* (1922, Once Upon a Time), a lost film said to be very slight, Dreyer returned to Germany for *Michael* (1924, *Heart's Desire*). The story of an elderly painter betrayed and cheated by his model (whom he has adopted as his son), *Michael* was enhanced by a lavish treatment from the producer Erich Pommer, the talents of two great cameramen, Karl Freund and Rudolph Maté, and a remarkable cast. The Danish and Hollywood actor and director Benjamin Christensen played the painter, the future character actor Walter Slezak played Michael, and the Austrian actress Nora Gregor – later to star in Jean Renoir's classic *La Règle du Jeu* (1939, *The Rules of the Game*) was the princess who comes between them. The film was quintessential Dreyer: a steady, unhurried contemplation of a crisis in two lives and its resolution by death.

*ove left: the 75-year-old Dreyer while
ecting* Gertrud. *Above, far left: awaiting
surrection – Inger (Brigitte Federspiel), who
d during childbirth, with her brother-in-law
ay Kristiansen) and father-in-law (Henrik
alberg) in* Ordet

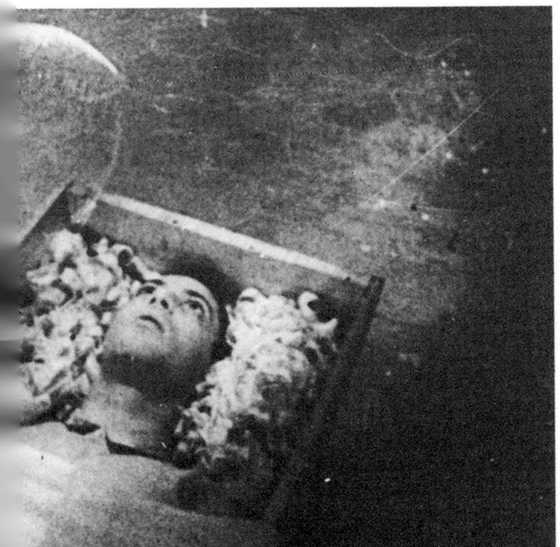

Silent martyr

Back in Denmark, Dreyer made *Du Skal aere din Hustru* (1925, *Thou Shalt Honour Thy Wife*), a deliciously ironic account of a demanding husband's come-uppance at the hands of the old family nurse, and then, after making the minor *Glomdalsbruden* (1926, The Bride of Glomdal) in Norway, moved to France for his best-known film, *La Passion de Jeanne d'Arc* (1928, *The Passion of Joan of Arc*). Concentrating Joan's trial into one day and consisting largely of interrogations, this late silent film seems to cry out for sound and yet, miraculously, to transcend that necessity. The brilliance of the editing, Rudolph Maté's photography, the performance in her only film by the great French stage actress Renée Falconetti, the marvellously expressive faces, the sublime and terrible ending – out of these Dreyer created a study of the interior life of a human being unequalled in its intensity. *The Passion of Joan of Arc* is a silent film in which light falling on a human face has the eloquence of a thousand words.

The film understandably estranged Dreyer from producers. It was a commercial failure, and an extravagant one at that. Dreyer had even constructed a vast château at Clamart, Paris, but it can hardly be seen in the picture. For all its critical acclaim, the film kept him idle until 1932 when, thanks largely to the financial backing of Baron Nicolas de Gunzburg, who played the lead, he was able to complete *Vampyr: Der Traum des Allan Gray* (*Vampyr: The Strange Adventures of David Gray*). Here Dreyer and Maté created a world of dream, a world of grey and white, of mist and phantoms, a world where no reality is certain, where every event is perhaps imagined, where a man may lie in his coffin and yet observe. There are few words and those, with a mainly amateur cast filming in three languages, are hard to understand, and so reinforce the feeling of a private universe, its laws the laws of sleep. *Vampyr* was a failure with the public and gained critical acceptance far too late. For 11 years Dreyer was out of films (though he toyed with various projects), returning to journalism in 1935.

Back to the stake

At last, in 1943, he was able to make *Vredens Dag* (*Day of Wrath*), and at last he had an international success. Set in the Denmark of the early seventeenth century, the film deals – often in details of savage cruelty – with the burning of a supposed witch, and its effects on the members of an involved family. Again there are landscapes of lyrical beauty, again an unflinching gaze at souls in spiritual torment, but this time no quiet resolution. The horror will go on.

More wasted years followed, with a minor feature *Två Människor* (1945, Two People), documentaries, and then in 1955 a little-seen version of Kaj Munk's play *Ordet* (*The Word*). Ten more years passed, during which time Dreyer became the director of a cinema. His career seemed finished but his last film, and his masterpiece, was still to come. In *Gertrud* (1964) he summed up his art. He had always disdained popularity, and there would be no compromise now. Dreyer's Gertrud, played by Nina Pens Rode, lives for an ideal love; rather than accept less, she chooses solitude. Dreyer made his films with the same creed. In 1968 he died, his script on the life of Christ unrealized.

JACK LODGE

Filmography

Films as scriptwriter only: **1912** Bryggerens Datter. **'13** Ballonekspiosionen; Krigskorrespondent (GB: The War Correspondent); Hans og Grethe; Elskovs Opfindsemhed; Chatollets Hemmelighed. **'15** Ned Med Vabnene; Juvelerernes Skraek. **'16** Penge (GB: Money); Den Hvide Djaevel; Der Skønne Evelyn; Rovedderkoppen; En Forbryders liv og Levned; Guldets Gift; Pavilionens Hemmelighed. **'17** Den Mystiske Selskabsdame; Hans Rigtige Kone; Fange Nr. 113; Hotel Paradis. **'18** Lydia; Glaedens Dag. *Films as director unless otherwise specified*: **'19** Praesidenten (+sc; +art. dir); Grevindens Aere (sc. only); Gillekop (sc. only). **'20** Blade af Satans Bog (+sc; +art. dir); Prästänkan (+sc) (USA: The Witch Woman; GB: Youth to Youth; retitled: The Parson's Widow). **'22** Die Gezeichneten (+sc) (GER); Der Var Engang (+co-sc; +co-ed). **'24** Michael (+sc) (GER) (USA: Chained; GB: Heart's Desire). **'25** Du Skal aere din Hustru (+co-sc; +art. dir) (GB: Thou Shalt Honour Thy Wife; retitled: Master of the House). **'26** Glomdalsbruden (+sc; +art. dir) (NOR). **'28** La Passion de Jeanne d'Arc (+co-sc) (FR) (USA/GB: The Passion of Joan of Arc). **'32** Vampyr: Der Traum des Allan Gray (+co-prod; +co-sc; +ed) (GER) (USA: Vampire; GB: Vampyr: The Strange Adventures of David Gray). **'36** Jungle Nera (co-sc. only) (IT). **'42** Mødrehjaelpen (short) (+sc) (GB: Good Mothers). **'43** Vredens Dag (+co-sc) (USA/GB: Day of Wrath). **'45** Två Människor (+sc; +co-ed) (SWED). **'46** Vandet på Landet/Bronde på Landet (short) (+sc). **'47** Landsbykirken/Den Danske Landsbykirke (short) (+co-sc) (GB: The Danish Village Church); De Gamle (short) (sc. only); Kampen Mod Kraeften (short) (+co-sc). **'48** De Naede Faergen (short) (+sc) (GB: They Caught the Ferry); Danmark Vågner (short) (sc. only) (unreleased). **'49** Thorvaldsen (short) (+co-sc); CTD (co-dir) (shot in 1929 and 1932). **'50** Shakespeare og Kronborg (short) (sc. only); Storstrømsbroen (short) (+sc). **'54** Et Slot i et Slot (short) (+sc); Rønne og Nexøs Genopbygning/Bornholms Genopbygning (short) (sc. only). **'55** Ordet (+sc) (GB: The Word). **'64** Gertrud (+sc). **'69** Diaries, Notes and Sketches/Lost Lost Lost (appearance as himself only) (USA).

After the great success of *Du Skal aere din Hustru* (1925, *Thou Shalt Honour Thy Wife*), its director Carl Theodor Dreyer was commissioned by the Société Générale de Films, which specialized in prestigious art films aimed at the international market, and whose products included Abel Gance's *Napoléon* (1927, *Napoleon*), Jean Epstein's *Finis Terrae* (1929, The End of the Land), and Maurice Tourneur's *L'Equipage* (1928, The Crew). Dreyer proposed three possible subjects: Marie Antoinette, Catherine de Médicis and Joan of Arc.

When Joan of Arc was finally selected it was decided to base the script partly on a recently published study by Joseph Delteil and partly on the original transcripts of the trial in Pierre Champion's 1921 edition. However, Dreyer and Delteil soon fell out and the director worked mainly from the transcripts, making Champion the film's historical advisor.

After some uncertainty the leading role went to Renée Falconetti, a theatrical actress, who was known, in 1927, for her roles in light, boulevard comedies. A surprising choice at first sight, perhaps, but Dreyer's defence of his decision provides the key to his whole conception of the film:

'Behind the make-up, behind the pose and that ravishing modern appearance, there was something. There was a soul behind that façade.'

The Passion of Joan of Arc is not a film about whether or not Joan was really inspired by visions. Nor is it particularly concerned with the religious and political whys and wherefores of the trial (in the way that George Bernard Shaw's play *Saint Joan* and Jean Anouilh's *L'Alouette* are, for example).

Dreyer is not concerned with historical accuracy or picturesque detail, but with psychological drama, or what Paul Schrader, previously a critic and now a film-maker, in his book *Transcendental Style* calls 'the spiritual progress of Joan's soul'. As Dreyer himself has said:

'I did not study the clothes of the time and things like that. The year of the event seemed as inessential to me as its distance from the present. I wanted to interpret a hymn to the triumph of the soul over life.'

For Dreyer the window into the soul is provided by the human face – 'everything human is expressed in the face', he once said, as 'the face is the mirror of the soul'. Hardly surprisingly, then, *The Passion of Joan of Arc* is a film in which intense close-ups of faces predominate. It is, as critic Tom Milne remarked, 'a symphony of faces'.

None of the cast wore makeup and the panchromatic film stock made their facial details stand out with extraordinary clarity, almost as if in etched relief. Indeed the effect is heightened by them being shot against what appear to be brilliant white walls – although, in fact, the interior sets were tinted yellow and the exteriors pink in order to achieve precisely this

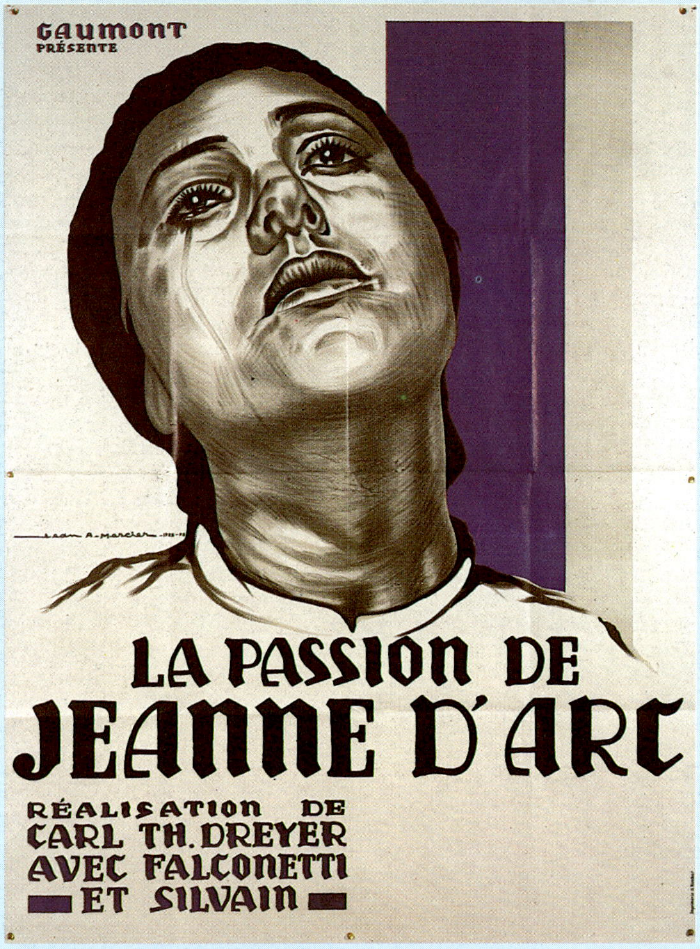

sense of brilliance.

Dreyer was concerned above all to penetrate beyond appearances, a desire he shared with many in the German silent cinema. Significantly, one of the art directors on the film was the renowned Hermann Warm, who co-designed Robert Wiene's expressionist classic *Das Kabinett des Dr Caligari* (1919, *The Cabinet of Dr Caligari*); whilst Dreyer's active, participatory camera style recalls F. W. Murnau's *Der Letzte Mann* (1925, *The Last Laugh*).

This creative use of outer appearances to express inner realities Dreyer called abstraction rather than Expressionism – which he defined as 'something that demands of the artist to abstract himself from reality in order to strengthen the spiritual content of his work'. By transcending the limitations of naturalism (which had come to dominate the film medium), Dreyer aimed at making a film that was not merely visual, but spiritual.

Thus the close-ups of the demonic faces of Joan's inquisitors, the threatening low-angle shots, the intensely expressive quality of the architecture, the dramatic high-contrast lighting, the remarkable mobile camera – all these elements contribute to an expressive climate that leads the spectator to empathize intensely with Joan's inner state.

Like many of Dreyer's films, *The Passion of Joan of Arc* was a critical success and a financial failure. In the light of its box-office losses, allied with the losses from *Napoleon* and the various problems caused by the arrival of sound, the Société Générale de Films broke their contract with Dreyer for a further film – leaving the director free to make the independently-produced *Vampyr: Der Traum des Allan Gray* (*Vampyr: The Strange Adventures of David Gray*) in 1932.

JULIAN PETLEY

Directed by Carl Theodor Dreyer, 1928

Prod co: Société Générale de Films. **sc:** Joseph Delteil, Carl Theodor Dreyer. **adap:** Carl Theodor Dreyer. **hist ad:** Pierre Champion. **photo:** Rudolph Maté. **set dec:** Hermann Warm, Jean Hugo. **cost:** Valentine Hugo. **ass dir:** Paul La Cour, Ralf Holm. **r/t:** 110 mins (commercial version, 86 mins). Original title: *La Passion et la Mort de Jeanne d'Arc*. Re-titled: *La Passion de Jeanne d'Arc*. Released in GB/USA as *The Passion of Joan of Arc*. Premiere, Copenhagen, 21 April 1928.

Cast: Renée Falconetti (*Joan of Arc*), Eugène Silvain (*Bishop Cauchon*), Maurice Schutz (*Nicolas Loyseleur*), Michel Simon (*Jean Lemaître*), Antonin Artaud (*Massieu*), Ravet (*Jean Beaupère*), André Berley (*Jean d'Estivet*), Jean d'Yd (*judge*), Jean Hemm, André Lurville, Jacques Arna, Alexandre Mihalesco, Robert Narlay, Henri Maillard, Jean Ayme, Léon Larive, Paul Jorge, Henri Gaultier.

1

Joan is brought before the judges (1); she refuses to recite the Lord's Prayer yet claims that God has sent her to save France. When questioned about her masculine attire she replies that when her mission is completed she will exchange it for a dress.

The judges – led by Bishop Cauchon (2) – continue to

3

6

The Passion of Joan of Arc

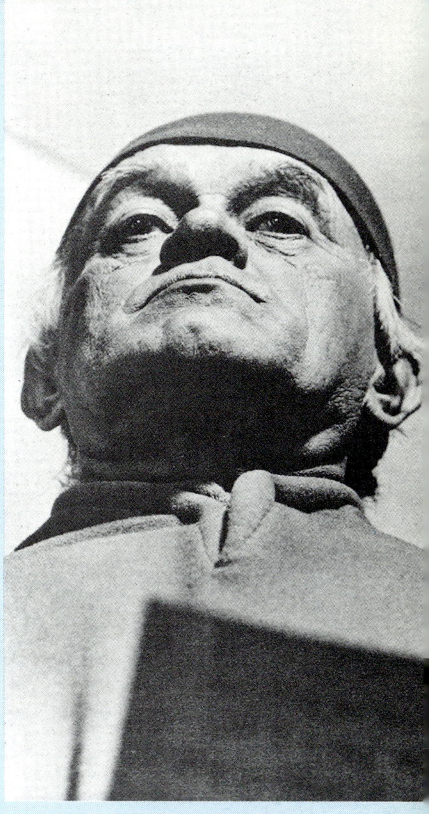

2

interrogate Joan, hoping to trap her in a blasphemy. Joan questions their right to judge her, however, and requests to be tried by the Pope himself. The judges dismiss the idea. Joan then tells them that she will be delivered from captivity soon, whereupon she is led out.

The judges decide to trick Joan into submission. They forge the King's signature and attach it to a letter of their own composition (3), recommending Joan to trust a priest they send to her cell.

Shortly after, the judges return to cross-examine Joan in her cell and succeed, through trickery, in extracting various 'blasphemous' statements out of her. Bishop Cauchon then gives orders to prepare the torture chamber. Though at first Joan refuses to sign an abjuration, the threat of the stake and her general state of physical and mental collapse (4) all finally force her to comply. Though saved from burning she is condemned to life-imprisonment.

While her hair is being shaved off (5), Joan regrets her action and makes a formal recantation. Preparing for death, Joan makes a confession to a young priest (6); then she is taken to the market-place where she is to be burnt at the stake (7). Meanwhile the crowd protests (8), accusing the judges of burning a saint, but they are ruthlessly suppressed.

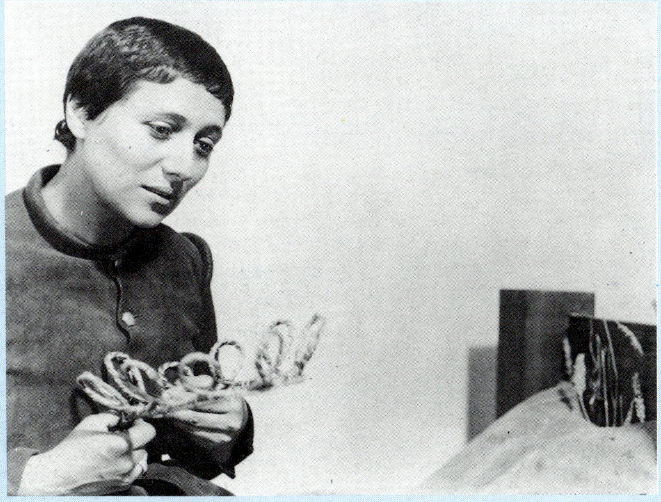

4

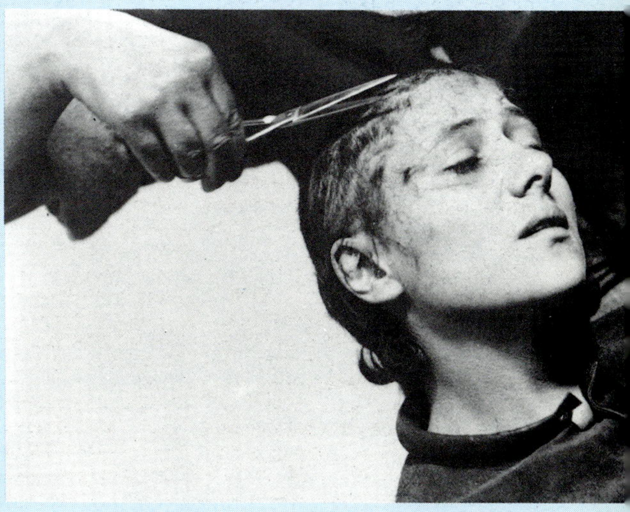

5

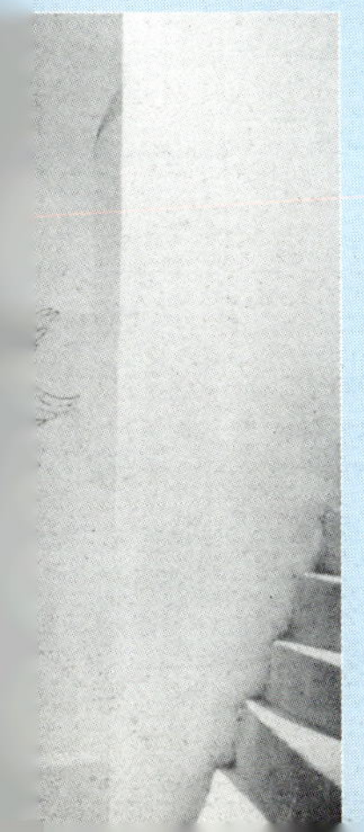

7

8

Lon Chaney

The Man of a Thousand Faces

The list is seemingly endless: old man, drunken husband, evil grandmother, would-be seducer, crazy-man, cripple, phantom, dope-addict, mad scientist, tragic circus-clown, pitiful hunchback . . . but it can be reduced to a single entry – Lon Chaney

Above: Lon Chaney makes up for his role as an ape-like hunchback – the alter ego of mad scientist Dr Lamb – in A Blind Bargain *(1922*

There came a moment in the history of movies when the real lives of the stars became stories that no scriptwriter dared offer the public; they seemed so far-fetched. It was as if the 'man-in-the-street' had begun to regard himself, subconsciously, in terms of a motion-picture scenario; or, adversely, as if movie melodrama had encouraged him to see how far-fetched reality often is.

Lon Chaney once hinted that he would never have wandered into the picture business if a stage-musical he was touring in had not run out of funds in Santa Ana, a stone's throw from Los Angeles. An actor ungraced with leading parts had to hustle to stay employed, and Chaney began to experiment with makeup and costume in order to prove his versatility. This professional need and practical initiative eventually resulted in an extraordinary career. Many of his films deal with fantasy and the supernatural, and it is easy to suppose that Chaney himself saw destiny carrying him forward – he was born and bred to enact silent stories, and behind his harsh features he nursed a sympathy for the handicapped and outcast, those incapable of joining in with society's glib chatter.

Alonso Chaney was born in Colorado Springs on April Fool's Day in 1886. Both parents were deaf and dumb – his father from the age of three, his mother from birth. But it was not a sorrowful household, and the maternal grandmother – who had produced four deaf-mute children – far from being a victim of self-pity, set about instituting better facilities for the deaf and dumb in Colorado. For Lon Chaney, the fact that people could be stricken mute – figures of fun and fear for the supposedly whole – was a way of life. It cannot have escaped his notice that, whereas his parents were substantially hindered in their enjoyment of the stage, the magic of silent movies was tailor-made for the compensatory instincts (such as acute eyesight and sensitivity) developed by the handicapped to overcome communication difficulties.

Imitating life

As if being a deaf-mute were not bad enough, Chaney's mother – always active and busy – contracted rheumatism so severely that she had to remain in bed for the rest of her life. His father kept up his barbering job – spared the small-talk that goes with lather and trims – and the nine-year-old Lon looked after his mother. Deaf and still, but always inquisitive, she was a demanding audience for whom the boy mimed the day's events.

While in his teens Chaney did odd jobs including work as a stage-hand at the Colorado Springs Opera House. Sometimes he was enlisted for crowd scenes, and once or twice he had a line of dialogue. When he was 17 he followed his brother John into travelling theatricals. He did anything and everything, not just acting but writing plays and painting scenery, making travel arrangements and doing song-and-dance routines. At 19 he married singer Cleva Creighton. They had a child (Creighton) Chaney, who became the actor Lon Chaney Jr), and Cleva's career soared briefly before instability and drinking ruined both her public and private life. At the height of one family quarrel she gulped down poison – although she survived her vocal chords were burned away.

Chaney left her, having won legal custody of his son, and met Hazel Hastings, a chorus girl. But she was already married to a man who had lost both legs; such circumstances would b

Top left: three confidence tricksters aim to exploit the healing powers of an old man – Thomas Meighan, Betty Compson, Joseph J. Dowling and Chaney star in The Miracle Man. *Above left: Blizzard, legless ruler of San Francisco's underworld, lives to have revenge on the surgeon who crippled him in* The Penalty *(1920). Above: Chaney with completed makeup in* A Blind Bargain

nting to any writer of fiction striving credibility. Both parties eventually divor- and Chaney's marriage to Hazel Hastings the secure basis on which he built his er.

he director Allan Dwan remembered meet- Chaney a short time after he had left the e-musical in Santa Ana:

picked up a new property man at Un- sal . . . He used to come around with funny h in his mouth and weird makeups. I guess was hinting – nobody goes around with a y nose on unless he wants to be noticed Finally, I said to him, "What the hell is Do you want to get in front of the lens?" aid yes, he'd tried acting once in a stock pany and had liked it. He was a property because he had to make a living. So I put to work as a couple of weird characters he caught on – people began to notice

y the middle of 1919 Chaney had appeared er one hundred pictures. He directed a few em and played romantic parts as well as ge idiots, ethnic heavies and exotics. He Krogstad in *A Doll's House* (1917), a five- version of Ibsen's play; a gang-leader in *Morgan's Girl* (1917); and von Tirpitz in *Kaiser – The Beast of Berlin* (1918), a aganda blast directed by Rupert Julian. In ummer of 1919 he appeared as Frog in *The cle Man*. Frog is a bogus cripple who plans xploit a blind faith-healer. With director ge Loane Tucker, Chancey worked extra hard on the 'fake' distortion of Frog's body and the theatrical exhilaration with which he is 'cured'. It is melodrama, made without compromise, but Chaney brings such conviction and tortured physicality to the idea of being crippled that he monopolizes the film. He was less an actor than a conjuror whose trick was his own physique.

Fortune in fear

The Miracle Man brought him better parts and billing, but Chaney was still some way from finding his own niche and laying the foundation of American horror movies. Throughout the Twenties Chaney made fear a major pull in pictures and identified the compelling fascination held by monsters and noble savages. Indirectly he came to influence a growing awareness of ambiguity in dark heroes and heroic villains, an element crucial to the gangster picture and *film noir*. He was Ricardo in *Victory* (1919); Blind Pew in *Treasure Island* (1920); he played dual roles as a gangster and the Chinaman (Chaney often played Orientals, making them as fancifully demonic and mythic as Dracula) who kills him in *Outside the Law* (1921); was Fagin to Jackie Coogan's Oliver in *Oliver Twist* (1922); and a crazed waxworks attendant in *While Paris Sleeps* (1923).

The quintessential Quasimodo

But it was in 1923 that Chaney played perhaps his most celebrated role as Quasimodo in *The Hunchback of Notre Dame*. Here was the epitome of the misfit, reaching out for understanding from a human shape twisted by a harness and with makeup that pre-figures John Hurt's in *The Elephant Man* (1980). Added to this physical appearance there is a glee and mobility about Chaney's Quasimodo; he is an ape who rules the high towers. When Charles Laughton came to play the part in 1939 he looked at Chaney's version and noticed the quality of dance in his performance:

'When he realised that he had lost the girl, his body expressed it – it was as though a bolt of lightning had shattered his physical self.'

Chaney returned to Universal to make *The Hunchback of Notre Dame* which made him a star. He subsequently received many offers but joined MGM at the request of Irving Thalberg, himself a recent 'defector' from Universal. Under the direction of Victor Sjöström, Chaney played a great scientist who has gone into humiliating exile as a circus clown in *He Who Gets Slapped* (1924). Also at MGM he was reunited with Tod Browning, the director whose cool, macabre vision had always made

the best use of his unique talents. In Browning's *The Unholy Three* (1925) Chaney plays a crook who dresses up as an old woman: it is his most sinister work, and it helped to dispel the idea that dear old ladies should be figures of sweet comfort.

Although Chaney had some straight parts, such as the tough sergeant in *Tell It to the Marines* (1926), he was generally allowed to explore the poetry of the maimed and the grotesque. In 1927 he played Alonzo the Armless in *The Unknown*, and in Browning's *London After Midnight* he was both the policeman and vampire. With the arrival of talkies Chaney signed a new contract with MGM in which he agreed to remake his silent successes. The talkie version of *The Unholy Three* (1930) was barely completed when he died of throat cancer.

Of all the silent stars, Chaney is perhaps least known today – although he is possibly the best appreciated. When he died he was considering the role of *Dracula* (1931), the part that eventually made Bela Lugosi a star. Had he lived beyond middle age there is every reason to suppose that he could have played many parts taken by Lugosi and Boris Karloff. Those actors owed their chance and their genre to him, for perhaps no-one but Lon Chaney would have recognized the fine line to be drawn between terror and pity. DAVID THOMSON

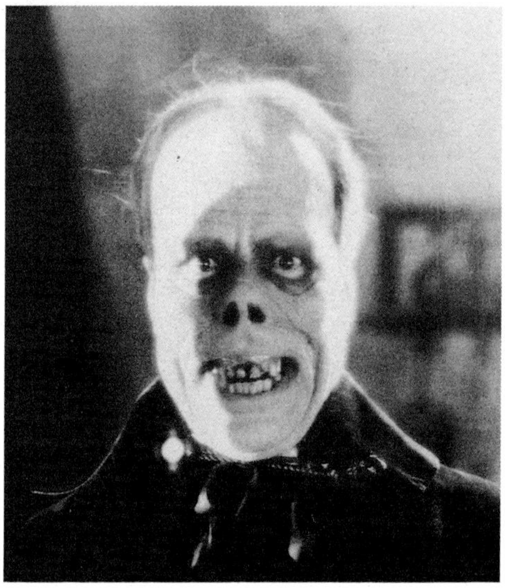

Chaney proving himself the *master of disguise and contortion as Quasimodo in* The Hunchback of Notre Dame *(top left); the armless knife-throwing circus-star in* The Unknown *(top right); an unladylike role as the crooked ventriloquist masquerading as Mrs O'Grady, seller of parrots, in the silent* The Unholy Three *(right); and as* The Phantom of the Opera *(above)*

Filmography

All films shorts unless otherwise specified: **1913** Poor Jake's Demise; The Sea Urchin; Red Margaret, Moonshiner; The Trap; Back to Life; Almost an Actress; Bloodhounds of the North. **'14** The Lie; The Honor of the Mounted; By the Sun's Rays; The Adventures of François Villon (serial); A Miner's Romance; Virtue Its Own Reward; The Small Town Girl (feature); Her Life's Story; The Lion, the Lamb, the Man; A Ranch Romance; Her Grave Mistake; The Tragedy of Whispering Creek; Discord and Harmony (feature); The Embezzler; The Lamb, the Woman, the Wolf (feature); The Forbidden Room; Richelieu (feature); The Pipes of Pan; Lights and Shadows; A Night of Thrills; Her Bounty; The Old Cobbler (feature); Remember Mary Magdalen; The Menace to Carlotta; Her Escape; The End of the Feud; The Unlawful Trade. **'15** Star of the Sea; Maid of the Mist; Threads of Fate; The Stronger Mind; The Measure of a Man; Such Is Life; Bound on the Wheel (feature); Quits: The Sin of Olga Brandt; The Grind; When the Gods Played a Badger Game; Where the Forest Ends; All for Peggy; The Desert Breed; The Stool Pigeon (+dir; +prod); Outside the Gates; For Cash (+dir; +prod); The Oyster Dredger (+dir; +prod; +sc); The Violin Maker (+dir; +prod); The Trust (+dir; +prod); Mountain Justice; The Chimney's Secret (+dir; +prod; +sc); The Girl of the Night; An Idyll of the Hills; Steady Company; The Pine's Revenge; Alas and Alack; The Fascination of the Fleur de Lis (feature); Lon of Lone Mountain; A Mother's Atonement (feature); The Millionaire Paupers (feature); Father and the Boys; Stronger Than Death; Under the Shadow. *All remaining films features unless otherwise specified:* **'16** The Grip of Jealousy; Tangled Hearts; Dolly's Scoop (short); The Gilded Spider; Bobbie of the Ballet; Grasp of Greed; The Mark of Cain; If My Country Should Call; Felix on the Job (short); Place Beyond the Winds; The Price of Silence; The Piper's Price (GB: Storm and Sunshine). **'17** Hell Morgan's Girl; The Mask of Love (short); A Doll's House; The Girl in the Checkered Coat; Fires of Rebellion; The Flashlight; Pay Me/Vengeance of the West; The Empty Gun; The Rescue; Anything Once; Triumph; Bondage; The Scarlet Car. **'18** The Grand Passion; Broadway Love; The Kaiser – The Beast of Berlin; Fast Company; A Broadway Scandal; Riddle Gawne; That Devil, Bateese; The Talk of the Town; Danger – Go Slow; The False Faces. **'19** The Wicked Darling; A Man's Country; Paid in Advance; The Miracle Man; When Bearcat Went Dry; Victory. **'20** Daredevil Jack (serial); Treasure Island; The Gift Supreme; Nomads of the North; The Penalty. **'21** Outside the Law; For Those We Love; Bits of Life; The Ace of Hearts; The Night Rose/Voices of the City. **'22** The Trap (GB: The Heart of a Wolf); Flesh and Blood; The Light in the Dark; Shadows; Oliver Twist; Quincy Adams Sawyer; A Blind Bargain. **'23** All the Brothers Were Valiant; While Paris Sleeps; The Shock; The Hunchback of Notre Dame. **'24** The Next Corner; He Who Gets Slapped. **'25** The Monster; The Unholy Three; The Phantom of the Opera; The Tower of Lies. **'26** The Black Bird; The Road to Mandalay; Tell it to the Marines. **'27** Mr Wu; The Unknown; Mockery; London After Midnight (GB: The Hypnotist). **'28** The Big City; Laugh, Clown, Laugh; While the City Sleeps; West of Zanzibar. **'29** Where East Is East; Thunder. **'30** The Unholy Three.

THE GOLDEN WEST

The silent Westerns carried on where real life left off, since the world they portrayed, although it still existed, was rapidly fading away in a glow of nostalgia

The Western is one of the finest creations of American culture, and the cowboy one of the great macho heroes of the world. Historically, the supreme era of the cowboy was short. It lasted from the end of the American Civil War in 1865 to the 1880s, when the cry was for beef to feed the hungry, growing nation. These were the days of the epic cattle drives up the famous trails like the Goodnight and the Chisholm, the days of the cattle empires, of the wide-open cow towns like Abilene and Dodge City, of range wars and murderous rivalries – the raw material of cowboy legend. But disastrous weather, bad management and the collapse of the beef market put an end to the boom; the arrival of homesteaders and the spread of barbed wire terminated the open range. Cowboys continued to exist and to ply their trade; but the old expansive, free-wheeling life had ended. Many cowboys moved on and the destination of some of them was Hollywood. By the Twenties, it was estimated that 500 a year came to Hollywood from ranches in Arizona and Colorado that were going broke.

The earliest Westerns therefore not only reconstructed the story and the life-style of the Old West – they overlapped with it and actually continued it. Real-life western characters appeared in films about their exploits: outlaws such as Al Jennings and Emmett Dalton and lawmen such as Bill Tilghman, last of the great western marshals. Tilghman made a number of films, actually interrupting the shooting of one of them to round up some bank robbers, thus mingling fantasy and reality with a vengeance. For the epic film *North of 36* (1924), the director Irvin Willat staged the first longhorn cattle drive for nearly thirty-five years, exactly replicating the conditions of the drives in the 1870s.

But for all the documentary-style realism of some of these Western reconstructions, the mass audience went to Westerns primarily for dashing heroes and plenty of action, preferably in impressive locations. So the films that the real-life cowboys helped to make in Hollywood gave worldwide currency to a romantic archetype which had been established even before the film industry came into being. The cowboy was seen as the embodiment of the virtues of the American frontier. These had been described by the historian Frederick Jackson Turner in 1893:

'That coarseness and strength combined with acuteness and inquisitiveness; that practical, inventive turn of mind, quick to find expedients; that masterful grasp of material things, lacking in the artistic but powerful to effect great ends; that restless, nervous energy; that dominant individualism working for good and for evil, and withal that buoyancy and exuberance which comes with freedom.'

These characteristics were blended with the essential elements of the chivalric gentleman of the Old World – courtesy, bravery and nobility – to create an ideal Westerner. This image was perfected by three men, all Easterners, all friends, all intoxicated by the heroic vision of the West and all destined to influence the Hollywood version of it. Owen Wister, a Philadelphian, made the cowboy the hero of his novel *The Virginian*, published in 1902. It was the first serious Western novel and gave the cowboy pride of place over the previously preferred heroes, the dime-novel favourites – the outlaw, the lawman, the pioneer, the trapper and the scout. Frederic Remington, a New Yorker, in his

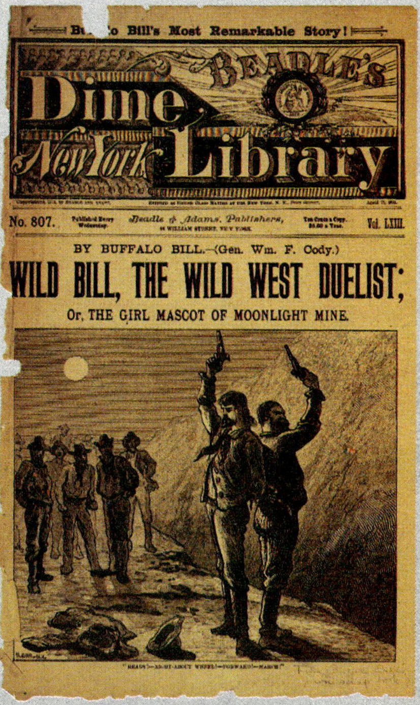

Above: Prentiss Ingraham wrote the dime novels signed by Buffalo Bill as well as 200 stories about the popular Western hero. Below: in The Covered Wagon, *the wagon train unwisely makes a stand against the Indians in a box canyon, open to attack from above*

paintings of cattle drives and round-ups, gunfights and hold-ups, recorded a West made up of swirls of action and colour, with manly cowboys at its centre. Theodore Roosevelt, aristocratic President, explorer and big-game hunter, preached in his life and in his books a militant Anglo-Saxonism of which the cowboy was the proud exemplar. The first epic Western film, *The Covered Wagon* (1923), was to be dedicated to his memory. The impact of the cowboy can be gauged from the fact that the terms 'Western film' and 'cowboy film' became interchangeable, although many Western films actually featured no cowboys as such.

Although the cowboy was being ennobled for the first time, the process was built on the tradition of the dime novels. From the 1860s onwards, as the West seized the imagination of America, a flood of cheap novels, written according to a few formulas, had poured from the presses, dramatizing and romanticizing the adventures of real and fictional Western heroes. Dime novels became one of the primary sources of film content, reinforced by stage melodramas with Western settings and the Wild West shows which popularized what became the great set-pieces of Western films – the stagecoach chase, the wagon-train attack and the cavalry charge.

One figure tapped all these sources of inspiration – Colonel William F. Cody, 'Buffalo Bill' himself. A real-life scout and buffalo hunter, he was taken up by the leading dime novelist, Ned Buntline, who started a long series of novels describing his fictional adventures. Cody took to the stage in 1872 in a rather bad melodrama called *The Scouts of the Plains* and, discovering that he lacked aptitude as an actor, launched his celebrated Wild West show in 1883. Towards the end of his life, he brought the wheel full circle by producing and starring in a film of his Western exploits, made in 1913 and known by various titles, including *The Adventures of Buffalo Bill*. His career is the perfect demonstration of how historical reality shaded into cinematic fiction.

It was inevitable that films would follow the lead of the stage and the printed page, and Westerns became a staple of the new entertainment medium early on. The first recorded Western is a one-minute vignette entitled *Cripple Creek Bar Room*, produced in 1898. The first Western story film, *The Great Train Robbery*, followed in 1903. Directed by Edwin S. Porter, it was actually filmed in New Jersey but told a classic story of robbery, chase and retribution. It had enormous success at the box-office and was extensively imitated. One thing it did not have was a hero. But in the cast was an actor called Gilbert M. Anderson, who was soon ready to remedy this defect. Overcoming an initial tendency to fall off his horse, he saw the potential in the cowboy hero, launched a new company (Essanay) and took a film unit off first to Colorado and then to California, where he began producing one- and two-reel Westerns, many of them featuring Anderson himself as a sentimental tough guy called Broncho Billy. Anderson, who appeared in hundreds of Broncho Billy films between 1908 and 1916, thus became the first Western hero. Business problems kept him off the screen for over a year and when he

Above: Frederic Remington's 1899 painting Missing *depicts a cavalry trooper captured by hostile Indians and unlikely to survive for long, since Indians soon killed their prisoners. Top right: an encounter between Indian warriors in* The Way of a Mother *(1913), supervised by Thomas H. Ince. Right: G. M. Anderson as Broncho Billy (right) in a 1913 story of a tenderfoot who gets tired of being pushed around and becomes a crack shot. Far right: in* White Oak *(1921), William S. Hart plays Oak Miller, a gambler obsessed with visiting revenge on the man who deceived his sister; the villain is finally killed by an Indian chief whose daughter he has betrayed. Below right: Harry Carey as a good-hearted outlaw in Ford's* The Scarlet Drop *(1918)*

of his romanticism, plots that were sentimental, melodramatic and heavily moralistic. In his films he played a succession of ramrod-straight, grim-visaged badmen with names like Black Deering, Blaze Tracey and Draw Egan, who were underneath it all chivalric and sentimental and whose moral regeneration was a central theme of the stories. In *Hell's Hinges* (1916), he actually burns down a sinful town, in a sequence eerily prefiguring Clint Eastwood's *High Plains Drifter* (1973). Hart's horse Fritz became the first of a long line of star movie horses who became as well-known as their riders. But Hart's popularity waned and the piety, sentimentality and comparatively slow pace of his films came to seem increasingly old-fashioned with the rise of a very different sort of star – Tom Mix. Hart refused to change his style and after a final film, *Tumbleweeds* (1925), he retired. *Tumbleweeds* represents the triumphant summation of Hart's vision of the West and takes place symbolically against the background of the end of the open range and the arrival of the homesteaders. It also contains a stunningly executed and majestically shot set-piece, the Cherokee Strip land rush, which ranks with the best of its kind in the genre.

Where Hart had prided himself on the authenticity of his films, Tom Mix's films were pure fantasy. He has first entered films in mid-1909 as a stockman and supporting player in a rodeo picture, *Ranch Life in the Great Southwest* (1910), and from then until 1917 he worked for the Selig company, turning out something like a hundred Westerns, one- and two-reelers, which he often wrote and directed as well as starring in. But in 1917 he moved to Fox and his career took off. The inspiration of his films was the circus and the Wild West show, where Hart's had been Victorian melodrama and photographic realism. Tom Mix's cowboy hero, flamboyantly costumed, involved himself in fast-moving, far-fetched stories, strong on stunts, action and comedy. Fleet of foot, keen of eye and effortlessly gallant, Tom Mix became the Doug Fairbanks of the sagebrush. He set the style and pattern for the Westerns of a host of rivals and imitators. Indeed from his own supporting casts emerged Buck Jones and George O'Brien, who were both to be promoted as Western stars by Fox.

Westerns received a tremendous boost in 1923 when Paramount released the first indisputable Western epic, *The Covered Wagon*. Based on Emerson Hough's novel, it began as a conventional programmer about a wagon boss falsely accused of a crime by his rival for the heroine's affections, but expanded to become the saga of wagons westward on the Oregon Trail in 1848. It exists now only in an incomplete print. Nevertheless it can be said that despite such assets as the grandeur of Karl Brown's photography, the documentary look imparted by eight weeks' location shooting to such large-scale action sequences as the wagon train's departure, the river crossing and a buffalo hunt, and the rich character comedy of Ernest Torrence and Tully Marshall as two old frontiersmen, it is a flawed film. The director James Cruze, whatever his strengths, was weak on action highlights and suspense, and the Indian attack on the wagon train and its rescue are clumsily mishandled.

But the film was a great box-office success, and it emboldened Fox to turn its new Western *The Iron*

Westerns drew for inspiration on dime novels, stage melodramas, rodeos and Wild West shows

returned he found that new idols had risen and his career faded.

The artistic possibilities in the Western became clear in the work of two of the cinema's great innovators – D. W. Griffith and Thomas H. Ince. Griffith in his years at Biograph brought his increasingly sophisticated technique and powerful visual sense to Westerns, imbuing such projects as *The Last Drop of Water* (1911), *The Massacre* (1913) and *The Battle at Elderbush Gulch* (1914) with truly epic qualities. Thomas H. Ince, the first producer to insist on fully detailed and comprehensive scripts for the guidance of the production team as well as the actors, and an organizational genius when it came to staging large-scale action, hired the Miller Brothers 101 Ranch Real Wild West Show, to provide him with a ready-made stock company of cowboys and Indians, longhorn cattle, stagecoaches and wagons. He turned out Westerns from his Inceville studios, one of the most successful of which was *Custer's Last Raid* (1912), directed by and starring Francis Ford (though Ince officially took the directorial credit). This film so impressed Carl Laemmle that he lured Ford away from Ince and set him to work at Universal, which was to become one of the major producers of Westerns. But Francis Ford was eventually to be eclipsed as a director by his younger brother John Ford and as an actor by Harry Carey and then Hoot Gibson, who both starred in many popular Westerns for Universal, some of them directed by the up-and-coming John (then known as Jack) Ford.

Ince, however, found a more-than-adequate replacement for Francis Ford in William S. Hart, who entered films in 1914 at the age of 44. Previously a stage actor, who had appeared not only in Shakespeare and *Ben-Hur* but also in such popular Western stage melodramas as *The Squaw Man* and *The Virginian*, Hart was an incurable romantic. He had been raised in the West, loved it and wanted to depict it realistically on the screen. First with Ince and later with Paramount, he succeeded in his aim, giving his films a gritty surface realism of austere, dusty townships and authentic cowboy costume and accoutrements. But with this went another side

Above: a dime-novel-reading cowboy (Ken Maynard) acts as guide to a circus in The Wagon Show *(1928) and becomes its star rider. Below: after an Indian attack, the train returns to the railhead in John Ford's* The Iron Horse. *Bottom: production shot of* The Vanishing American, *sympathetic to the Navajo Indians and filmed in authentic locations*

Horse (1924) into an epic. So the familiar story of a young man seeking the murderer of his father burgeoned into a full-scale reconstruction of the building of the transcontinental railroad. In John Ford, Fox had a director who could combine visual sweep and exciting action sequences, rich comedy interludes and acutely-observed details of everyday life to counterpoint the epic theme. In George O'Brien, Ford found a wholly convincing Western star, virile, natural and likeable. The result was one of the great achievements of the silent cinema. Other epics followed, such as Irvin Willat's *North of 36* and James Cruze's *The Pony Express* (1925). But none of them achieved the success of *The Covered Wagon* and *The Iron Horse*, and it became clear that large-scale evocations of nationalistic sentiment were not entirely to the public's taste. Interestingly, after his magisterial land-rush epic *Three Bad Men* (1926), John Ford was not to make another Western until *Stagecoach* (1939).

Programme Westerns, however, flourished and production of them trebled in the year following *The Covered Wagon*. Films on the streamlined, action-packed Tom Mix model were what was required, and in his wake a posse of immortals galloped across the screen. These were the men in white hats riding white horses, the paladins of the prairies, the idols of the Saturday matinées.

MGM launched a group of historical Westerns starring the stalwart Colonel Tim McCoy, a former Indian agent who had handled the Indians used in the making of *The Covered Wagon*. At First National, Ken Maynard starred in rousing Western adventures, whose spectacular set-piece highlights were to be reused constantly as stock footage throughout the Thirties. At FBO, Fred Thomson, a former Presbyterian minister and Boy Scout leader, now forgotten but idolized in his day, rode and fought his way into the hearts of a legion of young admirers. From Paramount between 1921 and 1928 (and thereafter in the sound era) came an impressive series of adaptations of the novels of Zane Grey, arguably the most popular of Western writers. With classic plots and evocative titles like *The Thundering Herd*, *The Vanishing American* and *Wild Horse Mesa* (all 1925), they generally starred steely-eyed Jack Holt or rugged Richard Dix. They also benefited from being filmed, as the contract with Grey specifically demanded, on the actual locations of the stories.

By 1926, however, a glut of cheap Westerns took the edge off the public demand and the coming of sound apparently signalled their doom. Short on that essential commodity, dialogue, they were dubbed old-fashioned and over-romantic. The vogue was for bang-up-to-date films that could exploit the new medium, and Westerns were eclipsed by gangster films with their screeching cars and machine-gun battles and by musicals – 'all-talking, all-singing, all-dancing'. Production of Westerns was cut by as much as 75 per cent and in 1929 *Photoplay* magazine declared: 'Western novel and motion picture heroes have slunk away into the brush, never to return.' JEFFREY RICHARDS

The First Hurrahs – the silent films of John Ford

Ford laid down the blueprints for his fifty-year career as a director in the last decade of the silents – when the American Dream still seemed a possibility

Although the bright vision of an ideal and idealized society that John Ford so often projected in his films dimmed with the passing of the years, it was always tinged with a romantic melancholy. As the son of an immigrant Irish family, Ford was principally preoccupied with belonging. The obvious unit to which to belong was the family – but the pressures of twentieth-century life tended towards the breakup of the family and the breakdown of the traditional values it symbolized. As early in his work as *Four Sons* (1928), Ford was charting the disintegration of a family. Mostly, however, his films of the Twenties hymn his adoptive country without qualification, and an optimism and excitement redolent of the nineteenth-century's expansive spirit shine forth from his two great silent Westerns, *The Iron Horse* (1924) and *Three Bad Men* (1926).

Lines of vision

The rediscovery of many of Ford's silent movies has enabled film historians, to whom they were long unavailable, to trace a visual, stylistic and thematic coherence and continuity with the director's later and more familiar work, a relationship that could not have been anticipated. Taken together, these silent films reveal the emergence of Ford's distinctive style. At Fox, he worked regularly with cameraman George Schneiderman who endowed the films with a soft, shimmering quality. But whatever the particular photographic idiom Ford adopted, and this changed radically in his talkies, it is the composition that remains the constant factor. Ford admitted to having 'an eye for composition' and his frames are unmistakable, composed with the ritual formality, formal symmetry and tableau groupings that might be expected from an apostle of order and hierarchy. His screen is bisected into neat and regular spatial areas by tent poles, hitching rails, sidewalks, gateways, stone walls, wooden fences, railway lines, the horizon. His delight in rituals such as parades, dances, trials and funerals is partly to be explained by the fact that they are conducted according to rules of formal patterning and positioning. Even non-ritualized events are turned into rituals by posings and framings. In *Three Bad Men*, for example, there is a scene in which Bull Stanley (Tom Santschi) carries his dead sister down the stairs of the saloon; Ford invests this with the formality of a funeral rite by framing and composition.

But within that compositional frame, as befits the image of Ford as a self-styled rebel, rogue and individualist, he gave his other talents free rein – powerfully evoking atmosphere and character, and infusing life and spontaneity into the script by the means of 'business', gesture and enlivening detail.

Ford's film career began as soon as he left high school aged 18 in 1913. He joined his brother Francis, a director and actor, at Universal as prop man, stunt man and assistant director. He made his debut as director, writer and star with a two-reeler, *The Tornado* (1917), the first of over thirty films he directed before leaving Universal to join Fox in 1920. Almost all his Universal films were Westerns and he regularly won critical praise for his handling of action, his comedy and his visual sense. One critic called his *The Outcasts of Poker Flat* (1919) 'an optic symphony'.

Only one of these Universal films has survived – *Straight Shooting* (1917), which was his first feature. It was one of 24 films Ford made with Harry Carey, usually cast in the continuing role of 'Cheyenne Harry', and is a fairly conventional homesteaders-versus-cattlemen drama. What is remarkable is that both in style and some thematic elements, *Straight Shooting* distinctly foreshadows Ford's mature masterpiece *The Searchers* (1956). Though it does not have the later film's depth and complexity, some of the compositions are identical and there is the same emotional commitment to the family and the land, the same feeling of anguish present in a funeral sequence and the same sympathy with an outsider hero, here Harry Carey, whose familiar gesture of holding his left arm with his right hand John Wayne deliberately copied for the concluding scene in *The Searchers*.

Above: John – or Jack – Ford (in front of rail-car) filming at Universal around 1920

At Fox, Ford began by working with their resident cowboy stars Buck Jones and Tom Mix before graduating to prestige productions with *Cameo Kirby* (1923), starring John Gilbert as a discredited riverboat gambler. Ford marked the promotion by changing his own name on the credits from Jack to John. The variety of films he handled at Fox allowed him to extend his range and deepen his poetic insights, but, characteristically anxious to preserve the image of the hard-nosed professional who was just doing a job of work, he told Peter Bogdanovich many years later:

'You didn't choose those things. They were thrown at you and you did the best you could with them.'

First rails West

Three films in particular stand out from the Fox period to indicate the sort of project that brought out the best in Ford: *The Iron Horse,*

Three Bad Men and *Four Sons*. For Davy Brandon (George O'Brien), hero of *The Iron Horse*, as for Ford himself, the railroad seems to be a mystical concept, compounded of progress and nationhood. The film shows people of many different nationalities (Irish, Italians, Chinese), working to build the transcontinental tracks, giving it a symbolic nature (co-operation, brotherhood, unity). Similarly, former soldiers of the Union and the Confederacy work side by side, symbolizing reconciliation. It is these aspects rather than the commercial or capitalist angle that Ford stresses and Davy Brandon personifies. It is an interpretation sanctified by the iconic presence of Abraham Lincoln, to whom the film is dedicated and whose dream of one nation undivided is realized by the completion of the railway line. Within the narrative, Ford creates a world teeming with life and rich in comedy, typified by the impromptu saloon trial and the reluctant visit to the dentist by the inevitable Irish labourer (played by J. Farrell MacDonald, a regular in Ford's movies). It is also worth noting as a tribute to their success that all the best action sequences in the film (the cavalry rescue of the besieged train, the saloon scenes, the dismantling of the railroad town and the meeting of the two lines at Promontory Point) were carbon-copied to form the highlights of Cecil B. DeMille's *Union Pacific* (1939).

The mainspring of *Three Bad Men* is Ford's Catholicism, another of the continuing threads in his work. At heart it is a deeply religious film – full of ritual imagery – with its story of a trinity of bad men sacrificing their lives to save the young hero and heroine (George O'Brien and Olive Borden) from outlaws and thereby winning love and forgiveness. It was a theme Ford reworked in *Marked Men* (1920) and *Three Godfathers* (1948). The setting is the Dakota Gold Rush of 1877 but, in classic populist fashion, the search for gold is made subordinate to land settlement and farming. The film duly ends with hero, heroine and curly-haired son at peace on their farm with fields of grain waving in the breeze. The major action sequence of the film is the complex, detailed and dynamically staged land rush, full of wagon crashes and near escapes, and punctuated by scenes of a fallen baby being snatched away from the thundering hooves of the horses, a newspaper being printed *en route*, and a delightfully incongruous penny-farthing bicycle being towed by a careering wagon.

America as the land of opportunity figures at the climax of *Four Sons*, which proved Ford's biggest box-office success since *The Iron Horse*. The film explores the tragic breakup of a family, the theme Ford was to return to in su later masterworks as *The Grapes of Wra* (1940) and *How Green Was My Valley* (194 In *Four Sons* the family is German and t central figure mother Bernle (Margaret Man loses three of her four boys in World War I. S is eventually rescued and taken from a d feated Germany to the USA by the fourth so who had emigrated there before the war a made a successful new life. In its visual sty emphasized perhaps by the use of sets fro F. W. Murnau's *Sunrise* (1927), the film sho the impact that the influx of German directo had had on the look of Hollywood movies.

Mother Ireland

The years at Fox allowed Ford to give visual l to another of his preoccupations – Irela Ford's dual images of an expatriate's drea Erin are reflected in the folksy, humorou anecdotal *The Shamrock Handicap* (1926) and *Hangman's House* (1928), a powerful, dar toned tale of the Irish 'Troubles'.

The Shamrock Handicap tells the famili story of a penniless Irish aristocratic fam taking their prize racehorse to the USA a winning a race. Ford transformed it into a fa tale, celebrating his two countries with equ enthusiasm: Ireland, the beloved homela lovingly and sentimentally evoked as a la

Left: *the parting of the ways in* Three Bad Men, *with Olive Borden and George O'Brien. Far left: George Stone, Buck Jones and Helen Ferguson in* Just Pals. *Above, far left: dramatic use of landscape by Ford in* Straight Shooting. *Above: an historic occasion re-created as east meets west in* The Iron Horse. *Below left: a mother (Margaret Mann) and her* Four Sons *(George Meeker, Francis X. Bushman Jr, Charles Morton, James Hall). Below right: another parting in* Mother Machree *(1927) – about an Irish woman's love for her son*

drenched in tradition and *noblesse oblige*; and the USA, the land of opportunity where fame and fortune await the immigrant. In Ford's vision the leisurely nineteenth-century pastoral idyll of old Ireland typically gives way to the bustle and knockabout of a vigorous new multi-racial society.

Hangman's House projects the other side of Ford's Ireland, an Ireland of bardic lore and Celtic myth, floating dreamily in a sea of mist. Shooting almost entirely in the studio, Ford created memorable images of foggy back-streets, mist-wreathed moors and marshes and shadowy keeps for a sombre tale of revenge, daring escapes and star-crossed lovers. Victor McLaglen, playing an exiled Irish freedom-fighter who returns to exact vengeance on a high-born Irish collaborator who has betrayed his sister, embodies the key Fordian themes – love of country, love of family and the poignancy of exile. And like *Four Sons*, the film shows how much Ford had absorbed the Germanic influence in lighting and staging.

American friends

Ford adopted a different style – open-air location shooting and sunlight – for his Americana. His first picture for Fox, *Just Pals* (1920), still a charming, fresh and irresistibly appealing tale, can be seen in some respects as a direct precursor of Ford's Thirties trilogy of small-town American life: *Doctor Bull* (1933), *Judge Priest* (1934), *Steamboat Round the Bend* (1935). The two pals of the title are Bim (played by the popular Western star Buck Jones), who is the resident bum of a small mid-Western town, and Bill (George Stone), a ragged orphan thrown off a freight train. Ford sketches their developing relationship with affection, warmth and an unerring eye for detail.

He was, however, always pessimistic about the nature of man and his capacity to live harmoniously with his fellows; prejudice is never far from the surface in his communities. Twice during *Just Pals* the respectable citizenry forms a lynch mob, first to ride Bim out of town, and the second time to string him up when he is falsely accused of attempting to rob the express office. This intolerance extends to the younger members of the community, who beat up Bill simply because he is a ragged outsider. But Ford resolves the tensions by providing in Bim a selfless, Lincolnian figure who takes the sins of society onto his shoulders and combats the forces of darkness. He does it by accepting the blame for the theft of the school fund to protect the schoolmarm he loves, and saves the town from disaster by foiling the express-office robbery almost at the cost of his own life. Significantly, despite his rejection and ill-treatment, Bim still feels part of the community, telling the robbers: 'You ain't gonna rob *our* town.'

The short story that he could enrich, expand and develop was Ford's preferred source of film material, but when he was handed hit plays to film he found himself unable to solve the problem of how to convey great stretches of dialogue interestingly. *Lightnin'* (1925) was such a project. The first half of the film is pure character comedy, establishing the shiftless, booze-centred existence of Lightnin' Bill Jones (Jay Hunt), his attempts to outwit his wife, and his binges with his drinking pal Zeb. Halfway through the film the plot takes over as two swindlers try to gain control of Lightnin' Bill's hotel, and the story culminates with a lengthy trial sequence, which is tedious, protracted and tiresome. Similarly, *Cameo Kirby*, evokes lovingly and characteristically an elegant Old South of riverboats, white-painted plantation buildings and Negro slaves strumming banjos – yet gets bogged down for the last half-hour in a series of expository dialogue exchanges in set-piece interiors. Despite these partial failures, Ford's silent films gave ample testimony of a major talent, and it was a talent that was to reach full fruition in the years ahead.

JEFFREY RICHARDS

Directed by James Cruze, 1923

Prod co: Famous Players-Lasky. **prod:** James Cruze. **sc:** Jack Cunningham, from the novel by Emerson Hough. **photo:** Karl Brown. **ed:** Dorothy Arzner. **mus arr:** Hugo Riesenfeld. **tech adv:** Col. T. J. McCoy. **length:** 9407 ft (approx. 125 minutes). New York premiere, 16 March 1923.

Cast: Lois Wilson (*Molly Wingate*), J. Warren Kerrigan (*Will Banion*), Alan Hale (*Sam Woodhull*), Charles Ogle (*Jesse Wingate*), Ethel Wales (*Mrs Wingate*), Ernest Torrence (*Bill Jackson*), Tully Marshall (*Jim Bridger*), Guy Oliver (*Joe Dunstan*), John Fox (*Jed Wingate*).

Although the great migration westward across North America in the mid-nineteenth century had been treated in earlier Westerns such as *Wagon Tracks* (1919), which starred William S. Hart, *The Covered Wagon* was the first film to reconstruct the experience on the scale of the historical events and to emphasize the epic nature of the achievement.

It was filmed almost entirely on location, mostly on the borders of Utah and Nevada, under conditions that were at times as arduous as those suffered by the original pioneers. This was a striking departure from the standard procedure of closely supervised studio shooting, to which only Robert Flaherty's *Nanook of the North* (1922) offered a real precedent. Natural occurrences such as an unexpected snowfall were worked into the script. A river crossing was staged exactly as the original travellers achieved it by caulking the wagons and driving them across. Real Indians, 750 of them, were recruited as well as 1000 local inhabitants, and most of the 500 wagons used were genuine and not built for the film. Considerable historical research was undertaken to make the film look as convincingly authentic as possible.

The project was made possible by the enthusiasm of Jesse L. Lasky, himself the grandson of a pioneer. As vice-president in charge of production at Famous Players-Lasky, he won the support of the president, Adolph Zukor, to provide a budget five times that of a normal Western at a period when public interest in the genre was on the wane. Thereafter, it was the drive and passion of the director James Cruze that bulldozed the film through to completion, although Lasky then intervened to demand further shooting to make a stronger ending. *The Covered Wagon* finally cost a phenomenal $782,000 instead of the $500,000 originally authorized; but it was a smash hit, recouping nearly five times its cost, and as late as 1935 was generally reckoned one of the five top-grossing films to that time.

Its success revitalized the Western and encouraged Fox to shoot their railroad-building epic, *The Iron Horse* (1924), as well as to make their own wagon-train spectacular, *The Big Trail* (1930). Certainly John Ford and Raoul Walsh, as directors of these two films, showed far more imagination and artistic power than James Cruze; but it was Cruze who had shown what could be done.

The Covered Wagon no longer exists in its original form. Dramatic incidents such as a prairie fire have been removed and much documentary-like detail trimmed to give more prominence to the characters and plot. Although characterization is fairly rudimentary, the heroine shows unusual spirit and, if the hero, Banion, is too stoical in not countering the accusations of the villain, Woodhull, there is a certain vigour to their enmity with Banion barely resisting the opportunity to gouge out Woodhull's eyes after beating him in a fight, and constantly being urged by his old scout friend Bill Jackson to kill Woodhull.

River crossings and Indian attacks on encampments have become familiar ingredients of the Western, and the big scenes of *The Covered Wagon* have been criticized for their static and unadventurous use of the camera. The newsreel-like limited coverage can be seen as working in the film's favour. As Kevin Brownlow has put it:

'The fact that the camera is not ubiquitous . . . helps the initial impression that *The Covered Wagon* is a documentary record of an original trek in 1848.'

When the film is seen today, the lack of a spoken soundtrack strengthens this impression. In any case, *The Covered Wagon* makes up for a lack of camera movement by the memorable images captured by the cinematographer Karl Brown, such as the wagons of the gold seekers passing their abandoned ploughs or the shot of an Indian at night on top of a bluff, silhouetted by the white smoke of the migrants' camp fires as he shoots an arrow, or the mass of Indians charging forward in a straight line viewed from one end.

The titles convey the flavour of the colloquial speech of the West and also point up the epic character of what is being shown. The opening title reads:

'The blood of America is the blood of pioneers – the blood of lion-hearted men and women who carved a splendid civilization out of an uncharted wilderness.'

The film also presents the Indian point of view, clearly indicating that they were fighting to preserve their way of life. Perhaps most criticism of the film as a depiction of history has centred on the wagon train's occupying a box canyon and thereby inviting Indian attack from the surrounding heights. Cruze later suggested that it showed a blunder on the leader's part but no criticism of him is made within the film.

Surprisingly, *The Covered Wagon* was never remade, although Ernest Torrence and Tully Marshall played the characters of Bill Jackson and Jim Bridger again in Paramount's *Fighting Caravans* (1931) and the studio would have made it into one of their early VistaVision spectaculars in 1955 if the proposed star, Alan Ladd, had not suddenly departed from the studio.

ALLEN EYLES

1

3

5

8

2

In May 1848 at Westport Landing (later Kansas City), the leaders of two wagon trains, Jesse Wingate (1, left) and Will Banion (1, right), watched by Wingate's deputy Sam Woodhull, agree to travel together on the 2000-mile trek to Oregon (2). Wingate's daughter Molly is engaged to Woodhull but attracted to Banion.

Woodhull refers to Banion's clouded past as an army officer and the two men argue (3). At the Platte river they brawl over the best way of crossing (4). Woodhull provokes the Indians by taking their ferry and shooting the owners; they destroy most of his section of the wagon train. Banion drives the other wagons across at a shallower point of the river (5).

The party crosses the Rockies to Fort Bridger, where Jim Bridger, a trader, has just learned of the discovery of gold in California. Consequently the train splits: Wingate's followers decide to continue to Oregon, while Banion leads a breakaway party heading for California. Molly is about to marry Woodhull when Bridger tells her that Banion's army reputation has been restored (6). Indians suddenly attack, wounding Molly (7) as they surround the wagon train (8). Banion's party returns to save the settlers.

By the following year Banion has struck it rich in California (9). His friend Bill Jackson foils Woodhull's final attempt to dispose of his rival. Banion rides to Oregon and is reunited with Molly (10).

4

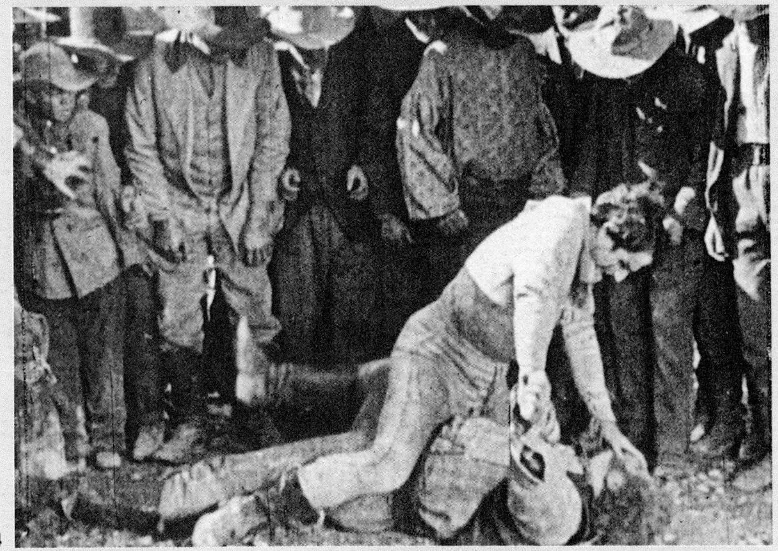

6

7

9

10

‘Rex Ingram, pageant-master’

. . . that is how fellow-Dubliner James Joyce, writing in his novel *Finnegans Wake*, described this artist of the silent screen. The director Michael Powell has meanwhile called his first employer in films ‘the greatest stylist of his time’. Certainly few film-makers since Ingram have been able to match his use of visual imagery in conveying mysticism and romance

Above left: Ingram and June Mathis relax during the shooting of The Four Horsemen of the Apocalypse. *Above: Paul Wegener as* The Magician, *with Alice Terry as his virgin captive and Stowitts as the dancing faun*

The Irish-born director Rex Ingram was one of the most glamorous figures in Hollywood in the Twenties. He was the outstanding romantic pictorialist of the silent screen; when the producer Dore Schary later considered the ‘top creative people . . . in the early days of films’, he named D.W. Griffith, Ingram, Cecil B. DeMille and Erich von Stroheim – in that order. Film-makers as diverse as Yasujiro Ozu, David Lean and Michael Powell have acknowledged their debt to him. Not the least of Ingram's achievements was the launching of great stars like Rudolph Valentino and Ramon Novarro, and his contributions to the careers of players of the calibre of Lewis Stone, Cleo Madison, Barbara La Marr, Paul Wegener, Ivan Petrovitch and Antonio Moreno. He also shone because he was extremely good-looking and charming and promoted an awareness of his work in audiences so that to the filmgoers of the Twenties ‘A Rex Ingram Production’ really meant something.

From Dublin's fair city

Born Reginald Ingram Montgomery Hitchcock in Dublin in January 1893, Ingram spent most of his childhood in his father's rectory in the village of Kinnitty. He was educated at St Columba's College, Dublin. In 1911, shortly after the death of his mother, he emigrated to the USA and worked at the rail stockyards in New Haven, before enrolling in the sculpture class of Lee Lawrie at the Yale School of Fine Arts. In 1913, inspired by the Vitagraph film *A Tale of Two Cities* (1911), he joined the Edison Company as an actor, designer and general handyman. Eventually he joined Vitagraph as a leading actor and scriptwriter, and from 1915 worked at Fox, providing scripts for such stars as Betty Nansen, Robert Mantell, Nance O'Neill and Theda Bara. After this apprenticeship he began directing at Universal, beginning with the melodrama *The Great Problem*, made in 1916 when he was only 23, and in all completing ten films at the studio. Set in exotic, colourful locations such as Hong Kong, Mexico, Italy and Russia, these films were distinguished by a fine pictorial sense, relentless pursuit of atmosphere and the use of deformed actors, especially dwarfs and hunchbacks. Notable are *Black Orchids* (1916), starring Cleo Madison as a *femme fatale* in a Gothic romance (remade by Ingram as *Trifling Women* in 1922), and *The Reward of the Faithless* (1917) which, with its scenes of sordid slums, was almost a blueprint for Erich von Stroheim's *Greed* (1925).

Fired by Universal in 1917 after disagreements with the studio, Ingram suffered a lean period. He made two films for the Paralta W.W. Hodkinson Corporation, but neither *His Robe of Honor* nor *Humdrum Brown*, both made in 1918 and starring Henry B. Walthall, was successful. Moreover, Ingram was disappointed by his brief and unhappy marriage to Doris Pawn, a Universal serial queen. He enlisted in the Royal Canadian Flying Corps, but was too late for active service in World War I

He returned to Universal and made *Under Crimson Skies* (1920), with Elmo Lincoln as a ship's captain involved in a revolution, and this was a success. Ingram was regarded at this time as a man to be watched.

Conquests at Metro

In 1920 he made two well-received melodramas for Metro, *Shore Acres* and *Hearts Are Trumps*, starring Alice Terry (b.1900) whom Ingram subsequently married. He then embarked on the film that was to make him famous, *The Four Horsemen of the Apocalypse* (1921), adapted from Vicente Blasco-Ibáñez's best-selling novel about World War I by the scriptwriter-producer June Mathis. It featured the unknown Rudolph Valentino in the role – of a libertine artist who fights for the French army – that set him on the road to stardom. Ingram was already aware of the young Latin's potential, and with Alice Terry and a fine supporting cast, he created an overwhelming box-office success. It was also a fine artistic achievement by the director, and stunningly photographed by his regular cameraman John Seitz. The film's range of settings, from Argentina to wartime Paris, from the Battle of the Marne to Lourdes, provided Ingram with ample opportunity to vary the atmosphere and he did so with characteristic ease.

The team next produced *The Conquering Power* (1921), based on Honoré de Balzac's novel *Eugénie Grandet*, which was more of a vehicle for Alice Terry – who played a miser's daughter vainly in love with her cousin, an

Above left: Zareda (Barbara La Marr) and her chimpanzee spy in Trifling Women. *Left: Ingram acting in an unidentified film from about 1913, with Helen Gardner. Below: Rudolph Valentino as Julio Desnoyers, artist, in* The Four Horsemen of the Apocalypse

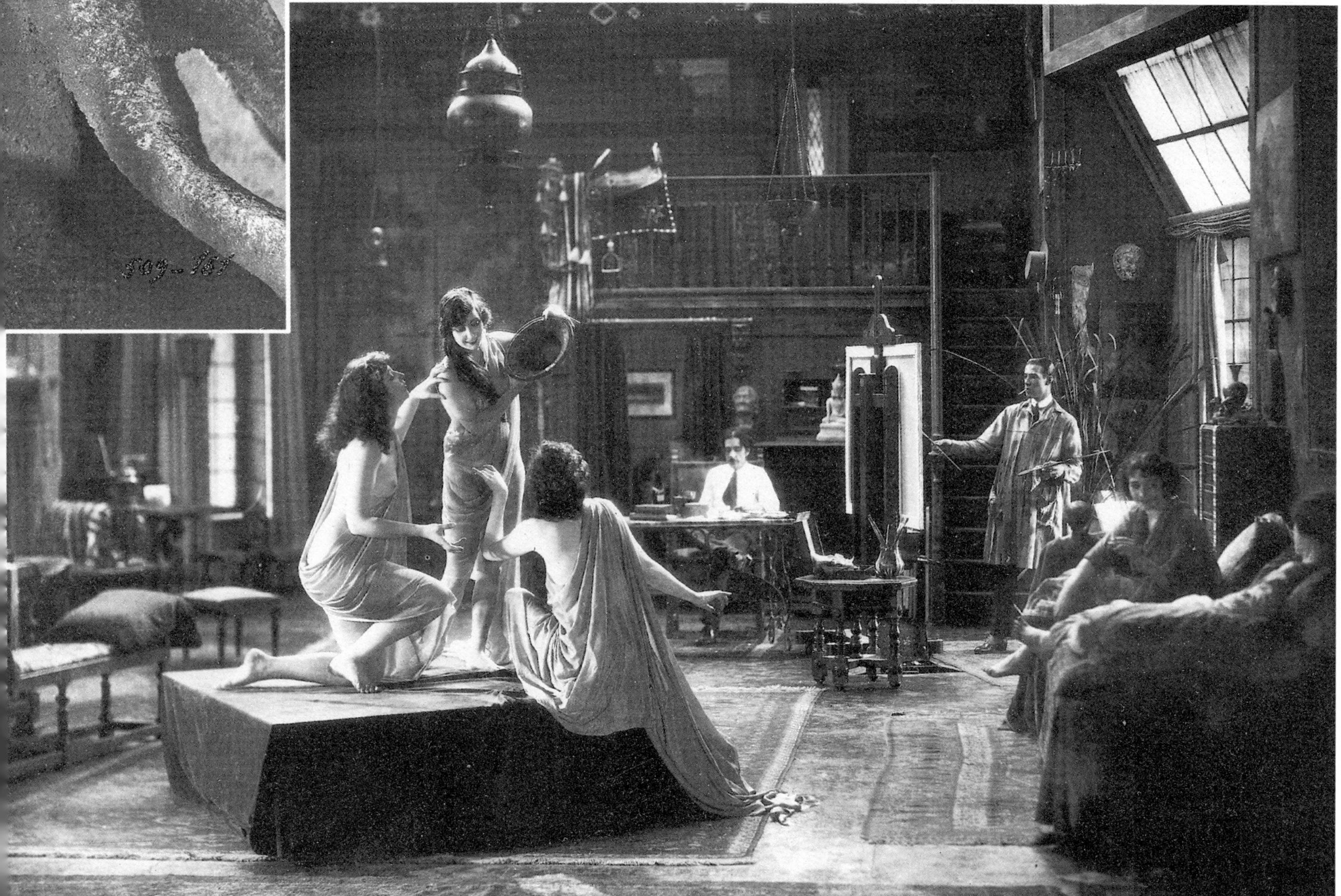

impoverished socialite – than for Valentino, who was rapidly becoming the hottest property in Hollywood. An insignificant comedy, *Turn to the Right*, preceded Ingram's next success *The Prisoner of Zenda* (both 1922), for which he discovered a new star, Ramon Novarro, to play Rupert of Hentzau; Lewis Stone and Alice Terry played the lovers Rudolph Rassendyll and Princess Flavia. By now Ingram had *carte blanche* at Metro, and in rapid succession came *Trifling Women*, with Barbara La Marr; *Where the Pavement Ends* (1923), a South Seas tragedy with Novarro and Terry; and the monumental *Scaramouche* (1923), a beautifully-shot romance of the French Revolution with Novarro, Terry and Stone.

Arabian sights

Ingram was by now considered one of the American cinema's major artists, and particularly attracted the admiration and friendship of Erich von Stroheim, who entrusted him with the second cut of the over-length *Greed*. Hollywood, however, was becoming more regimented and Ingram wanted to get away. He believed films should be shot at the locations of their stories, so in 1924 went to North Africa to film *The Arab*, a story about a white missionary's daughter (Alice Terry) in love with the son of a sheik (Ramon Novarro), also involving a plot to slay Christians. The same year Ingram refurbished the old Victorine studio at Nice on the south-east coast of France, and there produced his favourite film, the lavish and costly *Mare Nostrum* (1926), from another World War I novel by Blasco-Ibáñez, about love and espionage in the Mediterranean. Alice Terry was cast in a Mata Hari-like role as Freya Talberg who entices Ulysses Ferragut (Antonio Moreno), the Spanish captain of a sailing ship, the *Mare Nostrum*, to provide fuel for German submarines, one of which torpedoes an enemy ship causing the death of the captain's son. Freya is shot as a spy and Ulysses goes down with his ship after destroying the submarine, but the lovers – with Freya now become the goddess Amphitrite – are mystically reunited in the deep. *Mare Nostrum* (which, like *Greed*, was extensively cut by Metro before release) was well received in America and France, but along with *The Four Horsemen of the Apocalypse* it was withdrawn in the late Twenties because of anti-German content.

Ingram eventually became owner of the Nice studio after MGM turned down its option to buy it outright, and he subsequently rented it to the Hollywood company for future productions. He made two further films there for MGM, but as he hated Louis B. Mayer he insisted they were 'Metro-Goldwyn' productions. The first was the macabre and erotic *The Magician* (1926), based on Somerset Maugham's story with a central character inspired by the notorious occultist Aleister Crowley; he was portrayed by Paul Wegener who had impressed Ingram in *Der Golem: Wie er in die Welt kam* (1920, *The Golem*). Alice

Terry played the virgin hypnotized by th magician, who needs her heart for his ma experiments.

Back to the desert

Next came *The Garden of Allah* (1927), phot graphed by Lee Garmes, Ingram's replacemer for John Seitz who had returned to Hollywoo Shot on location in North Africa, it concerns

hree roles for Alice Terry. Above: as the bride ˚ a monk (Ivan Petrovitch, left) in the weltering, guilt-ridden The Garden of Allah. *bove right: as Freya going to her execution in* lare Nostrum. *Below: as the white girl whose ative lover (Ramon Novarro) drowns himself 'hen she is taken from him in* Where the avement Ends. *Right: the massacre of the wiss Guard in* Scaramouche

Trappist monk (Ivan Petrovitch) who abandons his faith, flees to the desert and marries a young girl (Alice Terry) but is overcome by guilt. Ingram no longer wanted to work in Hollywood, and with his MGM contract expiring, remained in Nice to make two films for other companies. *The Three Passions* (1929) combined romantic and religious themes in a labour-relations drama and starred Alice Terry as a flapper in her last film. Ingram's final picture, and his only talkie, was *Baroud* (1932), a story of love and tribal war in Morocco, in which he himself played the lead part of a Spahi regiment officer. A strange film, visually very beautiful, it was marred by execrable dialogue spoken by an international cast.

As a film-maker Ingram had come to the end of the road. In Nice he was an uncrowned king, and his friends read like a *Who's Who* of Twenties social and literary life. But he had legal difficulties with the studio and lost control of it. He did not really accept the sound film and his interest in movies waned. He was passionately in love with African life and culture (reputedly becoming a Mohammedan), and spent some years in Cairo before returning to Hollywood in 1936 where he spent his time on his writing and sculpture and occasional travels to Spain, Mexico and the Caribbean. He died in Los Angeles on July 21, 1950 and was survived by his charming and devoted wife Alice Terry. LIAM O'LEARY

Filmography

Films as actor Rex Hitchcock only unless otherwise specified: **1913** The Family's Honor (sc. only); Beau Brummel (as Rex Ingram). **'14** The Spirit and the Clay; Her Great Scoop; Eve's Daughter (orig. title: The Artist's Madonna); The Crime of Cain; The Evil Men Do; The Circus and the Boy; His Wedded Wife; The Upper Hand; Fine Feathers Make Fine Birds; The Moonshine Maid and the Man; The Necklace of Rameses; Goodbye Summer (as Rex Ingram). **'15** Snatched From a Burning Death. *Films as Rex Ingram*: The Blindness of Devotion (sc. only); A Woman's Past (sc. only); The Wonderful Adventure (sc. only); The Song of Hate (sc. only). **'16** Should a Mother Tell? (sc. only); The Great Problem (+sc); Broken Fetters/A Human Pawn (+sc); Chalice of Sorrow (+sc) (GB: The Chalice of Remorse); Black Orchids (+sc) (GB: The Fatal Orchids). **'17** The Reward of the Faithless (+sc); The Pulse of Life (+sc); The Flower of Doom (+sc); Little Terror (+sc). **'18** His Robe of Honor; Humdrum Brown. **'19** The Day She Paid. **'20** Under Crimson Skies/The Beach Comber; Shore Acres; Hearts Are Trumps. **'21** The Four Horsemen of the Apocalypse (+sup); The Conquering Power. **'22** Turn to the Right; The Prisoner of Zenda (+prod); Trifling Women (+sc). **'23** Where the Pavement Ends (+sc); Mary of the Movies (appearance as himself only); Scaramouche (+prod). **'24** The Arab (+sc). **'25** Greed (co-ed. only). **'26** Mare Nostrum/Our Sea (+prod); The Magician (+sc). **'27** The Garden of Allah. **'29** The Three Passions (+sc). **'32** Baroud (+prod; +co-sc; +act) (FR-GB) (FR: Les Hommes Bleus).

Rudolph Valentino

Rudolph Valentino flashed across the skies of America like a meteor and plunged to earth in the only dramatic moment of his life – his death. The suddenness of his illness and the swiftness of his death caused a wave of hysteria never seen before or since. The fantasy figure of all women of any age – he was the Great Lover

The Man

Few women in the world could fail to be thrilled at being torn from their escort and whirled into a tango so erotic as to be a virtual seduction – like Valentino's tango in *The Four Horsemen of the Apocalypse* (1921). What woman could resist the naked, animal appeal of a man who could with a slow, slow, upward sweep of narrowed eyes strip off her riding breeches, ignoring the outward jutting of her jaw and her masculine stance and ask, simply, 'Are you not woman enough to know?' as Valentino asks in *The Sheik* (1921)? Imagine the attraction of being able to bring to his knees a man who could bring wild, dangerous bulls to their knees in the bull ring, as Valentino does in *Blood and Sand* (1922).

In watching Valentino many women come as close as they ever will to a passionate, virile, caressing lover, submissive only to their beauty. His encompassing appeal to women has always fascinated male biographers and historians: animal magnetism, charisma, 'it' – his wide-eyed tender glances; flashing, passionate eyes; his grace, his love-making, his unashamed use of his body in his dancing. Some indefinable quality shines through Valentino and makes him irresistible.

He was Italian to the bone, with all the Italian charm and not a few of the Italian vices, and, like so many Italians of both sexes, he had a breathtaking beauty in the bloom of his youth which would run to fat after its brief flowering. A snapshot taken at the Paramount commissary when he was working on *Monsieur Beaucaire* (1924) shows unmistakable signs of a jowl, and his costumed pictures all show him in a very corseted waist-band.

The coming of sound would have presented no problem to him. He was a natural linguist who spoke fluent Spanish and French, indeed, a lot of the dialogue in *Monsieur Beaucaire* was spoken in French. His English is said to have been easy and colloquial, with a touch of a foreign accent. This could only have added to his romantic appeal. Weight, had he lived, would have been the constant battle. Dancing came as naturally to him as languages.

After graduating from the Royal Academy of Agriculture in Genoa he went to Paris (his mother was French), and he undoubtedly picked up ballroom dancing in the gay, carefree student world to which, as a 17-year-old boy, he naturally gravitated. It is unlikely that there would have been formal dances in the small town of Castellaneta in Southern Italy where his middle-class family lived and where he was born Rodolfo Guglielmi in 1895. When his money ran out in Paris he was still young enough simply to write home for a ticket back to Castellaneta.

At 18 the spirit of adventure was strong in him, and he sailed for America – again well supplied with money. 'Italy is too small for me', he told his brother.

He lived the same carefree life in New York that he had lived in Paris, but this time when his money ran out his Italian pride rose. Instead of writing for the fare home he deliberately lied to his family. He stole writing-paper from the Waldorf-Astoria Hotel, had a photograph taken of himself in hired dress clothes to prove how prosperous he was – and slept in Central Park. He may have been involved in a minor way in a blackmail and extortion racket and spent a few days in The Tombs prison until the charge was dropped.

His good looks, youth, natural charm, European courtesy and dancing ability saved him from starvation and possibly from more serious crime. He found a job as a dancing partner at the popular thé-dansants held by most of the expensive hotels and restaurants in New York.

At one of these he partnered Bess Dudley, whose friend Bonnie Glass was a professional dancer at nightclubs and theatres and who was looking for a new partner to replace future film-star Clifton Webb. The first step away from the farm had been taken, and he began on the precarious and bewildering path of show-biz.

The dancing act ended when Bonnie Glass married, and Valentino hitched a ride with Al Jolson's dancing troupe to Utah, and from there he reached San Francisco and the Italian Agriculture Society whose function it was to help immigrant farmers. In spite of his qualifications the Society required a deposit of $1000 before they were able to help him acquire land, but Valentino did not have $1000.

Chance directed his destiny when he ran into an old friend, the actor Norman Kerry, who was working with Mary Pickford on location in San Francisco. Kerry persuaded

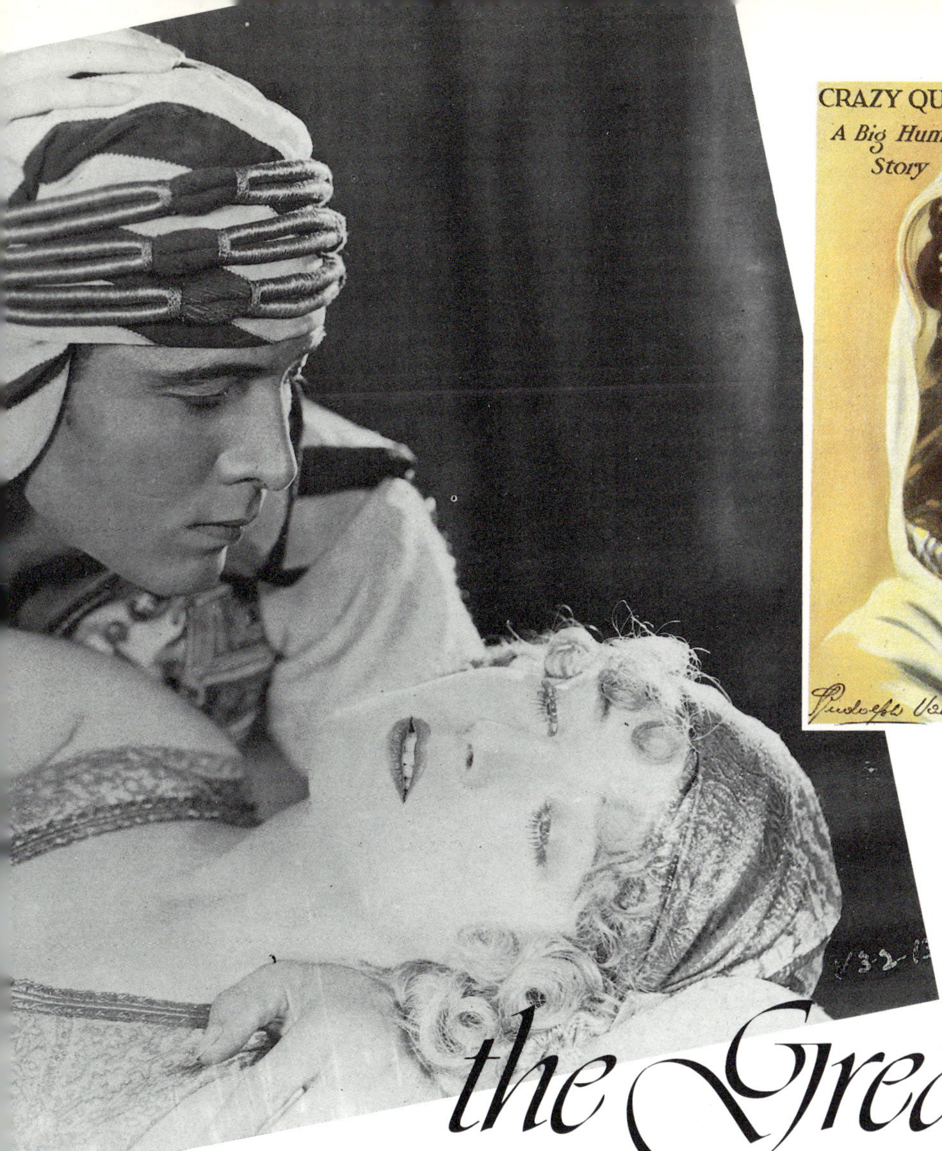

Far left: an unbilled role for Valentino in A Rogue's Romance *(1919) with Earle Williams. Left: as* The Son of the Sheik, *embracing the dancing-girl Yasmin (Vilma Banky) and (above) on a magazine cover. Below: playing an Argentinian libertine who later fights for France in* The Four Horsemen of the Apocalypse. *Below left: with Alla Nazimova in* Camille

the Great Lover

Above left: Don Alonza (Valentino) with Julietta (Helen D'Algy), the wife who, on their wedding night, is snatched from him by bandits in *A Sainted Devil* (1924)

Above: *The Eagle* has Valentino as an officer turned highwayman. By the time he made this film he was no longer under the influence of Natacha Rambova (below)

Valentino to try Hollywood. And so the traditional upward grind began. Weeks of no work, weeks of bit parts – mostly as 'heavies' – and eventually larger parts in undistinguished pictures. The money he earned went not on fast living, but on the Italian love of fast cars. Valentino was not a good driver. He was involved in many minor accidents. A faint scar on his right cheek is discernible in some pictures of him.

June Mathis, head of the script department and a power at Metro, saw in this young, unremarkable actor a rare and unrevealed magnetic personality and pressured the front office into casting him in *The Four Horsemen of the Apocalypse*. The meteor took off.

To the despair of the gossip writers Valentino was no partygoer, no womanizer and no drunkard. Only one scandal flared. After a brief, unconsummated marriage to actress Jean Acker, he fell in love with the extraordinary Natacha Rambova, a talented designer, and married her, in May 1922, before his divorce was finalized. The result of this was a charge of bigamy being brought against him, but it was very soon dropped.

Rambova had a disastrous effect on this easy-going young man. She forced him into quarrels with various studios, and said at one point they were so short of food that Valentino was forced to poach partridge and rabbit so that they could eat. She obliged him to live in the extravagant style she felt befitted a film star and encouraged his interest in spiritualism. He published a book of slushy poetry dictated from 'the other side' by his guide Black Feather.

This marriage lasted only long enough to give him the taste for extravagance which was nearly to bankrupt him, as well as the ulcers that he would ultimately die from in 1926.

The box-office receipts from the films following *The Four Horsemen of the Apocalypse* may have wavered, but his personal popularity never even flickered. His brother recalls that during periods of insolvency they lived on the quarters they charged for 'signed' photographs of him, requests for which came in sack-loads. Valentino was extremely short-sighted and is said, as a result, to have been refused enlistment in the Air Force during the war. This myopia may have accounted for those deep penetrating looks into the very souls of his leading ladies; those narrow-eyed glances so full of passion that they stirred the blood of American womanhood. Perhaps he was merely trying to get them into focus.

Above: Valentino taunting his victims – whoever they may be – in Blood and Sand. *r left:* Monsieur Beaucaire *with his brother ndré Daven)*

But the one quality that shines through oriously in every shot of every movie he ade is his astonishing grace. Freeze any me from any film and there is a picture of a llet dancer. And together with this balletic ace there was also the controlled balletic uscle power. He could lift a woman from the ound onto a horse in one breathtaking ooping movement as effortlessly and as ntily as if he were flicking a lace cuff.

f as a care-free, spendthrift youth of 18 lentino had had the prudence to put to one e a mere quarter of the $4000 he brought th him to America, he would undoubtedly ve become a fat, prosperous Californian mer. As it was he became immortal.

ELIZABETH LODGE

The Movies

Rodolfo Guglielmi reached Hollywood in 1917. Between then and 1920 he appeared in at least 17 films, in parts varying from tiny to fairly large. Young Guglielmi, known as Rodolfo di Valentina, played gangsters, co-respondents, and a variety of louche Italian types but not one of his films was in the least important. In *Eyes of Youth* (1919), however, he impressed, and he subsequently landed the part of the playboy Julio in an ambitious Rex Ingram production, *The Four Horsemen of the Apocalypse*. Ingram, who had met the actor before and borne him in mind, took a chance, and when he saw the impact of his new actor in the famous tango scene, he determined to build up that aspect of the part. But Valentino had more to contribute. The tone of the film becomes far darker with the wartime sequences, the hero matures and suffers, and Valentino reveals a versatility and command of varying emotion astonishing in one so inexperienced.

He was supremely lucky, here and in *The Conquering Power* (1921), to be guided by one of the greatest of Hollywood's silent directors in Rex Ingram. It was a benefit Valentino would not often enjoy. Of his twelve other major pictures, only the last two – *The Eagle* (1925), *The Son of the Sheik* (1926) – were directed by men of genuine stature. By then the influence of his wife Natacha Rambova was declining, and there was more room for directors with personalities of their own.

In 1921 Rambova had begun to dominate the actor's career, and *Camille*, also made that year, was more remarkable for her bizarre art-deco designs and for Alla Nazimova's striking performance than for Valentino's contribution. Ingram's *The Conquering Power*, a version of Honoré de Balzac's *Eugénie Grandet*, offered Valentino a chance for what was almost a character portrayal, and as an elderly man at the end he was entirely convincing. Had he missed stardom, he would still have been much in demand. He then broke with Metro, and *The Sheik* (1921), his first film for Famous Players-Lasky, saw the beginning of the legend.

The Sheik was a crude enough picture, and without Valentino's uninhibited eroticism might well have been nothing: as it was, it produced a phenomenal reaction among women, and soon led to the jealous reaction from men which was to hound Valentino for the rest of his life. The viciousness of anti-Valentino articles in *Photoplay*, a periodical capable of maintaining its spite against a star it disliked for a very long time, is still as astonishing as it is offensive. The furore suited the studio, and they rushed Valentino into four 1922 releases, of which only *Blood and Sand*, drawn like *The Four Horsemen of the Apocalypse* from a Vicente Blasco-Ibáñez novel, was worthy of him. Here again he showed that particular sense for the maturing of a character, for conveying the wearing effects of time and mischance, which he possessed to such a degree. At the beginning of *Blood and Sand* he is a happy, unaffected boy; at the end, for all his glittering virility, he has had enough of success, romantic and professional alike, and embraces his death almost willingly.

Nine Valentino films had been released in his first two years of stardom, so rapid and so concentrated was his ascent. Now, however, there was a hiatus for two years while he and Rambova quarrelled with the studio. There was more to be said for Rambova than is usually admitted. She was right to resent the trashy vehicles which wasted Valentino's talent. She was a brilliant designer. Her *Salome*, for Nazimova in 1922, may have been decadent, but the design was as successful in giving an overall unity to a movie as could be wished. And if she was fatally wrong in thinking that a doctrine of Film-as-Art was viable in Hollywood, that was not an ignoble error.

When Valentino returned to the screen in *Monsieur Beaucaire*, it was in a film designed by Rambova. The film has never been much liked, and certainly it could have done with a livelier director than the veteran Sidney Olcott, but in some ways it shows Valentino to enormous advantage. His sense of fun is delightful, and while he moves and poses more balletically than ever, he does it all with an ironic enjoyment that never fails to communicate itself to the audience.

His last three films were made after his final break with Famous Players-Lasky, and the last two were a triumphant end. Valentino and Rambova had separated, and Valentino made *The Eagle* with a fine director in Clarence Brown; the film also had an exceptionally witty script by Hans Kraly, writer of so many brilliant films for the director Ernst Lubitsch. In *The Eagle* Valentino plays a Cossack lieutenant who becomes a rather benevolent bandit, has to pose as a teacher of French, and has difficulty in escaping the Czarina's amorous advances. He relishes every moment of the role, knows he is irresistible and wickedly glories in it. Valentino in *The Eagle* is the acutest critic of his own tawdrier roles.

Unhappily, he had but one film left, *The Son of the Sheik*, again with a good director, George Fitzmaurice. By the time that it was shown, Valentino was dead. Behind the legend, behind the swooning and the loathing, there was an actor – a skilful professional with a wide range and an ever developing knowledge of his craft. He would have weathered sound more easily than other outright romantic stars: his wit would certainly have guaranteed that.

JACK LODGE

Filmography

1918 Alimony; The Married Virgin/Frivolous Wives (as Rodolfo di Valentina); A Society Sensation (GB: The Little Duchess) (as M. Rodolpho De Valentina); All Night (as M. Rodolpho De Valentina). **'19** The Delicious Little Devil (as Rudolpho De Valentina); The Big Little Person (as M. Rodolpho De Valentina); A Rogue's Romance; The Homebreaker; Out of Luck; Virtuous Sinners; Eyes of Youth. **'20** An Adventuress/The Isle of Love (as Rodolpho De Valentina); Stolen Moments (as Rodolfo Valentino); The Cheater; Passion's Playground (as Rudolpho Valentino); Once to Every Woman/Ambition; The Wonderful Chance (as Rudolph De Valentino). **'21** The Four Horsemen of the Apocalypse; Uncharted Seas (GB: The Uncharted Sea); Camille; The Conquering Power; The Sheik. **'22** Moran of the Lady Letty; Beyond the Rocks; Blood and Sand; The Young Rajah. **'23** Rudolph Valentino and the Eighty-Eight American Beauties (doc); Valentino in England (doc) (unfinished). **'24** Monsieur Beaucaire; A Sainted Devil. **'25** Cobra; The Eagle. **'26** The Son of the Sheik.

Possible appearances as extra in the following films: **1914** The Battle of the Sexes; My Official Wife. **'16** Seventeen; The Foolish Virgin. **'17** Patricia (one ep. only in series).

Douglas Fairbanks

Cutting

The first swashbuckling superstar, and among the silent screen's most revered idols, was the man known affectionately to fans the world over as 'Doug'

Top left: Wild and Woolly *(1917) featured a chubby young Fairbanks who, like good wine, improved with age. Top: swashbuckling his way to fame – Zorro, Lolita (Marguerite de la Motte) and Captain Ramon (Robert McKim) struggle in* The Mark of Zorro. *Above right: how's that? – in* The Three Musketeers. *Left: stealing hearts in* The Thief of Bagdad

Born Douglas Elton Ulman in Denver, Colorado, on May 23, 1883, Douglas Fairbanks entered the theatre in his teens and soon became a juvenile lead. Hollywood was quick to seize him, and Fairbanks made his film debut for the Triangle company in *The Lamb* (1915), the first of a series of movies built around his personality and glorifying the all-American 'Doug'. D. W. Griffith, the film's supervisor and one of the Triangle moguls, disliked Fairbanks' unrestrained exuberance, disapproved of his ideas that movies should mean perpetual motion and advised him to go into Keystone comedies. The public, however, thought differently, and their response encouraged him not only to persevere in films but to go into business for himself.

In 1916 he set up the Douglas Fairbanks Film Corporation to release his films through Paramount-Artcraft. From then on, almost to the end of his career, he would be his own master: not only the star of his films but also their creator, for he would supervise production, direction and writing to secure his vision.

ash

n 1919 Fairbanks, D.W. Griffith, Mary Pick-ord and Charlie Chaplin founded United Artists in order to release their own indepen-lent films.

Fairbanks' screen character in these years was that of a bright, breezy, virile and self-eliant American athlete, the product of a philosophy that Fairbanks personally believed n: he advocated keeping fit, active and happy n a series of ghost-written books with self-xplanatory titles such as *Laugh and Live*, *nitiative and Self-reliance* and *Making Life Vorthwhile*. His films reflected the restless nergy of their star, mingling action and omedy, and bore equally self-explanatory itles – *He Comes Up Smiling* (1918), *The Knickerbocker Buckaroo*, *His Majesty, the Amer-can* and *When the Clouds Roll By* (all 1919).

However, in 1920 – at the age of 37 – airbanks took the historic decision to desert he world of contemporary satire and comedy Vestern in which he had made his name and ackle a period adventure. *The Mark of Zorro* 1920) was modestly budgeted, took a fairly ecent and so still familiar period (Spanish alifornia) and featured a hero with a dual ersonality (fop and adventurer) similar to hose he had portrayed in his previous adven-ure films. To provide a final piece of insurance gainst the film's failure, Fairbanks completed *The Nut* (1921), a comedy along the old lines, to be rushed into release should *The Mark of Zorro* fail. But it did not; instead it launched Fair-banks into immortality.

It seems reasonable to assume that Fair-banks' involvement with the great creative talents of his partners in United Artists inspired him to emulate their cinematic achievements. At any rate, from *The Mark of Zorro* onwards he sought to surpass himself at every stage: he built the biggest set Hollywood had ever seen for *Robin Hood* (1922); he out-did all previous special-effects fantasies with *The Thief of Bagdad* (1924); and he mastered the new two-tone Technicolor for *The Black Pirate* (1927). As a result he became the 'King of Hollywood' during the Twenties. Appropriately married to 'America's Sweetheart' Mary Pickford, he held court in the palatial 'Pickfair' mansion for the moguls of moviedom and the real-life blue-bloods of Europe. Fairbanks' and Pickford's world tours were like royal progresses. In 1926 *Robin Hood* was showing at 11 of the 12 first-run cinemas in Moscow, completely eclipsing the newly released *Bronenosets Potemkin* (1925, *Battleship Potemkin*), and when Doug and Mary arrived in Russia 300,000 people turned out to meet them at the station. The Russians even made a film called *Potselui Meri Pikford* (1927, *The Kiss of Mary Pickford*), about a cinema usher who believes he is Douglas Fairbanks – such was the celebrity of this remarkable couple.

The flashing blade

It was Fairbanks who gave the swashbuckling film its distinctive shape, look and 'feel'. Cen-tral to his films was action, and all action scenes were carefully choreographed. Douglas Fairbanks Jr later said of his father that he 'tended to think of himself more as a dancer than just as an athlete.' Indeed, his action sequences come across like athletic dances rather than mere stunts. They appear effort-less, but this was only achieved after weeks of rehearsal and painstaking preparation: Fair-banks mastered the use of sword, bull-whip and longbow; he engaged the first of the great Hollywood fencing masters, Henry J. Uyt-tenhove, to help design his swordfights; and he often used a metronome to establish the rhythm of his movements. The sets were constructed to the dictates of the action: furniture was specially built to suit the length of his reach and grasp; hidden hand-holds were installed in the stonework of buildings to allow him to scamper up walls without a hint of effort. In *Robin Hood* a slide was concealed behind the curtain drapes down which Fair-banks slides in one of his most spectacular stunts; in *The Black Pirate* he plunges down a sail, supported ostensibly by a dagger but in fact by an intricate mechanism of piano wire; for *The Thief of Bagdad* his spectacular leaps in and out of huge jars were aided by concealed trampolines. The flow of the action was always helped by the fact that Fairbanks did many of his own stunts, and several of them became 'standards' reproduced by succeeding swash-bucklers. However, they never surpassed the impact created by the originals.

Perfection personified

The other outstanding feature of a Fairbanks film was its 'look'. No expense was spared. 'These things have to be done properly or not at all', he would say. He assembled the best art directors and production designers available,

"DOUGLAS FAIRBANKS
AS THE
GAUCHO"

Douglas
FAIRBANKS
DON JUAN
ALEXANDER KORDA

Above, far left: chivalry from director Allan Dwan (centre) as Mary Pickford takes the chair while visiting Robin Hood. *Above left: from a whiter-than-white outlaw to* The Gaucho, *bandit of the pampas and seducer of women (left, with Lupe Velez). Far left: eight years on but D'Artagnan is still played with panache in* The Iron Mask. *Bottom, far left: another tailor-made role in* The Private Life of Don Juan. *Above: piracy romanticized in* The Black Pirate

and as a result his films became triumphs of imaginative art direction, successively providing stunning evocations of twelfth-century England, seventeenth-century France, nineteenth-century Spain and Arabian Nights' Bagdad.

The Mark of Zorro, directed by Fred Niblo, actually looks rather homely when compared with the luxuries of Fairbanks' later extravaganzas, and the plot is wafer-thin, consisting of a series of encounters in which Zorro outwits the forces of oppression. But the film is entirely redeemed by the star's performance as the black-masked avenger out to champion the oppressed. His set-piece gymnastics reveal him to be a spirit of the air rather than of the earth, and established the Fairbanks image for posterity.

It was an image consolidated in *The Three Musketeers* (1921), in which he created the definitive screen D'Artagnan – romantic, ardent, excitable and at times absurd. The swaggering walk, the sweep of the hat, the deep formal bows, hands on hips and head thrown back in laughter – all actions to capture the spirit of the young Gascon swordsman. The period was extensively researched and the outcome was a series of lavish and intricately detailed seventeenth-century sets and sumptuous costumes. Unfortunately, much as the later *Robin Hood*, it suffers from a slow build-up and an overlong exposition of court intrigue, stolidly handled by the workmanlike but rarely inspired Fred Niblo. But this stolidity is effortlessly surmounted by Fairbanks in the plentiful action sequences that call on him to ride, fight and clamber over rooftops, gates and walls.

Robin Hood, directed by Allan Dwan, is by any standards one of the landmarks of the silent screen. The sheer size and visual splendour of the film still takes the breath away. Its sets, which included an entire medieval castle containing a 450 foot banqueting hall, dwarfed even those of D. W. Griffith's celebrated *Intolerance* (1916). Designed as a chivalric epic, the film put on display all the panoply and splendour of medieval chivalry as idealized by nineteenth-century Romanticism, striking exactly the right note of innocent simplicity and mythic grandeur. Robin Hood is – like almost all Fairbanksian heroes – a grown-up schoolboy, bashful and hesitant with women but dashing and endlessly energetic when it comes to racing round the castle and fighting his enemies against overwhelming odds.

Peter Pan of pictures

With Raoul Walsh's *The Thief of Bagdad* Fairbanks' films scaled new heights of visual magnificence. It was the ultimate Arabian Nights fantasy, inspired by the story of Prince Ahmed's quest for the rarest object in the world. William Cameron Menzies' sets were a triumph of stylized Orientalism, and the outstanding special effects included a winged horse, a flying carpet, a magic army, a dragon and a voyage to the bottom of the sea. Fairbanks, lithe and agile as ever and clad only in a pair of gossamer pants and moustache, glides and leaps his way through it all with undiminished enthusiasm.

For *Don Q, Son of Zorro* (1925) the setting is a romantically conceived Old Spain, a world of ruined castles, Flamenco dancers and rose gardens. Fairbanks plays Zorro's son Cesar, a student wrongly accused of murder and forced to adopt the mask of an avenger (Don Q) to prove his innocence. His character is that of a high-spirited young man who always chooses to enter a room by sliding down the bannisters, to enter a house by vaulting over the wall and to light a cigarette by cracking a bull-whip across an open fire. For the spectacular finale Don Q is joined by his father Zorro, and with the aid of split-screen photography Fairbanks appeared at the same time as both father and son.

The Black Pirate is the definitive pirate picture. Unburdened by reels of court intrigue and lengthy plot exposition, the film is unequalled (even among Fairbanks' swashbucklers) for its humour, stylized acrobatics and sheer *joie de vivre*. His next film, *The Gaucho* (1927), was completely different. Uncharacteristically dark-toned, it is a mystical drama of faith and redemption, complete with visions of the Virgin (Mary Pickford) and miraculous cures. Fairbanks is cast as a wild Byronic outcast of the pampas, swaggering, smiling, irreligious, cigarette clamped permanently between gleaming teeth. When his outlaw band capture the City of the Miracle, he tries to seduce the innocent virgin guardian of the shrine and is struck down with leprosy. But the girl wins him over to the faith, he is cured and helps rid the city of a military tyrant. As relief from the pious and high-minded plot there are episodes of riding, fighting, hairsbreadth escapes and tempestuous love-making with a tigerish mountain girl (Lupe Velez).

Joining the spirits in the sky

In 1929 Fairbanks and Hollywood celebrated the last silent swashbuckler. Although the action was fast and free-flowing *The Iron Mask* (1929) presented a very different Fairbanks from the carefree cavalier of previous years. Aged 45 and greying, he appeared for the first time as a middle-aged man, D'Artagnan grown old. It was as if he knew it was to be his swansong. During the course of the action the three musketeers perish and D'Artagnan is mortally wounded. The film ends with the 'ghosts' of the musketeers beckoning him to join them and his spirit leaving its mortal shell to stride off with them into the clouds.

It was effectively Fairbanks' last bow. His Hollywood talkies, beginning with an ill-advised and unsuccessful venture into high culture with *The Taming of the Shrew* (1929), showed a sharp decline in artistic quality. His marriage to Mary Pickford ended in divorce in 1935 (his previous marriage to Anna Beth Sully, which had produced Douglas Fairbanks Jr in 1909, had come to an end in 1918). He travelled the world restlessly and grew old. It was this that was hardest for him to bear. His son said of him: 'He was a natural Peter Pan. He always thought of himself in terms of youth and he loved life in terms of youth.' But by 1929 he was no longer young. His body and face began to show signs of ageing and his always chunky frame thickened while his hairline receded. In 1934 he went to England to make *The Private Life of Don Juan* for Alexander Korda, his best and last sound film, in which he gives a poignant performance as the ageing Great Lover. He was planning to go into production with 'Doug' Jr when he died on December 12, 1939. JEFFREY RICHARDS

Filmography

1915 The Lamb; Double Trouble. **'16** His Picture in the Papers; The Habit of Happiness; The Good Bad Man (+co-sc); Reggie Mixes In (GB: Mysteries of New York); Flirting With Fate; The Mystery of the Leaping Fish (short); The Half-Breed; Intolerance (extra); Manhattan Madness; American Aristocracy; The Matrimaniac; The Americano. **'17** In Again – Out Again (+prod); Wild and Woolly (+prod); Down to Earth (+co-sc; +prod); The Man From Painted Post (+sc; +prod); Reaching for the Moon (+prod); War Relief (short). **'18** A Modern Musketeer (+prod); Headin' South (+prod); Mr Fix-it (+prod); Say! Young Fellow (+prod); Bound in Morocco (+prod); He Comes Up Smiling (+prod); Arizona (+dir; +prod; +sc); Sic 'em Sam! (short); Fire the Kaiser (short). **'19** The Knickerbocker Buckaroo (+prod; +co-sc); His Majesty, the American (+prod; +co-sc. under pseudonym) (GB: One of the Blood); When the Clouds Roll By (+prod; +co-sc). **'20** The Mollycoddle (+prod; +co-sc); The Mark of Zorro (+prod; +co-sc. under pseudonym). **'21** The Nut (+prod); The Three Musketeers (+prod). **'22** Robin Hood (+prod; +co-sc. under pseudonym). **'24** The Thief of Bagdad (+prod; +co-sc. under pseudonym). **'25** Don Q, Son of Zorro (+prod). **'27** The Black Pirate (+prod; +co-sc. under pseudonym); Potselui Meri Pikford (USSR) (GB: The Kiss of Mary Pickford); Odna Iz Mnogikh (USSR) (GB: One of Many); The Gaucho (+prod; +co-sc. under pseudonym). **'28** Show People (guest). **'29** The Iron Mask (+prod; +sc. under pseudonym); The Taming of the Shrew (+prod). **'31** Reaching for the Moon (+prod); Around the World in 80 Minutes/Around the World With Douglas Fairbanks (+co-dir; +prod; +co-sc). **'32** Mr Robinson Crusoe (+co-prod; +co-sc). **'34** The Private Life of Don Juan (GB).

A POSTER ART and Revolution

Alongside the achievements – in every sense revolutionary – of the Soviet cinema of the Twenties went another incidental but important artistic leap forward. Film poster artists of the period began to create advertisements worthy of the great works of Sergei M. Eisenstein, Lev Kuleshov, Vsevolod Pudovkin, Alexander Dovzhenko and Dziga Vertov – posters to attract the public with visual effects as arresting as those found in the actual films.

The graphic arts in the early years of the Revolution underwent a period of almost unprecedented excitement and discovery. Before the Revolution, young Russian artists had discovered Futurism and Cubism; after 1917, the passionate search to create new arts appropriate to the new age, produced 'isms' of all sorts. The dominant movement among them, wholly aligned with the revolutionary spirit, was Constructivism. Transmitted to the West by the sculptor Naum Gabo and the artist Vladimir Tatlin, the central aim of Constructivism was the notion that the artist should replace the imitative formulas of the past with 'new forms' in which space would be an element, a material in its own right, combined with kinetic rhythms.

In practice this resulted in characteristic tendencies: a preference for angular forms and shapes that would be dynamic and arresting; a fascination with machinery and the shapes and objects of the modern world – skyscrapers, guns, motor cars and, naturally, cameras. Celebrating the possibilities of technology and allied to the Revolution, Constructivism had a social function rarely achieved by the avant-garde.

One of the central figures in Constructivism, Alexander Rodchenko applied the principles of the new art to poster design. Others who enthusiastically embraced it were artists like Nikolai Prusakov and the two Stenberg brothers and their followers (many of whom remain anonymous to this day). Their work stands as some of the most original and exhilarating graphic work ever applied to film advertising, or indeed to any other area of publicity.

DAVID ROBINSON

lassic designs from the late Twenties and early hirties. Opposite page: Nikolai Prusakov and eorgi and Vladimir Stenberg collaborated on his dynamic poster from Lev Kuleshov's Po akonu (1926, By the Law)

Above: Constructivist motifs by S. Semionov for Victor Turin's Turksib *(1929). Below: anonymous poster for Friedrich Ermler's* Oblomok Impery *(1929, Fragment of an Empire). Above right: poster by the Stenbergs for Buster Keaton's* The General *(1926), and (below) their poster for Alexander Dovzhenko's* Zemlya *(1930, Earth), which echoes the spareness of style used to portray conflict between peasants and kulaks*

Left: anonymous poster, in Constructivist style, for Dzi Vertov's Entuziazm *(1931, Enthusiasm). Below left: Mikhail Dlugach uses dynan montage effects for* Zement *(1928, Cement), directed Vladimir Vilner. Below: Prusakov employs ingeniou photo-montage, verging on t surreal, for his poster for O Leonidov and Yakov Protazanov's* Chiny i Liudi *(1929), Ranks and People)*

ON THE RED FRONT

The experimental ferment that followed the October Revolution of 1917 took the Soviet Union to the artistic forefront of world cinema during the Twenties

Lenin said: 'Of all the arts, for us the cinema is the most important.' What did he mean and to what extent were his hopes for the cinema realized in the Soviet Union during the silent film period?

First and foremost Lenin intended that the cinema should provide the new revolutionary regime with its most effective weapon of agitation, propaganda and education. The cinema had certain attractions for the Bolsheviks. By the time they seized power in October 1917, the cinema was already the most popular form of entertainment in the towns and cities – the idea of the cinema therefore did not have to be 'sold' to the urban population. In the countryside it was still very much a novelty, with all the advantages which that implied, if only the industry could organize itself to provide the necessary equipment and the appropriate films. That was, however, to prove in the event a big 'if'.

The silent film was particularly attractive to the new Soviet authorities. The population, more than two-thirds illiterate, spoke a wide variety of languages. Written communication could therefore be effective only in the long run as the educational level improved, whereas the Bolsheviks were anxious to develop quickly the class consciousness of the masses. The silent film was an overwhelmingly *visual* medium – at its best, indeed, a *purely visual* medium – and was accessible to all sections of the people, while the moving image cut more deeply into the popular memory than did the poster, also widely used at that time.

Of course the silent film had its limitations: the dependence on relatively few intertitles to clarify the narrative meant that silent film plots had to remain fairly simple; but in this context such simplicity was to prove an enormous advantage. Films were first used on the agit-trains that toured the country for purposes of agitation and propaganda during the Civil War of 1918–21. These agitational shorts (*agitki*) were simple and direct. Their dynamism and economy of style were to exercise a great effect on subsequent Soviet film-making, as indeed were the people involved with them. Several of the foremost directors cut their cinematic teeth on the agit-trains. These trains distributed material from the centre to the provinces and gathered other material in the provinces to be taken back to the centre and used in future journeys. The film material gathered by them provided the content of the earliest Soviet newsreels and documentaries and also the themes for an important genre of fictional feature films about the Civil War. In some ways the Civil War became for the Soviet cinema the equivalent of the Hollywood Western, a vehicle for mass entertainment laced with elements of historical and political legitimation of the society that produced it.

Vital parts of the Soviet cinema network – in production, distribution and exhibition – remained in private hands until the industry was nationalized in 1919. But the problems were only just beginning: many of the private entrepreneurs fled the country, taking their equipment, their talent and their expertise with them. The ravages of war, civil war and general neglect had left studios (or 'film factories', as they were called) and cinemas in tatters, while a ban by the Western powers on the export of film stock to the Soviet Union meant that the authorities had virtually no new materials to make their own films.

Before the Revolution Russia had produced none of its own film materials; all stock and equipment had been imported.The Western blockade therefore dealt a particularly heavy blow to the nascent Soviet film industry. Desperation led Lenin to approve a deal with a certain Jacques Cibrario, who promptly disappeared with the money he had been given but without providing the materials that had been paid for.

The disruption of war and civil war caused widespread starvation and epidemics. Hundreds of

Top: Eisenstein re-created the events of October, *with Nikandrov as Lenin. Above: Marfa Lapkina as the peasant heroine of Eisenstein and Grigori Alexandrov's* The Old and the New

thousands died and millions more suffered. Fuel was scarce and power supplies erratic. The Russian winters increased the toll. Clearly the Soviet cinema needed a massive injection of funds, but, equally clearly, the government had to concentrate its limited resources on the more immediate tasks of political survival. One positive step was taken: in 1919 the first State Film School was set up to train new cadres (groups of Party workers) of all sorts to people the cinema when times were better.

The advent of the New Economic Policy in 1921, with its limited return to private enterprise, provided temporary relief. The aim was to finance the restoration and development of the film industry from its own resources. Audiences were to be drawn to cinemas to see films that they were willing to pay to watch and the money that they paid was to be used to produce films that the authorities wanted them to view. Entertainment was to pay for propaganda.

Anatoli Lunacharsky who, as People's Commissar for Enlightenment, had overall responsibilty for the cinema, was the architect of this policy of pragmatism. He preferred that audiences should come voluntarily to the cinema and that the propaganda should be concentrated in the newsreel. He himself was the author of several screenplays for 'psychological salon dramas', some of which provided a vehicle for his actress-wife Natalya Rozenel.

But Soviet audiences wanted to see foreign and, above all, Hollywood films. Charlie Chaplin, Buster Keaton, Harold Lloyd and, especially, Mary Pickford and Douglas Fairbanks were the staple diet of the Soviet cinemagoer during the Twenties. When Pickford and Fairbanks visited the Soviet Union in 1926, they were mobbed by fans; a feature film *Potselui Meri Pikford* (1927, *The Kiss of Mary Pickford*), from an idea by Lunacharsky himself, was made around their visit; and their comments on Sergei M. Eisenstein's *Bronenosets Potemkin* (1925, *Battleship Potemkin*) as 'the greatest film ever made' were used to relaunch the film after its disastrous first run.

By 1928 the Soviet authorities felt able to turn their attention to the political tasks of the Soviet cinema and it was in that year that the box-office receipts from Soviet films exceeded those from imported films for the first time. The new regime was now secure, even if Stalin's imagination did not always allow him to admit it, and the task of rapid industrialization that lay at the heart of the First Five Year Plan (1928–32) meant that the cinema could no longer be left to its own devices. The 'industrial revolution' was to be accompanied by a 'cultural revolution' in which the cinema's vital

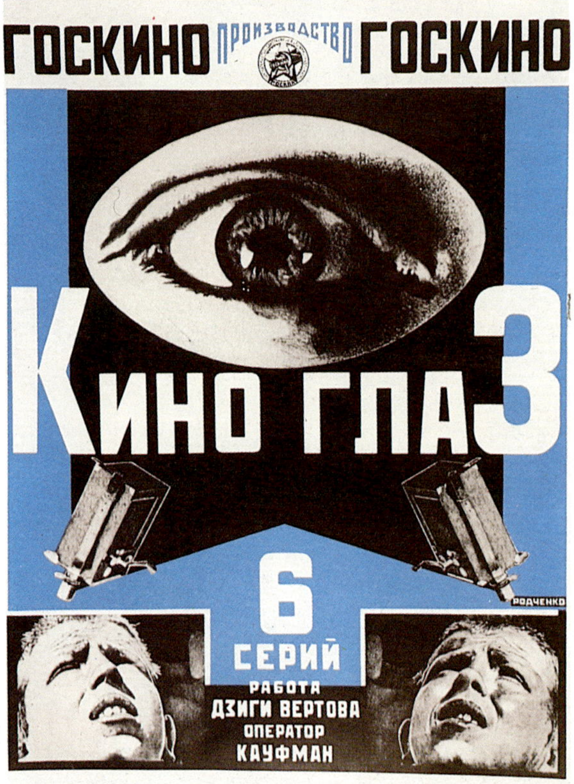

Top left: in The Extraordinary Adventures of Mr West in the Land of the Bolsheviks, *a hapless American tourist (Porfiri Podobed, bespectacled) is rescued from the 'Countess' (Alexandra Khokhlova), the 'Count' (Vsevolod Pudovkin) and an accomplice, who are showing him all the horrors he expects to find in the USSR. Centre top: an agit-train equipped to show and make films. Top right: poster for* Pokhozdeniya Oktyabriny *(The Adventures of Oktyabrina), a film of fantasy. Above right: Louise Poirier (Elena Kuzmina), a shopgirl, defending the Paris Commune of 1871 in* New Babylon. *Right: the pioneering documentarist Dziga Vertov. Above: Alexander Rodchenko's poster for Vertov's* Kino-Glaz *(1924,* Kino-Eye*)*

role was deemed to be the 'elevation of the cultural level of the masses'.

In March 1928 a Party Conference on Cinema outlined the tasks of the film industry and in 1929 a decree defined the responsibilities of the cadres of film workers. Despite reorganization of the industry in 1930, direct political control proved unexpectedly awkward to enforce. The attempt to impose it created its own troubles, and these were further complicated by the difficulties associated with the advent of sound and the refusal by many film-makers to recognize that sound was anything more than a passing novelty. Sound created problems in the West as well, but the by-now highly centralized organizational structure of the Soviet cinema turned those problems into nightmares.

Just as the political authorities had recognized the propaganda potential of the silent film, so a new generation of artists acclaimed the cinema as a new medium of artistic expression, as the new art form for the new epoch. Initially the political perspective merged with the artistic; but the political requirement of a medium of mass communication began to conflict with a need for artistic experiment, and the notion that here at last was an avant-garde which had the full support of the powers-that-be soon proved an illusion.

In addition to the functional attractions of the silent film, artists were drawn to the cinema as a relatively new medium untainted by a classical bourgeois tradition – unlike the theatre or literature, for instance – and with as yet untried but potentially limitless possibilities. For instance, the poet Vladimir Mayakovsky (1893–1930) tried his hand at writing three film scenarios in 1918. As the leading critic and scriptwriter Viktor Shklovsky (b. 1893) observed:

'Art forms "grow tired", burn themselves out, like flames. The change in forms is usually revolutionary. The cinema is the natural heir to the theatre and, possibly, literature.'

Others were more definite: 'The cinema is the new philosophy. . . the new international visual Esperanto of the future.' Since to many the new era was to be characterized by the modernization and industrialization of Russia, the mechanical base of the cinema was also seized upon by theorists such as G.M. Boltyansky:

'The mechanical possibility of unending reproduction and distribution of the works of the cinema make it, as distinct from the other arts, the sole and exclusive *expression of the era of the new culture.*'

One of the leading exponents of the new art form was Lev Kuleshov (1899–1970), who has been described as the 'father of the Soviet cinema'. Like so many film directors Kuleshov came to the cinema after the Revolution and, like others too, he was astonishingly young – only 18 in October 1917. Since there was no film stock with which to make feature films, Kuleshov had to channel his energies into the establishment in 1921 of his own workshop at the new film school. Here Kuleshov and his students rehearsed films that would never be produced, the so-called 'films without film'. It was at this time that Kuleshov first developed the idea that the distinctive nature of cinema, its superiority to the theatre, lay in the principle of *montage* or editing. Experiments suggested to him that each film shot acquired meaning from its immediate context, from the shots that preceded and succeeded it on the screen and therefore in the perception of the audience. By altering the context, by placing the original shot in different sequences, the whole meaning could be transformed. This discovery, of crucial significance to the subsequent development of Soviet film theory, was to become known as the 'Kuleshov effect'.

Kuleshov acquired some experience of actual filming by travelling in the agit-trains and he used the material he collected for his agitational film *Na Krasnom Fronte* (1920, *On the Red Front*). His first fictional feature film was the remarkable satire *Neobychainye Priklyucheniya Mistera Vesta v Strane Bolshevikov* (1924, *The Extraordinary Adventures of Mr West in the Land of the Bolsheviks*), one of the most successful Soviet silent comedies. This was followed by the detective thriller *Luch Smerti* (1925, *The Death Ray*) and the more psychologically-orientated *Po Zakonu* (1926, *By the Law*), set in the Yukon during the Gold Rush. Kuleshov made three more silent films and in 1929 produced his major contribution to film theory, *Iskusstvo Kino* (The Art of the Cinema), a book still not translated in full into English.

Kuleshov's great importance goes beyond his own films, for he influenced almost every other Soviet film-maker, not only through his development of the idea of montage but also because of his attempts to encourage a new style of 'naturalistic' acting specific to cinema and in some ways resembling the stage and film director Vsevolod Meyerhold's experiments with bio-mechanics in training actors to use their bodies in the theatre. Kuleshov called his actor, who lacked the artificiality associated with conventional stage training, a *naturshchik* and explained:

'Individuality is exceptionally important in a *naturshchik*. . . . The actor can serve directors of all tendencies; the *naturshchik* only the director who has taught him and a small circle of like-minded people.'

Many of Kuleshov's ideas were taken up by a small group of very young film-makers in Petrograd (later Leningrad), who included Grigori Kozintsev and who called themselves FEKS or the Factory of the Eccentric Actor. Central to their ideas was the notion of 'impeded form': people and objects were to be portrayed in unfamiliar contexts, thus alienating the viewer in the sense, later used by the German playwright Bertolt Brecht, of forcing him to see things in a new light. Their most important films were: *Pokhozdeniya Oktyabriny* (1924, The Adventures of Oktyabrina), an anti-capitalist political

allegory; *Mishka Protiv Yudenicha* (1925, Mishka versus Yudenich), a children's comedy which, in possible homage to Kuleshov, was subtitled 'The Unprecedented Adventures of Mishka the Paper-Boy Among the White Guards'; *Chertovo Koleso* (1926, *The Devil's Wheel*), a story of gangsters in Petrograd during the Civil War; *Shinel* (1926, *The Cloak*), based on Gogol's story about a poor clerk; *Bratishka* (1927, Little Brother), a comedy about a truck; *Soyuz Velikogo Dela* (1927, *The Club of the Big Deed – SVD*), concerning the Decembrist revolt in 1825 in St Petersburg; and finally a film about the Paris Commune of 1871, *Novyi Vavilon* (1929, *New Babylon*), for which Shostakovich wrote a memorable score.

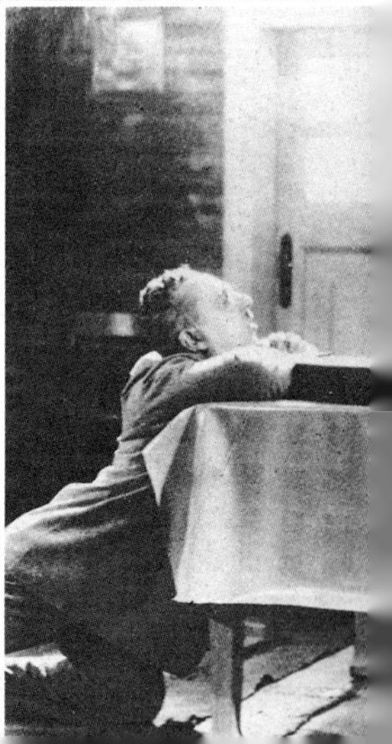

Far left: Vsevolod Pudovkin as The Living Corpse, *a drunkard who pretends to be dead so his wife can remarry. Below:* Earth *is a lyrical celebration of all that lives and dies. Below centre: Pudovkin's* Storm Over Asia *aroused protests for its satirical view of the British Occupation Forces in Mongolia. Bottom: Pavel Pol and Anna Sten in* The Girl With the Hatbox. *Bottom left: Alexandra Khokhlova, Vladimir Fogel and Sergei Komarov as three Yukon outcasts in* By the Law

One of Kuleshov's leading actors, and probably his most faithful pupil, was Vsevolod Pudovkin (1893–1953), who became an important director and retained in his own films much of the balance between actor's characterization and director's editing that Kuleshov preached. Pudovkin's first feature film was *Mat* (1926, *Mother*), about a woman who is led by the example of her son into political activism; this was followed by *Konyets Sankt-Peterburga* (1927, *The End of St Petersburg*), concerning World War I and the Revolution, and *Potomok Chingis-Khana* (1928, *Storm Over Asia*), a tale of the Civil War in Mongolia. Pudovkin's films, like those of Kuleshov, were among the most popular Soviet films of the Twenties. These directors employed and built upon the techniques developed by Hollywood with which audiences were familiar: their films had a clear plot and an individual hero and villain so that audiences found them accessible and were able to identify with the message that the director and his team were trying to convey.

In fact the bulk of Soviet films of this period tried to adapt American techniques to Soviet themes – the *Miss Mend* serial (1926) is a good example – and it was these Soviet films that Soviet audiences went to see rather than the works later acclaimed as masterpieces. Two of the leading figures of this popular cinema were Fyodor Otsep (1895–1949), who directed *Zhivoi Trup* (1929, *The Living Corpse*), based on Leo Tolstoy's play, and Boris Barnet, (1902–65), who directed *Devushka s Korobkoi* (1927, *The Girl With the Hatbox*) and *Dom na Trubnoi* (1928, *The House on Trubnaya Square*), two satirical comedies. Both men were disciples of Kuleshov.

In the world-famous masterpieces, as Party activists were quick to point out, form often seemed to outweigh content, so that they were 'unintelligible to the millions'. The films of Sergei M. Eisenstein (1898–1948) fell into this category, though the accusation of 'unintelligibility' reflected more on the accusers than the accused. Eisenstein was by no means alone among Soviet artists in thinking that a revolutionary *society* needed a revolutionary *culture* that would instil a revolutionary *consciousness* into the masses. This culture had to find new forms untainted by a bourgeois past and Eisenstein felt that the cinema was the ideal vehicle for this.

Eisenstein's movies shook the world of film but they generally flopped at the Soviet box-office

His silent films, beginning with *Stachka* (1925, *Strike*), were essentially experiments to find appropriate new forms. Traditional individual characterizations were abandoned as bourgeois relics in favour of symbolic ciphers representative of the mass and played by ordinary people who had no training as actors. Eisenstein called this 'typage' and it was a highly stylized form of caricature. The characterization of the sailors and the middle-class people of Odessa in his film about the failed 1905 revolution, *Battleship Potemkin*, is a good example. These figures were brought together by editing in a manner that challenged conventional narrative conceptions. In what Eisenstein described as 'intellectual montage', objects and characters were juxtaposed in a way that deliberately jarred on the audience: images commented on one another, forcing audiences out of complacent preconceptions and into a new consciousness of reality. The sequences showing Alexander Kerensky, leader of the Provisional Government after the February revolution in 1917, in the Winter Palace in *Oktyabr* (1927, *October*) are symptomatic. But the ironic analogy between Kerensky and the preening peacock on the tsar's clock was lost on contemporary audiences and confused them. Hence Eisenstein, though blazing a trail in terms of artistic theory and practice, failed to deliver the goods that the Party required and he fell into disgrace, though only temporarily, after the failure of his film on collectivization, *Staroye i Novoye* (1928, *The Old and the New*, sometimes known as *The General Line*).

There were of course many other directors active in the Soviet cinema. One of the most famous was the Ukrainian Alexander Dovzhenko (1894–1956), maker of *Zemlya* (1930, *Earth*), whose films evoked a pastoral folkloristic idyll. There was also an active film industry in Georgia, which produced such works as *Krasniye Diavolyata* (1923, *Little Red Devils*), *Moya Babushka* (1929, *My Grandmother*) and *Sol Svanetii* (1930, *Salt for Svanetia*).

Other artists went further in their search for forms appropriate to the revolutionary Soviet cinema by denouncing fictional feature films altogether. 'The film drama is the opium of the people. . . Long live life as it is!' wrote Dziga Vertov (1896–1954). He was the leading exponent of the inherent superiority of the documentary and newsreel format, the founder and leading member of the Cine-Eye group. He had begun working with film on one of the agit-trains during the Civil War and, while editing the *Kinonedelya* (Cine-Week) newsreels in 1918–19, made three documentary films from the material that he had collected. He went on to produce the series of *Kino-Pravda* (Cine-Truth) newsreels in 1922–25, the most famous of which is the *Leninskaya Kino-Pravda* (1925, Leninist Cine-Truth) depicting the reaction to Lenin's death in 1924 and initiating themes later developed in his sound films *Tri Pesni o Lenine* (1934, *Three Songs of Lenin*) and *Kolybelnaya* (1937, Lullaby). But the most important of Vertov's silent documentaries were *Shagai, Soviet* (1926, Stride, Soviet), *Shestaya Chast Mira* (1926, *A Sixth of the Earth*), *Odinadtsatyi* (1928, *The Eleventh Year*) and *Cheloviek s Kinoaparatom* (1929, *Man With a Movie Camera*), all depicting multifarious aspects of Soviet life with increasing virtuosity. In their manifestos the Cine-Eyes claimed to represent:

'. . . the art of organizing the necessary movements of objects in space and time into a rhythmic artistic whole, according to the characteristics of the whole and the internal rhythm of each object.'

They offered:

'Not a Pathé or a Gaumont newsreel (a newsreel of record), nor even a *Kino-Pravda* (a political newsreel), but a real Cine-Eye newsreel – a rapid survey of *visual* events interpreted by the film camera, pieces of *real* energy (as distinct from theatrical), brought by intervals to an accumulated whole by the great skill of montage.'

Through this montage the film-maker could organize 'life as it really is', improve upon it and 'see and show the world in the name of the world proletarian revolution'.

But by the end of the Twenties all this experimentation was giving way to the new orthodoxies of socialist realism. Soviet film directors initially wanted to use the new weapon of sound as an integral part of their concept of montage, with sound as counterpointing rather than merely illustrating the image; but the political situation had changed. Immersed in the world of collectivization and rapid industrialization, the Soviet cinema gradually adopted the tenets of socialist realism and attempted to 'describe not reality as it is but reality as it will be'. That became the clearly defined task of the Soviet cinema in the next decade.

RICHARD TAYLOR

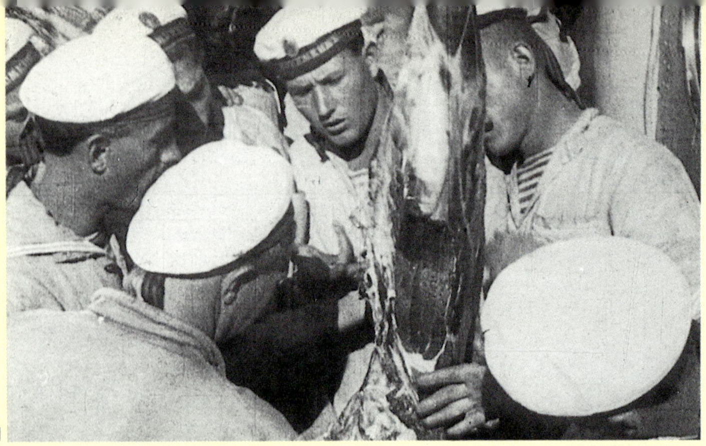

1

2

BATTLESHIP POTEMKIN

The most memorable and harrowing scene in *Battleship Potemkin* is that of the Odessa steps massacre. It is possibly the most celebrated sequence in the history of film, and the film itself numbers among the all-time greats.

Originally the *Potemkin* incident took up barely three pages of a massive script written by Nina Agadzhanova-Shutko, a revolutionary who had been active in the unsuccessful Russian revolution of 1905. The film was to be called, simply, *1905*. Shooting had begun in Leningrad, but because of poor weather conditions, the crew moved south to Odessa in the Crimea.

It is an indication of the genius of the director, Sergei M. Eisenstein, who was only 26 at the time, that, once in Odessa, he was rapidly able to see how a single incident could be made to encapsulate the whole period – with its conflict of forces, its triumphs and sufferings, its hopes and fears – far more vividly than a broad historical survey. And this provides the key to his whole approach, one which he developed into a theory that influenced all subsequent film-making.

Central to this theory was his concept of 'montage'. By selecting very specific images relating to a particular incident or circumstance and assembling them in a dynamic sequence of contrasts, conflicts and movements, he was able to transform a simple narrative into a profound emotional experience and a challenging political statement.

The Odessa steps sequence is the supreme example of Eisenstein's montage. Long-range shots of confusion and alarm as people under fire scramble in panic down the broad stone steps are intercut with close-ups of eyes in terror, lips in silent screams, feet stumbling, a bouquet crushed underfoot, a broken umbrella, bodies falling. Inserted into this complex imagery of general confusion are several highly personalized little vignettes. And cut into the whole assemblage of the crowd scenes are shots of the soldiers in their remorseless advance. Their feet, shown in military precision as they march forwards, are contrasted with the disorder of the escaping crowds. Close-ups of rifle-fire are juxtaposed to close-ups of the wheels of a runaway pram. The tempo gradually quickens into a horrifying crescendo of disaster.

The entire film is similarly constructed, with poetic rhythms and dramatic contrasts of imagery, pace and mood. Technique alone, however, is not enough to explain *Battleship Potemkin*'s extraordinary dynamism and passion, which sprang from the heady atmosphere of the Russian art world of the mid-Twenties when the gains of the 1917 Revolution had been consolidated and the air was bubbling with experiment, innovation and controversy. Eisenstein, caught up in this new spirit, had gravitated from architecture to the theatre, and from there to the youngest of the arts, the cinema, which was at the centre of the creative explosion.

In contrast to his later films, which he planned in great detail in advance, *Battleship Potemkin* grew out of Eisenstein's own excitement on realizing the potential of the Odessa steps. Some of the most famous effects were spontaneous. For example the evocative shots of mist over the sea were an inspired use of a natural phenomenon which would have spelt disaster to a lesser cameraman than the great cinematographer Eduard Tisse, who worked closely with Eisenstein throughout his life.

The whole film was shot in a week, and the editing took a further 12 days. It was premiered at the Bolshoi Theatre on December 21, 1925 to commemorate the twentieth anniversary of the 1905 revolution. Eisenstein and his close associate Grigori Alexandrov were still working on the film on the premiere night, according to an account by Alexandrov himself. And they rushed the final reel to the Bolshoi by motor-cycle, with Alexandrov driving and Eisenstein on pillion. The bike broke down in Red Square and they had to run the final stretch – the occasion was saved by an extra-long intermission between the fourth and fifth reels.

Battleship Potemkin was banned in almost all European countries outside the USSR for many years, and, with a few exceptions, could only be shown at private screenings. Its long-delayed British premiere was at a London Film Society screening in November 1929 and it was subsequently circulated – sometimes in the face of considerable police harassment – among film societies and workers' film clubs. Public interest in this and other great Soviet films of the period was, in fact, one of the main factors in the growth of the film society movement. The controversy provoked by the film led to campaigns for the relaxation of the censorship laws in many European countries, including Britain. Thus, *Battleship Potemkin* not only influenced the way in which films were made, but it also spearheaded a change in the way they could be screened.

NINA HIBBIN

Directed by Sergei M. Eisenstein, 1925

Prod co: Goskino. **sc:** Sergei M. Eisenstein, Nina Agadzhanova-Shutko. **photo:** Eduard Tisse, V. Popov. **ed:** Sergei M. Eisenstein, Grigori Alexandrov. **art dir:** Vassily Rakhals. **ass dir:** Grigori Alexandrov, Alexander Antonov, Mikhail Gomorov, A. Levshin, Maxim Strauch. **r/t:** 72 minutes. Russian title: *Bronenosets Potemkin*. Released in GB as *Battleship Potemkin*. Premiere, Moscow 21 December 1925.

Cast: Alexander Antonov (*Sailor Vakulinchuk*), Vladimir Barsky (*Commandant Golikov*), Grigori Alexandrov (*Lieutenant Gilyarovsky*), I. Bobrov (*young sailor*), A. Levshin (*an officer*), Repnikova (*woman on the steps*).

4

Russia, 1905. A huge crested wave breaks over the Black Sea, symbolizing the rising tide of revolution.

On board the battle-cruiser *Potemkin* the sailors are ready to mutiny. When they are given meat swarming with maggots (1) the limits of their tolerance are reached. They refuse to eat it. The admiral orders the rebels to be shot. Trapped under a huge tarpaulin (2), they appeal to the armed marines with the simple word, 'Brothers!'. The marines throw down their rifles and join the sailors in a violent struggle against the officers.

The men are victorious and the entire ship vibrates with triumph. But the mood changes when they discover that their leader has been shot. They make for Odessa (3) to bury him with honour.

The people of Odessa are aflame with the spirit of revolution, with quayside orators urging them to rise up. Crowds assemble on a huge stone stairway to cheer *Potemkin* from the shore (4). They organize a fleet of small boats to take provisions out to the crew (5).

Suddenly a line of tsarist militia appears across the top of the stairway, rifles cocked at the ready (6). The people hesitate, the soldiers fire and the stairway becomes littered with bodies (7). The crowd retreats in panic and disorder (8). The soldiers remorselessly advance. Children scream, a mother loses control of her baby's pram, which bounces down the steps.

The Russian fleet has assembled at the mouth of the harbour. The crew of the *Potemkin* raise the Red Flag defiantly, expecting attack. But as they set sail it becomes apparent that the other ships have gathered in support (9). The word 'Brothers!' seals their solidarity.

7

9

Thomas H. Ince - Father of the Western

The prolific producer and director Thomas H. Ince turned the studio-ranch he built in a Californian canyon into one of the world's most efficient and streamlined film factories – Inceville, where the first Western spectaculars were made, featuring full-blooded Sioux, gripping cowboy stories and a truly atmospheric terrain

Thomas Harper Ince was born at Newport, Rhode Island, on November 16, 1882, the son of stage performers John and Emma Brennan Ince. By the time Tom was 15 he had featured in over a dozen different shows and appeared on Broadway as a song-and-dance man. In 1910 he entered films as an actor for Carl Laemmle's Independent Motion Picture Company and was the director of the Mary Pickford unit that Laemmle sent to Cuba to make films out of the reach of the Patents Company.

In 1911 the New York Motion Picture Company (NYMPC) invited Ince out to their Bison Company studio in Edendale, California, where they made their own brand of Westerns. Ince later told *Photoplay*:

'I was offered a salary of $150 a week and in October I went west. The studio office was in the remains of a former grocery store which also provided a stage. Each story had a Colonel or a Sheriff or an Indian Chieftain . . . we made up Mexicans to play the parts of Indians. I had brought with me from New York as leading lady Ethel Grandin . . . and my cameraman was Ray Smallwood who became Miss Grandin's husband. Our first picture was *The New Cook* [1911], a single reel which was the standard length then, and it was freely predicted that I would be fired for wasting so much time on it.'

The reviewer of the film in *Moving Picture World* wrote that Ince, 'deserves to be complimented on the way he handled a rather threadbare scenario. The photography also is excellent . . . of really fine pictorial quality.'

Putting the Wild in Wild West

Towards the end of 1911 the NYMPC bosses Charles O. Baumann and Adam Kessel acquired the rights from the Pacific Electric Company to use their coast-road property – 18,000 acres that lay four miles to the north of Santa Monica – for shooting films. The studio itself was situated on the slopes of the entrance to the Santa Ynez Canyon. Around the same time, the Miller Brothers 101 Ranch Real Wild West Show, a circus that made its own movies, arrived from its spread in Oklahoma to winter on the California coast, and Ince was authorized to engage their entire company to make 'real' Westerns. This consisted of '350 people, including riders, actors, cowboys and girls, Indians, horses, steers, mules, equipment and paraphernalia.' The whole studio – the Miller 101 Bison Ranch – became popularly known as 'Inceville'. Said Ince:

'Our first plant at Inceville consisted of two dressing rooms (tents), one for the ladies and one for the gentlemen. Then we built a small platform upon which we staged our few interiors.'

Also used for shooting was a fishing village, inhabited by Japanese and Russian fishermen and their families, that lay on either side of the coast road and was sited between Inceville and Santa Monica.

Thus equipped, the studio embarked on the prolific production of its famous Westerns. The first to feature the Inceville Indians was the two-reeler *War on the Plains* (1912), starring Ethel Grandin, a film praised for it 'Historical accuracy, correct costuming, pe fect photography'. It was followed by *Th Indian Massacre*, *Custer's Last Raid* (both 1912 and many more. For *Custer's Last Raid*, a expensive three-reeler starring Francis Ford a General Custer, Ince re-created the Battle c the Little Big Horn and arranged with the U government to use, in addition to his residen company of Sioux, over a hundred reservatio Sioux as extras. Some of them had been ther when the real Custer lost his life in 1876 – the were the boys who followed the warriors an looted the dead soldiers.

Ince was personally involved in the produc tion and direction of all Bison's films from th autumn of 1911, when he first assumed res ponsibility for the brand, to the summer c 1912, when he divided the direction betwee himself and Francis Ford. At home, he and hi wife, the actress Elinor Kershaw, used thei kitchen as a projection room. She would ree out the film while he looked at it, cut it an assembled it. Then Ince would prepare scena rios from the material Elinor had found at th local public library that day.

In 1912 NYMPC joined with Universal and power struggle ensued within the company Ince recalled:

'. . . the near-battle which followed the leg fight over possession of our plant. . . . At on

The popularity of this type of film was already waning, however, and Ince introduced to the public a brand called Domino Films, whose Picturesque Productions featured Japanese star Tsuru Aoki and her company of players. Ince built a Japanese village in Santa Ynez for the series that included such films as *The Wrath of the Gods* and *The Typhoon* (both 1914), starring Aoki and her husband Sessue Hayakawa.

Inceville continued to grow and by 1914 contained a Spanish mission, a Dutch village with a real canal and an old windmill, an East Indian street, a Western town and a Sioux camp. There were about 520 inhabitants, all on the weekly payroll. The Indians who appeared in the Kay Bee and Broncho brand films were paid between $7 and $10 a week with their expenses covered. The chiefs were paid from $12 a week and were wholly responsible for their people. In 1916 Ince opened a school to provide a proper education for the Indians who worked for him.

Striking bargains

There was further expansion at the studio in 1914 and from then Ince's Kay Bee films were released by Henry E. Aitken's Mutual Masters Pictures. These included *The Bargain* (1914), the film that established William S. Hart as a major Western star. In 1915, in a further corporate shuffle, Aitken, now handling NYMPC's films, took Ince and Kay Bee into the new Triangle Film Corporation, along with D.W. Griffith's Reliance-Majestic and Mack Sennett's Keystone. Later that year the land-developer Harry Culver, who was working between Los Angeles and the Californian

bove left: Ince supervises the shooting of ivilization. *Above: the white chief of the* iceville *Sioux in 1914. Below: the Indians and* ieir *victims in* The Invaders *(1913), which Ince co-directed. Below right: William S. Hart, Ince's biggest Western star until they fell out, in* Truthful Tulliver *(1918). Bottom: Inceville on the Pacific Coast in 1915*

age of the proceedings, bloodshed was only verted by the belligerent attitude of our troop cowboys and Indians, all of whom were eady to do real fighting at the drop of a hat.'

The result of this legal wrangle was that YMPC surrendered the 101 Bison brand-ame to Universal's own Ince-inspired West-rns, while Kay Bee (the initials of Kessel and aumann) became the new brand for Ince's wn product.

In 1914 Ince made *The Battle of Gettysburg*, nploying eight hundred extras as soldiers in ie first week of shooting, and using eight ameras (perched at different angles) simul-ineously during each battle scene. One re-iewer said that film presented 'war scenes on larger scale than ever before attempted on ie screen. . . . Thomas Ince may properly egard it as his masterpiece.'

Above: scene from one of Ince's 'Japanese' films – The Wrath of the Gods. *Above right: Betty Ross Clark (left) and Betty Blythe as the 'other woman' in* Mother o' Mine, *a melodrama supervised by Ince in 1921*

resort town of Venice, offered free land to anyone who would build a movie studio in the area he named Culver City. Ince intended to build a new plant for NYMPC and obtained from Culver a 16-acre parcel of the dusty, sun-baked land along the road which became Washington Boulevard. The complex was briefly known as 'Incity'.

Ince himself ceased directing around this time to concentrate on production (working with a team of eight directors) and the expansion of his company. But he retained creative control of his films, developing the shooting scripts (including dialogue and camera positions) and personally assembling each and every film. He was especially noted for his efficient and penetrating editing. In 1916 he produced his great epic *Civilization*, the story of war and peace in a mythical country, which was a contribution to President Woodrow Wilson's peace effort during World War I, and he employed his best directors and photographers on its various parts. Irvin Willat, one of the cameramen, re-edited the film for Ince after a fire destroyed the first print. Willat added painted backgrounds behind the titles, a prologue and an epilogue, and he made an optical printer which enlarged stock shots of battle explosions to add realism.

In 1918 Ince fell out with Aitken, left Triangle and founded Ince Productions, building new studios at Culver City (a mile from the Triangle lot) and distributing his films through Paramount-Artcraft. The following year he began to release through Metro and formed Associated Producers, Inc. with Mack Sennett, Allan Dwan, Marshall Neilan, Maurice Tourneur and other producers and directors. This company merged with First National in 1922. Among the last significant films Ince produced were *Human Wreckage* (1923), a condemnation of drug abuse starring Bessie Love and Dorothy Davenport (the widow of the addicted star Wallace Reid), and *Anna Christie* (1923), with Blanche Sweet.

Ince's last voyage

On November 19, 1924 Ince joined newspaper magnate William Randolph Hearst's yacht to celebrate his own birthday and to discuss making pictures with Hearst's mistress, actress Marion Davies. Disregarding the orders of his doctor, who was treating him for ulcers and angina pectoris, Ince over-ate and over-drank, and became severely ill. He died at his home three days later. A heart attack brought on by acute indigestion was the official cause of his death, but it was also suggested that Ince had been shot by Hearst, who supposedly suspected him of having an affair with Davies. An investigation ordered by the district attorney of San Diego failed to provide any incriminating evidence, however.

The *Motion Picture News* of December 6, 1924 reported:

'Probably the most important gathering there since Hollywood became cinema capital of the world was held in Grauman's Hollywood Egyptian Theatre, Sunday at 11 o'clock. At this hour the entire industry from the highest to the lowest gathered to pay tribute to the memory of Thomas H. Ince.'

Cecil B. DeMille wrote:

'Under his remarkable showmanship-leadership and business ability, the motion picture art developed into an interpretive medium. When motion pictures are evaluated scores of years from now, Thomas H. Ince will be lauded internationally as largely responsible for changing a toy into an art. . . . He was one of the first to prove that real stories could be placed on the screen with tenderness and power. He will always rank as one of filmdom's greatest pioneers.' MARC WANAMAKER

Filmography

Shorts: **1910** His New Lid (actor only); Little Nell's Tobacco (+sc). **'11** Their First Misunderstanding (co-dir); The Dream (co-dir); Artful Kate; A Manly Man; The Message in the Bottle; The Fisher-Maid; In Old Madrid; Sweet Memories of Yesterday; For Her Brother's Sake (co-dir); In the Sultan's Garden; The Aggressor (co-dir); The New Cook; Across the Plains; The Winning of Wonega. **'12** War on the Plains; The Indian Massacre; The Deserter; The Battle of the Red Man; Blazing the Trail; The Crisis; The Lieutenant's Last Fight; His Message; The Colonel's Peril; The Hidden Trail; On the Firing Line; Custer's Last Raid; The Colonel's Ward; When Lee Surrenders; The Altar of Death (sup; +co-sc. only); A Double Reward; For the Cause; The Prospector's Daughter; The Law of the West. **'13** The Paymaster's Son; The Mosaic Law; The Shadow of the Past; With Lee in Virginia; Bread Cast Upon the Waters; The Drummer of the Eighth; The Boomerang; The Seal of Silence; The Invaders (co-dir); Days of '49. **'14** For the Freedom of Cuba; A Romance of the Sea; The Yellow Flame; O Mimi San (sup; +sc. only); The Battle of Gettysburg; The Gringo (sup; +co-sc. only); The Latent Spark (sup; +co-sc. only); The Rightful Heir (sup; +co-sc. only); Out of the Night (co-dir; +sup); Love's Sacrifice (co-dir; +sup); In the Cow Country (sup; +co-sc. only); The Hour of Reckoning; A Relic of Old Japan; The Typhoon (feature) (sup; +co-sc. only); The Wheels of Destiny; The Golden Goose (co-dir); The Worth of a Life (sup; +co-sc. only); The Brand; The Hateful God; The Bargain (sup; +co-sc. only); The Passing of Two Gun Hicks (sup; +co-sc. only); A Political Feud (co-dir; +co-sc); War's Women (sup; +co-sc. only). **'15** The Last of the Line (+co-sc); The Straight Road; In the Tennessee Hills (sup; + co-sc. only); Winning Back (sup; +co-sc. only); The First Love's Best; In the Switch Tower (sup; +co-sc. only); The Devil (feature); The Roughneck (sup; +co-sc. only); On the Night Stage (sup; +co-sc. only); Rumpelstiltskin (sup; +co-sc. only); The Conversion of Frosty Blake (sup; +co-sc. only); The Alien (feature); Keno Bates, Liar (sup; +co-sc. only). *All remaining films features unless otherwise specified:* **'15** The Coward (sup; +co-sc. only); The Disciple (sup; +co-sc. only). **'16** Peggy (sup; +sc. only); D'Artagnan (sup; +co-sc. only); Honor's Altar (sup; +sc. only); Bullets and Brown Eyes (sup; + co-sc. only); The Raiders (sup; +sc. only). **'17** Whither Thou Goest (sup; + co-sc. only); Ashes of Hope (sup: +sc. only). *Of the estimated 229 shorts and 239 features on which Ince was supervisor only, the most important include: Shorts:* **'12** The Post Telegrapher; On Secret Service. **'13** In the Ranks; An Indian's Honor; The Maelstrom; When Lincoln Paid; A Coward's Atonement; The Grey Sentinel; A Southern Cinderella; The Way of a Mother; A Slave's Devotion; An Indian's Gratitude; The Crimson Stain; The Banshee; Old Mammy's Secret Code; For the Love of the Flag; The Madcap; The Waif; The Struggle; Exoneration. **'14** The Romance of Sunshine Alley; A New England Idyll; In the Fall of '64; The Courtship of O San; The Wrath of the Gods, or the Destruction of Sakura Jima; In the Southern Hills; Out of the Dregs; A Frontier Mother; The Voice of the Telephone – Part 1; The Voice of the Telephone – Part 2; Shorty Turns Judge; Shorty and the Fortune Teller. **'15** The Face on the Ceiling; The Italian; The Scourge of the Desert; College Days; Pinto Ben. *Features:* **'15** The Iron Strain; Matrimony; The Golden Claw; The Forbidden Adventure; Aloha Oe; The Winged Idol; The Edge of the Abyss; Cross Currents. **'16** Hell's Hinges; The Return of Draw Egan; The Aryan; Civilization (re-released in 1930 with musical score and dialogue sequences). **'17** Somewhere in France; The Vagabond Prince. **'18** Blue Blazes Rawden; Borrowed Plumage; The Female of the Species; Flying Colours; Branding Broadway. **'20** Sex. **'23** Alice Adams; Human Wreckage; The Spoilers; Anna Christie. **'24** Galloping Fish; Tess of the D'Urbervilles. **'25** Playing With Souls.

Abel Gance: resting in peace

In recent years Abel Gance has been recognized as a great innovative director from cinema's silent days, but for most of his 62-year involvement in the business he was regarded with suspicion and his work neglected

Abel Gance, visionary, poet and film-maker, died in November, 1981 at the age of 92. For over fifty years he had been unable to make a film in the way that he wished, but before he died he had the consolation of knowing that his great work *Napoléon* (1927, *Napoleon*) – lovingly and extensively restored – was being shown to new and vast audiences in Europe and America. There the audiences, whose members were mostly not born when the film was made, were overwhelmed by an experience for which their cinematic knowledge had left them unprepared.

The creator of that experience was born in Paris on October 25, 1889. Although attracted to the arts from childhood, Abel Gance complied with his father's wishes and at 17 took a job in a solicitor's office. After only a year, however, he ran away to Brussels and became an actor. By 1908 he was back in Paris, playing small parts on the stage and in films, writing scenarios to eke out his income and, more importantly, making friends in the avant-garde artistic circles of the day. At the time those friends were little known, but included the painters Léger and Chagall, the symbolist poet Apollinaire, the writer Blaise Cendrars and the actor Séverin-Mars. Later, Cendrars and Séverin-Mars were to play important roles in Gance's work.

For some time film took second place in Gance's life, for all his attention was centred upon his play *La Victoire de Samothrace* (The 'Victory' of Samothrace). This poetic drama was destined for, and rejected by, the Théâtre Français. Gance's friend Edouard de Max then sent it to Sarah Bernhardt, who was enthusiastic. But with the advent of World War I the play remained unproduced, and after the war – Gance had been found unfit for military service because of tuberculosis – cinema became his abiding interest.

Raising Cain

During 1911 and 1912 Gance directed four short films for a small company that he had formed with a group of friends, but his real break came in 1914 when Louis Nalpas (head of Le Film d'Art, to which Gance contributed scenarios) gave him 5000 francs to direct a film for the company. The picture, *Une Drame au Château d'Acre* (The Drama at the Chateau d'Acre), was completed in five days. Nalpas liked it, and promised the young director a free hand on his next film, an opportunity that almost finished Gance's career. *La Folie du Docteur Tube* (1915, The Madness of Dr Tube) has been called the first purely experimental film. Gance and Léonce-Henry Burel, the cameraman who worked with him in the silent period, used distorting mirrors to such remarkable effect that the bewildered Nalpas, who considered that whatever the film was about it was not wartime entertainment, refused to release it. Discouraged, Gance bided his time and by turning out standard melodramas regained his producer's confidence. In 1917 he was given the chance to direct his first major film, *Mater Dolorosa* (Sorrowful Mother). Superficially a tearful bourgeois melodrama which would have been at home in any of the boulevard theatres of the day, the film easily transcends the genre.

Richly mounted, and beautifully photographed by Burel, *Mater Dolorosa* is the work of a director totally involved with his material, caring enormously for his characters, and believing passionately in his medium. It has two fine central performances from Emmy Lynn (a great star of early French cinema) as the grieving mother, and the stage actor Firmin-Gémier as her husband. Stage players of that period tend to look out of place in movies, but Firmin-Gémier acts with exemplary restraint for Gance. This control became a characteristic of Gance's work as actors instinctively recognized his faith in – and mastery of – his art. They submerged themselves in their characters, stars and extras alike. 'What actor wouldn't want to make pictures with this innovator, this marvellous director, this perfectionist?' asked Gabriel de Gravone, the actor Gance later used in *La Roue* (1923, The Wheel).

Mater Dolorosa and its successor *La Dixième Symphonie* (1918, The Tenth Symphony) were critical and commercial successes. In the latter, Gance's old friend Séverin-Mars played

Above: while shooting young Napoleon *winning a snowball fight, Gance (centre) rigged up a mobile camera to aid fluidity of movement*

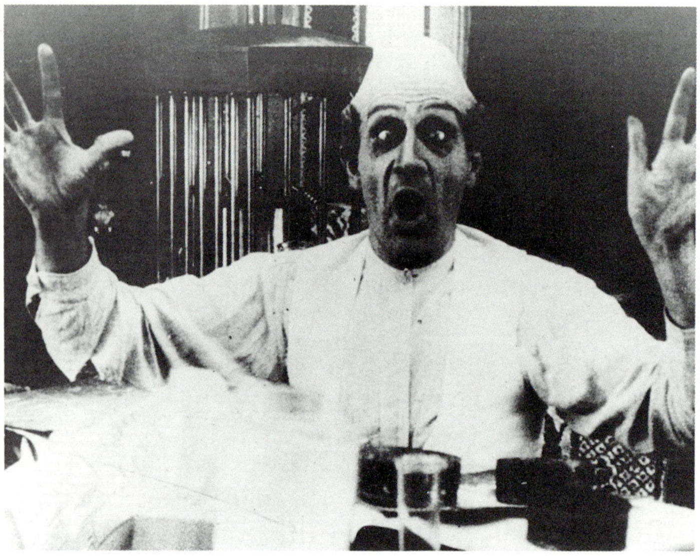

Above: a scene from one of Gance's more 'conventional' films, Lucrèce Borgia *(1935). Top: Séverin-Mars in* La Folie du Docteur Tube, *in which distorting mirrors and trick photography were used to startling effect. Top right: the war dead return from their graves in the silent* J'Accuse

Right: La Tour de Nesle *(1954,* The Tower of Lust*), an historical romance with sound, colour and technical know-how, but without Gance's old verve. Far right: Albert Dieudonné,* Napoleon *incarnate. Below right: a beautifully composed scene from* Mater Dolorosa. *Below left: Sisif (Séverin-Mars) in* La Roue

pposite Emmy Lynn. His presence would be
ucial in the two masterpieces which were to
llow.

During the production of *La Dixième Symonie* Gance was planning his great pacifist m *J'Accuse* (1918, I Accuse). He had been iefly mobilized into the Cinematograph Secon of the army, but was soon discharged. hen Charles Pathé – despite monetary difulties at Le Film d'Art – gave him permission go ahead with his project regardless of cost, ance rejoined the Cinematograph Section to m at the front. With the making of *J'Accuse*, e two sides of Abel Gance were combined for e first time: the film-maker provided spectalar crowd scenes, telling close-ups and even split-screen effect foreshadowing *Napoleon*; e visionary writer, in collaboration with aise Cendrars who had lost an arm in the war and experienced all its horror, provided a script startling in its scope and intensity. The basis is a simple romantic triangle of rivalry, jealousy and misunderstanding, and from this Gance rises to a bitter condemnation of the tragic misunderstandings of war. In a macabre climax of extraordinary power the survivor of two former rivals tells the people of his village about his vision of the war dead rising from the battlefields to return to their homes. They come, he says, to see whether the living are worthy of their sacrifice, and as the story is told Gance shows the 'return' of the dead. Some critics have since found that the pacifist message is blurred by the implication that the sacrifice was justifiable. Perhaps in 1918 that much had to be granted, but when the whole effect of *J'Accuse* is considered there can be no doubt of Gance's total outrage at the inhuman absurdity of war: 'I was accusing the war, I was accusing men, I was accusing universal stupidity.'

Life in the round

La Roue was made during a time of great personal sadness for Gance. He had fallen deeply in love with Ida Danis, a secretary at Le Film d'Art, and throughout the filming of *La Roue* she was seriously ill. On the day the first cut was finished she died. Gance also knew that Séverin-Mars had heart trouble and was unlikely to live long. Shortly after the film's completion he too died.

Only a 12-reel version of the original 32-reel, 3-part film survives, but even in this truncated form its impact is tremendous. Once again a love story serves as the framework for much wider concerns. Sisif, an engine driver, and his son Elie both love Norma, a girl whom Sisif rescued from a train wreck when she was a child and brought up as his own daughter. Believing this, Norma marries another man, and the desperation of Sisif and Elie leads to tragedy. But the railway is the soul of the film. Gance constructed Sisif's house among the marshalling yards at Nice, and the smoke, dirt and din are an ever-present background. Much of the drama takes place on Sisif's engine, and Gance used rapid cutting as never before, creating a musical rhythm reinforced by a score from the composer Arthur Honegger. The film became a symbolist poem with the imagery of the wheel dominating. At the end, as Sisif quietly dies in a hut in the mountains, the villagers below form a round dance – the final symbol – and it is clear that the wheel of the title is the wheel of Fate, that Sisif's suffering has from the beginning moved toward this ordained end.

In those terms *La Roue* can sound portentous, even silly. Perhaps Gance's thought, deprived of its images, is all too easy to criticize; *with* images it overwhelms, and the world that has at last welcomed *Napoleon* should no longer be deprived of *La Roue*.

Meeting his Waterloo

The years of work on *Napoleon* followed and were filled with the struggle to finance his six films covering the Emperor's life. With the coming of sound, interest in his efforts waned and even the innovatory split-screen techniques were shunned. When the film did appear it was often as a travesty of the original. His first sound film, *La Fin du Monde* (1930, The End of the World) received similar treatment, being so savagely mutilated by the producers that Gance disowned it. He never again enjoyed full creative freedom.

There were 19 further features, most of them commercial projects but including a new version of *J'Accuse* (1937), redesigned as a protest against the slide towards World War II, two refashioned versions of *Napoleon*, a film on the life of Beethoven – *Un Grand Amour de Beethoven* (1936, *Beethoven*) – which had flashes of the old grandeur, and some cheerful historical romances that would have been acceptable had anyone else done them.

In spite of all the restrictions Gance had to contend with, he continued to devise new techniques. To the Polyvision of *Napoleon* he added Perspective Sound (patented in 1929), Stereophony and Pictographe, another stereophonic system. The world took no notice. For Abel Gance, more than for anyone else, the end of the silent era coming just as his art achieved perfection had been a tragedy. But in 1927 Gance made this prophetic statement: 'A great film is a bridge of dreams, thrown across from one epoch to another.' And, with *Napoleon*'s rediscovery, this has proved to be the case.

JACK LODGE

Filmography

1909 Mireille (sc. only); Molière (actor only); Le Glas du Père Césaire (sc. only); La Légende de L'Arc-en-ciel (sc. only). **'10** La Fin de Paganini (sc. only); Le Crime de Grand-Père (sc. only); Le Roi des Parfums (sc. only); L'Aluminite (sc. only); L'Auberge Rouge (sc. only); Un Tragique Amour de Mona Lisa (sc. only). **'11** Paganini (sc. only); La Digue, ou Pour Sauver la Hollande (+sc); Cyrano et D'Assoucy (sc. only); Un Clair de Lune Sous Richelieu (sc. only); L'Electrocuté (sc. only). **'12** Le Nègre Blanc (+sc; +act); Il y a des Pieds au Plafond (+sc); Le Masque d'Horreur (+sc). **'14** L'Infirmière (sc. only); Un Drame au Château d'Acre (+sc). **'15** La Folie du Docteur Tube (+sc). **'16** L'Enigme de Dix Heures (+sc); La Fleur des Ruines (+sc); L'Héroïsme de Paddy (+sc); Fioritures (+sc); Le Fou de la Falaise (+sc); Ce que les Flots Racontent (+sc); Le Périscope (+sc); Barberousse (+sc); Les Gaz Mortels (+sc); Strass et Compagnie (+sc). **'17** Le Droit à la Vie (+sc); La Zone de la Mort (+sc); Mater Dolorosa (+sc). **'18** La Dixième Symphonie (+sc); J'Accuse (+sc). **'23** La Roue (+sc); Au Secours! (+co-sc; +prod) (GB: The Haunted House). **'27** Napoléon (vu par Abel Gance) (+sc; +act) (GB: Napoleon) (reissued with sound as: Napoléon Bonaparte, 1934). **'28** Marines (short) (+sc); Cristeaux (short). **'29** Napoleon auf St Helena (sc. only) (GER). **'30** La Fin du Monde (co-dir; +sc; +act). **'32** Mater Dolorosa (+sc). **'33** Le Maître de Forges (+sc). **'34** Poliche (+sc); La Dame aux Camélias (+sc). **'35** Le Roman d'un Jeune Homme Pauvre (+sc); Lucrèce Borgia. **'36** Ladro di Donne (IT) (dir; +sc. on French language version: Le Voleur de Femmes, 1937); Un Grand Amour de Beethoven (+sc) (USA: The Life and Loves of Beethoven; GB: Beethoven); Jérôme Perreau, Héros des Barricades (USA: The Queen and the Cardinal). **'37** J'Accuse (+co-sc) (USA: That They May Live; GB: I Accuse). **'38** Louise (+co-sc). **'39** Le Paradis Perdu (+co-sc) (USA: Four Flights to Love). **'41** La Vénus Aveugle (+sc). **'42** Le Capitaine Fracasse (+co-sc; +Italian language version: La Maschera sul Cuore). **'54** Quatorze Juillet 1953 (short) (+sc); La Tour de Nesle (+sc) (IT-FR) (USA: The Tower of Nesle; GB: The Tower of Lust). **'56** Magirama (co-dir; +co-prod; +sc. only). **'60** Austerlitz (co-dir; +co-sc only). (FR-IT-YUG) (GB: The Battle of Austerlitz). **'63** Cyrano et D'Artagnan (+co-sc) (SP-IT-FR) (USA: Cyrano and D'Artagnan). **'71** Bonaparte et la Révolution (+co-prod; +sc; +prologue).

1

3

On January 17, 1925, at the Billancourt studios in Paris, Abel Gance began the filming of *Napoléon*. He planned six long films covering the entire life of the Emperor and had, he thought, obtained sufficient funds to make a start from a Russian financier, Wengeroff, and the German industrialist, Hugo Stinnes. After a while the company moved to Corsica to shoot in the original locations. When they returned, they found that Stinnes had died; his assets were frozen, and Gance's finances collapsed. His actors, by now dedicated to the film, agreed to return whenever he could resume. Some six months later, a Russian named Grinieff came to the rescue. The first film, ending with Napoléon's invasion of Italy, was ready for release early in 1927. On April 7 came the triumphant first showing at the Paris Opéra, with two triple-screen sequences and a score by Arthur Honegger. It has now been discovered that this showing lasted three and a half hours; later that year a six-hour version was shown at the Apollo cinema.

At that high point, fate turned against Gance. With the coming of sound, no-one was interested in his achievements or his innovations. The film was shown in full in only eight European cities; in America, and in Europe too, after the first runs, shorter and increasingly travestied versions were the only ones available. Film historians came to speak of the piece as a monumental fiasco. What was on view bore them out. Of the five remaining parts, only the last, concerning Napoléon on St Helena, was ever made, and that by another hand. The respected Romanian director Lupu-Pick filmed *Napoléon auf St Helena* (Napoléon in Saint Helena) in Germany, from Gance's script, in 1929. But now, in almost its original form, *Napoleon* has returned, the result of thirty years of devoted labour by the English historian and film-maker, Kevin Brownlow, and the cooperation of the National Film Archive and archives and collectors across the world. Through Brownlow, and others, Gance's film can be judged as it was intended to be judged.

No film ever involved its audience more intensely. Others before Gance had set the camera free from constraint. Gance did more. He endowed the camera with a dynamic life of its own. For the pursuit across Corsica it was strapped to the back of a horse. Hand-held in the snowball battle at Brienne, it is a combatant, pelted but victorious. Swinging on a giant pendulum over the storm at sea and the storm in the Convention, it rocks in a dizzying frenzy. If the camera is a magical presence, the editing of the images which that camera caught is more astonishing still. Not only is there the intensely rapid cutting which Gance had introduced in *La Roue* (1923, The Wheel); there are the three simultaneous images of the triptych (now only one, for in a time of despair Gance destroyed those of the storm in the Convention, and the Bal des Victimes, which had been added in 1928, leaving only that of the march into Italy); and there are multiple-image effects, employing in the fight in the dormitory up to nine divisions of the screen. And, incredibly, all this was done with the eye alone, laboriously matching and cutting without the aid of an editing machine.

The triptych of Italy works supremely well. Sometimes the action spreads unbroken across all three screens. Sometimes the central image is balanced by contrasting or complementary images on the outer screens. Often the left-hand screen carries a mirror image of the right. Gance said that the centre was prose, the wings poetry, the whole was cinema. And so it proves. It has been claimed, against Gance, that Polyvision (as Gance called his triptychs) 'breaks the thread' of cinema by preventing the spectator from concentrating on the succession of single images which is cinema's essence. But it seems an arbitrary view of cinema. There is room in film for one image to play against – or with – another, and when the two or three are linked by a score as brilliant as Carl Davis' for the recent revival in Britain, then it can be, not a lack of concentration, but rather a gathering up of the spectator into a total experience which cinema seldom provides.

It would be wrong, however, to see *Napoleon* as entirely a display of new forms and new sensations. The quieter moments are as rewarding in their way: the gentle comedy of Napoléon's embarrassed courtship, the lovely invention (if invention it is) of the document-eaters who eat suspects' files and so save them from the guillotine, the trial of character in Italy between the new commander and the old generals, the sidelong view of the Revolution from Napoléon's obscure window and, above all, everything that concerns the girl Violine, played by Annabella with such surpassing tenderness. These by themselves would have made Gance's film a masterwork.

JACK LODGE

Directed by Abel Gance, 1927
Prod co: Westi/Société Générale de Films. **sc/ed:** Abel Gance. **photo** (tinted in part): Jules Kruger, Léonce-Henry Burel. **ass ed:** Marguerite Pinson. **art dir:** Alexandre Benois, Schildknecht, Eugène Lourié. **mus:** Arthur Honegger. **r/t:** various. Paris premiere, 7 April 1927.
Cast: Albert Dieudonné (*Napoléon*), Vladimir Roudenko (*Napoléon as a boy*), Gina Manès (*Joséphine*), Nicolas Koline (*Tristan Fleuri*), Annabella (*Violine*), Alexandre Koubitsky (*Danton*), Antonin Artaud (*Marat*), Edmond Van Daële (*Robespierre*), Harry Krimer (*Rouget de Lisle*), Damia ('La Marseillaise'), Henri Baudin (*Santo-Ricci*), Maurice Schutz (*Paoli*), Léon Courtois (*Gen. Carteaux*), Philippe Hériat (*Salicetti*), Alexandre Bernard (*Gen. Dugomier*), Jean Henry (*Junot*), Marguerite Gance (*Charlotte Corday*), Abel Gance (*Saint-Just*), Pierre Batcheff (*Gen. Hoche*), Georges Cahuzac (*de Beauharnais*), Jean d'Yd (*La Bussière*), Maxudian (*Barras*), Genica Missirio (*Murat*), Le Petit Henin (*Eugène de Beauharnais*), Roger Blum (*Talma*), Philippe Rolla (*Gen. Masséna*).

9

At the military college of Brienne, the boy Napoléon and his 'army' win a mock military battle in the snow (1). Angry at the release, by his rivals, of his pet eagle, the boy stirs up a great pillow fight in his dormitory. He is punished, but the eagle returns (2).

In 1789, Napoléon is present when Rouget de Lisle introduces the Marseillaise to the revolutionaries (3). He returns to Corsica to attempt to bring the island over to the Revolution (4), but fails, and escapes in a boat. Engulfed in a storm, while a political storm shakes the Convention (5), Napoléon is saved by his brothers. The eagle settles on their boat. Napoléon reaches France.

1793: Napoléon is a staff officer at the siege of Toulon (6). He stays at the inn of Tristan Fleuri, who had been a servant at Brienne. Violine, Fleuri's daughter, loves him. Given command of the assault by Dugomier, Napoléon wins his first victory in a torrential storm.

In Paris the Terror rages. Marat is murdered (7), Danton executed, Napoléon imprisoned.

1794: July. Saint-Just fails to save Robespierre. Refusing to fight the Royalists, Napoléon is sent to the Office of Topography. In October he is restored to command, and saves the Revolution. Violine sees him again, but at the Bal des Victimes he is captivated by Joséphine de Beauharnais. Violine watches from afar as he pursues Joséphine. Napoléon takes command of the Army of the Alps, and marries Joséphine (8). That night, Violine enacts her own imaginary wedding ceremony.

In the Hall of the Convention, Napoléon speaks with the ghosts of the Revolution. He joins his army, wins over the officers, and leads his men triumphantly into Italy (9).

2

4

5

7

8

Louis Delluc's writings on film were innovative and outspoken – he was frank in his criticism of French movies of the time and was eager that they should follow the example set by Hollywood. His own films were technically advanced and commercial, making him a major influence in the expansion of his native cinema

Louis Delluc

At the time of the Armistice in 1918, the French national spirit was at a low ebb and French cinema was suffering one of its most severe creative crises. One man, Louis Delluc, did more to restore the quality of French film at this time than any other. He did so – much like François Truffaut and Jean-Luc Godard forty years later – by first writing the most trenchant criticism of his generation, and then putting his theories into practice on the screen.

Louis Delluc was born on October 14, 1890, at Cadouin in the Dordogne. By 1910 he was embroiled in journalism, and although he was more attracted by the theatre in his early years, after 1915 (the same year he married the actress Eve Francis) he was drawn to the art of the cinema. During his late twenties he became a regular reviewer for the daily paper *Paris-Midi* and was chief editor of *Le Film*. In 1921 he founded *Cinéa*, a weekly journal, and in its pages he expounded his lively speculations on film.

Creative criticism

Prior to Delluc, most so-called film reviewers were under the thumb of French producers and distributors, often to the extent of being paid by the line for their resumés of a movie's virtues. Delluc, however, catered for an altogether more discriminating public: the devotees of the Ballets Russes, and those who knew of the innovative pronouncements on stage design of Gordon Craig, and writers like the Surrealist Louis Aragon, and Symbolist Apollinaire, and artists Picasso and Fernand Léger.

As early as 1917, Delluc had been attacked for being too effusive in his praise of American movies. He admired the work of Thomas H. Ince and especially Charles Chaplin and D. W. Griffith – who was known in France more for *Broken Blossoms* (1919) than for either *The Birth of a Nation* (1915) or *Intolerance* (1916), the two films generally considered his masterpieces. Delluc extolled the simplicity of Chaplin's art – a directness of appeal and imagery, the roots of which could be traced back to the conventions of medieval painting.

His view of French film was more disenchanted. He felt that Louis Feuillade, the master of the serial, had plunged into decline after 1914, and suggested that the French had no gift for the action cinema that was so brilliantly dominated by the Americans. Instead he thought they ought to return to the lack of self-consciousness and the lack of artifice practised by Lumière and his disciples, saying that it was through the straightforward depiction of reality, such as great events and natural phenomena, that 'the artisan finds the path to art'.

Patriotic profundities

He and the directors whose work he did admire (Abel Gance, Germaine Dulac and Jean Epstein among them) looked eagerly at the Swedish films of Victor Sjöström and Mauritz Stiller with their use of natural locations and their unassuming decor. 'The French cinema must be *cinema*, the French cinema must be *French*!' was the exhortation that Delluc had printed on the masthead of *Cinéa*.

Delluc's best writings were, like American film critic Pauline Kael's today, quickly collected and issued in book form – *Cinéma et Cie*, *Photo-génie*, *Charlot* and *La Jungle du Cinéma*. He wrote eight screenplays, all but one of which he directed himself, between 1919 and 1923. His first script was for Germaine Dulac's *La Fête Espagnole* (1919, The Spanish Fête), a torrid story of the rivalry of two men for the same wayward woman. Ironically this wealthy temptress runs off with yet another admirer, while the two original adversaries proceed to dispose of each other in a duel.

Inset, above: a line drawing of Louis Delluc. Above: Delluc's wife, Eve Francis, starring in La Femme de Nulle Part. *Right: Gabriel Signoret as a man devastated after he has killed his wife in* Le Silence

Le Silence (1920, Silence), Delluc's first film as director, was described at the time as 'a monologue in images' concerning a man who

Critic and Craftsman

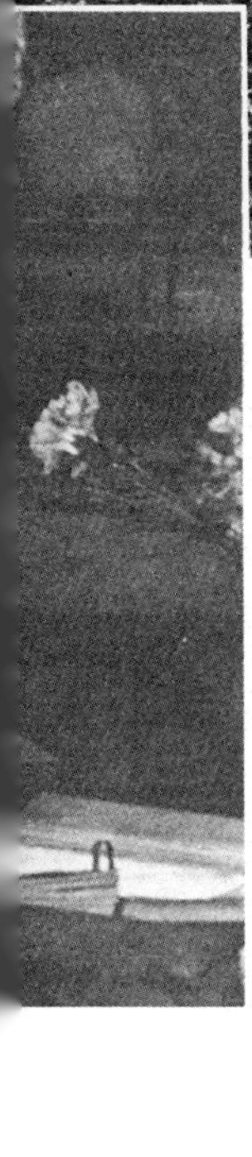

Left: Eve Francis, Jean Toulout and Gaston Modot in La Fête Espagnole. *Bottom left: Alban (Philippe Hériat) is confronted by his fiancée (Ginette Maddie, standing) and his real love (Eve Francis) in* L'Inondation

is overwhelmed by remorse for having killed his wife. The film itself has vanished apart from a handful of tantalizing production stills.

His next film, *Fièvre* (1921, Fever), was, according to the cinema historian Georges Sadoul, the best directed by Delluc. The emphasis was on atmosphere rather than plot, and the photography established an impressionist mood with its welter of close-ups and revealing glimpses of dingy bars.

Although Delluc coined the word cinéaste, and now has the reputation of a somewhat fastidious aesthete, his own films sought a wide public. He acknowledged the commercial pressures and exigencies that marched side by side with the art of the film. Cinema for him resembled a bullfight in that it gathered together 'not the masses, but the crowd. And the crowd includes everybody. The crowd comprises the world'. And he wrote, 'the masters of the screen are those who speak to the public at large.'

Eve Francis starred in the majority of Delluc's films, and imposed herself on his most well-known work, *La Femme de Nulle Part* (1922, Woman From Nowhere). This perfectly-wrought tale of persuasion and lost youth is striking for its use of natural landscape and for Delluc's startlingly sophisticated deployment of flashback. A middle-aged woman (Eve Francis) returns to the sumptuous villa where once she led a life of luxury and security. But a taste for romantic adventure has changed her ways, and she recognizes the impossibility of immersing herself again in the bourgeois round. She walks away down a dusty road, not with the jaunty step of, say, the Tramp's girl (Paulette Goddard) at the close of Chaplin's *Modern Times* (1936), but with the truculent hauteur of a more contemporary actress, like Monica Vitti or Jeanne Moreau.

Final deluge

Inspired by Sjöström's *Karin Ingmarsdotter* (1920, *God's Way*), Delluc's final film was *L'Inondation* (1923, The Flood), in which a river floods the surrounding countryside. Delluc made his river the Rhône as it passes through the Vaucluse district, and his film excels in physical and bucolic detail.

On March 22, 1923, Delluc died, heavily in debt and overcome by the ravages of tuberculosis. He was only 33, and yet he had created a legendary name for himself. He should now be praised for his pioneer work in deep-focus cinematography, intercutting and the control of narrative structure in general. He also helped to introduce the idea of the 'film society' in France and arranged the first screening in Paris of *Das Kabinet des Dr Caligari* (1919, *The Cabinet of Dr Caligari*). The Prix Louis Delluc, awarded annually to the best French film, perpetuates his attainments. PETER COWIE

Filmography

1919 La Fête Espagnole (sc. only). **'20** Fumée Noire (co-dir; +sc); Le Silence (+sc). **'21** Fièvre (+sc); Prométhée Banquier (actor only); Le Chemin d'Ernoa/L'Américain (short) (+sc); Le Tonnerre (+sc). **'22** La Femme de Nulle Part (+sc). **'23** L'Inondation (+sc).

Probably the most famous avant-garde film in cinema history, *Un Chien Andalou* (An Andalusian Dog) was in fact conceived as an attack on the esoteric 'formalism' of avant-garde French films in the Twenties. Luis Buñuel and Salvador Dali aimed to shock audiences with the violence of their imagery but they knew their audiences would be drawn from the artistic élite of the day – painters, poets, composers, film-makers – and not the average Parisian cinemagoers.

Thus the brutality of a human eye (actually an animal eye) being sliced with a razor and the sickening sight of putrefying donkeys were intended as a physical assault on the arty, abstract pretensions of artists who thought themselves avant-garde.

The inspiration for the film came from a line by the nineteenth-century poet Comte de Lautréamont (1846–70):

'Beautiful as the chance meeting of an umbrella and a sewing machine on a dissecting table.'

Lautréamont himself predated

Un Chien Andalou

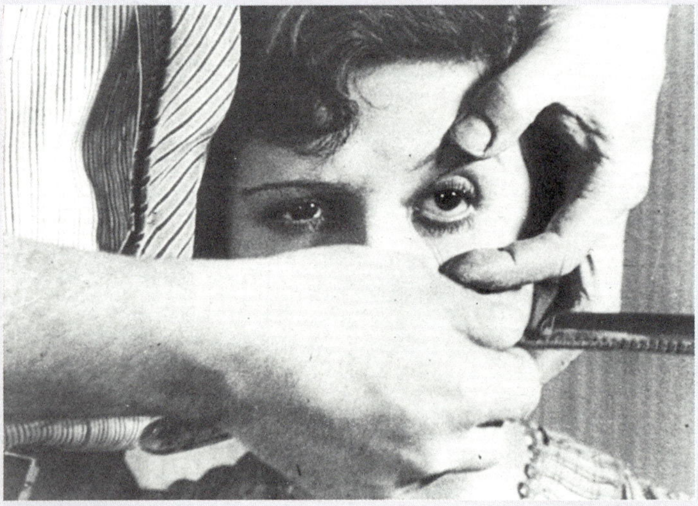

1

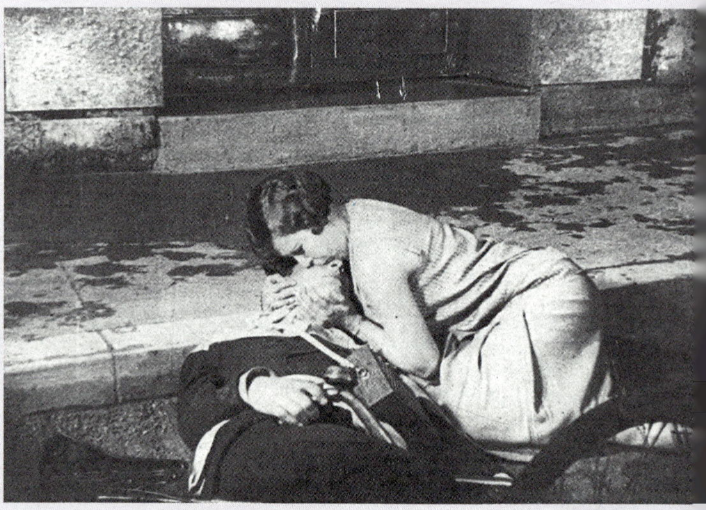

2

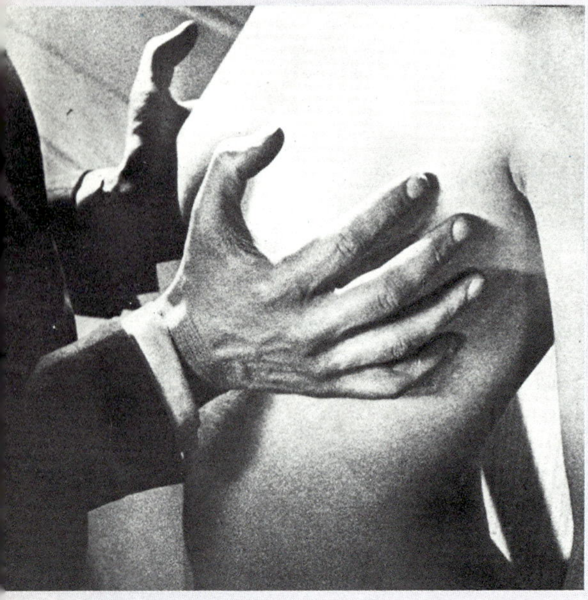

4

5

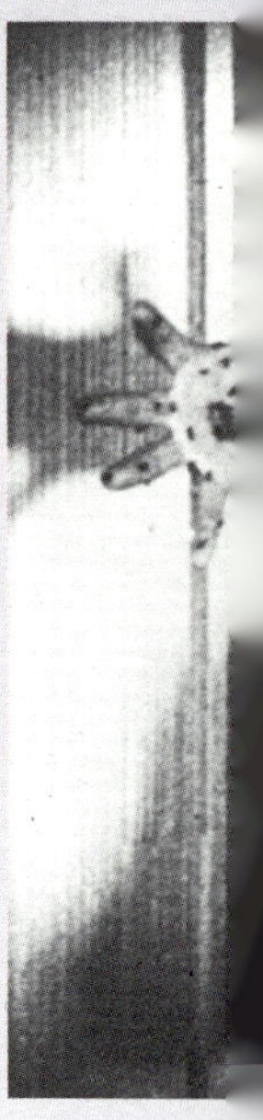

6

the Surrealist period in the arts, but his fondness for imagery of a bizarre 'unnatural' kind clearly anticipated the work of the Surrealists and stimulated the painter Dali and the film-maker Buñuel to look for such images in the collision of everyday reality and the workings of the human subconscious. It is important, therefore, to take account of the 'realistic' aspect of *Un Chien Andalou* – the streets of Paris, the apartment rooms, the beach – since they provide a half-believable landscape into which 'foreign' elements (a severed hand, dead donkeys and so on) are placed in order to create a sense of nightmare where the real and the macabre combine in images that defy reason but trigger emotional responses in the spectator.

Dali's paintings are among the best known in all Surrealist art but in *Un Chien Andalou* his images come vividly to life. Controversy still rages over whether he slaughtered the donkeys and stole the severed hand from a mortuary for those particular sequences, and his severest critics, among them the English novelist George Orwell, accused him of having a sick mind.

Those charges would not have worried Dali. It was a principle of Surrealist art that 'insanity' would be a major source of inspiration – a direct channel from the subconscious mind to the process of artistic creation. But the film is not devoid of meaning. Dali himself described it as:

'The pure and correct line of conduct of a human who pursues love through wretched humanitarian, patriotic ideals and the other miserable workings of reality.'

Buñuel, who appears in the film's opening sequence smoking a cigarette and sharpening the razor, was equally fervently committed to the sense of revolt that the film embodies. The shot of the young man kneading the woman's breasts through her dress is followed by a shot of her naked breasts (and the man's hands on them) in a sequence that anticipates Buñuel's explicit treatment of sexual desire in his subsequent films.

In translating male fantasy to the screen, Buñuel not only outraged the moral climate of his day, but also criticized the repression of desire that can lead to sexual abuse. As the film-maker Jean Vigo remarked in 1930 in his lecture *Vers un Cinéma Social* (Towards a Social Cinema) it was 'a kick in the pants to those who have sullied love in rape'.

In the shooting of the film Buñuel was surprisingly conventional. David Curtis has commented on this in his book *Experimental Cinema*:

'He treats his subject as though he were making a popular thriller presenting just enough continuity and theme to reinforce the illusion of reality.'

However bizarre the sequences, they are clearly located in film-space and the cuts from long shot to close-up are thoroughly consistent with the style of narrative film-making.

Neither Dali nor Buñuel expected the film to be a *succès de scandale* and to attract an audience outside the intellectual élite. Typically Buñuel attacked those who found 'beauty' or 'poetry' in the film and asserted that it was intended as 'neither more nor less than a despairing call to murder'. The spirit of anarchy signalled in this remark was to become even more apparent in his subsequent film *L'Age d'Or* (1930, The Golden Age) after which, apart from one documentary, Buñuel directed no more films until 1947. To look back at *Un Chien Andalou* is to be reminded of the combination of realistic and surrealistic images that was to characterize Buñuel's celebrated post-war films from *Los Olvidados* (1950, *The Young and the Damned*) to *Cet Obscur Objet du Désir* (1977, *That Obscure Object of Desire*). These may have shed some of the virulence of his early career in image-making but have lost none of the humour and imagination of this first notorious film. MARTYN AUTY

Directed by Luis Buñuel, Salvador Dali, 1928
Prod: Luis Buñuel, Salvador Dali. **sc:** Luis Buñuel, Salvador Dali. **photo:** Albert Dubergen. **ed:** Luis Buñuel. **art dir:** Pierre Schilzneck. **mus:** Beethoven, Wagner, a tango. **r/t:** 17 minutes.
Cast: Pierre Batcheff (*the cyclist*), Simone Mareuil (*the woman*), Jaime Miravilles, Salvador Dali, Luis Buñuel.

A title reads 'Once upon a time'. A man is smoking a cigarette and sharpening a razor. The eye of a young woman is slit with the razor (1).

'Eight years later' a young cyclist rides down a street in a strange frilly costume. A young woman sees him from her window and rushes out when he falls off his bicycle (2). In the room the cyclist's hand is crawling with ants. A woman, dressed in masculine style, is in the street poking at a severed hand with a stick (3). She is run over by a car. In the room the cyclist grabs the young woman and paws her breasts, seen clothed and then naked (4). The woman runs away. The cyclist attempts to follow her but is slowed down by the weight of two priests and two grand pianos on which are lying two decaying donkeys (5). The cyclist's hand is trapped in the door and is once again crawling with ants (6).

'Towards three in the morning' a stranger arrives and tears off the bizarre costume which the cyclist has resumed. 'Sixteen years before' in the same room, the stranger gives the cyclist some books. The books become revolvers (7) and he shoots the stranger who falls dead in a country meadow.

The woman arrives on a beach where she embraces a man in knickerbockers. Among the pebbles are the vestiges of the cyclist's costume. 'In the spring' the man and the woman are buried to their waists in sand (8).

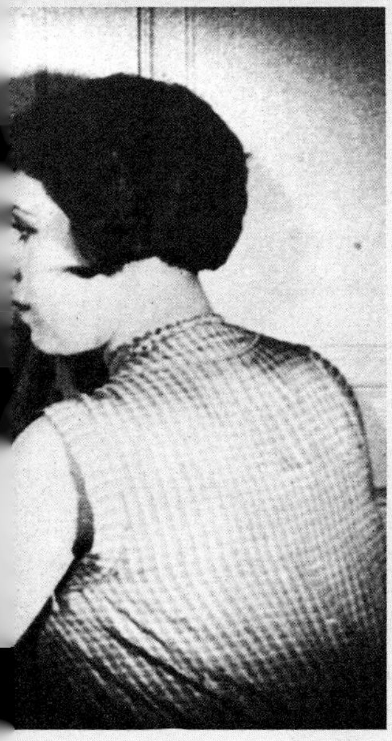

7

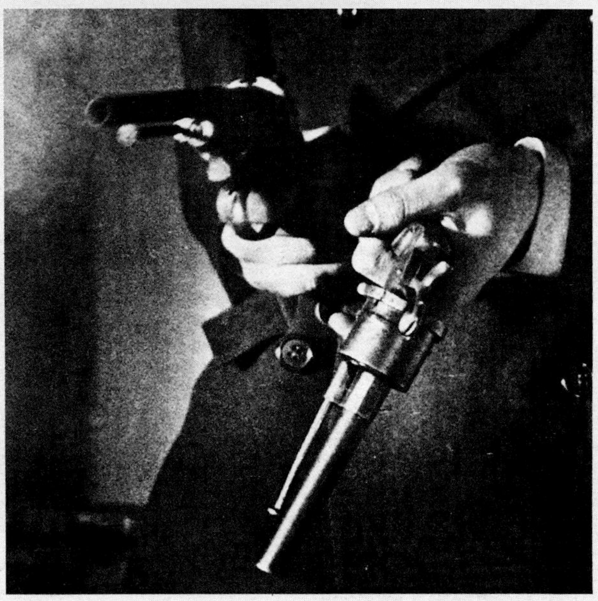

S

Charles Chaplin is the universal clown. His figure is recognized and his comedy instantly understood by hundreds of millions of people of every race, and his name and fame have endured since before World War I

It is no small part of Chaplin's magic and mystery that he rose to his unprecedented pinnacle of popularity from origins as humble and unpromising as might be imagined. He was born on April 16, 1889, according to his own account in East Lane, Walworth, London. Some uncertainty, though, has always surrounded the place of his birth: no birth certificate is recorded for him, and at various times publicity people attributed different locations to the event. Early in his film career, indeed, Chaplin fancifully claimed he had been born in Fontainebleau, France.

Certainly, however, he spent his earliest years in south London, in the Kennington district that was a favourite residential area for Victorian vaudeville performers. Charles Chaplin Senior was a music-hall ballad-singer whose portrait appears on a number of illustrated song sheets of the period. Until alcoholism – the occupational hazard of the music halls – overtook him, he seems to have been fairly successful, and the family was probably reasonably comfortably off at the time of Chaplin's birth. Within a year or so, however, his parents separated. His father died when young Charles was 12, and Mrs Chaplin, herself a not very successful music-hall singer, was left to bring up Charles and his older half-brother Sydney alone. According to Chaplin's own biography, they suffered periods of extreme poverty. When Mrs Chaplin eventually succumbed to the strains and declined into permanent mental breakdown, the two boys spent long periods in orphanages and institutions.

Chaplin's career as an entertainer seemed destined. He claimed that his first appearance before an audience was at five, when he stepped on stage at the Aldershot Canteen theatre to take over from his mother whose voice suddenly failed her. At eight, he joined Jackson's Eight Lancashire Lads, one of the juvenile variety troupes then popular. He later obtained favourable press notices as a child actor in the legitimate theatre, and played the West End and lengthy provincial tours as Billy the Page Boy in *Sherlock Holmes*.

Meanwhile, Sydney Chaplin had become a star comedian with the Karno comedy companies. Fred Karno, a former acrobat, had created what he accurately called his 'Fun Factory' in Camberwell Road, London. Here he rehearsed and equipped the several sketch companies which for many years proved the English music-hall's richest school of comedy. Sydney Chaplin persuaded Karno to engage his brother for a sketch called 'The Football Match'. Within a couple of years Charlie had become a leading comedian, and the star of companies that Karno sent on American tours during 1910-11 and 1912-13.

It was on the second of these tours that he was offered a year's contract with Mack Sennett's Keystone film company. Hesitantly, persuaded largely by the $150 a week that doubled his salary with Karno, he joined Sennett in California. Chaplin was at first uneasy in the new medium. He was disturbed by the chaos of the Sennett studios, and the Sennett slapstick comedians found his more refined style of comedy too slow. Little love was lost between Chaplin and his first director, Henry Lehrman, and he resented, equally, taking direction from his young, lovely and volatile co-star comedienne Mabel Normand.

His first film, *Making a Living* (1914), in which he was dressed as a dubious dandy, was indifferent, though well received by the trade press of the time. For his second film, a five-minute improvisation shot during the event which gave it its title, *Kid Auto Races at Venice* (1914), however, he adopted the costume that was to become world-famous. According to legend, it was made up from various items borrowed from other Sennett comedians: Fatty Arbuckle's huge trousers; Charles Avery's tiny jacket; a derby hat belonging to Arbuckle's father-in-law; Ford Sterling's boots, so oversize that they had to be worn on the wrong feet; and Mack Swain's moustache, sharply pruned.

Charles Chaplin

y-two years a King

Chaplin later wrote:

'I had no idea of the character. But the moment I was dressed, the clothes and the make-up made me feel the person he was. I began to know him, and by the time I walked on to the stage he was fully born.'

Over the next 22 years the character was to be refined and elaborated: the hero of *City Lights* (1931) or *Modern Times* (1936) is altogether more complex than the little Tramp of the first frantic Sennett slapstick shorts as he scurries on one leg around corners, clutching his hat to his head while being chased by Keystone Kops or angry, bewhiskered giants. But the general lines of the character – the range of emotions from callousness to high sentiment, and of his actions from nobility to larceny, the supremely human resilience and fallibility of his nature – were fairly soon defined.

Above left: Chaplin directs The Gold Rush. *Of the 87 films he was associated with, he directed 69 (5 jointly with Mabel Normand). Left: Perhaps the most famous figure of the twentieth century, the Tramp took to the road in over 50 movies. Below: Charlie causes chaos at* The Rink *– with Edna Purviance, Eric Campbell and Albert Austin*

Chaplin spent 1914 at Keystone, serving a valuable apprenticeship to his art, and making 35 films. From the twelfth of these, *Caught in a Cabaret*, he began to take a hand in the direction, and from the twentieth, *Laughing Gas*, he was permanently established as his own director. Seen today, these films are mostly primitive. The stock jokes involve intoxication, illicit flirtations, mallets, dentists, jealous husbands, cops, dough, dynamite, lakes to be fallen into, cars to crash, benches and boxing rings from which to fall. Already, however, in *The New Janitor* for example, Chaplin was trying out subtler skills as a story-teller and actor.

These skills were to be developed further and faster at Essanay, the company Chaplin joined in January 1915 in the first of a series of much-publicized changes of employer that would dramatically increase his earnings. Chaplin was at first unhappy in Essanay's Chicago studio, though he knocked out a lively little comedy about the film business, aptly titled *His New Job* (1915). When he moved to the company's West Coast studio he took with him a new cameraman, Roland Totheroh, who was to work with him for over thirty years. At Niles, California, Chaplin began to build a company around himself, and his most important discovery was Edna Purviance, a beautiful stenographer with no screen experience. She was to remain his ideal leading lady for the next eight years. The warm and feminine quality of Edna's screen personality – in sharp contrast to the amusing madcap Mabel Normand – was probably partly responsible for the growing element of romantic yearning in Chaplin's work. This was most evident in two of Chaplin's earliest Essanay films, *The Tramp* and *The Bank* (both 1915). At the same time Chaplin was becoming more ambitious – he was taking more time over his films, and going on location. For *Shanghaied* (1915), he even blew up a small schooner to provide a dramatic climax. In his last film for Essanay, *Police* (1916), he first introduced touches of a social irony that anticipated *The Kid* (1921) and *The Pilgrim* (1923).

With Chaplin's next move, his salary soared to $10,000 a week, with extra bonuses. He spent 16 months over the 12 two-reelers he made at his Lone Star studio for Mutual release. They were polished gag structures, mostly inspired by a location or a situation, as their titles – *The Floorwalker, The Fireman, Behind the Screen, The Rink* (all 1916) and *The Cure* (1917) – suggest. Some of them are feats of virtuosity: *One a.m.* (1916) is virtually a solo

turn, with Charlie returning home inebriated to battle with a keyhole, a folding bed, a tigerskin rug and other domestic hazards; *The Pawn Shop* (1916) includes a long unbroken take of an autopsy on a customer's alarm clock. Other films, including *The Vagabond* (1916) and *The Immigrant* (1917), exploited Chaplin's developing gifts for drama and pathos.

A new distribution agreement with First National Distributors enabled Chaplin to fulfil his ambition of building his own studio, where he was to work for the next 24 years. His contract called for eight films to be made in eighteen months; instead, they took five years, and included at least three masterpieces. The first, *A Dog's Life* (1918), sharpened the henceforth ever-present element of social satire, drawing parallels between the existence of the Tramp and his faithful mongrel dog. Chaplin next boldly defied accusations of bad taste in making comedy out of life at the front in World War I; the men who best knew that life took *Shoulder Arms* (1918) to their hearts, and today Chaplin's comic metamorphosis of the war may give a more vivid sense of those days than a more solemn dramatic treatment. *Sunnyside* (1919) is an uncharacteristic and only modestly successful pastoral comedy. *A Day's Pleasure* (1919) is a delightful slice of humble life, the misadventures of a little man taking his Ford and family on an outing; one of the children in the film was played by Jackie Coogan, whose uncanny acting ability partly inspired Chaplin's next film, *The Kid*. Here, a melodrama about an unmarried mother and her abandoned child provides the motive for a rich comedy about the Tramp's unwilling adoption of the foundling and the odd comic-pathetic bond that grows between them. After finishing the film, Chaplin decided to make a return visit to his homeland and to tour Europe. This was, perhaps, the peak of his career: few celebrities until this time had aroused the furore that attended every public appearance, or the adulation he received from the great men of the world.

The two films that he made on his return, *The Idle Class* (1921), a slapstick situation comedy with Chaplin in two roles, and *Pay Day* (1922), another slice-of-life comedy in which little Charlie is given a job, home and nagging wife, were only moderately successful; but with *The Pilgrim* his critical reputation soared again. This story of an escaped convict, who steals the clothes of a bathing priest and is mistaken for the new pastor of a little Midwest township, provided opportunities for nice irony at the expense of bigotry, hypocrisy and small-town manners.

Only when the First National contract was worked out was Chaplin free to make his first feature film for release by United Artists, the distribution organization he had formed in company with Douglas Fairbanks, Mary Pickford and D. W. Griffith four years before. *A Woman of Paris* (1923) was his first, long-contemplated attempt at serious drama. It was intended to launch the loyal Edna Purviance as a dramatic actress, and her elegant, restrained performance merited the chance, though her subsequent career was to be short-lived. Adolphe Menjou subtly partnered her and became a star. Chaplin himself appeared only in a walk-on part.

The film took the stuff of Victorian melodrama – the tragedy of a village girl turned courtesan and torn between an artist and a playboy – but applied to it an extremely sophisticated visual style, which was to influence the subsequent course of film comedy. To Chaplin's enduring chagrin, however, *A Woman of Paris*, despite its enthusiastic press proved a commercial failure, but he was to recover his losses and his confidence with two of his best comedy features, *The Gold Rush* (1925) and *The Circus* (1928).

From the Thirties onwards, Chaplin greatly slowed his output, taking not less than five years on each film. By the time he embarked on *City Lights*, sound pictures had arrived, and Chaplin had witnessed the downfall of other great silent comedians. He decided not to risk the voiceless character he had created or his vast international market by trying dialogue. *City Lights* is a silent movie with musical accompaniment. It is based on a series of comic variations built around an ironic melodrama about a blind girl and the sad little Tramp whose efforts give back the sight that enables her to see his pathetic reality. In *Modern Times* which marked the last appearance of the Tramp, he risked a few moments of comic gibberish, though elsewhere retained his old mimetic comic style. With this film Chaplin first attracted the hostile and persistent line of

·riticism that charged the comedian with ·xceeding his 'proper' brief, and setting himself ıp as a philosopher. It was a criticism that nevitably attached no less to *The Great Dictator* 1940), a comic satire on totalitarianism. For ıll the anger underlying the laughter, Chaplin ater said that had he known the truth about Hitler's concentration camps he would not ıave had the temerity to make the film.

A feeling for the dark and macabre had ıever been far absent from Chaplin's films, and t surfaced most strongly in *Monsieur Verdoux* 1947), the story of a French Bluebeard wife-iller between the wars. The philosophic ·ontrast that Verdoux draws between his own ind of murder and the kind that is licensed by var was not popular in the Cold War years, ınd the character was made a weapon of that ·ersecution that led to Chaplin's permanent xile from America in 1953.

.eft: a fruitful union that produced 15 comedy lassics. Far left: the Tramp dines with the 'runk millionaire (Harry Myers) in City *ights. Above, far left: Chaplin's film debut* Aaking a Living *as a bogus lord who charms he ladies (Minta Durfee, Alice Davenport). Above left: diagnosing the end for an alarm lock in* The Pawn Shop, *with Albert Austin. Below: Marie (Edna Purviance), her masseuse Nelly Bly Baker) and a neurotic friend Malvina Polo) in* A Woman of Paris. *Below eft: the* Limelight *deserts an old clown – with laire Bloom. Below right: keeping abreast of* A Countess From Hong Kong

Chaplin's last American film was a nostalgic tribute to his youth in the backstreets and variety theatres of London. Full of autobiographical references, *Limelight* (1952) tells of the friendship and mutual support of an old, failed, alcoholic comedian and a dancer struck with psychosomatic paralysis. Reversing the process, in Britain he made a film about America: *A King in New York* (1957) is a bitter and ferocious comedy about the paranoia and persecution of the McCarthy era. It is at its best where Chaplin relies upon pathos, casting his own son Michael as a Fifties parallel to *The Kid*, the child's mind and conscience brutalized by society as the Jackie Coogan character suffered in his body.

At 77 Chaplin made one last film. A pleasant romantic comedy, *A Countess From Hong Kong* (1967) might have been more successful and more kindly received if he had not made the mistake of using international stars – Marlon Brando and Sophia Loren – unsuited to his style of working. He never wholly retired, however. Almost until the end of his life he continued to work on the preparations of a film to be called *The Freak*. Having composed the music for his sound films, he continued to create new scores for reissues of his silent pictures. Barely a year before his death in 1977, Chaplin steeled himself to add music to *A Woman of Paris* for reissue, despite its painful memories. He had worked for more than eighty years; the 62 of them spent in pictures established a record not likely to be beaten.

DAVID ROBINSON

Filmography

Shorts unless otherwise specified: **1914** Making a Living (actor only); Kid Auto Races at Venice (actor only) (GB: Kid Auto Races); Mabel's Strange Predicament (actor only); Between Showers (actor only); A Film Johnnie (actor only); Tango Tangles (actor only); His Favourite Pastime (actor only); Cruel, Cruel Love (actor only); The Star Boarder (actor only); Mabel at the Wheel (actor only); Twenty Minutes of Love (sc;+act. only); Caught in a Cabaret (co-dir; +sc; +act); Caught in the Rain (+sc; +act); A Busy Day (+sc;+act); The Fatal Mallet (co-dir; +sc; +act); Her Friend the Bandit (co-dir; +co-sc; + act); The Knockout (sc; +act. only); Mabel's Busy Day (co-dir; +co-sc; +act); Mabel's Married Life (co-dir; +co-sc; +act); Laughing Gas (+sc; +act); The Property Man (+sc; +act); The Face on the Barroom Floor (+sc; +act); Recreation (+sc; +act); The Masquerader (+sc; +act); His New Profession (+sc; +act); The Rounders (+sc; +act); The New Janitor (+sc; +act); Those Love Pangs (+sc; +act); Dough and Dynamite (+sc; +act); Gentlemen of Nerve (+sc; +act); His Musical Career (+sc; +act); His Trysting Place (+sc; +act); Tillie's Punctured Romance (feature) (actor only); Getting Acquainted (+sc; +act); His Prehistoric Past (+sc; +act). **'15** His New Job (+sc; +act); A Night Out (+sc; +act); The Champion (+sc; +act); In the Park (+sc; +act); A Jitney Elopement (+sc; +act); The Tramp (+sc; +act); By the Sea (+sc; +act); His Regeneration (guest app. only); Work (+sc; +act); A Woman (+sc; +act); The Bank (+sc; +act); Shanghaied (+sc; +act); A Night in the Show (+sc; +act). **'16** Carmen/Charlie Chaplin's Burlesque on Carmen (short and feature versions) (+sc; +act); Police (+co-sc; +act); The Floorwalker (+prod; +co-sc; +act); The Fireman (+prod; +co-sc; +act); The Vagabond (+prod; +co-sc; +act); One a.m. (+prod; +sc; +act); The Count (+prod; +sc; +act); The Essanay-Chaplin Revue of 1916 (compilation); The Pawn Shop (+prod; +sc; +act); Behind the Screen (+prod; +sc; +act); The Rink (+prod; +sc; +act). **'17** Easy Street (+prod; +sc; +act); The Cure (+prod; +sc; +act); The Immigrant (+prod; +sc; +act); The Adventurer (+prod; +sc; +act). **'18** A Dog's Life (+prod; +sc; +act); Chase Me Charlie (compilation); Triple Trouble (co-dir; +co-sc; +act); Shoulder Arms (+prod; +sc; +act); The Bond (+sc; +act) (GB: Charles Chaplin in a Liberty Loan Appeal). **'19** Sunnyside (+prod; +sc; +act); A Day's Pleasure (+prod; +sc; +act). *All remaining films features unless otherwise specified:* **'21** The Kid (+prod; +sc; +act); The Nut (guest); The Idle Class (short) (+prod; +sc; +act). **'22** Pay Day (short) (+prod; +sc; +act). **'23** The Pilgrim (short) (+prod; +sc; +act); A Woman of Paris (+prod; +sc; +act; +mus. for 1976 reissue); Souls for Sale (guest); Hollywood (guest). **'25** The Gold Rush (+prod; +sc; +act; +mus. for 1942 reissue). **'26** A Woman of the Sea/The Sea Gull (add. dir; +prod; +co-sc) (unreleased). **'28** The Circus (+prod; +sc; +act; + mus. for 1970 reissue); Show People (guest). **'31** City Lights (+prod; +sc; +mus; +act). **'36** Modern Times (+prod; +sc; +mus; +act). **'40** The Great Dictator (+prod; +sc; +co-mus; +act). **'47** Monsieur Verdoux (+prod; +sc; +mus; +narr; +act). **'52** Limelight (+prod; +sc; +mus; +chor; +act). **'57** A King in New York (+prod; +sc; +mus; +act) (GB). **'59** The Chaplin Revue (compilation) (+prod; +sc; +mus; +narr). **'67** A Countess From Hong Kong (+sc; +mus; +act) (GB).

Chaplin also appears in: 1915 Introducing Charlie Chaplin (*short*). *'38* Charlie Chaplin Carnival; Charlie Chaplin Cavalcade; Charlie Chaplin Festival. *'66-74* The Chaplin Documentary (*unshown*). *'67* The Funniest Man in the World; Stimulantia *ep* Upptackten (*SWED*).

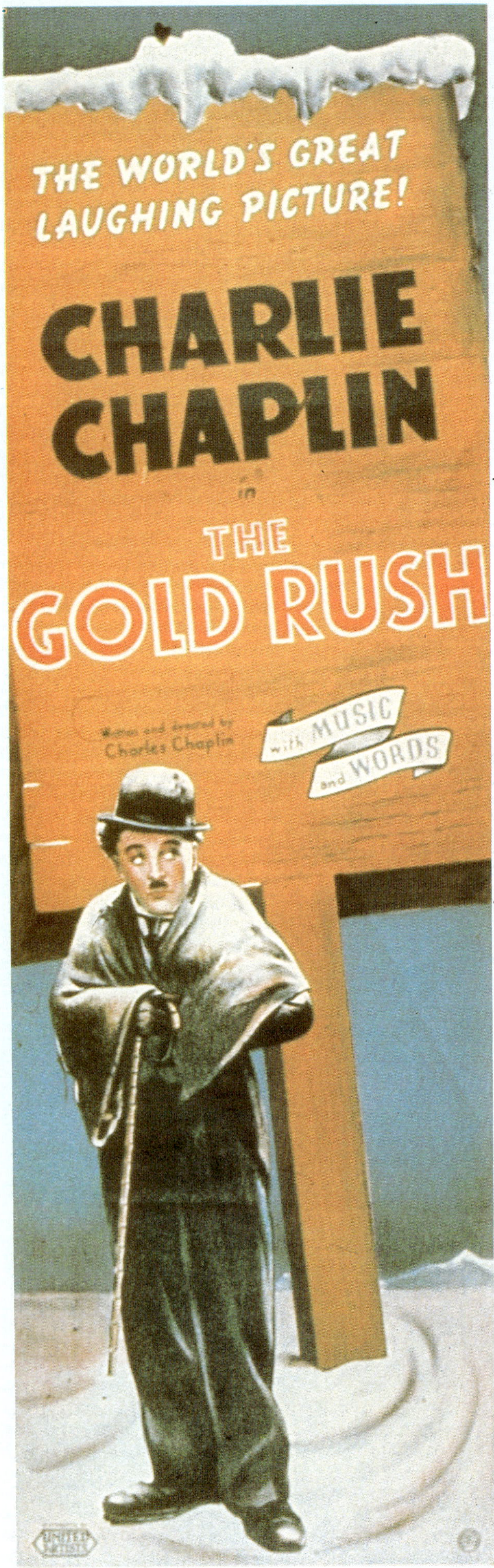
THE WORLD'S GREAT
LAUGHING PICTURE!
CHARLIE
CHAPLIN
in
THE
GOLD RUSH
Written and directed by
Charles Chaplin
with MUSIC
and WORDS
UNITED ARTISTS

1

2

4

5

6

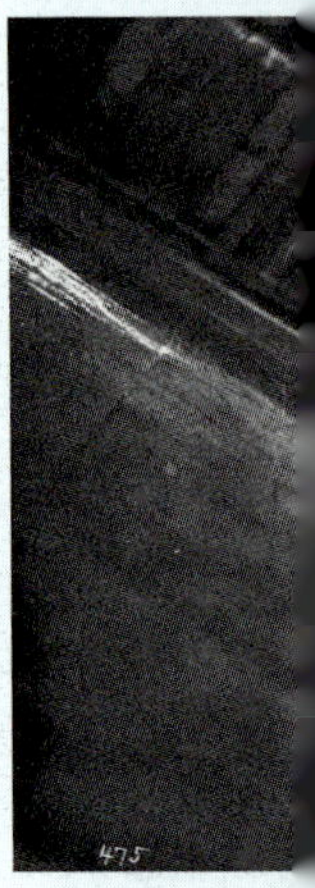
7

8

3

The Klondike gold rush of 1898: an endless line of prospectors winds its way up the snow-covered Chilkoot Pass. One lone adventurer among the rest, Charlie follows his own path, which is beset by a bear and a blizzard. Along with another fortune-hunter, Big Jim, Charlie seeks shelter (1) in the hut of the fearsome Black Larsen. When their food gives out, the three draw lots and Larsen is sent out into the wilderness in search of provender.

Back in the hut, Charlie and Big Jim's Thanksgiving dinner consists of one of Charlie's boots (2). The starving Jim hallucinates and sees Charlie as a plump chicken, ripe for slaughter. Defending himself (3), Charlie accidentally shoots a passing bear, solving the food problem. They finally leave the hut to go their own ways. Larsen steals Jim's mining claim and fells him with a spade, but is killed in an avalanche. Charlie meanwhile lands in a little mining town. He falls in love with saloon-girl Georgia (4), who pretends to encourage him to spite her tough boyfriend Jack (5).

Excitedly, Charlie, staying in the hut of a kindly prospector, prepares a New Year's Eve party for Georgia and her friends. They forget to come (6), but Charlie, falling asleep, dreams of triumphs as the perfect host.

Big Jim arrives in town, suffering from amnesia. He persuades Charlie to lead him to his gold strike, having forgotten its location. Only after hair-raising adventures in a hut balanced on the edge of a precipice (7) do they find Jim's mountain of gold.

Now millionaires, Jim and Charlie return home by ship (8). Press photographers persuade Charlie to pose in his prospector's rags, but he tumbles into the steerage where Georgia, also going home, thinks he is a stowaway and offers to pay his passage. The misunderstanding is explained, and Charlie invites the photographers to take an engagement picture of himself and his newly-found fiancée.

Directed by Charles Chaplin, 1925

Prod co: Charles Chaplin Productions, for United Artists. **prod/sc:** Charles Chaplin. **photo:** Roland H. Totheroh. **tech dir:** Charles D. Hall. **assoc dir:** Charles Riesner, Henri d'Abbadie d'Arrast. **prod man:** Alf Reeves. **length:** 8498 ft (approx. 94 minutes).

Cast: Charles Chaplin (*a lone prospector*), Georgia Hale (*Georgia*), Mack Swain (*Big Jim McKay*), Tom Murray (*Black Larsen*), Malcolm Waite (*Jack Cameron*), Henry Bergman (*Hank Curtis*), Betty Morrissey (*Betty*), John Rand, Albert Austin, Heinie Conklin, Allan Garcia, Tom Wood (*prospectors*).

The Gold Rush was the first comedy feature which Charles Chaplin made for release by United Artists. Though he had formed the distribution company with D. W. Griffith, Douglas Fairbanks and Mary Pickford in 1919, the only previous Chaplin film made for United Artists release was the drama *A Woman of Paris* (1923), which had proved a critical triumph but a commercial disaster. Chaplin has described how he 'strove, thought and brooded' for weeks, trying to get an idea. 'I kept saying to myself: "This next film must be an epic! The greatest!"' The idea finally came to him one Sunday morning after breakfast with the Fairbankses at their home, Pickfair. Looking at stereoscopic views of Alaska and the Klondike, he was particularly struck by:

'. . . a view of the Chilkoot Pass, with a long line of prospectors climbing up over its frozen mountains, with a caption printed on the back describing the trials and hardships endured in surmounting it. This was a wonderful theme, I thought, enough to stimulate my imagination. Immediately ideas and comedy business began to develop, and, although I had no story, the image of one began to grow.'

Further inspiration came from his reading a book on the Donner Party disaster, in which a group of 160 pioneers were snowbound in the Sierra Nevada, having missed the route to California. Only 18 survived out of the original 160, and hunger and cold drove them to cannibalism and to roasting their moccasins for food. Chaplin was always fascinated by the macabre and this tragic affair was to inspire what is perhaps his most famous comic invention – the eating of the boot with all the airs of a gourmet, picking the nails as if they were the bones of some dainty game bird, and treating the laces as spaghetti. He later reflected:

'It is paradoxical that tragedy stimulates the spirit of ridicule because ridicule, I suppose, is an attitude of defiance: we must laugh in the face of our helplessness against the forces of nature – or go insane.'

After six months pondering over likely comedy sequences, Chaplin began shooting on February 8, 1924 without a script, relying on gag sequences and gag inspirations and the stimulus of set and location to suggest the narrative line. This was generally his method in silent days: he could afford the extravagance of time it involved, since he had at his disposal the facilities of a permanent studio and crew. Shooting was completed on May 21, 1925: out of the total shooting time of 405 days, 170 days were actually occupied in filming. The remaining 235 'idle days', as they were recorded on the shooting schedules, were mostly used to allow the director-star to work out his next inspirations.

Parts of the film – notably the spectacular opening scene of the trail of prospectors – were shot on location in the high sierras of the California Rockies, at Mount Lincoln, where Chaplin had brought several hundred down-and-outs and hoboes who worked with enthusiasm, and provided their own costumes. Back in Hollywood, however, Chaplin built another mountain. The contemporary publicity for the film proudly announced that the construction required 239,573 feet of timber, 22,750 linear feet of chicken wire, 22,000 feet of burlap, 200 tons of plaster, 285 tons of salt and 100 sacks of flour.

Chaplin sought a new leading lady to replace the loyal Edna Purviance, who had now grown too mature for youthful roles in his pictures. An early candidate was Lita Grey, who instead became, briefly and unhappily, Mrs Chaplin.

The eventual choice was Georgia Hale, a beautiful and spirited actress whom Josef von Sternberg had discovered as an extra and cast in his notable first film *The Salvation Hunters* (1925). Sternberg later, ungallantly, attributed her lively performance in *The Gold Rush* wholly to Chaplin's direction. When she was put under contract to Paramount, Sternberg speculated that directors 'must have been shocked to find that attributes she had been credited with were not hers'. After *The Gold Rush*, she made a few more films and then became a dancing teacher in California. Of the supporting players Mack Swain, as Big Jim, and Henry Bergman, as the kindly prospector, were old Chaplin faithfuls. Tom Murray, who played Black Larsen, had been the sheriff in Chaplin's *The Pilgrim* (1923).

Sternberg recalls Georgia Hale's surprise at working for more than a year in a film after the three-week schedule of *The Salvation Hunters*. Even for those years the film was expensive; Chaplin reckoned the overall cost of production as $923,886. In 1942 Chaplin reissued the film, slightly cut and with a new synchronized musical score and narration spoken by himself.

DAVID ROBINSON

Alias Harold Lloyd

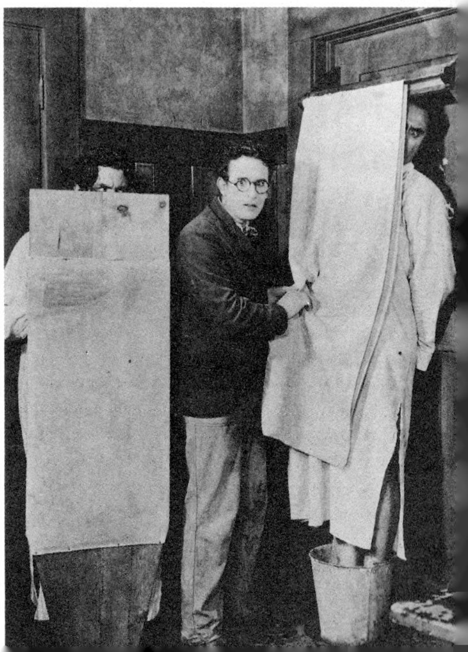

With a character based on Charles Chaplin's Tramp, a face as impassive as Buster Keaton's and a helplessness reminiscent of Harry Langdon's, one funnyman needed to find something unique to separate him from the crowd. He found a straw hat, a pair of glasses, an unassuming suit and a terrifying skill for stunts . . . and became Harold Lloyd

Now the least regarded of the great silent comedians, Harold Lloyd was very much a product of his times. In their different ways, Charles Chaplin, Buster Keaton and even Harry Langdon created timeless characters, but Lloyd's bespectacled youth belonged to the exuberant, booming Twenties – his ambitions, his fantasies and his failures were those of his audiences too. So when seen now, Lloyd's films develop a new layer of interest: the charm of their background. Behind the wild escapades of a film like *Safety Last* (1923), a summer's day in Los Angeles goes on its way, almost becoming a documentary movie on its own. And because from the start his films involved such rapport with the audience, Lloyd still needs an audience now. Seen on television, they simply do not work, but put them before a live audience – ideally one with children – response is immediate and the magic returns.

Harold Clayton Lloyd was born in Nebraska on April 20, 1893 (d. 1971) and, like so many of his contemporaries, he entered the movies almost by accident. In his youth, mainly spent in Omaha, he had drifted somewhat, but occasional work with stock companies made him think seriously of a career in the theatre. So when in 1911 he and his father (by then separated from Lloyd's mother) moved to San Diego in California, Lloyd picked up again with old theatrical acquaintances and worked, in a modest way, on the stage. In a bad spell in 1913, employed as an extra with an Edison outfit in San Diego, he decided that he would give the movies a further try, and went on to Los Angeles. It would be three years before he emerged from obscurity.

Lucrative Luke

He played extra roles and small parts in forgotten films, mainly at Universal, where he made the acquaintance of his future producer, Hal Roach. When Roach formed a small production company, Lloyd appeared for him as a low-life comic character known as Willie Work. This venture failed; Lloyd spent a short time with Mack Sennett at Keystone, made no impression there, and by the end of 1915 was back with Roach. Then came a partial success. Roach and Lloyd – each of them later claiming credit for the idea – devised a character, not far removed from Chaplin's Tramp, whom they dubbed 'Lonesome Luke'. Chaplin's clothes were much too big; Luke's were much too small – but surviving films and stills of Luke leave no doubt of the resemblance in style. Derivative and crude as the Luke films were, they were profitable, and in two years Lloyd made over fifty of them. The early ones were one-reelers, the last few stretched to two. Then, towards the end of 1917, came the inspiration that changed Lloyd's life. He created an identity that was to become his particular 'trademark' and make him recognizable throughout the world – the 'glasses' character.

As Lloyd himself put it later on, 'I would be an average, recognizable American youth and let the situations take care of the comedy'. The spectacles, of course, were crucial. They not only made him look innocent, but gave him a scholarly look as well. He was the kind of young man who would break off writing a suicide note to look up the spelling of 'sepulchre' in the dictionary (as in *Never Weaken*, 1921). The earliest 'glasses' films were an immediate success. Roach's distributors, Pathé, began to take Lloyd seriously. He was on his way to becoming a star.

The 'glasses' films also began as one-reelers, but expanded to two, and eventually three. By 1920 Lloyd had mastered the form and the character, and three of his last shorts – *Get Out and Get Under* (1920), *I Do* (1921) and *Never Weaken* – must rank among his finest work. In *Get Out and Get Under*, Lloyd plays the owner of a recalcitrant car, a theme very much of its time and one to which he would often return. *Never Weaken* has him among the high girders of a partially completed building, believing that the sculpted angels past whom he is carried mean that he has actually reached heaven. There had been two of these 'thrill' pictures (as Lloyd called them) before – *Look Out Below!* (1919) and *High and Dizzy* (1920) – and two of the feature films would return to the same situation. The image Lloyd's name evokes in most people's minds is that of him clinging to some protruding part of a high building. But in fact only five of his 190-odd films see him scaling the heights, the most famous of them *Safety Last*.

Lloyd's leading ladies

For some three years Lloyd's leading lady had been the young Bebe Daniels, already a gifted comedienne. In 1919 Daniels left to join Cecil B. DeMille, and Lloyd replaced her with Mildred Davis. Davis was pretty, blonde and somewhat characterless, but Lloyd fell in love with her, married her (the marriage lasting until her death in 1969), and played opposite her until she retired in 1923. His next six features starred the vivacious and charming Jobyna Ralston – even Lloyd must have known in his heart that she was a great improvement on Mildred Davis.

In 1919 an event occurred that could have changed the whole course of Lloyd's career. While making a short called *Haunted Spooks* (1920) a supposed dummy bomb exploded and severely injured him. A property man had

Top, far left: a certain Tramp gave Lloyd's Lonesome Luke hero (here with Bebe Daniels) some stiff competition. Top centre: Speedy *the reluctant hero horses around. Top right: Lloyd as 'Glasses',* Girl Shy *(1924) and crazy. Above, far left: allowing himself to be walked all over in* The Freshman. *Above left: a prototype superman? – Lloyd proving his nerves of steel* Never Weaken *while putting his own* Safety Last *(far left). Centre left: sensing a presence as* The Kid Brother *(1927). Left: South American trouble Twenties style – Lloyd with timid giant Johan Aasen in* Why Worry?, *his last film for the great comedy producer Hal Roach*

been at fault. Lloyd was not blinded, though for some time that was feared, but he lost the thumb and forefinger of his right hand, and in some of his films the specially constructed glove which he wore can clearly be seen.

Lloyd's move into features in 1921 was a virtual accident. *A Sailor-Made Man* (1921) and *Grandma's Boy* (1922) were both planned as shorts, but contained so much material that they inevitably grew into features. In the first the strain is apparent: in the second the feature length is clearly apt. Lloyd conveys a coherent story and an interesting character – a coward who is conned into courage – and has time to relax and take things at the pace they demand. He made ten features in the eight years before the advent of sound. They were not all triumphs. *Doctor Jack* (1922) is a dull comedy about a country doctor and is both unfunny and tasteless, the humour being at the expense of lunatics and Negroes; *Why Worry?* (1923) – the last film with Roach before Lloyd gained his independence – is a mechanical comedy about a South American revolution saved only by the marvellously devoted giant-figure of Johan Aasen; and *Hot Water* (1924) has two classic sequences (Lloyd and the turkey; Lloyd taking the in-laws out for a car ride) but very little else to recommend it.

A gaggle of gagmen

Some of the better films suffer a little from their method of construction. Lloyd employed a large team of gagmen, permanently there to devise situations. They were superb at their job and, as well as finding the 'situations', they polished and refined them, inventing outlandish 'toppers' for them – and these sequences could last for up to fifteen minutes. But then the gag sequences – his 'islands', as Lloyd called them – had to be connected and integrated into the story. Here the invention, even in such celebrated successes as *Safety Last* and *For Heaven's Sake* (1926), sometimes broke down.

When Lloyd had a strong story which could be developed logically without undue reliance on the 'islands', he produced masterpieces. In *The Freshman* (1925) he is a naive youth going about winning acceptance at college in quite the wrong way. He triumphs in the end, but his road there is hard, and his humiliations on the way are lacerating. *The Kid Brother* (1927) is a more mature version of *Grandma's Boy*, with

Above: in true Boy's Own *style the novice 'Glasses' character heads* Back to the Woods *in a 1919 short. Right: this ain't no way to treat a lady (specially when she's your mother-in-law) – Lloyd demonstrating the unreliability of the Butterfly Six and landing himself in very* Hot Water *in the process*

Lloyd eventually winning the respect of his tough father and brothers. The climax is a fight that is genuinely thrilling and full of inspired gags. His final silent movie was *Speedy* (Lloyd's own juvenile nickname), a model comedy made in 1928. Here, a dreamy baseball fan (Lloyd) not only meets the great Babe Ruth but singlehandedly (save for an intelligent dog – Lloyd's dogs and cats are worth a study in themselves) routs the crooks who are trying to eliminate the last surviving horse-drawn trolley-car in New York. Swift, economical, beautifully timed and attractively shot on location in New York (a new departure for Lloyd), *Speedy* falls little short of the great comedies of Keaton and Chaplin. But before Lloyd could progress any further sound arrived, changing the whole basis of comedy and undermining him.

Who directed Lloyd's films? Each of them carries a director's credit, but Lloyd always claimed that he was in total charge and made the vital decisions. He felt that the director simply kept things rolling smoothly while he was involved with his own performance. Basically this must be true – for it is the way most silent comics worked – but perhaps not entirely. Lloyd's three main directors were Fred Newmeyer, Sam Taylor, and Ted Wilde. Newmeyer directed the later shorts and the first three features; a former baseball pitcher, then a property man with Roach, he was a rough and ready worker who did nothing of note after Lloyd. Sam Taylor, whom Lloyd promoted from gagman, co-directed the next five features with Newmeyer, and had a solo credit for *For Heaven's Sake*. However, Taylor did work successfully elsewhere, directing Bea Lillie, John Barrymore, Mary Pickford and Douglas Fairbanks. His was a more sophisticated talent, and it seems fair to accord him some credit for the increasing finesse visible in Lloyd's work. Finally, Ted Wilde, another ex-gagman, directed the last two silent features – *The Kid Brother* and *Speedy* – both of which are beautifully visualized films. The scene in *The Kid Brother*, with Lloyd up a tree calling to a fast disappearing Jobyna Ralston, is not merely charming – it is a scene that depends entirely on good direction. To the finale of *Speedy* too, someone brought a completely new feeling for place and the use of camera angles, and Wilde received a nomination for the Oscar for Best Director for that film.

Eternally fresh

Finally though, as with all silent comedy, it is the character that is the essential feature. There was much more variety in Harold Lloyd than may appear at first sight. The basis may always be the eager young man, delighted by all the novelty of the twentieth century, but the facets were different. They ranged from the languid millionaire of *A Sailor-Made Man* and *For Heaven's Sake* to the go-getter of *Safety Last*; from the nervous youth of *Girl Shy* (1924) to the desperate trier of *The Freshman*, but they were all Lloyd, and each was what the Freshman so wanted to be – 'a regular fellow'.

JACK LODGE

Filmography

Shorts unless otherwise specified: **1913** From Italy's Shore; Samson and Delilah (feature); Damon and Pythias (feature). **'14** Wizard of Oz (feature). **'15** Just Nuts; Miss Fatty's Seaside Lovers; Lonesome Luke; Once Every Ten Minutes; Spit-Ball Sadie; Soaking the Clothes; Pressing His Suit; Terribly Stuck Up; A Mixup for Maisie; Some Baby; Fresh From the Farm; Giving Them Fits; Bughouse Bellhops; Tinkering With Trouble; Great While It Lasted; Ragtime Snap Shots; A Foozle at the Tea Party; Ruses, Rhymes and Roughnecks; Peculiar Patients' Pranks; Lonesome Luke, Social Gangster. **'16** Lonesome Luke Leans to the Literary; Luke Lugs Luggage; Lonesome Luke Lolls in Luxury (GB: Luke Lolls in Luxury); Luke, the Candy Cut-Up; Luke Foils the Villain; Luke and the Rural Roughnecks; Luke Pipes the Pippens; Lonesome Luke, Circus King; Luke's Double; Them Was the Happy Days; Luke and the Bomb Throwers; Luke's Late Lurchers; Luke Laughs Last; Luke's Fatal Flivver; Luke's Society Mixup; Luke's Washful Waiting; Luke Rides Roughshod; Luke, Crystal Gazer; Luke's Lost Lamb; Luke Does the Midway; Luke Joins the Navy; Luke and the Mermaids; Luke's Speedy Club Life; Luke and the Bangtails; Luke the Chauffeur; Luke's Preparedness Preparations; Luke, the Gladiator; Luke, Patient Provider; Luke's Newsie Knockout; Luke's Movie Muddle/Luke's Model Movie/Director of the Cinema; Luke Rank Impostor; Luke's Firework Fizzle; Luke Locates the Loot/Luke Locates the Lute; Luke's Shattered Sleep. **'17** Luke's Lost Liberty; Luke's Busy Day; Luke's Trolley Troubles (GB: Luke's Tramcar Tragedy); Lonesome Luke, Lawyer; Luke Wins Ye Ladye Faire; Lonesome Luke's Lively Life; Lonesome Luke on Tin Can Alley; Lonesome Luke's Honeymoon; Lonesome Luke, Plumber/Luke's Plumbing Blunders/Lonesome Luke's Plumbing Mishaps; Stop! Luke! Listen!; Lonesome Luke, Messenger; Lonesome Luke, Mechanic (GB: Luke, Motor Mechanic); Lonesome Luke's Wild Women; Over the Fence; Lonesome Luke Loses Patients; Pinched; By the Sad Sea Waves; Birds of a Feather; Bliss; Lonesome Luke From London to Laramie; Rainbow Island; Love, Laughs and Lather; The Flirt; Clubs Are Trump; All Aboard; We Never Sleep; Move On; Bashful. **'18** The Tip; The Big Idea; The Lamb; Hit Him Again; Beat It; A Gasoline Wedding; Look Pleasant, Please; Here Come the Girls; Let's Go; On the Jump; Follow the Crowd; Pipe the Whiskers; It's a Wild Life; Hey There!; Kicked Out; The Non-Stop Kid; Two Gun Gussie; Fireman, Save My Child; The City Slicker; Sic 'Em Towser; Somewhere in Turkey; Are Crooks Dishonest?; An Ozark Romance; Kicking the Germ out of Germany; That's Him; Bride and Gloom; Two Scrambled; Bees in His Bonnet; Swing Your Partners; Why Pick on Me?; Nothing But Trouble; Hear 'Em Rave; Take a Chance; She Loves Me Not. **'19** Wanted – $5000; Going! Going! Gone!; Ask Father; On the Fire/The Chef (GB: The Chef); I'm on My Way; Look Out Below!; The Dutiful Dub; Next Aisle Over; A Sammy in Siberia; Just Dropped In; Crack Your Heels; Ring Up the Curtain; Young Mr Jazz; Si, Senor; Before Breakfast; The Marathon; Back to the Woods; Pistols for Breakfast; Swat the Crook; Off the Trolley; Spring Fever; Billy Blazes, Esq; Just Neighbours; At the Old Stage Door; Never Touched Me; A Jazzed Honeymoon; Count Your Change; Chop Suey and Co; Heap Big Chief; Don't Shove; Be My Wife; The Rajah; He Leads, Others Follow; Soft Money; Count the Votes; Pay Your Dues; His Only Father; Bumping Into Broadway; Captain Kidd's Kids; From Hand to Mouth. **'20** His Royal Slyness; Haunted Spooks; An Eastern Westerner; High and Dizzy; Get Out and Get Under; Number Please. **'21** Now or Never; Among Those Present; I Do; Never Weaken. *All remaining films features unless otherwise specified*: A Sailor-Made Man. **'22** Grandma's Boy (+co-sc); Doctor Jack. **'23** Safety Last; Why Worry?; Dogs of War (short) (guest). **'24** Girl Shy; Hot Water. **'25** The Freshman (GB: College Days). **'26** For Heaven's Sake. **'27** The Kid Brother (orig. title: The Mountain Boy). **'28** Speedy. **'29** Welcome Danger (sound and silent versions). **'30** Feet First. **'32** Movie Crazy (+prod). **'34** The Cat's Paw. **'36** The Milky Way. **'38** Professor Beware (+prod). **'46** Mad Wednesday (orig. title: The Sin of Harold Diddlebock). **'62** Harold Lloyd's World of Comedy (compilation) (+prod; +ed). **'63** The Funny Side of Life/Harold Lloyd's Funny Side of Life (compilation) (+prod; +ed).

No reliable listings exist for Lloyd's bit parts in Universal and Edison films 1913–14.

1

When asked why he thought *The General* appeared to be so much more authentic as a picture of the American Civil War than *Gone With the Wind* (1939), Buster Keaton replied unassumingly, 'Well, they went to a novel for their story. We went to history'. The film is based on William Pittenger's *The Great Locomotive Chase*, recalling the author's part in a curious episode when a party of Unionists led by Captain Anderson seized a Confederate train. The chase was enough to recommend it to Keaton as a comedy subject. The principal change he made to the story was to tell the incident from the Southern point of view rather than from that of the raiders: 'You can always make villains out of the Northerners, but you cannot make a villain out of the South.' Another advantage of the change of sides was that it enabled Keaton's heroes to end up on top – the original historical episode ended somewhat grimly with the apprehension of the hijackers and the subsequent execution of several of their number.

The dramatic action and comic inventions are perfectly integrated: the story never seems to be merely an excuse for comic business, nor do the gags seem like ornaments planted on the narrative.

'I took that page of history and I stuck to it in all detail . . . And I staged the chase exactly the way it happened'.

Every shot looks as authentic as a Civil War photograph by Matthew Brady. However, Keaton had to abandon his original plan to shoot in the exact locations that Pittenger and his companions had traversed 65 years before, since he needed a region where there was still narrow-gauge track on which to run the two ancient locomotives that were renovated for the film. *The General* was eventually shot in the breathtaking mountain and pine-forest scenery of Oregon: Keaton's insistence that his engines should be fuelled with wood resulted in a forest fire during shooting. This preoccupation with authenticity was also extended to the scenes of the railway marshalling yards, to the battle sequences (Keaton seems to have borrowed the entire Oregon State Guard) and to the astonishing scene of a collapsing bridge that sends a locomotive hurtling to the bottom of a deep ravine – where it is reputed to lie to this day.

'The moment you give me a locomotive and things like that to play with, as a rule I find some way of getting laughs out of it.'

The General is an anthology of the greatest railway gags, and its inventions are still pillaged by other comedians. A whole series of gags is developed from Johnnie's problems when he runs out of boiler fuel: when all seems lost he passes under a bridge occupied by the enemy; as they pelt him with logs he gratefully retrieves them to stoke his engine.

Perhaps the film's most memorable image is the fade-out of the opening sequence. Rejected by Annabelle, a dejected Johnnie sits on the driving bar of his locomotive, which begins to move, carrying him off into the roundhouse where his immobile body traces a series of complex arcs. The effect was not obtained without considerable risk. Keaton recalls the train driver's advice:

' "A fraction too much steam with these old-fashioned engines and the wheel spins. And if it spins it will kill you right then and there". We tried it out four or five times and in the end the engineer was satisfied that he could handle it. So we went ahead and did it. I wanted a fade-out laugh for that sequence; although it's not a big gag it's cute and funny enough to get me a nice laugh.'

Finally, however, *The General* is memorable less for its gags than for the lone, brave, beautiful foolish little figure in single-minded pursuit of the two things he loves most in the world and which have been stolen from him. His love for 'The General' is passionate and touching: when he is carried off on the driving-bar he becomes part of his own machine. His feeling for Annabelle Lee is as intense. This most charming of Keaton heroines is played by Marion Mack, who sportingly accepts her rough handling – at one point she is bundled into a sack and flung around with the freight. Keaton recalled that she had enjoyed working on the film, and in retrospect the lady confirmed this. In those days, Keaton remembered:

'They kept their leading ladies looking beautiful at all times. We said to thunder with that, we'll dirty ours up a bit and let them have some rough treatment.'

Keaton's heroine charmingly parodies the characteristically feminine and dependent heroine of the period. Helping Johnnie to stoke when the fuel situation is desperate, she rejects a log with a knot in it and throws it overboard; then she hands up a tiny pencil-like chip which seems to her more acceptable. In the heat of the chase she decides to tidy and sweep out the cab. The exasperated Johnnie grabs her, shakes her violently – and then suddenly plants a small, quick kiss on her cheek. It is a rare, rich moment which reveals Keaton's singular ability for combining unsentimental tenderness and illuminating character comedy.

DAVID ROBINSON

Directed by Buster Keaton, Clyde Bruckman, 1926

Prod co: Buster Keaton Productions, Inc. **sc:** Keaton, Bruckman, from *The Great Locomotive Chase* by William Pittenger. **photo:** J. Devereaux Jennings, Bert Haines, Elmer Ellsworth. **ed:** J. Sherman Kell, Harry Barnes. **tech dir:** Frank Barnes. **prod man:** Fred Gabourie. **cost:** J.K. Pitcairn, Fred C. Ryle. **sp eff:** Jack Little. **length:** 7500 ft (approx. 90 minutes).

Cast: Buster Keaton (*Johnnie Gray*), Jackie Lowe, Jackie Hamlon (*boys who follow Johnnie*), Marion Mack (*Annabelle Lee*), Charles Smith (*Annabelle's father*), Frank Barnes (*Annabelle's brother*), Frank Agney (*recruiter*), Frederick Vroom (*Confederate General*), Glen Cavender (*Captain Anderson*), Ross McCutcheon, Charles Phillips, Jack Dempster, Red Thompson, Anthony Harvey, Ray Hanford, Tom Moran, Bud Fine, Jimmie Bryant, Al Hanson (*raiders*), Jim Farley (*Union General Thatcher*), Joe Keaton, Mike Donlin, Tom Nawn (*Union officers*).

2

3

4

5

6

7

8

Johnnie Gray is engineer of the Western and Atlantic Flyer Company's locomotive 'The General' (1). When the American Civil War breaks out he immediately tries to enlist for the Confederate South (2), but is refused because he is more useful to the cause as an engineer. Unaware of this, his girlfriend Annabelle shuns him as a coward (3).

A year later Annabelle, still estranged from Johnnie, is travelling as a passenger on the train when it is hijacked by Union spies. Johnnie sets off in pursuit of both his stolen loves in the 'Texas' and unwittingly crosses enemy lines (4). Entering the house where Annabelle is being held captive, he overhears enemy plans to launch a surprise attack the following morning (5). Having rescued the girl, he repossesses 'The General' and sets off towards the Southern lines (6), pursued by the Union army. His information enables the South to prepare an ambush, and Johnnie takes his place in the Confederate front lines after luring the 'Texas' – now held by the Union – to its doom across a burning bridge (7). When he finds himself the sole survivor of the guncrew, he takes over the cannon. Although the first ball misses the enemy, it comes down on a dam – unleashing a terrible flood that washes away the remaining Union forces.

Johnnie comes marching home, takes prisoner a Union General who has been hiding in the cab of the locomotive, and is rewarded with a commission. As an unending parade of soldiers pass by, Johnnie sits on the side of his engine with the now worshipping Annabelle on one arm, the other fixed in salute (8).

Buster Keaton

The Great Stone Face

Keaton was the comic who greeted the hostile world without a flicker of emotion, and overcame its physical hazards with a series of breathtaking but coolly calculated stunts. His refusal – or inability – to register either elation or despair must have stemmed from a belief that triumph and tragedy inevitably follow each other, and that neither is worth getting excited about

He came to the Venice Film Festival in September 1965 when they presented Samuel Beckett's *Film*, directed by Alan Schneider and starring Buster Keaton. He came down the aisle as the audience applauded him after the morning press show, a tiny solemn figure in a precarious state of preservation, with the urbane Los Angeles theatre-owner Raymond Rohauer like a puppet-master at his elbow. On the big screen his face, only revealed at the end of Beckett's work, bore the imprint of a terrible despair; in the flesh, too, there was nothing reassuring about his frailty. What did he think of the film which, seemingly at odds with his life's work, was in no way a comedy? 'What I think it means is that a man can keep away from everybody, but he can't get away from himself.' Within five months, at the age of 70, Buster died.

As some consolation, it could be said that Keaton had been able to witness at least a part of the restoration of his true status in screen history, a process which has continued steadily since the Sixties thanks to Rohauer's tireless cataloguing of copyrights, resurrection of prints, and licensing of commercial reissues. Not that *The Navigator* (1924) and *The General* (1926) were unknown in Europe (the British Film Institute had maintained them in its library and programmed them at the National Film Theatre for years), but the full perspective of Keaton's creative genius had been impossible to assess. It wasn't until a decade after his death that, for instance, *The Cameraman* (1928), narrowly rescued by MGM from negative decay, reappeared in Britain, and *Spite Marriage* (1929) was revived at the London Film Festival. Where Charles Chaplin has never been forgotten and Harold Lloyd has somehow never needed protection, Keaton had become thought of by the mid-Thirties as a mere pie-throwing extra from the Mack Sennett days. While he was seldom out of work, and apparently accepted his anonymity without rancour, his downfall followed the classic path (also trodden by Georges Méliès and D.W. Griffith among others) in being both ill-deserved and unavoidable.

Born in a trunk

Joseph Francis Keaton was born on October 4, 1895, the year in which cinema, too, was just beginning. His parents were members of the Mohawk Indian Medicine Company, a travelling vaudeville show, along with Harry Houdini, escapologist extraordinary, and were in Kansas when the baby arrived. Joe H. Keaton was Irish (although maybe with some Indian blood) and a former Wild West adventurer and journalist, whose stories lost nothing in the telling. With his tiny wife Myra, the pipe-smoking, card-playing, musical daughter of a travelling showman, he presented a knockabout acrobatic comedy act into which their son was absorbed shortly after the baby crawled on stage one night to the delight of the audience.

Called 'Buster', according to the legend he repeated throughout his life, for having been picked up unhurt after falling down a flight of stairs at six months (the experience was referred to by Houdini as a 'buster', the stage slang for pratfall), the boy proved to be the making of 'The Three Keatons': he upstaged his parents by the simple process of being thrown about, walked on, and used as a punchbag. Dressed in the same grotesque wig and sideburns as his father, wearing the same dress suit, white waistcoat and spats, he was subjected to such violence that the Keatons were often challenged by legal authorities to prove that 'The Human Mop' was in fact undamaged by his treatment. A typical gag involved his being hit in the face with a broom, his response being several seconds of complete lack of expression before he said 'Ouch!'. From such ordeals

Buster learned comic timing, physical endurance, and above all the discipline of 'freezing' all emotional reaction.

As early as 1912, 'The Three Keatons' were invited to appear on film, but Joe Keaton would have nothing to do with the nickelodeons which, in his eyes, were devaluing and destroying true theatrical entertainment. But Buster had seen hundreds of films by the time he was 21, and when the end came of the Keaton family show (the result partly of his father's hostility and drunkenness, partly of the fact that, small as he was, Buster was simply too big to be conveniently hurled around), it was an easy step for him to move into two-reelers. After a chance encounter with Fatty Arbuckle in New York, he turned down a Winter Garden Theatre engagement of $250 a week in order to appear in movies at $40 a week, beginning with *The Butcher Boy* early in April 1917. This was also the first film of Arbuckle's new Comicque Film Corporation.

Above left: teeing off in the earliest of The Three Ages *(1923) – the others were Ancient Rome and modern America. Top, from left to right: the end of the road in* The Garage *– Keaton's last film with Fatty Arbuckle; a cinema projectionist dreams of love in* Sherlock, Jr, *with Kathryn McGuire; umbrella trouble in* Steamboat Bill, Jr. *Above: Keaton's* Neighbors *(1920) were the girl he loves (Virginia Fox) and her father (Joe Roberts). Below: Friendless waits for Brown Eyes to yield milk in* Go West *(1925)*

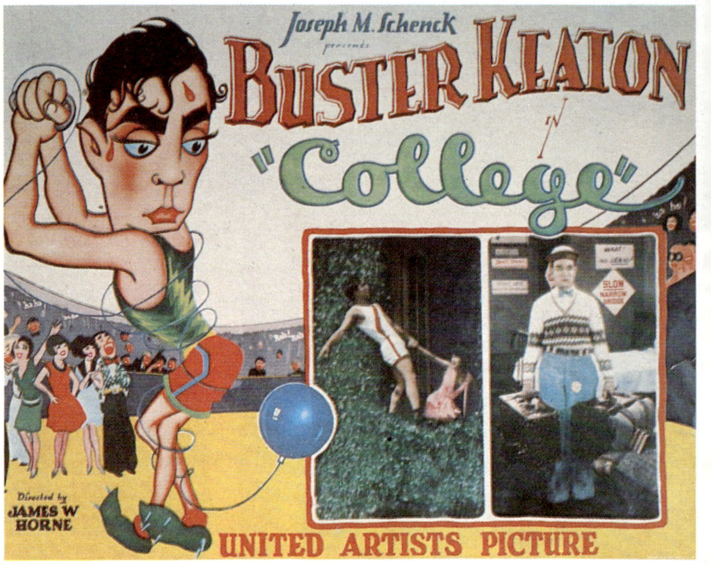

Above: a sailor takes up position in The Love Nest *(1923). Top right: a cyclone blows the front of a house on top of* Steamboat Bill, Jr *– fortunately a window is open; in performing the stunt, Keaton only allowed himself two inches to spare on either side. Above right: in* College *(1927) Keaton is a bookworm who tries to succeed at athletics to win a girl*

supervised by Joseph M. Schenck, and with the support and encouragement of both men Buster was immediately spellbound by both the technical and the creative side of film-making.

'One of the first things I did was tear a motion picture camera practically to pieces and found out the lenses and the splicing of film and how to get it on the projector – this fascinated me.'

After another five films – *A Reckless Romeo, The Rough House, His Wedding Night, Oh, Doctor!* and *Fatty at Coney Island* (all 1917) – the whole team moved to California. It took with it Keaton's family and one of the Talmadge sisters, Natalie. Very much in the shadow of her more famous sisters Norma and Constance, Natalie worked in a secretarial position at the studios where the Keatons met her. She became a special favourite of Myra's.

Accidents will happen

It was a foregone conclusion that Buster and Natalie would marry, not that there weren't many other girls in his life. As part of the Hollywood community, among a dazzling circle of friends including Chaplin, Douglas Fairbanks, W.S. Hart and Rudolph Valentino, the private and habitually non-committal Buster found himself to be, like Arbuckle, very public property, his existence stage-managed for the benefit of the press. His marriage in 1921 gives the impression (as indeed do his two subsequent marriages, to Mae Scribbens in 1933 and to Eleanor Norris in 1940) of having occurred without his full comprehension, like the innumerable natural disasters in his films. With Natalie came the rest of the Talmadge family, who enlisted Louise Keaton (Buster's sister) as a stand-in for Norma, shared the Keaton residence (a huge Italian Villa was built for them all at Beverly Hills in 1925), and determined after the birth of their two sons that Natalie should have no more children. The divorce was not until 1932, a final blow when Keaton's fortunes were already in battered shape, but the marriage had finished years earlier. The Talmadges don't even rate a mention in Keaton's 1960 'autobiography', *My Wonderful World of Slapstick*.

Buster made six two-reelers with Arbuckle in California – *A Country Hero* (1917), in which Joe Keaton also appeared, *Out West, The Bell Boy, Moonshine, Good Night, Nurse!* and *The Cook* (all 1918). He was then drafted in mid-1918 and spent seven months entertaining the troops in France. During this time he caught an ear infection that rendered him partially deaf for the rest of his life. When he returned in 1919, it was to find Arbuckle preparing to move into feature production, though they completed three more two-reelers together – *Back Stage, The Hayseed* (both 1919), and *The Garage* (1920). Joseph Schenck then offered Buster his own company on a handshake deal, and what was to be the golden era of Keaton comedy was under way, sadly and ironically aided by the collapse of Arbuckle's separate career following the scandal of 1921. From 1920 to 1923 Keaton made one feature (*The Saphead*, 1920) and 19 shorts, followed by 10 further features in the five years to 1928 when he changed producer.

If it was thanks to his brother-in-law (Schenck was married to Norma Talmadge) that Buster had no shares in his own company and finally made 'the biggest mistake of my life' by moving to MGM, it was also under Schenck's protection that he enjoyed in the last glorious years of silent cinema a seemingly limitless freedom to make whatever he liked, with no budgetary strings and no front-office interference. He was in peak condition as an athlete, he was inexhaustible on less than five hours sleep a night, he could drink copiously without side-effects, and if he needed a steam-engine or an ocean liner, they bought him one. But after this period never again would he have total control of his creativity, and never again would his films reflect the sheer uncluttered exuberance of his comic timing and his magical visual sense.

The hallmark of a Keaton comedy is the energy of its central character, all the animation that others display on their faces being expressed by Buster in a headlong ballet of acrobatics which he performed himself, in long-shot and without cuts. There is no trickery about the log-bouncing scene in *The General*, or Buster's high dive from the top of the ship in *The Navigator*, or the vaulting ease with which he skims down the riverboat decks in

bove: during a rail chase in The General, *ohnny sees a log blocking the line ahead. He truggles to the front of his engine with another og and at the vital moment throws it on to the bstacle, bouncing it clear . . .*

teamboat Bill, Jr (1928) and all the way up gain a moment later. In *Spite Marriage*, a ingle shot follows his desperate battle with the illain from one end of the luxury yacht to the ther where, flung into the ocean, he is carried y the current back to the lifeboat trailing at he stern and hauls himself up over the side to esume the struggle. During his career, as he ften reported in later years, he broke every one in his body. In *The Paleface* (1921) he ropped 85 feet from a suspension bridge into a et, he was nearly drowned under a waterfall n *Our Hospitality* (1923), and during the train equence in *Sherlock, Jr* (1924) he actually roke his neck yet continued stunting and filming despite months of blinding headaches.

Where there's a will . . .

Nevertheless, it's not as a stuntman but as a unique tragi-comic personality that he survives as the most fascinating of the silent comedians. As if pursuing a redefinition of his private experience, his films illustrate the purgatorial struggles of an inconsequential reject, habitually bullied by a scornful father or disdainfully ignored by an unappreciative girl, who by sheer persistence and ingenuous courage (physical danger never seems to occur to him as a possibility) battles his way to social acceptability. In his tenacious war against the forces of evil, his endurance in restoring the rightness of things, and his enigmatic face that gives nothing away – no promises, no denials – he is one of the screen's great martyrs. Yet at the same time, he has an uncanny gift for adapting technology to provide unexpected comforts; he uses a swordfish for protection, a boiler for a bedroom and a lobster-pot for an egg-holder in *The Navigator*, lazy tongs for a traffic indicator and a telephone for controlling a horse in *Cops* (1922), and can whip up a brisk asbestos suit in order to survive burning at the stake in *The Paleface*. As if in reward for his ingenuity, and for his obvious innocence, Providence is on his side, carrying him placidly off in an airborn canoe at the end of *The Balloonatic* (1923), or dropping the two-ton façade of a building over his body – he stands exactly where an empty window-frame drops over him – in that hair-raising shot from *Steamboat Bill, Jr* (even the cameraman, legend has it, couldn't bear to watch) leaving him dusty but unscathed.

At his best, Keaton's films found their least enthusiastic audience. While *The General* looks like a masterpiece today, it was a disaster when first released. Yet his MGM comedies of the early Thirties, *The Passionate Plumber, Speak Easily* (both 1932) and *What! No Beer?* (1933), uneasily teaming him with Jimmy Durante, and contemptuously regarded by Keaton himself, were huge moneyspinners. He took refuge from them, and from a movie business becoming increasingly incomprehensible, in prolonged periods of alcoholism, and waited through 17 lacklustre years of mediocrity, bit-parts, and gag-writing for other, lesser comedians, until, with *Sunset Boulevard* (1950) and *Limelight* (1952), the world began to notice him again. Then television provided a new home, and the final decade of his life afforded him a comfortable income from chat-shows, television commercials, and personal appearances at which, with a growing awareness, his audiences showed a genuine interest in the films that at first release had been taken so casually for granted. If the magnificent photography was now somewhat dimmed by chemical changes, Buster's own technical virtuosity still took the breath away. And as a symbol of the average man, struggling to find his place in a hostile society but unable to 'get away from himself', the great stone face speaks today with ever-increasing clarity. PHILIP STRICK

Filmography
As actor only in shorts: **1917** The Butcher Boy; A Reckless Romeo; The Rough House; His Wedding Night; Oh, Doctor!; Fatty at Coney Island/Coney Island (GB: Coney Island); A Country Hero. **'18** Out West; The Bell Boy; Moonshine; Good Night, Nurse!; The Cook. **'19** Back Stage; The Hayseed. **'20** The Garage. *As co-director, co-scriptwriter and actor in shorts unless otherwise specified:* One Week; Convict 13; The Scarecrow; Neighbors; The Round Up (actor only, uncredited); The Saphead (feature) (actor only). **'21** The Haunted House; Hard Luck; The High Sign; The Goat; The Playhouse; The Boat; The Paleface. **'22** Cops; My Wife's Relations; The Blacksmith; Screen Snapshots, No. 3 (guest); The Frozen North; Day Dreams; The Electric House. **'23** The Balloonatic; The Love Nest. *Features:* The Three Ages (co-dir; +act); Our Hospitality (co-dir; +act). **'24** Sherlock, Jr (co-dir; +act) (GB: Sherlock Junior); The Navigator (co-dir; +act). **'25** Seven Chances (dir; +act); Go West (dir; +act). **'26** Battling Butler (dir; +act); The General (co-dir; +co-sc; +act). *As actor only unless otherwise specified:* **'27** College. **'28** Steamboat Bill, Jr; The Cameraman (prod; +act). **'29** Spite Marriage; The Hollywood Revue of 1929 (guest) (GB: Hollywood Revue) (+guest in German version: Wir Schalten um auf Hollywood). **'30** Free and Easy/Easy Go (+Spanish version: Estrellados); Doughboys (prod; +act) (GB: Forward March) (+actor only in German version: De Fronte, Marchen; and in Spanish version, title unknown). **'31** Parlor, Bedroom and Bath (prod; +act) (+actor only in French version: Buster se Marie; and in German version: Casanova Wider Willen); Sidewalks of New York (prod; +act); The Stolen Jools/ The Lost Jools/The Slippery Pearls (guest). **'32** The Passionate Plumber (prod; +act) (+actor only in French version: Le Plombier Amoreux); Speak Easily (prod; +act). **'33** What! No Beer? (feature) (actor only). *Shorts as actor only unless otherwise specified:* **'34** The Gold Ghost; Allez Oop; Le Roi des Champs Elysées (feature) (FR). **'35** The Invader/The Intruder/An Old Spanish Custom (feature) (GB); Palooka From Paducah; One Run Elmer; Hayseed Romance; Tars and Stripes; The E-Flat Man; The Timid Young Man. **'36** Three on a Limb; Grand Slam Opera (+co-sc); La Fiesta de Santa Barbara (guest); Blue Blazes; The Chemist; Mixed Magic. **'37** Jail Bait; Ditto; Love Nest on Wheels. **'38** Life in Sometown, USA (dir. only); Hollywood Handicap (dir. only); Streamlined Swing (dir. only). **'39** Pest From the West; Mooching Through Georgia; Hollywood Cavalcade (feature). **'40** Nothing But Pleasure; Pardon My Berth Marks; The Taming of the Snood; The Spook Speaks; The Villain Still Pursued Her (feature); Li'l Abner (feature); His Ex Marks the Spot. **'41** So You Won't Squawk; She's Oil Mine; General Nuisance. *Features as actor only unless otherwise specified:* **'43** Forever and a Day. **'44** San Diego, I Love You. **'45** That's the Spirit; That Night With You. **'46** God's Country; El Moderno Barba Azul (MEX). **'49** The Loveable Cheat; In the Good Old Summertime; You're My Everything. **'50** Un Duel à Mort (+co-sc) (FR); Sunset Boulevard. **'52** Limelight; Ça c'Est du Cinema (compilation) (FR); L'Incantevole Nemica/Pattes de Velours (IT-FR); Paradise for Buster (short made for private showings only). **'56** Around the World in 80 Days. **'57** The Buster Keaton Story (tech. consultant only). **'60** The Adventures of Huckleberry Finn. **'62** Ten Girls Ago (unreleased) (CAN). **'63** Thirty Years of Fun (compilation); Its a Mad, Mad, Mad, Mad World; The Sound of Laughter (compilation). **'64** Pajama Party. **'65** Beach Blanket Bingo; Film/Project One; How to Stuff a Wild Bikini (GB: How to Fill a Wild Bikini); Sergeant Deadhead; The Big Chase (unreleased); The Rail Rodder/L'Homme du Rail (short) (CAN); Buster Keaton Rides Again/Buster Keaton (doc) (as himself). **'66** The Scribe (short) (CAN); A Funny Thing Happened On the Way to the Forum. **'67** Due Marine e un Generale (IT) (USA: War Italian Style).
Keaton was uncredited as gag-writer on: 1938 Too Hot to Handle (*+co-sc*). *'40* Comrade X. *'44* Bathing Beauty. *'48* A Southern Yankee (GB: My Hero). *'49* Neptune's Daughter.

The tears of a clown...

Harry Langdon and Larry Semon were among the most adored of the silent comics, with their ridiculous antics often tinged with pathos. And yet by trying to gain independence their careers failed and they faded rapidly into insignificance

'Comedy is the satire of tragedy', readers of *Theatre Magazine* were told in 1927. 'Most deliciously comic moments on the outside are full of sad significance for those who realize the sinister characterization of the situation.' The writer was no would-be critic but Harry Langdon, the flustered, baby-faced clown of *The Strong Man* (1926) and *Long Pants* (1927), who had only just been catapulted to fame and fortune.

Yet only a few months after the publication of Langdon's article – 'The Serious Side of Comedy Making' – the tragedy and sad significance were all in his own life. The starring vehicles he personally directed won neither popular nor critical approval; there were money problems, talkie problems. His career dwindled to odds and ends, with him appearing in impoverished shorts and scriptwriting for Laurel and Hardy. When he died in 1944 he was working as a supporting player for Monogram and Republic.

Pride before a fall

Langdon's rise and fall were spectacularly meteoric, but others followed the same pattern. There was also Larry Semon, a pasty-faced, bowler-hatted loon, described by *Picturegoer* in 1925 as 'One of the three best-loved comedians in filmland', when he had just bridged the gap between shorts and features. He joined the band of popular clowns with continental nicknames: in France he was Zigoti; in Italy, Ridolini. But like Langdon, success made him attempt too much. By 1928 he was bankrupt and looking for work in vaudeville; he died the same year aged 39 after a nervous breakdown and pneumonia.

Of the two, Langdon had the greater talent. Born in 1884 to Salvation Army workers, he moved into vaudeville in the hope of escaping poverty. By 1903 he had developed a sketch called 'Johnny's New Car', in which Johnny battled with his shrewish wife and an equally domineering car that finally exploded. The sketch, with variations, kept Langdon in business for 20 years; then he joined the director Mack Sennett and worked in two-reelers.

As in vaudeville, he frequently appeared henpecked and put-upon, but Langdon's screen persona gradually developed new, strange traits. He became a creature of awesome innocence – the world's oldest baby, fumbling about in an adult world full of sophisticated women, gangsters and curious

Above: Harry Langdon in drag for one of a series of shorts he made for Hal Roach. Right: lost but laughable – Langdon looking lonesome, and Semon standing not at all at ease in Spuds. *Top, far right: Langdon hits out in another Roach comedy. Below, far right: Harry Logan (Langdon) puts up a poster of his loved one Betty Burton (Joan Crawford), whilst Nick Kargas (Tom Murray) sleeps on below in* Tramp, Tramp, Tramp

objects. Faced with the incomprehensible, Langdon performed delicate ballets of curiosity and indecision, like a child at the seaside nervously testing the water. *Long Pants* contains some classic examples of Langdon's skills at pantomime. Urgently needing a policeman, he tries to catch the attention of a dummy – conveniently propped on a seat nearby – by staging imaginary crimes, throwing a fit and staring with exquisite incredulity. There is also Langdon's courtship, on a bicycle, of the film's *femme fatale*, during which he circles her car, balancing on the handlebars, to ludicrous but touching effect.

Four smart chaps

Sennett placed Langdon in the hands of a talented trio of gag writers and burgeoning directors in Harry Edwards, Arthur Ripley and Frank Capra. When Langdon moved into independent feature production in 1926 he wisely took them with him. Whatever the extent to which Capra and his companions moulded Langdon, the characterizations and

larry
Langdon

social attitudes in Langdon's films certainly paved the way for Capra's own development, and he went on to make Oscar-winning films like *Mr Deeds Goes to Town* (1936). The team worked on several successful movies together: *Tramp, Tramp, Tramp* (1926), Langdon's first feature, shows a big shoe company stamping on the smaller ones. In *The Strong Man*, Langdon defeats the corrupt forces threatening a small town. In *Long Pants*, big-city vice is deliberately set against small-town virtue.

Langdon subsequently tried to survive without his collaborators. *Three's a Crowd* (1927) moved into Chaplin territory, with jokes built over a sentimental melodrama. In *The Chaser* (1928) Langdon mixed some customary clowning involving the problems of getting an egg from a chicken with acid observations on marriage and the sexes. The spy comedy of *Heart Trouble* (1928) represented a further change in subject-matter. None of these films has been widely reappraised, but parts of *The Chaser*, at least, suggest that Langdon might have been able to use his peculiar talents successfully if sound and hard times had not overtaken him.

Fall guy

By the time films talked Larry Semon was dead and it would be difficult to imagine his madcap visual comedy surviving far into the Thirties. Semon adopted the screen character of a dumb-bell, forever in a whirlwind of accidents and chaos – but he functioned primarily as a machine-like component of stunts, falls and chases. Magical tricks were part of Semon's home background as his father was Zera the Great, a stage musician and acrobat. Semon worked first as a cartoonist for the New York *Sun* and began acting in and directing films at

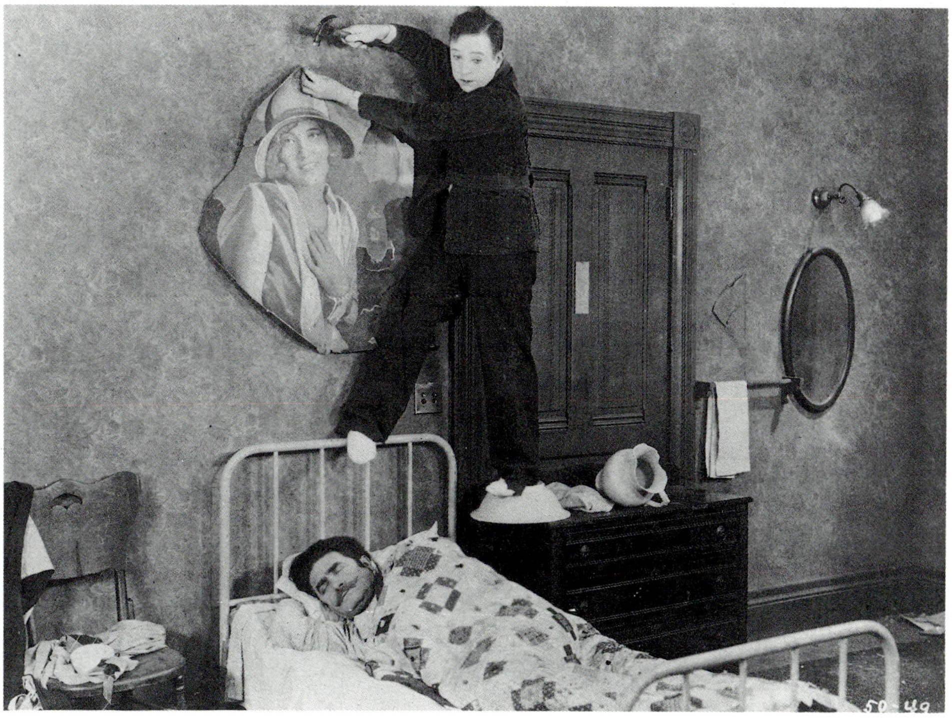

the Vitagraph studios.

By the mid-Twenties, hectic two-reelers like *The Sportsman* (1920) and *The Sawmill* (1922) had made Semon one of the biggest stars in his field, but he was unable to master the feature format, for which his talents were never properly suited. Disagreements with Vitagraph forced him into independent production. He was obsessed with filming Frank L. Baum's fantasy *The Wizard of Oz* and finally managed to do so in 1925 with a script co-written by Baum's son. But the plot, as usual with Semon, was smothered with gags, including falls from trees, dives into mudbaths, funny business with bees, ducks and lollipops. Semon directed and played the Straw Man and Oliver Hardy, who was a frequent partner, appeared as the Tin Man.

The *Wizard of Oz* was one of his many obsessions. Semon always worked with zeal and became increasingly worried over his reputation, which sagged after dishevelled features like *The Perfect Clown* (1925) and *Spuds* (1927). His short films do display an antic charm, but Semon doomed himself to a comparatively minor place in cinema history when he claimed that 'a comedy is only as funny as its gags. The comic is of secondary importance.' GEOFF BROWN

Above left: Larry Semon looking to clean up with Lucille Carlisle in an unidentified comedy made in the early Twenties. Above right: Carlisle, Oliver Hardy and Semon in The Perfect Clown *– sadly this unsuccessful feature did not live up to its title. Right: Semon as a farm hand in the film he had always longed to make –* The Wizard of Oz

Larry Semon: filmography

All films shorts unless otherwise specified. As director and co-scriptwriter: **1916** The Man From Egypt; Losing Weight; A Jealous Guy; The Battler; Romance and Rough House; There and Back; A Villainous Villain; Loot and Love; Sand Scamps and Strategy; She Who Last Laughs; Tubby Turns the Tables; Rah! Rah! Rah!; More Money Than Manners; Jumps and Jealousy; His Conscious Conscience; Help! Help! Help!; Hash and Havoc; Bullies and Bullets. **'17** Footlights and Fakers; Dubs and Drygoods; Rips and Rushes; Cops and Cussedness; Boasts and Boldness; Hazards and Home Runs; Guff and Gunplay; Bombs and Blunders; He Never Touched Me; Jolts and Jewelry; Pests and Promises; Rips and Rushes; Big Bluffs and Bowling Balls; Shells and Shivers; Masks and Mishaps; Flatheads and Flivvers; Worries and Wobbles. *As director and actor:* Slips and Slackers; Plans and Pajamas; Chumps and Chances; Risks and Roughnecks; Gall and Golf; Plagues and Puppy Love. *As director, scriptwriter and actor unless otherwise specified:* Rough Toughs and Roof Tops. **'18** Guns and Greasers; Rooms and Rumours; Babes and Boobs; Stripes and Stumbles; Meddlers and Moonshiners; Whistles and Windows; Rummies and Razors; Romans and Rascals; Spies and Spills; Boodle and Bandits; Skids and Scalaways; Hindoos and Hazards; Bathing Beauties and Big Boobs; Dunces and Dangers; Huns and Hyphens; Mutts and Motors; Bears and Bad Men; Frauds and Frenzies; Pluck and Plotters; Humbugs and Husbands. **'19** Traps and Tangles; Scamps and Scandal; Well I'll Be; Passing the Buck; The Star Boarder; His Home Sweet Home; The Simple Life; Between the Acts; Dew Drop In; Dull Care; The Head Waiter. **'20** The Grocery Clerk; The Fly Cop (co-dir; + sc; + act); School Days; Solid Concrete; The Stage Hand; The Suitor; The Sportsman. **'21** The Hick; The Bakery; The Rent Collector; The Fall Guy; The Bell Hop. **'22** The Sawmill; The Show (co-dir; + sc; + act); A Pair of Kings; The Counter Jumper; Golf; The Agent. **'23** No Wedding Bells; The Barnyard; The Midnight Cabaret; The Gown Shop; Lightening Love; Horseshoes (co-dir; + sc; + act). **'24** Trouble Brewing (co-dir; + co-sc; + act); Kid Speed (co-dir; + co-sc; + act); Her Boy Friend; The Girl in the Limousine (feature) (dir; + act). **'25** The Dome Doctor; The Cloudhopper; The Wizard of Oz (feature) (co-dir; + co-sc; + act); Go Straight (as himself); The Perfect Clown (feature) (actor only). **'26** Stop, Look and Listen (feature) (dir; + co-sc; + act). **'27** Oh What a Man; The Stunt Man; Spuds (feature); Underworld (feature) (actor only). **'28** Dummies; A Simple Sap.

Harry Langdon: filmography

All films shorts unless otherwise specified: **1924** Picking Peaches; Smile Please; Shanghaied Lovers; Flickering Youth; The Cat's Meow; His New Mama; The First Hundred Years; The Luck of the Foolish; The Handsome Cabman; All Night Long; Feet of Mud. **'25** The Sea Squawk; Boobs in the Wood; His Marriage Wow; Plain Clothes; Remember When?; Horace Greeley, Jr; The White Wing's Bride; Lucky Stars; There He Goes. **'26** Saturday Afternoon; Tramp, Tramp, Tramp (feature); Ella Cinders (feature); The Strong Man (feature) (+ prod). **'27** Fiddlesticks; Soldier Man; Long Pants (feature); His First Flame (feature); Three's a Crowd (feature) (+ dir). **'28** The Chaser (feature) (+ dir); Heart Trouble (feature) (+ dir). **'29** Hotter Than Hot; Sky Boy. **'30** The Head Guy; The Fighting Parson; The Big Kick; Shirt Shy; The Shrimp; The King; A Soldier's Plaything/A Soldier's Pay (feature); See America Thirst (feature). **'32** The Big Flash. **'33** Tired Feet; The Hitch Hiker; Knight Duty; Tied for Life; Hooks and Jabs; Marriage Humour; The Stage Hand (+ sc); Leave It to Dad; On Ice; Pop's Pal; A Roaming Romeo; Hallelujah, I'm a Bum/New York/The Heart of New York/Happy Go Lucky/The Optimist (feature) (GB: Hallelujah, I'm a Tramp); My Weakness (feature). **'34** Trimmed in Furs; Circus Hoodoo; No Sleep on the Deep; Petting Preferred; Counsel on de Fence; Shivers. **'35** His Bridal Sweet; The Leather Necker; His Marriage Mixup; I Don't Remember; Atlantic Adventure. **'37** Wise Dogs (feature) (dir only) (GB). **'38** A Doggone Mixup; Sue My Lawyer; Mad About Money (feature) (GB) (orig. title: Stardust) (USA: He Loved an Actress); There Goes My Heart (feature); Block-Heads (feature) (co-sc. only). **'39** Zenobia (feature); The Flying Deuces/Sons of the Legion (feature) (co-sc. only). **'40** Cold Turkey; Goodness! A Ghost (feature) (+ sc); Misbehaving Husbands (feature); A Chump at Oxford (feature) (co-sc. only); Saps at Sea (feature) (co-sc. only). **'41** All-American Co-Ed (feature); Double Trouble (feature); Road Show (feature) (co-sc. only). **'42** What Makes Lizzy Dizzy?; Tireman, Spare My Tires; Carry Harry; Piano Mooner; House of Errors (feature). **'43** A Blitz on the Fritz; Blonde and Groom; Here Comes Mr Zerk; Spotlight Scandals (feature). **'44** To Heir Is Human; Defective Detectives; Mopey Dope; Hot Rhythm (feature); Block Busters (feature). **'45** Snooper Service; Pistol Packin' Nitwits; Swingin' on a Rainbow.

THEY HAD FACES THEN

The great silent stars of Hollywood enjoyed an international fame and mass worship that the world had never known before

In 1919, three men sat down in the Palace of Versailles: they were playing a board game in which the pieces were the bloodied parts of Europe that had been fought over in the remorseless stalemate of World War I. The French Premier Georges Clémenceau, the British Prime Minister David Lloyd George and the American President Woodrow Wilson could have been forgiven for thinking that they were the most powerful and therefore the most important and best-known people alive. They were the figureheads of the new nation states. But they were not in pictures, and their political eminence was being surpassed by the new volatile celebrity of movie stars.

A couple of years later, Charlie Chaplin completed *The Kid* (1921) and struck this deal with First National: they would distribute the film in return for a payment of $1.5 million to Chaplin; once they had recouped that investment, Chaplin received 50 per cent of the net profits; and after five years the picture reverted to him. Chaplin decided he would take a trip to England and the rest of Europe. He would go by sea, on the *Olympic*:

'It had been ten years since I had left England, and on this very boat with the Karno Company; then we had travelled second class. I remember the steward taking us on a hurried tour through the first class, to give us a glimpse of how the other half lived. He had talked of the luxury of the private suites and their prohibitive price, and now I was occupying one of them, and was on my way to England. I had known London as a struggling young nondescript from Lambeth; now as a man celebrated and rich I would be seeing London as though for the first time.'

In London, wherever he went, Charlie was mobbed. In the space of Chaplin's lifetime, theatrical stardom had gone from being hailed and followed on a few city streets to being known all over the world. Although he and the picture business could only see box-office in 1921, stardom had a political dimension. Stardom was not simply the use of attractive personalities to sell motion pictures. It was the promotion of a supposedly desirable concept of personality that would rapidly take on ideological connotations. In proving the impact of new media, it established a new relationship between power and the masses. Henceforth, leaders would have to compete with movie stars. Adolf Hitler, Benito Mussolini and Franklin D. Roosevelt were faces and voices that penetrated every household. By the late Thirties, Chaplin had come to believe it was his duty to join with the great dictators in speaking to the public. Over forty years later, a second-rate star, Ronald Reagan, was given a fresh chance at inspiring the audience in the role of President of the United States.

More than anyone alive, Chaplin epitomized the dynamic of universal recognition. In 1921 (and for several years before and after), no other human image could have been identified by so many in the world. Charlie was the movies; his name and his sentimental resilience were synonymous with the

jazzy but soft-hearted entertainment provided by the medium. Look and be transported; it had happened to Charlie himself, and the audiences knew that their own adoration had made the Tramp one of the richest men in the world.

Stardom may be the crucial communicative discovery of the movies. It also characterized the medium's grasp of story-telling. Ever since the days of Florence Lawrence, the 'Biograph Girl', film companies had appreciated how far audiences liked to see certain lovely and arousing personalities in film after film. A title could sell a picture, some indication of genre was helpful, but a picture of a star was most persuasive. So film companies began to assess possible stories as 'vehicles' for their stars. Whereas action had been the prevailing feature of very early films – a rush of business seen in long shot – stardom insisted on the close-up, and it brought the movies the reverie of introspection:

Rudolph Valentino (top) died on August 23, 1926. His New York lying-in-state and the funeral cortège a week later (centre) drew huge crowds. Pola Negri (above) was among the mourners and claimed they had planned to marry

Below: one Sunday in the summer of 1926, friends dropped in at Richard Barthelmess' place and others at Constance Talmadge's. They joined up at her Malibu beach house. From left to right on the fence are: Roscoe (Fatty) Arbuckle, Mae Murray, Ward Crane, Virginia Valli, Ronald Colman, Bessie Love, Jack Pickford, Rudolph Valentino and Pola Negri. Scattered through the middle row are: Louella O. Parsons (columnist), Carmel Myers, Alan Forrest, Bert Lytell, Claire Windsor, Richard Barthelmess, Constance Talmadge, Beatrice Lillie, Josephine Lovett, Julanne Johnston, Agnes Ayres, John S. Robertson and Marshall Neilan (director). The bottom row includes: Antonio Moreno, Prince David Mdivani, Charles Lane, Alf Goulding, Marcel de Sano, Manuel Reachi (Agnes Ayres' husband), Harry d'Abbadie d'Arrast (director), Natalie Talmadge Keaton, Captain Alastair MacIntosh (Constance Talmadge's husband), Mrs Antonio Moreno and Blanche Sweet. List from Motion Picture, *October 1926*

'What is Little Mary thinking?' Stars were those loved by the camera, and capable of inspiring love in the anonymous masses when intense images of their yearning faces were projected in the dark but public places built for movies. Stardom is the force that invites the viewer's imagination to come up onto the screen. Tycoons and producers reckoned it was enough to get people into the theatres, but the greatest films involve that extra, fantastic journey.

This is a kind of sleep-walking, an indulgence in fantasy that can seem morbid, escapist or mad. In other words, stardom has an irrational undertone at odds with those modern disciplines of hard work, civic duty and common sense. There is the beginning of a widespread, often unconscious, feeling of shame that goes with star worship, and which demands the occasional fall and humiliation of some of these demi-gods. The ostensible leaders of society did not enjoy the competition of these movie ghosts, and thus the establishment was always ready to condemn stars and the frivolity that believed in them.

Granted that latent antagonism, it is surely very important in the history of stardom that Chaplin, Douglas Fairbanks and Mary Pickford could demonstrate that stars might be radiant public servants and happy examples, like royalty given the extra good luck of casting. They were the three greatest stars of the time, and they went on tours of America to promote the sale of Liberty Bonds in support of the war effort. It is said that they sold $3 million-worth. Chaplin was excused for not going back to Britain to enlist, while Doug and Mary apparently fell in love in that open car that seemed to be forever flanked by cheering crowds who had the movies' faith in true love.

Of course, they were both married – Doug to Beth Sully, and Mary to the actor Owen Moore. They were both anxious about what the public would think of convenient divorces. Chaplin told them to live together, and get it out of their systems; but they had aspirations towards respectability and a deep longing to be both honest and popular, to be admired for themselves. It is the moment at which a star wants to be more than his or her screen roles. So they contrived their divorces, and in 1920 they married. The public rejoiced – this was like a movie romance come true. The nation's athletic hero and 'America's Sweetheart' made a dynasty of stereotypes, and a kind of royal household for the raw, insecure Hollywood community as they held court at Pickfair, the Beverly Hills property that Doug bought, developed and gave to Mary as a wedding present.

Once married, Doug and Mary went on a triumphal tour of Europe, to be greeted by immense crowds wanting to touch Mary and see Doug do some flamboyant jumps. They were a better couple than anyone knew – Doug a natural and inoffensive show-off, Mary a sweet face and a quick business brain. Before marrying, they had made a commercial pact, forming United Artists with Chaplin and D.W. Griffith. The festival of their honeymoon was not just a holiday. It was also a publicity gesture, all the more effective in that it was not cold-blooded – stars must always believe in their own story. The couple did weary of the lack of privacy. They went to Germany where they were less well known,

Above: Mary Astor was already a star in the Twenties, and this portrait of her by Ruth Harriet Louise shows why. Above right: Betty Blythe as The Queen of Sheba (1921), nearly topless in pre-Hays Office style. Far right: Doug and Mary as proud proprietors of their studios on Santa Monica Boulevard in February 1922. Right: a 1927 portrait by Marland Stone of Dolores Costello, newly a star

because of wartime banning of their films. But not being recognized hurt them more, and they quickly slipped back into the limelight – royal figures, but prisoners too.

Pickfair was a model for new success enjoying itself in the Twenties, a party for Hollywood celebrities, for writers, artists, sportsmen and the reject royalty of old Europe. But the Pickfair party was robust, good-natured and generally wholesome – Doug was romantic and Mary practical, but they were both conservatives at heart and already older than the fast set. Doug remained a star of the silent era, with *Robin Hood* (1922), *The Thief of Bagdad* (1924) and *The Black Pirate* (1927); but he was getting into his forties, a little stiffer than screen high-jinks ever suggested, and thoroughly rattled when the new career of his son, Douglas Fairbanks Jr, invaded his aura of swashbuckling sun-tan. Mary was ten years younger, but she made far fewer films after 1923 – in part because she felt trapped as an *ingénue*, and also because she spent more time worrying over United Artists. As for Chaplin, his work fell away to a trickle, as if celebrity added weight to his pondering.

The stardom of these three endured, but it had been won in the years 1914–20. A new generation of stars really marks the Twenties, typified by Rudolph Valentino and Gloria Swanson. Valentino had not much more than seven years in pictures. His stardom was defined by his premature, tragic death and by the feeling of fatality being allied to his erotic potency. He was sexy in a way that dated Doug and Mary. There was also an air of scandal and sleaziness to Valentino that matched the public's growing instinct that stars might be vulnerable, unhealthy and hiding guilty secrets.

Valentino only came to America in 1913. He worked as a gardener and a dancer, and he had quite a few small movie jobs before June Mathis, head of the script department at Metro, got him a lead part in *The Four Horsemen of the Apocalypse* (1921). Valentino would make another 13 films as a 'Latin lover', dark-eyed, soulful, brooding, exotic and with hints of masochism and violence adding to his romantic lustre. But here was a star whose public reputation exceeded the reality and perhaps daunted the man. Valentino lost one wife, allegedly

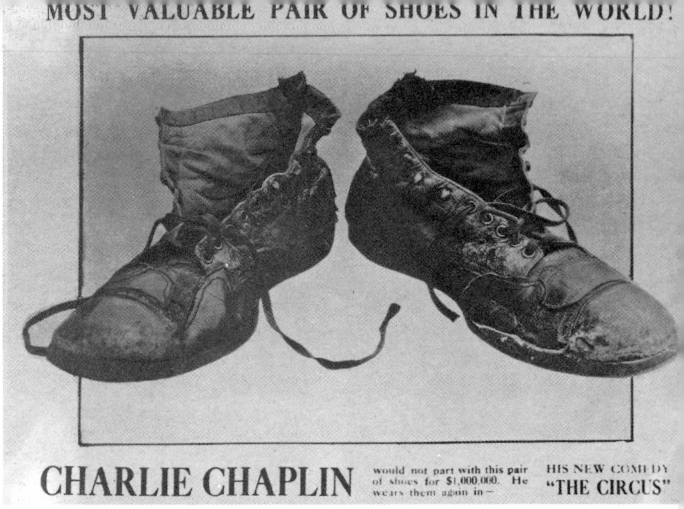

Above: Gloria Swanson with the MGM executive Irving Thalberg on St Valentine's Day, 1934. Her MGM contract was the kiss of death to her career – she made only one film (on loan to Fox). Her successful comeback was with Paramount in 1950. Top: based on the autobiography I, Mary MacLane, *this 1918 Essanay production starred and was written by Mary MacLane, who relived her experience of six lovers. Top right: despite having dined off a boot in* The Gold Rush *(1925), Chaplin had the pair intact for* The Circus *(1928)*

because he could not please her as fully as a laboratory-technician lover could. His second wife, Natacha Rambova, dominated him and sought to organize his career. They had separated before he died, in New York in 1926, aged 31, the victim of an ulcer and of press innuendo about gay inclinations.

More than a hundred thousand people came to the funeral parlour to see his humbled but fabled body. Pola Negri sent an arrangement of 4000 roses. Hollywood potentates such as Adolph Zukor and Joseph Schenck served as pallbearers. Huge crowds watched the cortège pass by. His last film, *The Son of the Sheik* (1926), had just opened, and its portrait of a romantic hero, filled with dark, morbid urges, became part of the Valentino legend that linked love and death, stardom and ruin.

Gloria Swanson had been a teenage bathing beauty for Mack Sennett, but it was only in 1918, under the guidance of Cecil B. DeMille, that she gained stardom. She was the new woman – sexy, shrewd, carefree and assertive – liberated from the Victorian codes that had previously dictated the hopes and fears of screen women. For Paramount, she made such films as *Male and Female* (1919), *Prodigal Daughters* (1923) and *Manhandled* (1924). Swanson was a fresh, home-grown heroine, much

Valentino and Swanson summed up modern sex-appeal in the Twenties

more vivacious and amusing than might be deduced from her comeback performance in *Sunset Boulevard* (1950).

Like several others, Swanson fought her studio and branched out on her own to star in and produce several films, including the ill-fated *Queen Kelly* (1928), in which she refused to be overawed by either her co-producer Joseph Kennedy or her director Erich von Stroheim. A few years after the coming of sound, she temporarily retired.

Sound would become the bluntest measure the studios had to control their stars; it was also a technical departure that made it far harder for independent stars to go it alone. The moguls had very mixed feelings about their properties: they needed them, and milked their fame, working them as hard as possible; but they envied their glory, their looks and their reckless living, especially if it required a studio cover-up.

The stars of the Twenties were not as free as Chaplin or Pickford. They were as vulnerable as all pretty people are to time and fickle taste – today, for instance, Lois Moran, Barbara La Marr and Carmel Myers are just vivid faces who each had her moment. Stars were owned by studios, and they were the test cases of the contract system. Some were well looked after: Irving Thalberg appreciated and promoted Lon Chaney, the only great star of ugliness; and for a time Joseph Schenck gave Buster Keaton his greatest creative liberty. Others were treated badly: Lillian Gish was dismissed as out-of-date, and Louise Brooks was regarded as out-of-line. There were also the scandals that made the first great wave of Hollywood paranoia in the early Twenties. Fatty Arbuckle could never fully extricate himself from a Labor Day weekend party and the body that was left in the aftermath. Mabel Normand and Mary Miles Minter were both damaged beyond repair by their involvement with the murdered director William Desmond Taylor. The death of the actor Wallace Reid accelerated legends that many stars lived on booze and drugs.

These scandals reflect two new professions, inseparable from stardom. There is the newspaper gossip writer always looking for revelations about the stars – the trade that would include Hedda Hopper, Louella Parsons, *Confidential* and the *National Enquirer*. To ward off these reporters, the studios and the stars hired publicity people, press agents and managers to concoct, write and spread a more favourable legend. Neither side was especially fond of the truth, and so it is that the history of stardom is recorded in biased, sensational and mercenary printed materials – hand-outs and exposés, alike in their hysterical tone.

The stars had faces, to be sure, but they also had an army of necessary supporters – still photographers, doctors, agents, accountants, lawyers, confessors, makeup men, hairdressers, costumiers and astrologers. The studio system played on their vulnerability, just as it flattered and indulged them. It wanted their films, but it flinched from salary demands that recognized how much the pictures grossed. So it was that the men who spent their working days glorifying stars might abuse them in private, dumping them when fortune shifted and exploiting them personally. Love and dislike, glory and envy – the star's life soon became an ordeal.

But Hollywood made all of America dream of going west for its big opportunity. The studios imported actors and actresses from Europe: some were abandoned, some stayed to change the notion of stardom – Pola Negri, Greta Garbo, Marlene Dietrich, Ronald Colman. When sound became standard, so Hollywood cleaned house. One generation of stars yielded to another, trained in the theatre, able to play dialogue. The era of the face and the image gave way to the power of total screen presence. John Gilbert was replaced by Clark Gable. And the public absorbed every small gesture in these new people: Gable's grin and his insolent redneck vitality became an ideal of uncomplicated American decency. The stars were advertisements for a way of life, front runners in the pursuit of happiness.

DAVID THOMSON

Speechless Hitchcock

ight at the end of his long and distinguished areer, Alfred Hitchcock could be charac-rized without argument as the last of the reat silent directors, because the basis of his yle was and always had been the sort of raphic visual story-telling that he had learnt ı the silent cinema. But then, the visual was ways his first consideration. When he suc-eded, at the age of 20, in getting himself ken on in 1919 by the newly set-up British vision of Famous Players-Lasky, it was first of ll as designer of the title-cards which were ıen important and profuse in silent pictures. nd when he began to participate more act-ely in the actual making of movies, it was imarily as art director and set designer, and nly incidentally as scriptwriter, assistant dir-tor and general odd-job man.

he first steps

he five films he made, in any or all of these apacities, with the director Graham Cutts etween 1922 and 1925 do not seem to ave survived. But in *The Pleasure Garden* 925), the first complete feature he directed all y himself, there are some remarkable indi-ations of his mature style and preoccupations, pecially in the vivid conjuring up of a seedy ackstage atmosphere in the early sequences. appears unlikely that he found much to terest him in the film's melodramatic story-ne, or in that of his next film, now lost, *The ountain Eagle* (1926).

But with *The Lodger* (1926) suddenly every-ing changed. It was the first chance itchcock had to pursue on screen his spare-me interest in murder, mayhem and the arker recesses of the human psyche. It was ased on a best-selling novel by Mrs Belloc owndes, suggested by the story of Jack the ipper, and starred Ivor Novello. Hitchcock boldly shaped the story in largely atmospheric terms, building up the feeling of panic in the streets while the killer is on the loose and the disturbed mental state of the unjustly-suspected hero, in a style more German than British or American. The film's producers shelved it as too difficult until they found that they needed some new product in a hurry – at which point they brought in Ivor Montagu, subseqently a frequent collaborator of Hitchcock's, to advise. Montagu told them to cut out a lot of titles, get Hitchcock to reshoot a couple of sequences which had been skimped to stay within budget, and release it. This they did, to universal acclaim, and Hitchcock became at one stroke the leading director in British cinema.

ight: production shot from The Mountain *agle, with Hitchcock and his future wife Alma eville. Below: Roddy (Ivor Novello, right) is lsely accused of theft*

By the time of his last film, *Family Plot* (1976), Alfred Hitchcock was the only director still active who had been making feature films in silent days. He never forgot the lessons he had learned from those early movies. In them can be found the clues to everything Hitchcock was to become at the height of his career

No thrillers

Though with hindsight it is possible to say that he had found his true bent with *The Lodger*, in which he even (more or less accidentally) made the first of those little screen appearances that were later to become his trade mark, he does not seem to have felt then (or really ever) that he should confine himself exclusively to the thriller genre. Indeed, none of his other silent films is even remotely a thriller. In *Downhill* (1927) he continued the happy working relationship with Ivor Novello in a story, told with amazing flair and visual invention, of a public-school boy who goes picturesquely to the dogs after being expelled over a misunderstanding. *Easy Virtue* (1927) was based on one of Noel Coward's recent stage successes. But it takes nearly half the film to get to the opening of Coward's play, all the rest being a charmingly light-hearted account of just how the heroine, a lady with a slightly shady past, has come to marry into the very stuffy family whose inquisitiveness and narrow-mindedness bring about her downfall.

Hitchcock's other film of 1927, *The Ring*, is a love story with a boxing background about the rise of a prize-fighter and the effect this has on the course of his marriage to a girl who

Which is Hitch?

1

2

3

(1) *Hitch with Joel McCrea in* Foreign Correspondent *(1940). (2) Production shot with Farley Granger in* Strangers on a Train *(1951). (3) As a silhouette advertising Reduco (right) in* Rope *(1948). (4) With Jane Wyman in* Stage Fright *(1949). (5) In a newspaper*

6

7

8

'ar left: Betty (Betty Balfour) has her assets ıspected at a theatrical agency in Champagne. eft: Carl Brisson plays a boxer who stars at 'ıe fairground in The Ring. Right: The lanxman Peter (Carl Brisson) is happy with is wife Kate (Anny Ondra) but she is pregnant y another man, his best friend

: almost equally attracted to the reigning hampion. The film is full of little Hitchcock ɔuches, some of them bordering on the naive, ke the mirroring of the idea of a mismatch by ıe presence of side-show Siamese twins at the 'edding, but nonetheless effective in the graıhic telling of the story. *The Farmer's Wife* 928) took Hitchcock off in another direction ıat he was not afterwards to pursue – the road rural comedy of Eden Philpotts' play. *hampagne* (1928) Hitchcock regarded as an lmost unmitigated disaster, mainly because e was not allowed to use the story he had 'ritten, and had to improvise something fairly onsensical about a rebellious heiress at the ıst moment. All the same, it does have ɔuches of typical Hitchcockian insolence, esecially during the heroine's rather impraccal search for a job.

Blonde Venus

The Manxman (1929), based on Hall Caine's best-selling novel about a love triangle on the Isle of Man, is remarkable in Hitchcock's output for the directness with which it expresses sensuality and desire. It would be tempting to see Anny Ondra as the first of Hitchcock's ice-maiden blonde heroines with fire down below, except that there is nothing prim, let alone icy, about her at all.

Clearly, Hitchcock enjoyed working with her as he starred her in his next film, *Blackmail* (1929), his first reversion to the thriller genre since *The Lodger*. That, of course, was when it was to be a completely silent film and so it would not have mattered that a Czech actress played a suburban Londoner. But the producers decided that the last reel should use this new gimmick, sound; then, at Hitchcock's urging (and backstage plotting), they agreed that it could be made over into a complete talkie. Anny Ondra was dubbed – in a primitive but effective fashion – and went back to Germany, where she married the boxer Max Schmeling. Hitchcock had his biggest triumph since *The Lodger* and went on to a new career in talkies. JOHN RUSSELL TAYLOR

Nearly all of Hitchcock's films carry his trade mark of a rief personal appearance, sometimes devised with great ngenuity and usually having some comic aspect amidst background of suspense

4

5

'ice in The Lodger (1926). (6) With Gregory ːck in The Paradine Case (1947). (7) With ımera in Young and Innocent (1937). (8) 'ith boy in Blackmail (1929). (9) With ːorge Sanders in Rebecca (1940). (10) Last ɪpearance in Family Plot (1976)

10

9

THE LODGER

The Lodger was Alfred Hitchcock's third film, but it was the first from a subject of his own choosing, and the one which the director himself considered the first real 'Hitchcock movie'. Hitchcock worked closely on the script with the writer Eliot Stannard, scenarist of all his silent movies. What had led him to the story, he said, was not so much Mrs Belloc Lowndes' novel as a stage version of it which he had happened to see. Looking back on *The Lodger* with the benefit of hindsight, it is now possible to notice a great deal in it which, maybe subconsciously at the time, appealed to Hitchcock as his kind of material.

His famous 'transfer of guilt' theme is plain enough. Whether the lodger is guilty of the 'Ripper' murders is kept from the audience (he isn't – being played by Ivor Novello, he couldn't be); the guilt of Joe, the policeman who is jealous of his girl's interest in the lodger, and corrupted in his duty by that jealousy, is underlined. Another of the director's favourite situations, the irruption of the bizarre, the unbelievable, into a mundane setting (here the Buntings' little terrace house which has never seen anything out of the ordinary), makes a first appearance, as does a lesser but noteworthy Hitchcockian topic – the irresponsibility of the media in spreading panic and confusion. Here, too, is Hitchcock's liking for the riveting opening: this time a close-up of the latest murder victim, shot against glass to enhance the gleam of her golden hair.

Some have seen too much of a young man's exuberance in the film. This was certainly the view of Hitchcock's distributors, who at first pronounced the film unreleasable. His previous film, *The Mountain Eagle* (1926), made like his first in Germany, was still on the shelf as well, and he must have been worried. The distributors were persuaded to change their minds by Ivor Montagu, engaged to do what he could for the picture. Montagu thought it much too good for any radical interference, so contented himself with a cosmetic job on the titles and a minimum of reshooting. And (daringly in view of his bosses' philistine propensities) he employed the artist McKnight Kauffer, whose posters were a feature of London life at the time, to design the credits and titles in a highly stylized script, thus adding a further Germanic touch to something that looked much more likely to have come out of Ufa than Islington. Anyway, someone persuaded the powers-that-be, the film was released, was a triumph (the British trade paper *The Bioscope* calling it the greatest British picture yet), and Hitchcock's future was assured.

That the movie is Germanic perhaps needs qualifying. Only at the end, as the lynch mob has the lodger trapped in the railings in Hyde Park, is there any overt symbolism, and even then the allusion to Christ does not precisely force itself on the viewer. Long passages with the lodger off screen are treated in a perfectly matter-of-fact way. But with the lodger present, all that had rubbed off on Hitchcock as he made his first two films in Germany comes to the fore. There is the famous shot, through a plate glass ceiling, of the lodger's feet as they pass to and fro over the Buntings' heads; there is the emphasis on stairs, on shadowed faces, on night and fog; there is a feeling that outside the house the city is an implacable enemy. It is likely that Hitchcock had seen Karl Grune's *Die Strasse* (1923, *The Street*). That film had the same contrast between home and safety and city and menace, and the same evocation of the city with dazzling street signs set against ink-black streets.

In *The Lodger* Hitchcock made the first of his token appearances. In an early establishing shot of a newspaper office he is a shadowy figure looming in the foreground; at the end he watches the lynching from a terrace above. Some of the more far-fetched criticism of his work has sought a deep significance in Hitchcock's appearances. But as he told François Truffaut when they talked about *The Lodger*, he had to fill up the spaces somehow, and he hadn't all that many extras on hand. Probably the truth is that he enjoyed it; he obviously loves his bit in *Blackmail* (1929).

The Lodger is not a masterpiece, then; rather a young man's brilliant beginning. It is not over-exuberant either; the trickery is well spaced out and firmly under control, and one or two of the more *outré* effects were eventually cut out by Hitchcock. But discounting those two 'prentice efforts, it was a very good first card, and he had exactly 51 left to deal before he was finished.

JACK LODGE

Directed by Alfred Hitchcock, 1926
Prod co: Gainsborough. **prod:** Michael Balcon. **sc:** Alfred Hitchcock, Eliot Stannard, from the novel by Mrs Belloc Lowndes. **photo:** Baron Ventimiglia, Hal Young. **ed/titles:** Ivor Montagu. **art dir:** C. Wilfred Arnold, Bertram Evans. **ass dir:** Alma Reville. **r/t:** 88 minutes.
Cast: Ivor Novello (*the lodger*), June (*Daisy Bunting*), Marie Ault (*Mrs Bunting*), Arthur Chesney (*Mr Bunting*), Malcolm Keen (*Joe Chandler*).

London is terrorized by a series of murders, all of blonde girls, all killed on a Tuesday. As news of the latest killing (1) spreads, a strange young man, Jonathan Drew, takes a room at the house of Mr and Mrs Bunting (2, 3). The Buntings have a daughter, Daisy, who is courted by Joe Chandler, a young policeman, but she is clearly attracted to the lodger (4), and Joe is deeply jealous. The lodger's mysterious comings and goings (5), his reticence, his apparent concern with the killings, arouse Joe's suspicions. When the lodger is at home, he paces the floor restlessly over the heads of the Buntings, and they are certain that something is wrong.

Eventually Joe, unbalanced by his jealousy (6), accuses the lodger, who is pursued by a lynch mob, flees to Hyde Park, and is trapped in the railings (7). News of another killing arrives at that moment, and the lodger's innocence is established. It transpires that his sister was one of the killer's earlier victims, and that he had been obsessed with finding the murderer. Daisy and the lodger are married. With some trepidation, the Buntings visit them in the lodger's mansion (8).

2

4

6

8

JAPAN
an eye for silence

Early Japanese film-makers were slow in developing the possibilities of sound. But this may have been of their own design, as they made silent films with skill, grace and flair

So much material on the Japanese silen cinema has been lost or mislaid througl natural disasters and the lack of preservatior facilities that it is impossible to assess the worl of many Japanese directors in any detail However, it is known that a surprising numbe of silent films were made in the Thirties anc this is due to two historical circumstances. Ir most of Europe and America, sound film equip ment had been fully established by about 1930 but the new technology was slow in reachin Japan and was mainly confined to the bi cities. There was also much resistance t sound by the *benshi* – indefatigable commen tators who translated the intertitles and gen erally 'explained' the story for audiences a over the country. A third reason offered b several Japanese film-makers was that direc tors in the Thirties alternated talkies wit silent films because they justifiably felt them selves masters of silent technique and wer loath to surrender to the demands of canne theatre', as seen in many foreign feature films

The Twenties saw the beginnings of the tw genres which were to dominate Japanes cinema in subsequent decades: *jidai-geki* period/costume dramas set before 1868; an

shomin-geki, lower middle class contemporary dramas. Of the former, the main exponent was Daisuke Ito, a consummate technician who greatly influenced the *chambara* (swordplay) film, giving it a modern relevance and a critical-social view which was to be continued by many other directors. From the few existing examples of the work of Ito and his contemporaries, it is clear that they developed a virtuoso camera style years before their American and European counterparts. Swift, fluid tracking shots and giddy pans abound as the camera follows impeccably choreographed fights with bodies hurtling through the paper walls of houses and armies battling in courtyards. This palpable enjoyment in film-making's physical aspects and the camera's freedom of movement was carried over into the Thirties in such films as Tsuruhiko Tanaka's *Beni Komori* (1931, *The Red Bat*), an episode from a long newspaper adventure serial with incredibly frenetic fights, some split-screen effects and a crazy, cliff-hanging finale.

A similar virtuosity and enjoyment can be found in Tomu Uchida's *Keisatsukan* (1933, *Police*), a startling pre-echo of post-war American location thrillers with a plot which also pre-dates *Manhattan Melodrama* (1934) and *Angels With Dirty Faces* (1938). Here, Uchida deals with a police investigation in the depths of the city, with much detailed location shooting in grimy little lanes, streets and bars culminating in an ambush and chase between cop and hoodlum (who are schoolboy friends) featuring rapid travelling shots which look almost impossible to shoot.

Leading Japanese directors at this time were deeply interested in, and fully aware of, developments in foreign cinema, notably American and German – for example, it is easy to understand why Heinosuke Gosho, with his swiftly-cutting montage style, should have been influenced by Ernst Lubitsch's *The Marriage Circle* (1924). The European-American cinematic styles of F. W. Murnau and Josef von Sternberg came together in a strange 1934 film by Minoru Murata called *Muteki* (*Foghorns*), set in late nineteenth-century Yokohama, with a delicate delineation of place and a steely narrative taking in both German and Russian fatalism. The camera style is again very mobile and slinky, moving around dock areas, marshlands and steamy bars, triumphantly acknowledging the last great flowering of the international silent cinema. Murata was also co-director with Kaoru Osanai of one of the first Japanese art movies, *Rojo no Reikon* (1921, *Souls on the Road*), in itself a relatively experimental piece featuring a Mary Pickford-like Japanese actress.

Far left: two lonely Souls on the Road *– this film's scriptwriter, Kiyohiko Ushiwara, later went to Hollywood to study with Charles Chaplin. Above left: a movie of 1919 being shot with the first Bell and Howell camera to be imported to Japan. Left:* The Red Bat *– an episode from a series of swordplay dramas. Below: insane images in* A Page of Madness

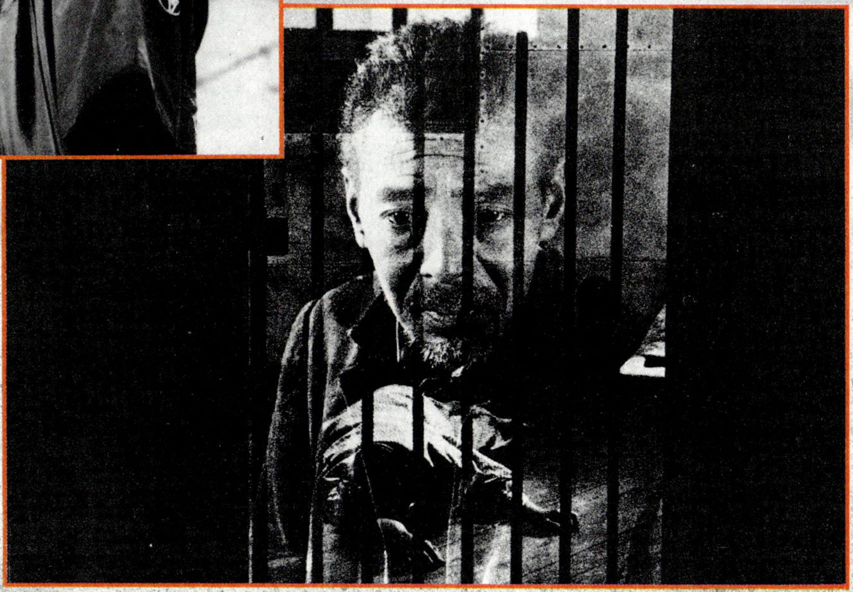

Above: Teinosuke Kinugasa's Crossroads. *Right, from top to bottom: silliness in the snow during* Days of Youth*; a typical shot from director Yasujiro Ozu in* Passing Fancy*; a woman turns to prostitution in* Nightly Dreams.

Far right: Caresses *(top) directed by Heinosuke Gosho, and (bottom)* Daigaku wa Deta Keredo *(1929,* I Graduated, But. . .*) in which an unemployed graduate has to tolerate living with his fiancée and his mother*

Although Teinosuke Kinugasa did not visit Europe until the late Twenties, the two silent films available from his considerable output testify to his awareness of the changing face of film styles. Produced independently and a commercial failure, *Kurutta Ippeiji* (1926, *A Page of Madness*) mixes European influences with specifically Japanese modes of expression. Made entirely without intertitles and set in a lunatic asylum, its sense of everyday abnormality is conjured up in several hallucinatory sequences seen through the eyes of the inmates (with human figures reduced to obscene, contorted blobs through the bars of cells) which make it one of the most advanced film works from any country. Kinugasa also makes much play between extreme stillness and sudden eruptions of movement within the set, again using a free-flowing camera. Although less formally innovative, his later *Jujiro* (1928, *Crossroads*) reworks elements of German Expressionism in its nightmarish vision of Yoshiwara, the famous entertainment quarter, which is symbolized by a huge, glittering, revolving globe. The hero's torments are often paralleled by transformations in the set design, allied to a wonderful sense of movement as the camera tracks along gaudy streets or cranes up to balconies filled with excited 'customers'.

Although the appearance of American film posters in most of his early movies shows where his influences lay, Yasujiro Ozu developed a specifically Japanese style from the very beginning of his career. His earliest known feature, *Wakaki Hi* (1929, *Days of Youth*), establishes the pattern of middle-class drama that he was to make his own, with a bright collection of young players and a gentle humour that manifests itself in the bantering by-play of the snowy holiday scenes. It also reveals the basic principles of his style – the abundance of static set-ups viewed from a low, floor level – yet there were also, in the early Thirties, many short, sharp travelling shots (along office desks or following characters down streets) which were gradually to be discarded in later years. In the prolific period up to his first sound film *Hitori Musuko* (1936, *The Only Son*), Ozu took in marital dramas, children's fantasies, thrillers with a knowing American look and sharply-pointed studies in domestic relationships which were to form the basis of his mature work. The popularity of the probing family tragi-comedy *Umarete Wa Mita Keredo* (1932, *I Was Born, But . . .*) has somewhat overshadowed other key works from this period like *Sono Yo no Tsuma* (1930, *That Night's Wife*), the compact study of a poor wife, her husband turned thief, and a sympathetic policeman, remarkable also for its opening robbery sequence shot like a Warner Brothers melodrama. Apart from his richly humorous response to children Ozu, in the early Thirties, developed an almost Renoir-like respect for male friendships, usually fathers trying to make out with recalcitrant children or schoolfriends helping each other to find jobs, as in *Tokyo no Gassho* (1931, *Tokyo Chorus*), *Dekigokoro* (1933, *Passing Fancy*) and *Tokyo no Yado* (1935, *An Inn in Tokyo*). Standing slightly apart from these is *Ukigusa Monogatari* (1934, *A Story of Floating Weeds*), a richly observed, picaresque love story about a travelling theatrical company, embellished with much attractive location shooting.

The atmospheric power of these generally modest films emanates from Ozu's remarkable eye for set-ups and the physical detail of the shots. He often cut away to an object – a clock, a tray, a bundle of clothes – which simply, yet justly, shades in a feeling or a moment of characterization. These are also allied to his famous 'pillow' shots which establish images of an open space or devices like a line of washing to usher in the next scene. Ozu's humour, which erupts sometimes in the most unexpected places, often derives from gags in the American-style but is more frequently a matter of beautifully gauged looks and exchanges embedded in a precise editing style.

Parallel productions

The careers of Ozu's distinguished contemporaries in the *shomin-geki* genre, Heinosuke Gosho and Mikio Naruse, developed along similar lines but with some intriguing differences. Gosho had the distinction of making the first Japanese sound movie, a rather rough, bucolic comedy called *Madamu to Nyobo* (1931, *The Neighbour's Wife and Mine*), but returned to silent films several times in the following years. *Izu no Odoriko* (1933, *The Dancing Girls of Izu*), a film based on the amatory adventures of a group of entertainers, is a good example of his shooting methods, taking in extensive location work and a subtle alternation of close shots with distant vistas. Gosho, like his contemporaries, inscribes the surface quality of his films with such detail that the characters emerge with a novelistic density seemingly unattainable in the cinema of other countries. In Gosho's case, the accumulation of detail is allied with a breaking down of the narrative into thousands of shots, so that each scene is constructed through a swiftly flowing montage of close-ups, mid-shots, and continuity shots of people entering and leaving rooms, all based on an intuitive feeling for the right distance between camera and object. These techniques are fully explored in *Aibu* (1933, *Caresses*), a sensitive, occasionally sentimentalized drama with a medical background which, judging by the abundance of dialogue intertitles, may once have been envisaged as a sound film. Gosho's direction of his actors is so meticulous, however, that he justifiably turns it into a 'silent play for faces'.

Swinging Thirties

Unlike Gosho and Ozu, Naruse did not work in the silent Twenties, his earliest films dating from 1930, but he continued the silent tradition for several years before he started to make sound films in 1935. His early movies are somewhat melodramatic yet his shooting style and use of evocative decor suggest an informed film sense, at times weakened by a penchant for swinging his camera around rooms. From *Yogoto no Yume* (1933, *Nightly Dreams*), *Kimi to Wakarete* (1933, *Apart From You*) to *Kagirinaki Hodo* (1934, *Street Without End*), there is a gradual refinement in silent technique so that in *Street Without End* all the elements come together in extremely elegant, flowing patterns of movement. Equally intriguing is the fact that the films belong irrevocably to the important 'feminist' phase of Japanese cinema in the Thirties, with the female characters invariably proving stronger than the men. This reaches sublime heights in the climax of *Street Without End* where the woman rejects her family and strides out through the hospital corridor in a great tracking shot which sets the seal on a sequence remarkable for its high emotional fervour.

The silent work of Ozu, Gosho and Naruse has gradually become available in recent years, but much other silent work is difficult to come by, particularly that of Yasujiro Shimazu (who was Gosho's teacher and virtually the founder of *shomin-geki*) and Hiroshi Shimizu, a truly individual master who loved children, buses, travelling shots and long-distance shooting. Therefore further discoveries are needed before it will be possible to place this crucial phase in the development of Japanese film history in its true perspective.

JOHN GILLETT

HAROLD
YD

I Was Born, But...

Mono no aware is a phrase which is central to Japanese culture and to the films of Yasujiro Ozu. It has its origins in Zen and, like most Zen concepts, it is not easy to translate into a Western language: it means something like balance and contemplation, a sad but total acceptance of the way things are. Ozu's is by no means the only work by a Japanese director to which it applies (it can be found in films as different as those of Akira Kurosawa, Nagisa Oshima and Kaneto Shindo), but his pictures are suffused with it, and none more delicately than his last silent feature, *I Was Born, But . . .*, largely remade by him as *Ohayo* (*Good Morning*) in 1959.

The two Yoshi boys are confronted with the kinds of pressures that are inflicted daily on children because, as Mr Yoshi says, 'It's a problem they'll have to live with for the rest of their lives.' Uprooted from their home town of Azabu because of their father's career, the first piece of advice they hear is the removal man saying of their father, 'That's the way to get ahead. You could learn from him.' Bullied by the local kids, the Yoshi boys are extricated from a fight by their father with the bland imperative: 'This place is our new home. You ought to be friendly with those boys!' – as though it were a matter of free choice. Recruiting the *sake* delivery boy to deal with the bully Kamekichi, they find that even here their father's job gets in the way: the delivery boy will not tell off the boss's son because 'his folks buy a whole lot more than yours do'.

And yet *I Was Born, But . . .* is not a Hollywood-style saga of misunderstood youth. Mr Yoshi is acutely aware of his sons' dilemma: 'Just so they don't become an employee, like me,' he says, as he and his wife bend tenderly over their sleeping children. And it remains a comedy: the tensions are expressed in scenes of wry humour. Returning home from his first day's work, Mr Yoshi discovers that the boys have played truant. He berates them as he changes from his business suit into his kimono. 'Why didn't you go to school and become somebody?' he asks, standing there in his long johns. The kids'-eye view of the lecture is shown in a close shot of his stockinged feet topped by a short expanse of hairy leg and the bottom end of the long johns.

The film's major confrontation is an even more delicately controlled sequence. Invited to the boss's house to see some home movies, the Yoshi boys are deeply humiliated to see their father making funny faces for Mr Iwasaki's camera. They walk home in the dark, sulkily throw their clothes on the floor and end up tearing things from the shelves in frustration. Their father returns with a small present for them, which they eye inquisitively but cannot bring themselves to accept. Finally, they burst out with, 'You're a nobody. You're a nothing.' Father spanks one while the other attacks him with a ping-pong bat. It is a scene in which comedy and a dreadful awareness of the conflict are delicately balanced – the 'sympathetic sadness' of *mono no aware*.

I Was Born, But . . . is as rigorously patterned as any Japanese art work. Scenes recur – waiting at the level crossing, for instance – as do details, for example the sparrow's eggs which are supposed to confer invulnerability from bullying but which, when fed to the family dog, make its hair fall out. The entire film is shot from Ozu's standard low angle, replicating the viewpoint of a Japanese sitting cross-legged on the floor. Interiors are often introduced by a lateral tracking shot across a neutral section of wall – a device which, in *I Was Born, But . . .*, is also used to draw parallels between Mr Yoshi's office and the children's rows of school desks.

The recurring features and camera style confer on the film a kind of serenity. When, at the end, the boys accept their father's position – they urge him to go and say good morning to the boss, and go off with their arms round the shoulders of the boss's son – the sense of compromise is distinctly limited. The acceptance that the film portrays emphatically denies the voluntary blindness that would make it reactionary, and opens the way to the transcendence of *mono no aware*. It is, in a very Japanese way, a beautiful film. NICK RODDICK

Directed by Yasujiro Ozu, 1932
Prod co: Shochiku-Kamata. **sc:** Akira Fushimi, Geibei Ibushiya, from a story by Akira Fushimi, James Maki (Yasujiro Ozu). **photo:** Hideo Shigehara, Yushun Atsuta. **art dir:** Takashi Kono. **ass dir:** Kinkichi Har. **r/t:** 86 minutes (original r/t: 100 minutes). Japanese title: *Umarete Wa Mita Keredo*. Released in USA/GB as *I Was Born, But . . .*
Cast: Tatsu Saito (*Yoshi, the father*), Hideo Sugawara (*Ryoichi, the elder son*), Tokkankozo (*Keiji, the younger son*), Mitsuko Yoshikawa (*the mother*), Takeshi Sakamoto (*Iwasaki, the boss*), Seiji Nishimura (*the schoolmaster*), Shoichi Kofujita, Zentaro Ijima, Chishu Ryu.

The Yoshi family, with their two sons Ryoichi and Keiji, move from Azabu to a suburb of Tokyo so that Mr Yoshi can advance his career (1). While Mr Yoshi pays a courtesy call to his new boss, Mr Iwasaki (2), the boys encounter a gang of kids led by the bully Kamekichi (3). Mr Yoshi strikes up a good relationship with his boss, a home-movie fanatic (4), but the boys are reluctant to go to school and end up playing truant for the day. They are found out, and Mr Yoshi tells them off for not taking advantage of their education (5).

The boys establish themselves in the local gang, and the boss's son Taro invites them to his house for one of his father's home-movie sessions. Mr Yoshi is also there, and Ryoichi and Keiji are ashamed to see him on the screen, clowning for the boss's camera (6). They go home early and, when Mr Yoshi returns, a family row develops. The boys accuse their father of being a nonentity and he is finally forced to spank Ryoichi while Keiji, his loyalties torn, sides with his brother (7).

In the morning, the boys refuse to eat. Mrs Yoshi brings some rice balls out to them, but they remain steadfast. Finally, Mr Yoshi comes out to join them, and they give in. Father and sons eat the rice balls (8), and the family is reconciled. Ryoichi and Keiji accept that their father has to be polite to his boss, and they themselves are happy to consolidate their friendship with Iwasaki's son.

2

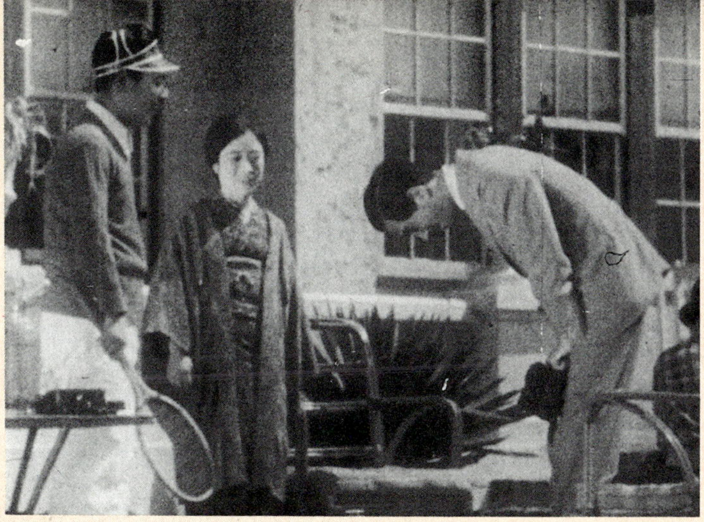

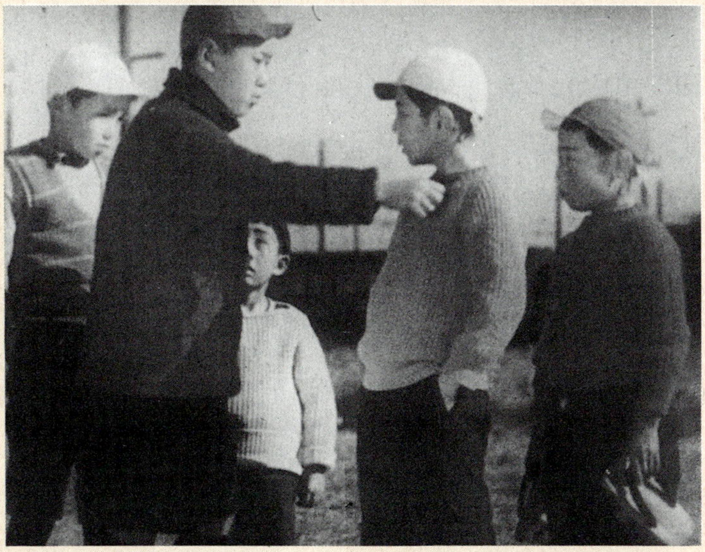

4

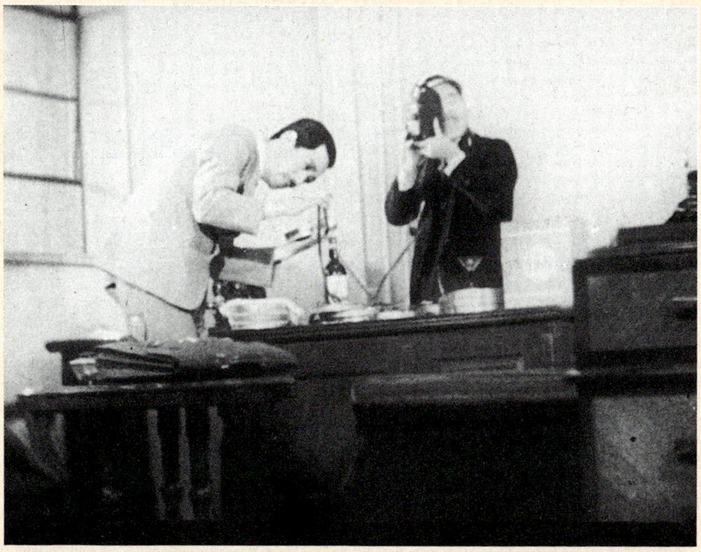

6

8

Ufa–Pride of Germany

Above: poster for Lang's The Girl in the Moon. *Left:* Zuflucht *(1928, Refuge) starred Henny Porten (right) and was produced by her for Ufa. Above left: Erich Pommer, director Robert Siodmak and Ufa script-editor Robert Liebmann. Top: the Neubabelsberg studios*

Vith its two great Berlin studios, its ranks of talent and its onsistent quality output, Germany's giant film-production ombine helped maintain national self-esteem during the ark days following World War I

he most celebrated film company outside of ollywood during the silent era was Ufa Jniversum Film Aktien Gesellschaft – Universe lm Company Limited). Despite defeat in Vorld War I, runaway inflation and the ollapse of the mark, Germany was able to ecome the largest centre for commercial film roduction in Europe – and Ufa led the way.

Ufa was originally founded as part of the war fort. General Ludendorff, Chief of Staff to Field arshal von Hindenburg, recognized that film as vitally important for propaganda and orale, and proposed that in the national terest film companies should merge to form a ngle production combine. To this end, he tablished under the German High Command photographic and film office known as Bild nd Film Amt (BUFA). The film industry llowed his lead by setting up the Deutsch chtbildgesellschaft (German Cinemato-aphic Company, DEULIG) for propaganda on e civilian front.

fa united

s a further result of this united push by army, overnment and industry, the large Ufa com-ne was founded in November 1917 with pital of 25 million marks, about one-third of hich came from the government, the rest om various industrial sources. Several lead-g companies, including Davidson's Projek-ons AG Union, German Nordisk, Vitascop d the Austrian Sascha-Film, became af-ated to Ufa. The resources of these com-nies – their studios (notably Tempelhof, near erlin), prominent first-run theatres and con-act artists – were all amalgamated under the a banner. By 1919 Ufa had at its disposal ch talented directors as Ernst Lubitsch (and s writer Hans Kräly), Max Mack, Gustav icky and the Hungarians Mihály Kertész (the future Michael Curtiz) and Alexander Korda, and stars Pola Negri, Asta Nielsen, Fritz Kortner and Emil Jannings.

The mission of Ufa, intensified after the war, was to promote German tradition and culture in as many films of artistic merit as possible, often in the form of spectacular historical productions, and films that demonstrated German talent and professionalism. German films of the time exhibited an extraordinary flair that outpaced anything the film industries of the Allied conquerors in Europe could produce. France, and especially Britain, lagged far behind, though France began to catch up in the mid-Twenties.

Following the Armistice in November 1918, the government's financial interest in Ufa was bought out and the industry took over the combine. Ufa was vitally concerned with developing Germany's markets abroad (especially in view of the deeply rooted unpopularity of Germany in Europe), and acquired cinemas in Spain, Holland, Switzerland and Scandinavia, concentrating on neutral countries where such penetration was possible so soon after hostilities, and before the rapid decline of the mark following the Treaty of Versailles and the punitive reparations imposed by the Allies.

German gold

Led by Ufa, the German film industry rallied, and in 1922 production was up to 472 movies, declining though to the 200s as inflation bit deeply. These films were obviously of a very mixed standard, but the so-called 'Golden Age' of German cinema – the Twenties – had begun. Ufa's power grew when in 1921 it merged with Erich Pommer's Decla-Bioscop. This company, itself the result of a merger the year before, brought Ufa new capital of 30 million marks, the great film-making estate Neubabelsberg near Berlin, and Germany's outstanding film producer in Pommer himself.

It was Pommer (1889-1966) who had produced Decla-Bioscop's *Das Kabinett des Dr Caligari* (1919, *The Cabinet of Dr Caligari*), bringing in Robert Wiene to direct when Fritz Lang, whom he actually wanted, proved unavailable. Pommer approved the use of Expressionist sets in this very modestly budgeted film, setting a famous style that would be adopted in many German films of the Twenties, including Ufa's *Der Golem: Wie er in die Welt kam* (1920, *The Golem*), directed by Paul Wegener and Carl Boese, and *Faust* (1926), directed by F. W. Murnau. Pommer also pressed Ernst Lubitsch to leave comedies, the field in which he had established himself, and turn to spectacular historical films designed to show off German studio proficiency. They were vehicles mostly for the sensuous actress Pola Negri, who starred at Ufa in Lubitsch's *Madame Dubarry* (1919, *Passion*) and *Sumurun* (1920, *One Arabian Night*), while Henny Porten appeared in *Anna Boleyn* (1920, *Deception*) with Emil Jannings, who also starred in *Das Weib des Pharao* (1922, *The Loves of Pharaoh*). Lubitsch next turned to intimate, erotic dramas such as *Die Flamme* (1923, *Montmartre*), with Pola Negri, the type of film that earned both director and star their tickets to Hollywood.

Fritz Lang built his Ufa career entirely in terms of spectacular films: *Dr Mabuse der Spieler* (1922, *Dr Mabuse, the Gambler*), *Die Nibelungen* (1924), *Spione* (1928, *The Spy*), *Frau im Mond* (1929, *The Girl in the Moon*). His greatest production of the period, *Metropolis* (1927), was also Ufa's most ambitious project of the Twenties, with, according to Lang, a colossal budget of about 5 million marks though Ufa claimed that it went up to 8 million. The film also took 17 months to make with 310 shooting days; by the time it was finished, the company was in dire financial straits. In 1927 it was taken over by the financier Dr Alfred Hugenberg. Backed by the Deutsche-Bank, Ufa had its capital raised to 45 million marks. Hugenberg, a right-wing nationalist, committed the company to producing propagandist

Above left: one of Otto Hunte's sets for Lang's medieval epic Die Nibelungen. *Left: Emil Jannings as Henry VIII in Lubitsch's* Anna Boleyn. *Below left: Jannings as the professor*

Sorcerers of light

The period of German cinema dominated b Ufa was noted for the outstanding technic efficiency of the studios. The productions wer characterized by elaborate set design togethe with excellent black-and-white cinematog raphy. The two outstanding cameramen wer Fritz Arno Wagner (1889–1950) and Ka Freund (1890–1969), who both worked ex tensively at Ufa.

Wagner began as a newsreel camerama and shot his first feature in 1919. He wa director of photography on such atmospher silent masterpieces as Fritz Lang's *Der Müd Tod* (1921, *Destiny*) and *Spione* (1928, *The Spy* F. W. Murnau's *Nosferatu, eine Symphonie d Grauens* (1922, *Nosferatu, the Vampire*), Arthu Robison's *Schatten* (1923, *Warning Shadows* Arthur von Gerlach's *Zur Chronik von Grie huus* (1925, *The Chronicles of the Grey Hous* and G. W. Pabst's *Die Liebe der Jeanne Ne* (1927, *The Love of Jeanne Ney*). He stayed on i Germany during the Third Reich, working in the post-war years but with little furth opportunity to develop his art.

Karl Freund, on the other hand, went Hollywood in 1929, having shot such classi as Paul Wegener and Carl Boese's *Der Golen Wie er in die Welt kam* (1920, *The Golem* Murnau's *Der letzte Mann* (1925, *The La Laugh*) and *Tartüff* (1925, *Tartuffe*), E.

:ormented by desire for Lola-Lola (Marlene Dietrich) in Sternberg's *The Blue Angel*, with Rosa Valetti. Above: one of Hans Poelzig's remarkable sets for *The Golem*

newsreels. Ufa became responsible for 80 per cent of German newsreel production and, with their massive chain of cinemas and contracts with independent cinemas, was able to force their films on the German public. And it was with their help that Hitler finally came to power.

Cities of darkness

During the late Twenties the German cinema became notable for what might be termed its street or city films. Narrative films began to show the more tragic aspects of city life, the 'mean streets' that hid people whose lives were in one way or another disturbed. F. W. Murnau was to exploit this in one of his finest films at Ufa, *Der letzte Mann* (1925, *The Last Laugh*). G. W. Pabst in particular created such films with a heavy emphasis on crime and sex – *Die freudlose Gasse* (1925, *The Joyless Street*), dealing with the dark years of inflation, the psycho-analysis orientated *Geheimnisse einer Seele* (1926, *Secrets of a Soul*), and, for Ufa, *Die Liebe der Jeanne Ney* (1927, *The Love of Jeanne Ney*), featuring the streets of Paris – where it was shot on location – rather than those of Berlin.

As was to be expected, the Germans were in the forefront when it came to the introduction of sound. As early as 1918, a sound system known as Tri-Ergon was developed, anticipating the recording of sound on film, and based on experiments dating back to the nineteenth century to record sound by means of light. The rights to this system, held by Ufa from 1924, were acquired by the American company Fox in 1926. The Germans merged their various sound film interests in 1929 in a syndicate called Tobis-Klangfilm set up by the electrical combine AEG and Siemens. Though the Aafa Film company made Germany's first sound picture, *Dich hab' ich geliebt* (1929, I Loved You), Ufa remained in the lead, making its sound debut with *Melodie des Herzens* (1929, *Melody of the Heart*), produced by Pommer. The ratio of sound to silent films quickly grew – for example, from three per cent in September 1929 to thirty per cent in January 1930 – and it was Pommer who invited Josef von Sternberg from America to direct *Der blaue Engel* (1930, *The Blue Angel*), the early Ufa talkie classic, made in both German and English, that launched Marlene Dietrich as a star. But the Golden Age was over, and in 1933 the industry came under the control of Joseph Goebbels, Hitler's Minister for Propaganda and Public Enlightenment.

Ufa became state-owned in 1937. *Munchhausen* (1943), a spectacular fantasy designed to celebrate the company's twenty-fifth anniversary, was perhaps its final flourish; Ufa ceased to exist in 1945, and Deutsche Film Aktien Gesellschaft (DEFA), East Germany's state-owned film organization, took over the Neubabelsberg studios. There was an abortive attempt to resurrect Ufa's great name in 1956, but the new company quickly foundered.

ROGER MANVELL

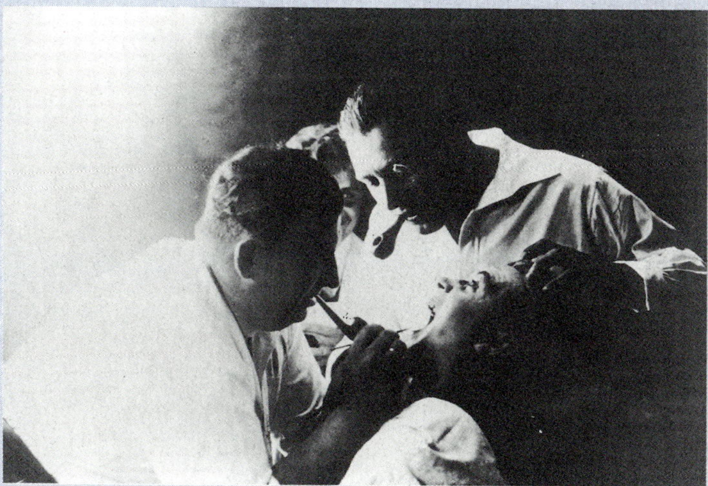

Above: Karl Freund (left), Fritz Lang and 'patient' in a bizarre production shot from *Metropolis*. Above left: Fritz Arno Wagner (right) at Neubabelsberg in 1928

)upont's *Varieté* (1925, *Vaudeville*) and Lang's *Metropolis* (1927). Freund also began as a newsreel cameraman and also, like Wagner, pecialized in the chiaroscuro effects associated vith the more stylized German studio films lealing with mystery and the supernatural. His and Wagner's work has been described in Roger Manvell and Heinrich Fraenkel's book *The German Cinema*:

'If photography can be defined as painting a scene with light, this is what these artist-photographers achieved, using selected points of highlight framed with shadows, building compositions of light and shade, flooding the image with mist, dissolving it with superimpositions, giving it magic by means of multiple exposures, and creating vast perspectives with illusory height and depth through the Schüfftan and other processes for marrying sections of models to sections of life-size sets. Theirs was the technical skill and artistry which realized in terms of two-dimensional images in black-and-white, shadow and light, mist and illumination the imaginary visions of directors as different as Lang and Pabst, Wiene and Murnau, and the men who designed and built their sets.'

The German cinematographers (especially Freund) and designers made use throughout the Twenties of special effects, including the substantial use of models and trick photography. Most celebrated at the time was the Schüfftan Process, which saved millions of marks in production costs. It was devised by the cinematographer Eugen Schüfftan (1893–1977). An inclined mirror was used to reflect a photographic image of a miniature representation of the whole of the upper section of a vast set, joining this reflected image to the full-scale structure on the studio floor, which represented only the lower section of the set in which the actors actually appeared. This action area was photographed by the cameraman through the plain glass of the lower part of the mirror plate which, stripped of its silver, allowed the full-scale part of the set to join up with the small mirrored image placed above it. Freund used this process extensively in the filming of *Metropolis*.

In America Freund continued to create superb photographic images in such films as *Dracula* (1931), *The Good Earth* (1937), for which he won an Academy Award, and *Key Largo* (1948), while also directing *The Mummy* (1932), and other movies. ROGER MANVELL

METROPOLIS
EIN FILM VON FRITZ LANG
IN DEN HAUPTROLLEN:
BRIGITTE HELM • GUSTAV FRÖHLICH,
ALFRED ABEL, RUDOLF KLEIN-ROGGE, THEODOR LOOS, FRITZ RASP, HEINRICH GEORGE
AN DER KAMERA: KARL FREUND, GÜNTHER RITTAU
UFA FILM IM VERLEIH DER PARUFAMET

1

2

4

5

6

7

8

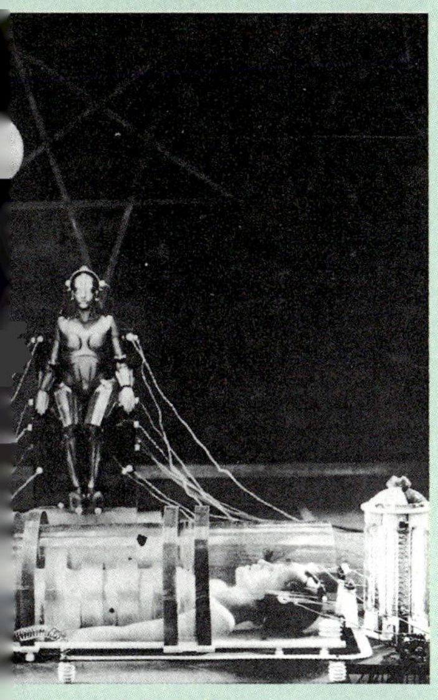

3

Directed by Fritz Lang, 1927

Prod co: Ufa. **prod:** Erich Pommer. **sc:** Fritz Lang, Thea von Harbou, from her own novel. **photo:** Karl Freund, Günther Rittau. **sp eff photo:** Eugen Schüfftan. **art dir:** Otto Hunte, Erich Kettelhut, Karl Vollbrecht. **sculpture:** Walter Schultze-Mittendorf. **cost:** Anne Willkomm. **r/t:** 120 minutes.

Cast: Alfred Abel (*John Fredersen*), Gustav Frölich (*Freder*), Brigitte Helm (*Maria*), Rudolf Klein-Rogge (*Rotwang*), Fritz Rasp (*Slim*), Theodor Loos (*Josaphat*), Erwin Biswanger (*No. 11811*), Heinrich George (*foreman*), Olaf Storm (*Jan*), Hanns Leo Reich (*Marinus*).

In Metropolis, a giant city of the twenty-first century, everything is done by enormous machines run by an army of ant-like slave workers (1). They live in labyrinthine underground slums, while the minority ruling class lives above ground in the 'eternal gardens' (2). They are not conscious of being tyrants, but one day Freder, son of the city's Master John Fredersen, notices a beautiful young woman – Maria – with a clutch of hungry children at the gates of the gardens (3). Moved by her beauty, he sets out in pursuit of her, and discovers the squalor of Metropolis' hidden power centre (4).

In the subterranean tenements he finds Maria; she has been urging the restless workers to have patience and wait for salvation from 'the forgotten Christ'. Their meeting is discovered by Freder's father, who then instructs his principal scientist Rotwang to make a robot in the image of Maria in order for her to gain the worker's confidence in the rulers, and so put a stop to all revolutionary tendencies.

Rotwang kidnaps Maria and creates an android (5) with the idea of furthering his own designs – which are ultimately to displace Fredersen as Master and take power himself. The ensuing revolt (6), urged on by the false Maria who has gone beserk, is all too effective: the pumps stop turning and all the underground areas occupied by the workers are flooded. Freder and the real Maria – who has managed to escape – lead the worker children out of danger (7). The workers, realizing how they have been misled, burn the robot.

Seeing the collapse of all his plans, Rotwang goes mad. John Fredersen sees the error of his ways (8), and with the joining of Maria and Freder's hands in front of the cathedral, Capital and Labour are united – by love.

Fritz Lang quickly established himself at the forefront of German cinema. He had been an enthusiastic art student, but during World War I he became interested in the theatre and cinema, and began to write film scenarios in order to gain an entrée into the cinematic world. He began by writing scripts for the great serial specialist of the time, Joe May, and by 1919 had progressed to direction with *Der Halbblut* (The Half-Caste), a film made in only five days. From there he moved on to bigger things such as the two-part *Die Spinnen* (1919–20, *The Spiders*), but after preparing the script of a big two-part spectacle *Das Indische Grabmal* (1921, *The Hindu Tomb*), which he also intended to direct, he found himself baulked by Joe May and determined to work for himself from then on. The first major film he made after this decision was *Der Müde Tod* (1921, *Destiny*, which recounted three historical horror stories. It turned into a big international success, and Lang's future career seemed assured.

However, Lang was not one to sit back and take the easy option. Instead, he launched into three of the largest and most expensive productions to be made in Germany, or indeed anywhere else in the world at that time. First came the two-part story of an insane master-criminal *Dr Mabuse der Spieler* (1922, *Dr Mabuse, the Gambler*), then the even bigger *Die Nibelungen* (1924). The latter, also in two parts, required enormous sets and vast crowd scenes in order to evoke the stories of Siegfried and Kriemhild, characters from the set of German legends previously quarried by the composer Richard Wagner in his *Ring*-cycle music.

Scarcely had Lang finished with this vast project than he embarked on *Metropolis*, a vision of the future written, as had been the three previous films, by himself and his wife Thea von Harbou.

From the outset *Metropolis* was conceived as both a colossal spectacle and as a film-with-a-message. The message, if any, has always been a subject for controversy – not surprisingly, for Lang's political attitudes during the Twenties were sufficiently far to the left for him to be rootedly anti-Nazi and later to get him into trouble with the Hollywood witch-hunters. In contrast, Thea von Harbou's politics were sufficiently to the right for her to stay on happily in Germany after Hitler's rise to power, and become one of the most successful screenwriters of the Third Reich. Thus, as a product of both minds *Metropolis* takes on no less than the whole problem of Capital versus Labour, postulates a gigantic slave community dominated by a small elite in the year 2000, imagines a slave revolt, and invents a solution to reconcile the warring elements.

Of course the 'solution' is, as Lang later ruefully admitted, monumentally naive and banal: simply that love conquers all, and that 'the intermediary between the hand and the brain is the heart' ('That's a fairytale – definitely' added Lang). But even if, on a political level, the idea is simplistic and sentimental, it has to be admitted that it effectively identifies the keystone in *Metropolis*' gigantic construction, for the structure is more emotional and visual than reasoning. The story as a whole is seen as a battle between light and dark, good and evil, rather than something so prosaic as management and labour. Indeed, in the view of the film's creators it was about magic and the dark ages as against the illumination of modern science. Taking this approach, it is possible to argue that all the good in the story comes from science, and all the bad from magic, especially in the person of the magician Rotwang. But as the magical element was minimized in the shooting, Rotwang comes over instead as just another mad scientist and the distinction becomes hopelessly blurred.

What does remain as impressive as ever is the mastery with which Lang stages his dramas. Evidently he had learnt, like most other directors in Germany at the time, an enormous amount from Max Reinhardt's stage spectacles: his management of the huge crowds of robot-like slaves – and of the rebellion when, spurred on by the false Maria, they go on a rampage of destruction – is as stunning as anything in that line before or since. True, the characters are dwarfed by their environment and reduced to stereotypes, but with so much else going on to interest and amaze, who is going to stop and argue? Certainly not the film's first audiences: even in America *Metropolis* was taken as a model of how to do things, and Lang was deluged with offers to come and make films of equal quality in Hollywood. But he refused. Why should he go when he had resources just as vast at his disposal in Germany, and far more freedom than he could ever hope for in America? Or so he thought in 1927. JOHN RUSSELL TAYLOR

1

4

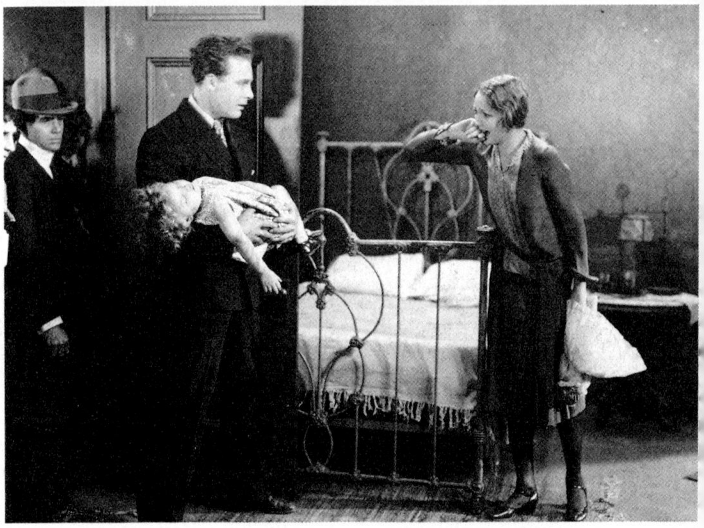
7

Directed by King Vidor, 1928
Prod co: MGM. **sc:** King Vidor, John V. A. Weaver, Harry Behn. **titles:** Joe Farnham. **photo:** Henry Sharp. **ed:** Hugh Wynn. **art dir:** Cedric Gibbons, Arnold Gillespie. **length:** 8538 feet (approx. 95 minutes).
Cast: James Murray (*John*), Eleanor Boardman (*Mary*), Bert Roach (*Bert*), Estelle Clark (*Jane*), Daniel G. Tomlinson (*Jim*), Dell Henderson (*Dick*), Lucy Beaumont (*mother*), Freddie Burke Frederick (*Junior*), Alice Mildred Puter (*daughter*).

When it was resurrected to the tuneful accompaniment of the Wren Orchestra during the London Film Festival of 1981, *The Crowd* finally, and with justification, assumed its place among the immortal achievements of the screen.

King Vidor's masterpiece has, like its hero, suffered the vagaries of fortune. Acclaimed on its first release, it was nevertheless frowned upon by many intellectual critics. Harry Alan Potamkin, for example, wrote in the serious film journal *Close Up*:

'The theme was enormous: ineffectual man, doomed by prophecy, caught within the indifference or hostility of the mass. But the vast scope of such a scheme is immediately reduced to a trite duplication of the irony-and-pity, human interest *feuilleton*.'

Then, as the sound era developed, *The Crowd* grew less familiar as a staple of repertory cinemas, and soon became a name to conjure with in history books.

But the zest of a specially written score by Carl Davis has revealed the captivating rhythms of *The Crowd* – its ability to chart an American tragedy without lurching into a morass of sentimentality or unremitting gloom. MGM was approaching its peak as a studio when Vidor, whose *The Big Parade* (1925) had earned a rich dividend for the company, persuaded the production chief Irving Thalberg to embark on an experimental movie – *The Crowd*.

For a start, the leading man was an unknown, James Murray, who was so disbelieving of his opportunity that he did not bother to turn up for his first screen test with Vidor. Secondly, there was no vaulting passion, no overwhelming romance or glamour – just the workaday relationship of John, the man in the crowd, with his little wife Mary (Eleanor Boardman).

The concept, however, appealed to Thalberg. And the fate of James Murray's John was uncanny in its prescience, for the scenes of his fighting for a place in job queues would be matched in the aftermath of the Wall Street Crash of 1929. The experience of this ordinary man is enriched by Vidor's description of domestic life: a visit from the wife's family, the romping with children, the little explosions of exasperation – as when a milk bottle squirts its contents into John's face, and he exclaims to his wife, 'Why can't you tell me when things are full?'

The Crowd belongs among the most audacious films of the Twenties as far as visual technique is concerned. Vidor sets his hero in a huge office, surrounded by rows of identical desks, each occupied by a worker as obedient and cowed as John. Outside Fritz Lang's *Metropolis* (1927), the concept of people as automata had not been so fiercely evoked. When the young John realizes that his father has died, he advances up a broad staircase towards the camera, the walls on either side stretching away in painful perspective, stressing the void in the boy's life.

Vidor's remains a disenchanted view of 'the crowd'. People swarm around someone at times of triumph or grief – the death of John's little daughter in a street accident, for instance – but ignore him at others. Anyone who sets his face against the tide of the crowd

2

3

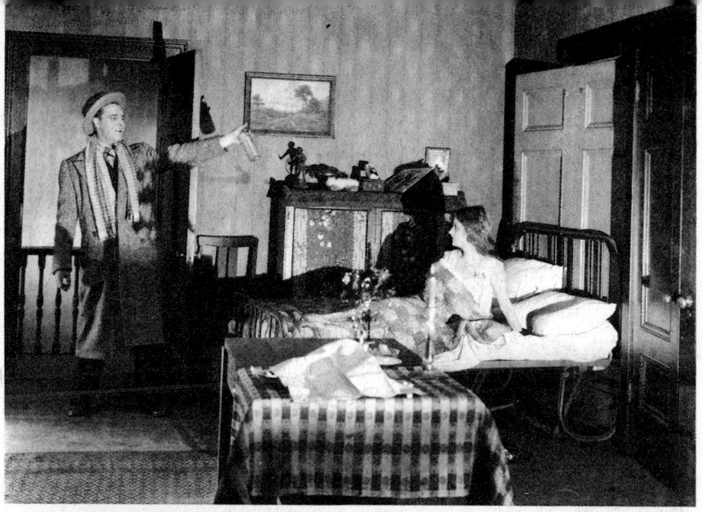

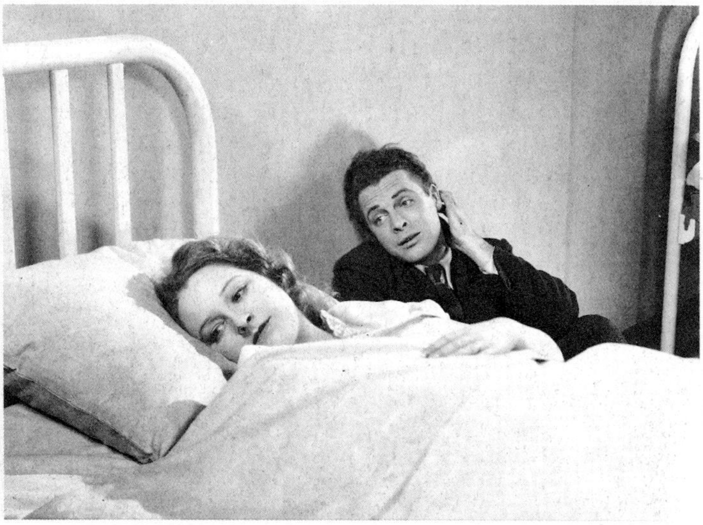

6

9

must be prepared to be swept aside. Once John loses his job, he is out of step with his comrades. The delicate fabric of his daily round collapses. His marriage grinds down. He discovers traits in his character that appal him as much as they aggravate others. Yet at the end he is viewed as a member of the crowd once more, protected by the surrounding mass as they laugh uproariously in a vast variety theatre. Seven different endings were mooted, including one showing John and Mary celebrating round a Christmas tree; but Vidor insisted on a bitter-sweet finale.

The Crowd was shot in the Culver City studios of MGM, but also on location in Detroit and New York City. Some of the most exhilarating sequences unfold in Manhattan, with its hectic traffic and the awesome novelty of the skyscrapers; and in Brooklyn's Coney Island, where John and his family go for an outing. A tragic appendage to the success of *The Crowd* was the decline and eventual death of James Murray from alcoholism and sheer dejection during the Thirties. His female co-star, meanwhile, Eleanor Boardman, was married to King Vidor and later to another director, Harry d'Abbadie d'Arrast, and in *The Crowd* exemplified the finest in silent acting craft.

PETER COWIE

On July 4, 1900, a baby son is born to the Sims family. The mother dies at birth, and the father follows her just 12 years later. Young John faces the future with courage, travelling to New York City in search of fame and fortune – and winning for his pains a post as a clerk in a huge office (1). During a trip to Coney Island with a friend, John meets Mary and they fall in love with each other (2). They are married and enjoy a rapturous honeymoon at Niagara Falls.

Married life is not all roses. John leaves the apartment and gets drunk one night while Mary's relatives are visiting (3), and as the months pass the couple grow increasingly irritated with each other (4). A baby brings temporary relief (5), and is followed by another.

John's unexpected win in an advertising-slogan contest enables him to buy Mary a new dress (6). But in the very moment of celebration, their little daughter is struck down by a lorry in the street (7) and dies of her injuries.

John is haunted by guilt, and loses his concentration at work. Soon he is fired (8), and refuses offers of employment from Mary's supercilious brothers. Mary too turns against him (9), and John, accompanied only by his small son, makes a botched attempt at suicide. On the way home, he stumbles on that miracle – a job: juggling balls in the air as a sandwich man. Not much, but enough to earn a few dollars and to win back the affections of his wife. Together they go to a show, and are finally shown laughing – in the midst of 'the crowd'.

The Enduring Craft of HENRY KING

Henry King's career was one of the most remarkable in Hollywood history. An actor in films as early as 1913, he began to direct in 1915 and worked for such companies as Pathé, Mutual, the American Film Company, Inspiration, Paramount, Goldwyn and United Artists and, from 1930, prolifically for Fox. He was still making pictures in the Sixties.

His greatest gift lay in telling stories in visual terms, and even in the sound era the pictorial element was still pre-eminent in his work. His first major success, the silent *Tol'able David* (1921), was compared favourably with the films of D. W. Griffith, and the great masters of the Soviet film took it as a model. In later years, with films like *State Fair* (1933), *Jesse James* (1939), *Wilson* (1944), *Twelve O'Clock High* (1949) and *The Gunfighter* (1950), King brought the highest standards of craftsmanship and excellence to commercial studio projects.

He recorded the interview from which the following extracts are taken in 1977. At that time, according to which reference books are to be believed, his age was between 85 and 89. He was still piloting his private plane and working on new scenarios. He died in 1982.

David Robinson

I was on the stage for only three and a half years, but I packed a lot of experience into that. I worked 52 weeks of the year because I wanted to gain experience. I worked in touring stock companies, travelling all over the States.

I first went into pictures as an actor, and I went into it because it was more certain than the stage. The man who engaged me said in the pictures you get your money every week. Now in the theatre you work for your living, and what I couldn't stand when I first went into pictures as an actor was all the sitting around. So I had a desk put in my dressing room, and I got to writing. With all the plays I knew from the theatre, I could take a little of this and a little of that . . . and they thought they were great screen stories. Then I wrote an original – well, it leaned a little on a play I knew – and sold that for $75. I played in it. They called it *The Brand of Man* (1915, episode from the serial *Who Pays?*), and it was quite successful.

Spoiling for a fight

I got into direction because of a fight scene. Tom Santschi and Bill Farnum had shot a fight scene for *The Spoilers* (1914), in which they beat each other to a pulp. It was the talk of the country and it was imitated in every film that had a fight in it. Well, we were doing a film with a fight scene, and I said to the director, 'Oh don't let's do *The Spoilers* fight yet again. People are sick of seeing it. You're going on location today. Let me write out the fight scene and see how you like it.'

Now when I was about eight years old I was in a little town called Ellaston, Virginia, and I vividly remembered a fight I had seen there, between two coloured men. I wrote the scene just as I remembered that fight. And when the director came back I showed it to him, and he said, 'But this is just a jumble' – because you see I had written it in little short scenes, close-ups of a hand reaching for a stone, and so on.

So he said, 'You'd better direct it yourself' which I did. Then there came a message from the lab, where the man in charge was the brother of the editor. 'We've got a lot of scraps of film', they said, and in turn the editor told me, 'But this is no use – some of the scenes are only six inches long. You can't have shots less than three feet'. 'Is that a law?' I asked her.

So we put it together, and I made a few changes, and the director saw it, and the

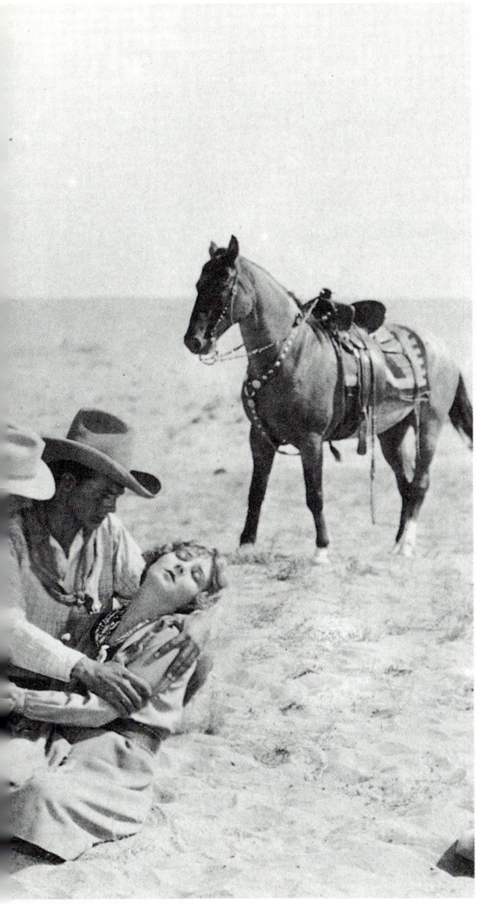

management saw it, and they all agreed it was the most exciting fight they had ever seen on the screen. So they decided I ought to be directing, not acting.

Tall story

My biggest success for the American Film Company was my last film there, *Six Feet Four* (1919). I made it at 5800 feet, a thousand feet longer than the usual programme picture length. I suggested that the studio released it as a feature picture, which they did. They had a big success with it which decided them that they would go into feature production after this. They had great plans for me, but I had already gone to Thomas H. Ince's studio.

Far left: King shooting the historical romance Romola *on location in Italy in 1924. Left: Gary Cooper (centre) and Vilma Banky in* The Winning of Barbara Worth *(1926)*

I made one film for Ince – *23½ Hours Leave* (1919). It was a wartime comedy. Ince had hired an efficiency expert to make the studio run more economically, and when I finished the picture – Mr and Mrs Ince were on vacation – this man said to me, 'You're $20,000 over budget. We're not taking up our option to renew your contract.' So I said, 'That's all right, because the option's expired anyway and I've signed elsewhere', which I had. That was on the Saturday. Mr and Mrs Ince came back from their holiday over the weekend and ran the film, and Mrs Ince said, 'Tom, this is the best film we've made'. And on the Monday Ince went looking for me, but I had gone. And he was so mad he fired the efficiency expert.

Tol'able behaviour

When they looked at *Tol'able David*, people talked about art, art, art – but I'd never heard the word used about a motion picture. I was making a motion picture, an entertainment, and I just set out to make it as well as I could. I set out as seriously as someone might who was writing a book. But there was a great deal of me in *Tol'able David*. It was made just about eighty miles from where I was born. I knew the people. I knew what that boy's desires were. His experiences were things I had known as a child. A very tragic story of my youth was in that film. I had a dog. A boy and his dog could be very close. A man claimed our dog had killed some sheep, and he convinced my mother he must take the dog and kill it. I took my father's revolver, but my mother chased me and outran me and stopped me. In that way little bits of myself rubbed off onto the film. Every picture that you do has something of yourself, your friends, something you've learned, something that's at the back of your mind.

I only met D. W. Griffith once. That was after the screening of *Tol'able David*, and Richard Barthelmess – the leading man of *Tol'able David*, who'd starred in a lot of Griffith films – took me to meet him. 'Too good, dear boy', he said. 'Too good. Too good.'

Shooting abroad

I wanted to do *The White Sister* (1923) in Italy, because I felt it would be impossible to do it in the States. I've been a location man all my life. I always prefer to go back to nature, to go to the real places. The studio made no objection. Then, however, when I'd been three months in production, they discovered I was going to kill off the hero before the end of the picture. So they sent a couple of writers out to Italy. And they wrote a lot of endings, but they couldn't do one better than ours. So the studio head said he'd back that one. And when the picture was finished they realized they had the right ending.

Shooting in sound

In the late Twenties you heard nothing but sound, sound, sound. And some of the early sound pictures I saw made me think what a terrible mistake sound was. I reckoned I was in the business of telling stories, and that what mattered was to make the sound support the picture. At that time I was making a picture called *She Goes to War* (1929). So I added a song, and a few bits of dialogue. But then I started thinking about the problem of sound. Technicians coming in from radio were dictating policy, but I determined from the start that I was still going to be director. Well, I had a story, and I found my locations and built the exteriors and interiors together. The technicians said they would never do, because there were echoes. I said, 'I'm so glad you told me you couldn't do this, 'cause I know a man who can.' So they said they'd try after all.

The sound on *She Goes to War* was wonderful. We had much less trouble than in the studios when they were building everything for sound and everything seemed so dead.

Hogging the screen

I made two films with Will Rogers. He was the salt of the earth, the nicest, easiest, most amusing and wonderful man you could

Below: maternal reason prevails in Tol'able David, *with Richard Barthelmess and Marion Abbott. Below left and far left: King's romantic drama* The White Sister *and his mother-love weepie* Stella Dallas *(1926) starred his discovery Ronald Colman*

Above: King's classic war drama starred Gregory Peck as an officer cracking up. Above right: Will Rogers and the prize-winning Blue Boy in State Fair. *Below: Jason Robards and Joan Fontaine in King's last film,* Tender Is the Night *(1962)*

imagine. Those two films, *Lightnin'* (1930) and *State Fair* (1933), were the highlights of my life. In *State Fair* we had this enormous hog. I bought two hogs, one to play the part and one to understudy. And then I had to get a valet for the hogs. Rogers used to sit in the pen with the hog, Blue Boy.

Rogers would sometimes change a line, but the meaning was always there. His reputation as an ad libber was not entirely deserved. He was a very serious man about his work.

Missouri breaks

Jesse James (1939) I call not so much a Western as a mid-Western, because you expect to have a lot of cowboys in a Western. This was one of Nunnally Johnson's classic scripts; from somewhere he had got hold of the editorials from a Missouri newspaper of the time of Jesse James, written by an editor who was very sympathetic to the James family. And out of this he had fashioned something original.

At the time Darryl F. Zanuck of 20th Century-Fox wanted me to direct *Stanley and Livingstone* (1939). I convinced him, however, that his script for that film was a mess, so eventually he agreed to let me do *Jesse James*. 'It'll only show in Missouri and a few other parts though, while *Stanley and Livingstone* is a subject with international appeal', he said. As it turned out *Jesse James* was a huge box-office success – not that a film that makes a lot of money is necessarily a good film, but it does mean that a lot of people have seen it. After that I made *Stanley and Livingstone*. The script was better by that time: I suggested that they centre it on Stanley's quest.

The motion picture is my first love. I've never made a film that didn't have some little bit of me in it. I never made motion pictures for money. Fortunately, though, they paid me to do them. . .

From an interview with Henry King by David Robinson in 1977.

Filmography

Films as actor only unless otherwise specified: **1913** A False Friend; The Split Nugget; Back to the Primitive; The Birthmark; The Padre's Strategy; A Perilous Ride; Love and War in Mexico; A Romance of the Ozarks; A Woman's Heart; The Legend of Lover's Leap; The Mysterious Hand; The Apache Kind; Jim's Reward; An Actor's Strategy; The Message of the Rose; The Outlaws Gratitude; The Tenderfoot Hero; His Last Crooked Deal; Playing With Fire; The Medal of Honor; A Mexican Tragedy; For Her Brother's Sake; The Mate of the Schooner Sadie; When Brothers Go to War; Magic Melody; When the Clock Stopped; Turning the Tables; Melita's Sacrifice; Her Father; You've Got to Pay; Love Life and Liberty; The Moth and the Flame. **'14** The Eternal Duel; The Power of Print; The Measure of a Man; The Rat; The Will o' the Wisp. **'15** Who Pays? (12-part serial) (+dir); Saved From Himself; The Acid Test; The Bliss of Ignorance; Letters Entangled; Tomboy; Should a Wife Forgive? **'16** The Sand Lark; Faith's Reward. *Films as director:* Little Mary Sunshine (+act); Joy and the Dragon (+act); Shadows and Sunshine. **'17** Twin Kiddies (+act); The Climber (+act); Told at Twilight (+act); Sunshine and Gold (+act); Souls in Pawn; The Bride's Silence; The Unafraid; The Upper Crust; Scepter of Suspicion; The Mainspring (+act); Southern Pride; A Game of Wits; The Mate of Sally Ann; Vengeance of the Dead. **'18** King Social Briars; Beauty and the Rogue; Powers That Pray; The Locked Heart (+act); Hearts or Diamonds (+act); Up Romance Road (+act); All the World to Nothing (+act); Hobbs in a Hurry (+act); When a Man Rides Alone (+act). **'19** Where the West Begins; Brass Buttons; Some Liar; A Sporting Chance; This Hero Stuff; Six Feet Four; 23½ Hours Leave; A Fugitive From Matrimony; Haunting Shadows. **'20** The White Dove; Uncharted Channels; One Hour Before Dawn; Dice of Destiny; Help Wanted – Male. **'21** When We Were Twenty-One; The Mistress of Shenstone; Salvage; The Sting of the Lash; Tol'able David (+prod; +co-sc). **'22** The Seventh Day (+prod); Sonny (+prod; +co-sc); The Bond Boy (+prod). **'23** Fury (+prod); The White Sister (+prod). **'24** Romola (+prod). **'25** Sackcloth and Scarlet (+prod); Any Woman (+prod). **'26** Stella Dallas; Partners Again; The Winning of Barbara Worth. **'27** The Magic Flame. **'28** The Woman Disputed (co-dir; + prod). **'29** She Goes to War (+exec. prod). **'30** Hell Harbor (+prod) (GB: Hell's Harbour); The Eyes of the World (+exec. prod); Lightnin'. **'31** Merely Mary Ann; Over the Hill. **'32** The Woman in Room 13. **'33** State Fair; I Loved You Wednesday (co-dir). **'34** Carolina; Marie Galante. **'35** One More Spring; Way Down East. **'36** The Country Doctor; Ramona; Lloyds of London. **'37** Seventh Heaven. **'38** In Old Chicago; Alexander's Ragtime Band. **'39** Jesse James; Stanley and Livingstone. **'40** Little Old New York; Maryland; Chad Hanna. **'41** A Yank in the RAF; Remember the Day. **'42** The Black Swan. **'43** The Song of Bernadette. **'44** Wilson. **'45** A Bell for Adano. **'46** Margie. **'47** Captain From Castile. **'48** Deep Waters. **'49** Prince of Foxes; Twelve O'Clock High. **'50** The Gunfighter. **'51** I'd Climb the Highest Mountain; David and Bathsheba. **'52** Wait Till the Sun Shines, Nellie; O. Henry's Full House *ep* The Gift of the Magi (GB: Full House). **'53** The Snows of Kilimanjaro; King of the Khyber Rifles. **'55** Untamed; Love Is a Many Splendored Thing. **'56** Carousel. **'57** The Sun Also Rises. **'58** The Bravados. **'59** This Earth Is Mine; Beloved Infidel. **'62** Tender Is the Night.

No complete listings exist for King's work before 1919.

END OF THE SILENTS

Once the sound film proved its profitability, silent movies were doomed to the boneyard of cultural and industrial history, despite their proven artistic virtues

Above: the camera had great mobility at the end of the silent period and even outdoors the director could shout instructions above the noise. A production shot from The Woman Disputed *(1928), starring Norma Talmadge as a prostitute loved by two officers, Austrian and Russian, on opposing sides in a war. The film was released in two versions – one silent, the other with a Movietone soundtrack of music and effects*

It was a dog that killed the silent cinema. If that seems far-fetched, consider an alternative scenario. If the director Malcolm St Clair had had the nerve to shoot Rin-Tin-Tin, as he threatened to do on numerous occasions when the beast persisted in savaging cast and crew, Warners would have had great difficulty, deprived of their bread-winner, in surviving until 1926, let alone being able to pour vast sums into the development of sound. Given a year or so of grace, silent movies would have survived until the Depression, the East Coast bankers would have been unable to provide the money needed for sound, and the silent films, already in the late Twenties achieving new heights year by year, would have been ready as the nation emerged from its economic miseries for a different battle – with television.

It was not to be. On August 6, 1926 came the New York premiere of *Don Juan* with sound effects and synchronized score in the Vitaphone process, together with several musical short films; other similar programmes followed, with Fox's Movietone emerging to rival the Warners' Vitaphone. On October 6, 1927 the sensational premiere of *The Jazz Singer* took place. On July 8, 1928 the first all-talking picture, *Lights of New York*, was shown. By the end of the year, all the Hollywood major studios were committed to making sound films, although the occasional silent feature was still appearing in 1929. As the Thirties came in, the victory of the sound film was complete.

Throughout the American film industry, in those years of uncertainty, there was something not far short of panic. With their fears that their voices might not be suitable, actors were the most at risk. Their employers submitted them to 'voice tests'.

The scenarist Frances Marion was a fascinated observer:

'Long queues lined up for these tests, and as they were herded forward to face their destiny, fear was paramount, although here and there you could catch a cocky expression of confidence, one who had had prior stage experience and harboured no doubt of passing the test.'

Most of them did in fact pass. They endured elocution and singing lessons, and one studio even made its character players read Shakespeare; but employers were not going to lose performers of tried popularity if there was any way of avoiding it. There were many reasons why such actors as John Gilbert, Buster Keaton and Richard Barthelmess faded from the scene, but inadequacy of voice was not one of them. Perhaps Norma Talmadge was the only real casualty of sound. Eventually the actors could breathe again.

Producers and directors watched and waited, cautious and uneasy. MGM's production chief Irving Thalberg thought that sound was a useful adjunct to technique, but that it would not replace the silent film. Nevertheless, Thalberg himself worked with the sound expert Douglas Shearer, his brother-in-law, on the new methods, and kept his options open. Harold Lloyd wrote:

'No-one can predict and everyone is predicting what its effects will be. Apparently it will multiply many times the emotional appeal of the screen, opening unguessed possibilities.'

That statement exactly illustrates the way in which the industry let this thing happen in almost total ignorance of the consequences. 'Emotional appeal' was precisely what sound *took away* from the movies. Silent film was an unreal experience. The thinking mind ceased to work; images and music took the spectator near to dream; imagining dialogue helped him to identify. Sound broke the identification, ruptured the dream. Some may say that was all to the good. What is certain is that it happened.

A number of the earliest sound films made such extravagant profits that audiences may well be thought to have welcomed them undiscriminatingly. So, no doubt, many people did; but it is interesting to note that there was a minority, small but vocal, who resented the sound films bitterly. Fan magazines of the time contained many letters lamenting the change, and in the trade papers, too, exhibitors made similar complaints. Allowance must be made for the defective nature of much early sound equipment – in local cinemas in 1930 the audience had to sit for some ten minutes before the dialogue became intelligible – and also for the fact that satisfied customers tend not to write letters; but the undercurrent of discontent was there, and the essence of it was that the spectator was not drawn into the film as he or she used to be. What was not realized – what is often not realized even today – was that audiences were faced with a new art. The sound film was not just a silent film with words tacked on, but a new form that had to reconcile the real (the accurate recording of speech) with the unreal (the two-dimensional image), while the silent film had been a harmonious unity.

When the major studios realized that sound was not a passing fancy, they looked feverishly for the kinds of talent which they believed that sound demanded. Stage actors, stage directors and writers of stage dialogue were imported lavishly. The old directors, scenarists and gagmen would stay on to help the newcomers out of any difficulty. The 'dialogue director' was born. This functionary looked after spoken scenes, leaving camera angles and such to the experts; and as dialogue tended to be spoken very slowly in the interests of clear recording, the results could be peculiar. A notorious example is John Ford's *The Black Watch* (1929), a vigorous action movie slowed down unbearbly by very static dialogue scenes directed by Lumsden Hare, a talent imported from the theatre. The dialogue director still got occasional credits in the late Thirties, but his influence was by then hardly making itself felt.

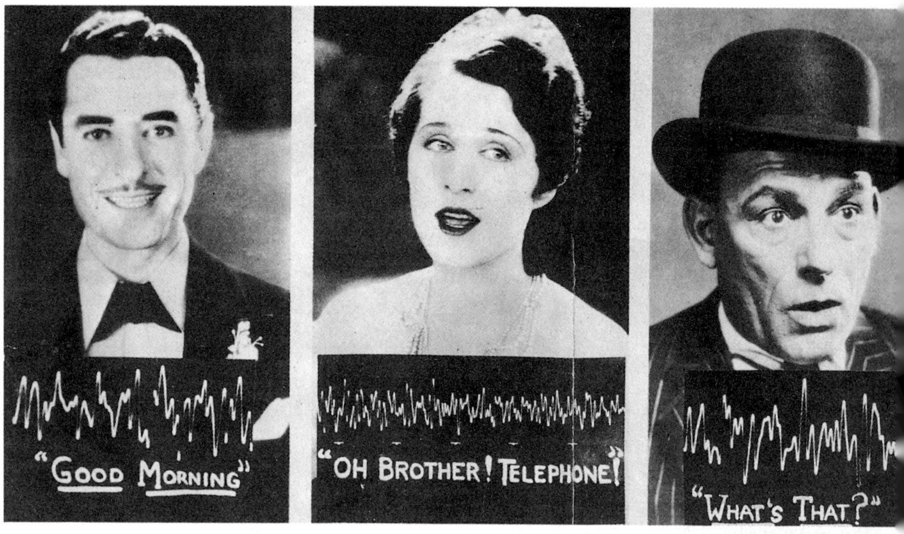

Very few of the newcomers lasted. The old scenarists adapted rapidly, the cultured tones of the stage actors were found to be unnecessary (or worse, for the mass audience could not identify with people who talked like that), and the silent directors weighed up the situation and found their individual ways around the difficulties. Within a year, most of Broadway's emigrants could go back home.

Directors found that their greatest difficulties stemmed from the various sound men who for a while tried to dominate the studio stages. These men knew little about filming and a great deal, nominally, about recording. As already mentioned, they influenced the delivery of lines. They also had very definite ideas about the impossibility of outdoor recording, and not until Raoul Walsh's *In Old Arizona* (1928) did a film-maker go against expert opinion and produce a perfectly satisfactory outdoor feature talkie. John Ford, however, had paved the way with a three-reel comedy, *Napoleon's Barber* (1928), that he too wished to shoot outdoors. In a book-length interview, Ford told the director and

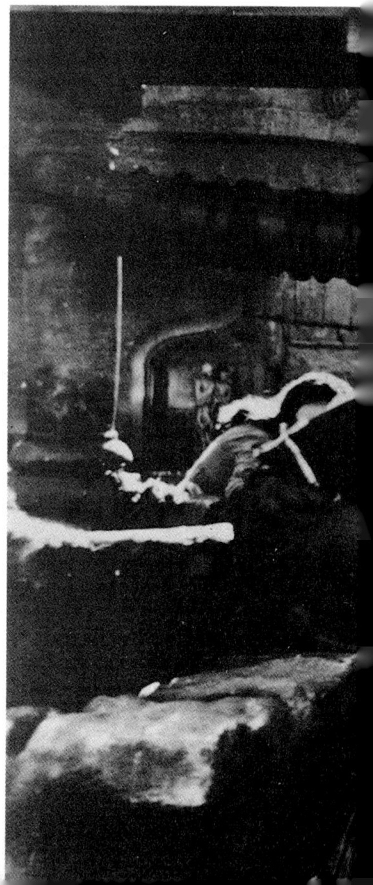

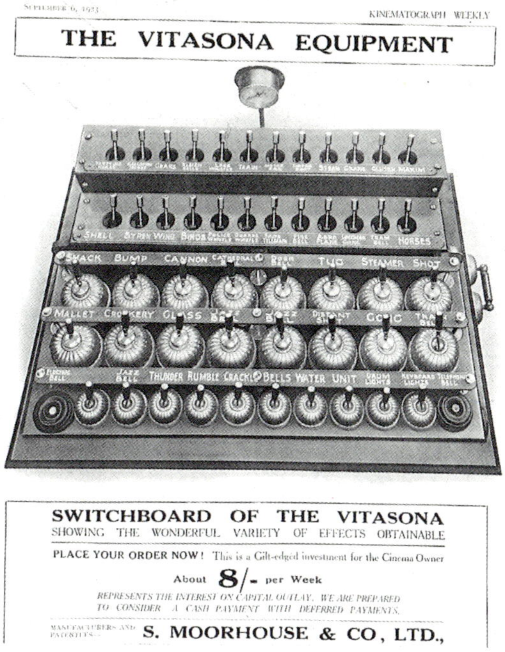

critic Peter Bogdanovich how the sound men reacted:

'They said it couldn't be done, and I said, "Why the hell *can't* it be done?" They said, "Well, you can't because –" and they gave me a lot of Master's Degree talk, so I said, "Well, let's try it".'

They tried it, and it worked. Similarly, it was discovered that the sound-proofed camera did not need to remain in the cumbersome booth of the primitive sound era, and the invention of the microphone-boom gave the camera greater mobility still. In two sound films of 1929, David Butler's *Sunny Side Up* and Rouben Mamoulian's *Applause*, the camera was on the prowl as it had been in the old days, and the one genre that had not been possible before, the musical, got off to the best of starts.

In other film-producing countries, events took a similar course, but studios could afford to wait a while and study the success of the American experiment. The German industry, at any rate, did not suffer any invasion of new people from the theatre, for most German directors and actors had stage backgrounds, and the influence of Max Reinhardt and other noted stage producers had been there for a long, long time.

In Britain there was a certain amount of looking back with regret. 'I considered,' wrote the director Anthony Asquith, 'that the silent film was a self-sufficient art-form which had found its artistic feet,' whereas now, he went on, 'the visual and the oral are indispensable elements.' Few of his contemporaries saw as clearly as Asquith did here the

Far left: Rin-Tin-Tin switches off the power in Tracked by the Police *(1927), the story of which was written by Darryl F. Zanuck. Top, far left: voice tests for John Gilbert, Norma Shearer and Lon Chaney. Above left and centre: advertised in the* Kinematograph Weekly *in 1923, Vitasona was a short-lived method of adding sound effects in the cinemas. Above: Germanic lighting as Nell (Elissa Landi) hides from Bill (Cyril McLaglen), who plots to marry her although she loves another, in* Underground, *set partly in the London tube. Below: Otto Matiesen in* Napoleon's Barber, *John Ford's first talkie*

Above: Garbo was still silent in her second Hollywood film, made in 1926, but effectively portrayed a woman who brought her men and herself to disaster. The film, based on a Blasco-Ibáñez novel, was initially directed by Mauritz Stiller, who had come with Garbo from Sweden, but he was soon replaced by Fred Niblo. Below: the farmer (George O'Brien) sees a vision of the big city evoked by his mistress (Margaret Livingston) in Sunrise. *Below right: Alice (Anny Ondra), having the night before stabbed a would-be rapist to death, is reluctant to use the bread-knife in* Blackmail, *during a breakfast conversation dominated by the word 'knife'*

uniqueness of the silent film, and his words were those of a man making the best of a bad job. Certainly his sound films never approached the adventurousness of such silents as the dramatic *Underground* (1928).

At about the same time, Alfred Hitchcock was even more guarded. 'Talk is the essential propulsion of the stage play,' Hitchcock said, 'but it is only an aid in the case of film. The ideal of the film is to present its story.' 'Only an aid': Hitchcock would bear that in mind throughout his career, and would never allow talk to dominate. His first sound film, *Blackmail* (1929), taught him what would work and what would not, because *Blackmail* was three films in one. It began life as a silent and some passages, such as the brilliant opening, were entirely wordless. Then came long dialogue exchanges, static, slow and dull. The third element was experimentation with unrealistic sound, as in the famous scene where the word 'knife' was allowed to dominate a conversation. Here again sound was a gain indeed.

It is often written, and sometimes believed, that the first years of sound set the cinema back many years; and it is true that many of those early 'talkies' were exactly what that term implies. But paradoxically it is also true that sound was used more excitingly then than it ever has been since. In addition to *Blackmail*, René Clair's *Sous les Toits de Paris* (1930, *Under the Roofs of Paris*), Rouben Mamoulian's *City Streets* (1931), Howard Hawks' *Scarface* (1932) and many others could be cited. A lesser-known example is the Russian Boris Barnet's *Okraina* (1933, Outskirts), where the first reel was a symphony of natural sound, and the only dialogue was a line spoken by a horse. By the mid-Thirties, however, such delights were rare. Sound was no longer a thrilling new toy, and its possibilities were largely unexplored.

Perhaps one of the reasons was that in America, at any rate, the sound film was very much a child of its times. When it took its first steps, in the course of 1927 and 1928, the nation was being swept along by an optimistic surge of prosperity, and the rising stock market rivalled, even outran, baseball as the first thing a reader looked for in his morning paper. The market had its hiccups, and there were bad days in March and December of 1928, but it was quick to recover. Golden days seemed to stretch limitlessly ahead, and it appeared to be a time when new enterprises could not miss. So by mid-1929 (the stock market peaked in September) the sound film was established. When on Tuesday, October 29 the great Crash came, and America entered on the long years of the Depression and slow recovery, the initial impetus was sufficient to carry the studios

Adventurous directors were keen to experiment with innovative uses of sound in the early years

along for a few years. In fact, the only immediate impact of the Wall Street Crash seems to have been that the drying up of his sources of finance destroyed William Fox's carefully-engineered attempt to gain control of Loew's, Inc., and with it the glittering prize of MGM.

But all too soon the staggering profits of the early sound years withered, retrenchment was forced on the studios, salaries were cut, personnel were laid off, and caution ruled. It was no time for adventure. By 1934 the sound film was playing it safe.

There could never be a turning back. The silent film had to die. In all history no art had died before, but then no art had been an industry too, or rather, none had depended so entirely upon an industry for its artefacts. It had lasted, all in all, a mere 35 years, and it had perished at a moment when, artistically, its future was exciting as never before, though this can be seen more clearly in retrospect than was perhaps possible at the time. But for the silents to come, in a third of a century, from a peep-show parlour to *Napoléon* (1927, *Napoleon*) and *Sunrise* (1927), and to die then, was a tragedy of modern times.

JACK LODGE

GENEALOGY OF THE CINEMA

Photography

The **camera obscura**, which 'projects' sunlit exteriors into a darkened room, was developed in the sixteenth century

1803: Thomas Wedgwood and Humphrey Davy obtain photographic images but are unable to fix them

1827: Nicéphore Niépce produces a permanent image on a bitumen-coated pewter plate exposed for eight hours

1834: William Henry Fox Talbot begins experimenting on fixing positive images onto sensitized paper

1839: Louis J. M. Daguerre demonstrates the **Daguerreotype** which fixes an image onto a sensitized copper plate. The French government buys the process to offer it freely to the world

In the same year, John William Herschel calls his fixed images 'photographs'

1840: Talbot develops the **Calotype** which fixes an image with only a brief camera exposure

1847: Abel Niépce de Saint-Victor describes the first practical method for producing negatives on glass

1851: F. Scott Archer uses collodion, a sensitized material which enables instantaneous exposures

1855: Alexander William Parkes discovers the plastic base of cellulose, later developed into celluloid

1868: J. W. Hyatt and Isaiah Hyatt market celluloid

1872: Eadweard Muybridge begins experimenting with photographing moving objects

1874: Jules Janssen builds the **revolver photographique** which records the transit of Venus across the face of the sun

1879: Ferrier produces the first photographic film

1882: Etienne Marey perfects his **fusil photographique**, a device similar to the *revolver photographique*

1888: Marey designs the **Chronophotographe**, a camera using roll film

1889: Kodak celluloid roll film becomes available

1891: Thomas Edison and W. K. Laurie Dickson invent the **Kinetograph**, a camera for recording moving images

In the same year, Edison and Dickson invent the **Kinetoscope**, a machine for viewing moving pictures

Projection

Shadow shows are known from the earliest recorded times. In the seventeenth century, the magic lantern is used to project simple pictures

1798: Etienne Robertson develops the **Phantasmagoria**, a more sophisticated magic lantern

1839: Henry Langdon Childe further develops the magic lantern by introducing dissolving views

1853: Franz von Uchatius develops the **Kinetiscope** which projects moving drawings

1866: L. S. Beale devises the **Choreutoscope**, a slide which allows the magic lantern to project moving drawings

1870: Henry R. Heyl demonstrates the **Phasmatrope** which projects moving photographic images

1880: Reynaud develops a Praxinoscope capable of projecting moving images

1881: Muybridge demonstrates the **Zoopraxiscope**, which projects moving pictures based on photographs

1892: Reynaud uses the Praxinoscope to publicly project the **Pantomimes Lumineuses**, hand-painted transparent bands which tell a simple story

Persistence of vision

The principle that an image is visually retained for a short time after observation has ceased was observed in ancient times

1826: Dr John Ayrton Paris markets the **Thaumatrope**, a card which, when spun, gives the illusion of movement

1829: Joseph Antoine Plateau publishes a thesis explaining retinal perception and the persistence of vision

1830: Michael Faraday experiments with the visual illusions created by a revolving wheel

1833: Plateau develops the **Phenakistiscope**, a revolving disc which gives the illusion of motion

In the same year, Simon Stampfer develops the **Stroboscope**, an identical device

1834: William George Horner develops the **Zoetrope**, a revolving cylinder which gives the illusion of motion to the pictures inside

1877: Emile Reynaud patents the **Praxinoscope**, a cylindrical device using mirrors to give the illusion of motion

1878: Reynaud develops the **Praxinoscope-Théâtre**, a more sophisticated version of the Praxinoscope

---

1895–6: the Lumière's **Cinématographe**, Robert W. Paul's **Theatrograph**, Edison's **Vitascope**, Max and Emil Skladanowsky's **Bioscop** all project moving films

INDEX

Note: page references in *italics* refer to main entries